CAMBRIDGE LIBRAI

Books of enduring scl.

Travel and Exploration

The history of travel writing dates back to the Bible, Caesar, the Vikings and the Crusaders, and its many themes include war, trade, science and recreation. Explorers from Columbus to Cook charted lands not previously visited by Western travellers, and were followed by merchants, missionaries, and colonists, who wrote accounts of their experiences. The development of steam power in the nineteenth century provided opportunities for increasing numbers of 'ordinary' people to travel further, more economically, and more safely, and resulted in great enthusiasm for travel writing among the reading public. Works included in this series range from first-hand descriptions of previously unrecorded places, to literary accounts of the strange habits of foreigners, to examples of the burgeoning numbers of guidebooks produced to satisfy the needs of a new kind of traveller - the tourist.

Diary of William Hedges, Esq. (Afterwards Sir William Hedges)

The publications of the Hakluyt Society (founded in 1846) made available edited (and sometimes translated) early accounts of exploration. The first series, which ran from 1847 to 1899, consists of 100 books containing published or previously unpublished works by authors from Christopher Columbus to Sir Francis Drake, and covering voyages to the New World, to China and Japan, to Russia and to Africa and India. Three volumes, published in 1887, are devoted to the diary of William Hedges (1632–1701) who in 1681 became the first Agent of the East India Company at its new base in Bengal. The first volume contains a transcription of the diary itself; Volume 2 contains a collection of documents relevant to Hedges' time in India; and Volume 3 is a documentary history of Thomas Pitt, grandfather of Pitt the Elder and Governor of Fort St George, who appears frequently in Hedges' diary.

Cambridge University Press has long been a pioneer in the reissuing of out-of-print titles from its own backlist, producing digital reprints of books that are still sought after by scholars and students but could not be reprinted economically using traditional technology. The Cambridge Library Collection extends this activity to a wider range of books which are still of importance to researchers and professionals, either for the source material they contain, or as landmarks in the history of their academic discipline.

Drawing from the world-renowned collections in the Cambridge University Library, and guided by the advice of experts in each subject area, Cambridge University Press is using state-of-the-art scanning machines in its own Printing House to capture the content of each book selected for inclusion. The files are processed to give a consistently clear, crisp image, and the books finished to the high quality standard for which the Press is recognised around the world. The latest print-on-demand technology ensures that the books will remain available indefinitely, and that orders for single or multiple copies can quickly be supplied.

The Cambridge Library Collection will bring back to life books of enduring scholarly value (including out-of-copyright works originally issued by other publishers) across a wide range of disciplines in the humanities and social sciences and in science and technology.

Diary of William Hedges, Esq. (Afterwards Sir William Hedges)

During his Agency in Bengal, as well as on His Voyage Out and Return Overland (1681-1687)

VOLUME 3: CONTAINING DOCUMENTARY CONTRIBUTIONS TO A BIOGRAPHY OF THOMAS PITT, GOVERNOR OF FORT ST. GEORGE; WITH COLLECTIONS ON THE EARLY HISTORY OF THE COMPANY'S SETTLEMENT IN BENGAL; AND ON EARLY CHARTS AND TOPOGRAPHY OF THE HÚGLÍ RIVER

WILLIAM HEDGES
EDITED BY HENRY YULE

CAMBRIDGE
UNIVERSITY PRESS

CAMBRIDGE UNIVERSITY PRESS

Cambridge, New York, Melbourne, Madrid, Cape Town, Singapore,
São Paolo, Delhi, Dubai, Tokyo

Published in the United States of America by Cambridge University Press, New York

www.cambridge.org
Information on this title: www.cambridge.org/9781108010924

© in this compilation Cambridge University Press 2009

This edition first published 1887
This digitally printed version 2009

ISBN 978-1-108-01092-4 Paperback

WORKS ISSUED BY

The Hakluyt Society.

THE DIARY

OF

WILLIAM HEDGES, Esq.

(Illustrative Extracts from Records.)

No. LXXVIII.

THOMAS PITT.

GOVERNOR OF FORT ST GEORGE

FROM A PAINTING BY KNELLER, AT CHEVENING.

THE DIARY

OF

WILLIAM HEDGES, Esq.

(AFTERWARDS SIR WILLIAM HEDGES),

DURING HIS AGENCY IN BENGAL;

AS WELL AS ON HIS VOYAGE OUT AND RETURN OVERLAND

(1681-1687).

ILLUSTRATED BY COPIOUS EXTRACTS FROM UNPUBLISHED
RECORDS, ETC.,

BY

COLONEL HENRY YULE, R.E., C.B., LL.D.,

PRESIDENT OF THE HAKLUYT SOCIETY.

VOL. III.

CONTAINING DOCUMENTARY CONTRIBUTIONS TO A BIOGRAPHY
OF THOMAS PITT, GOVERNOR OF FORT ST, GEORGE;

WITH COLLECTIONS ON

THE EARLY HISTORY OF THE COMPANY'S SETTLEMENT IN BENGAL;

AND

ON EARLY CHARTS AND TOPOGRAPHY OF THE HÚGLÍ RIVER.

LONDON :

PRINTED FOR THE HAKLUYT SOCIETY,

4, LINCOLN'S INN FIELDS, W.C.

M.DCCC.LXXXIX.

COUNCIL

OF

THE HAKLUYT SOCIETY.

CONTENTS OF THIS VOLUME.

PREFATORY NOTE TO VOL. III.

THESE volumes have, through many hindrances, got completed at last. The copious Index, without which a book of this kind is almost useless, forms a keystone to the structure, which has been, in this case, a somewhat laborious task ; but the labour has been mitigated through the help contributed by some friends, whom I here heartily thank without naming them.

At the end of the Preface to Vol. II, it was mentioned that Mr. SCHARF, C.B., had recently identified at Chevening a portrait of THOMAS PITT's wife, JANE INNES. I have now to thank that generous friend for a sketch of the picture by his own accomplished hand, of which a reduction is presented opposite page clviii. My thanks to Lord STANHOPE are also due for the permission to publish this drawing.

Just as the sheets of Index have been passing through the press, I have obtained, through the kind effort of Dr. JOHN ANDERSON, a photograph from the portrait of ELIHU YALE at Yale College, U.S.A., which affords another most interesting illustration of these documents.

This completes four entirely unpublished portraits of Anglo-Indian notables of the seventeenth century, with which I have been enabled, through the kindness of various friends, to add value to this compilation, viz., those of THOMAS PITT and of his wife, of Sir STREYNSHAM MASTER, and of ELIHU YALE.

H. YULE.

ERRATA AND ADDENDA.

In Vol. II, p..ccix, line 24.   For " 1600" read " 1700"
  ,,   p. ccxcii, line 28.   For " 1671-2" read "1691-2"

In Vol. II, in regard to ELIHU YALE, of whom notices are given at pp. ccxcii-xciv, and whose correspondence with Governor Pitt frequently occurs in the present volume, I owe to the kindness of Dr. JOHN ANDERSON, late Keeper of the Museum at Calcutta, interesting particulars, of which I was entirely ignorant.

ELIHU YALE was born at New Haven, New England, 5th April 1648.

His grandfather, DAVID YALE, belonged to a family possessing a landed estate near WREXHAM, and (1613) married ANN MORTON, whose father eventually became Bishop of DURHAM. He died in 1617. The widow, in the following year, married THEOPHILUS EATON, a London merchant, and in 1637 EATON, with his wife and step-children, sailed for America in the *Hector*.

ELIHU was the third child of THOMAS YALE (third child of DAVID YALE and ANN MORTON). After the death of EATON, in 1657, his widow returned to England, accompanied by her family, including her grandchild ELIHU. THOMAS YALE returned to America in 1659, leaving his son behind. The latter was chosen to the service of the E.I. Company 24th of October 1671.[1]

YALE married the widow of JOSEPH HYNMERS, with whom he came into possession of a large fortune. She was presumably of PORTUGUESE blood, her name being JERONIMA DE PAITA.

ELIHU YALE died in London, 8th July 1721, and was buried at WREXHAM, with the following epitaph :

> " Born in AMERICA, in EUROPE bred,
> In AFRICA travel'd, and in ASIA wed,
> Where long he liv'd and thriv'd, at LONDON dead.
> Much good, some ill he did, so hope that all's even,
> And that his soul thro' mercy's gone to Heaven.
> You that survive and read, take care,
> For this most certain exit to prepare ;
> For only the actions of the just
> Smell sweet and blossom in the dust."

YALE was married a second time, as there are records extant of his widow and administratrix, Katherine by name. By his first wife he had two sons, who both died before him. He left three daughters : (1) CATHERINE, who married

---

[1] *Court Book* of that date. The final nomination was apparently 11th Nov. 1671, given erroneously in Vol. II, p. ccxcii, as 1670.

DUDLEY NORTH, grandson of the Earl of GUILDFORD ; (2) ANN, who married
Lord JAMES CAVENDISH, son of the Duke of DEVONSHIRE ; and (3) URSULA,
unmarried.

ELIHU YALE, during his later years, was a benefactor to " His Majesty's
College of CONNECTICUT", and his gifts were so highly appreciated by the
trustees that by a solemn act, dated 12th September 1718, they gave the
seminary the now famous name of YALE COLLEGE.

A portrait of YALE, by " E. SEEMAN, 1717", was presented to the College in
1789 by DUDLEY NORTH, son of YALE's daughter CATHERINE ; and an
engraved likeness of him was also sent to the College at an earlier date.   Under
this was placed the following MS. inscription :

> " *Effigies clarissimi viri D. D.* ELIHU YALE *Londinensis Armigeri.*
>
> " En vir ! cui meritas laudes ob facta per orbis
>   Extremos fines inclyta fama dedit,
>   Aequor trans tumidum gazas adduxit ab Indis,
>   Quas Ille sparsit munificenti manu
>   Inscitiae tenebras, ut noctis luce coronae
>   Phoebus, ab occiduis pellit et Ille plagis.
>   Dum mens grata manet, nomen laudesque Yalensis
>   Cantabunt Soboles unanimique Patris."

Capt. ALEXANDER HAMILTON, a writer much given to gossiping detraction,
says that YALE was probably a most arbitrary Governor, as he hanged his groom
for riding out on his horse for two or three days without his master's leave, a
disgraceful proceeding, for which he was called to severe account in England.
And PENNANT, in his *Outlines of the Globe*, states that the site of Fort ST.
DAVID, with a small district adjoining, was purchased by ELIHU YALE from a
Mahratta prince for £30,000.

Other particulars are given in Dr. ANDERSON's Note.   His facts have been
gathered from (1) *Statistical Account of the Towns and Parishes in the State
of* CONNECTICUT, issued by the Conn. Academy of Art and Science, Vol. I,
No. 1, NEW HAVEN, 1811 ; (2) *Catalogue of the Paintings belonging to* YALE
College, p. 3 ; (3) *Hist. of* YALE *College*, NEW HAVEN, 1766 ; (4) PENNANT'S
Tour in WALES, Vol. II, 1784, corrections, etc., p. 191, etc.

I have tried in vain to trace any copy of the engraved portrait of Mr. YALE
above referred to, nor is it now to be found in the College.   But just in time for
introduction in this volume I have received, through Dr. Anderson's kindness,
a photograph of the picture presented to the College by Mr. DUDLEY NORTH.

Vol. II., p. clxxxiii.   Here ought to be inserted the following curious notice
regarding Sir T. Grantham, contributed by Mr. Albert Gray, a member of our
Council and the editor of *Pyrard*.

" *Modern Reports*, vol. iii, p. 120.

" 2 and 3 James II, 168⅞.

" Sir THOMAS GRANTHAM'S *Case.*

" He bought a monster in the Indies, which was a man of that country, who
had the perfect shape of a child growing out of his breast as an excrescency, all
but the head.

" This man he brought hither and exposed to the sight of the people for profit.

" The Indian turns Christian, and was baptised and was detained from his master, who brought a *homine repleg'*[1]: the sheriff returned that he had replevied the body, but doth not say the body in which Sir Thomas claimed a property · whereupon he was ordered to amend his return, and then the Court of Common Pleas bailed him."

In Vol. II., p. ccliii, add the following :

I am indebted to a friendly and appropriate communication from Mr. J. H. Mayo, of the India Office, for the following extract, in which Sir S. Master comes forward.

" *Church of* ST. GEORGE THE MARTYR, QUEEN SQUARE, BLOOMSBURY."
  [*Extracted from* " *Select Views of London*", *by* JOHN B. PAPWORTH, London, 1816, 8vo., p. 57.]

" On the west side stands the Church of S. GEORGE THE MARTYR. The erection of this edifice was occasioned by the great increase of inhabitants in the parish of S. ANDREW, HOLBORN. Several of those who resided at the extremity of the parish having proposed to erect a chapel for religious worship, Sir STREYNSHAM MASTER and fourteen other gentlemen were appointed trustees for the management of the business. In 1705 they contracted for the building of a chapel and two houses for £3,500, intending to reimburse themselves by the sale of pews. The edifice being finished the next year, they settled annual stipends for the maintenance of a chaplain, an afternoon preacher, and a clerk ; but the commissioners for erecting fifty new churches in the metropolis purchased the building, caused a certain district to be appointed for its parish, and had it consecrated in 1723, when it was dedicated to S. GEORGE, in compliment to Sir STREYNSHAM MASTER, who had been Governor of FORT S. GEORGE, in the EAST INDIES."

On this Mr. Mayo remarks :

" I had imagined that like other Georgian Churches this one was named in compliment to the King, with ' The Martyr' for a difference to distinguish it from the adjoining parish of S. GEORGE, BLOOMSBURY. It had always puzzled me, however, how two adjoining parishes, created at the same period, should both have been named after S. GEORGE ; but the matter is now explained.

" The Church of S. GEORGE, BLOOMSBURY, has a statue of the King on top of the spire. If S. GEORGE THE MARTYR had had a spire, the builders might possibly have crowned it with the effigy of Sir S. MASTER !

" The building (as chapel) seems to have been finished in 1706, so Sir STREYNSHAM enjoyed the benefit of a place of worship in the vicinity of his residence in RED LION SQUARE for nearly 20 years."

---

[1] For *homine replegiando*, a writ to bail a man out of unlawful imprisonment.

In the present volume (III.) the following early letters of T. PITT's ought to have found their proper place near the beginning, but they were not discovered till the first sheets had been printed off.

"*To* Mr. THOMAS ROLT (Agent in PERSIA).

"*ffrom aboard ye Ship* Bengall Merchant *in* GOMBROONE *Roade* ye 6th June 1676.[1]

" Worp¹ Sʳ:

"Last night in Capt: Clarkes boat my Purser and Mate came aboard, and this night are taken very ill, either it is by being poysned or by being drubt like doggs by yᵉ: Shawbanders men as they say and will give under their hands was yoʳ: only order, my Purser haueing about him 600: and odd *abasses*, wᶜʰ: I am certaine is all that hee hath in ye world, and the Peones tooke it from him as drubt them ; my Mate likewise 250: *abasses*, wᶜʰ: is all gonn, and their Cloathes tore all to peeces; yᵉ: place is brought to a fine pass, yᵗ: Christians, especially English, must turne Moors as to their habitt to please yoʳ: Worpˢ: humors ; If this bee an amicable conclution as you promised (to kill our men), and cause them to be balled to and fro ye street like doggs, I will p'sue noe longer that method ; to yoʳ: Worpᵖ: 1 haue sent my accott: inclosed, and desire yoʳ: Worpᵖ: that you will bee pleased to order mee yᵉ: Ballance to bee sent off in my boat, or else I must take some other Course for ye procureing of it, and at last if not procurable, I shall charge yoʳ: Worpᵖ: on ye Credᵗ: Side of my accᵗˢ: with my owners, and for wᵗ: taken when yᵉ: house was broke open with the Chest I may happily refer till a fitt time, and place presents for Justice. Sʳ: it was as I am certaine yoʳ: Worpᵖ: is Sensible yᵗ: my desire is peace ; wᶜʰ: I hope Still may bee complyed withall. Sʳ: yoʳ: Worpᵖ: as I understand hath been pleased to say yᵗ: I refused to receive Mʳ: CLAUELLS concerns, wᶜʰ: I deny, and if yoʳ: Worpᵖ: please to lade them on us I shall take ye greatest Care of it imaginable, as it was Mr: CLAUELLS order to receive wᵗ: soever yoʳ: Worpᵖ: was pleased to lade upon us wᶜʰ: I acquainted you with, and in my boat I have for the secureity of ye money if you please to Send it I have sent a booye and ropes in the boat. Soe desireing yoʳ: Worpˢˢ: orders this night p' my boat, this being all as offers at p'sent from him as shall still Subscribe himselfe

" Sʳ yoʳ Worpˢ: Serua¹:

"THOS: PITT.''

To President *and* Council *at* SURAT.

"*from abord ye* Bengall Merchant *in* GOMBROON *Roade* ye 8ʰ: June 1676.[2]

" Honourable &ca:

" Sᵐ: haueing been at one of yoʳ: Subordinate factories, GOMBROONE in PERSIA, and I being Imployed by Mʳ: WALTER CLAUELL, Mʳ: MATTHIAS VINCENT, and Mʳ: JOHN SMYTH, whoe haue all Sustained wᵗʰ my Selfe a vast Losse, caused wholly and Solely by yᵉ: Worpˡˡ. THOS: ROLT. his base and vnjust actions for the verity of wᶜʰ: I appeall to these papers inclosed, and some other intelligence as I am certaine will bee giuen of itt, all being soe Publikely knowne, soe yᵗ: I supposed itt to bee convenient in our owners behalfe to aply my Selfe to yoʳ: Honoʳˢ: &ca: Counsell for Justice ; which I doubt not of obtaining ·

"I remain Sʳ:

" Yoʳ: Honoʳˢ: &ca: most humble Seruant

" Tʜᴏs: Pɪᴛᴛ."

These letters show that Pitt's voyages to Persia had begun at an earlier date than I was aware of when writing p. ix.

———

P. xxii.   Last line.   Insert the No. " 3."

P. xxiii.   4th line from bottom.   For *supra* read " Vol. ɪɪ."

P. xxvii.   Last line.   For *supra* read " Vol. ɪɪ."

P. lvi.   2nd line from bottom.   For " Fying" read " Flying."

P. lxii.   In 2nd line of Pitt's letter to his wife the letters " pa" have dropped out of " pacquet."

P. lxv.   In 4th line of Curgenven's letter.   For " Ridont" read " Ridout".

P. clxiii.   In para. (19).   *Dele* " and Kinsman"; and for " lxxxvi" read "lxxxvii".

LIST OF ILLUSTRATIONS IN THIS VOLUME.

FACSIMILE AUTOGRAPHS.

---

[1] By error on the plate " 1687-1690"

V.

DOCUMENTARY CONTRIBUTIONS
TO A
BIOGRAPHY OF THOMAS PITT,

INTERLOPER, GOVERNOR OF FORT ST. GEORGE, AND PROGENITOR
OF AN ILLUSTRIOUS FAMILY.

———————

IN the *Diary of William Hedges* we find repeated reference to a
Captain Pitt or Pitts (as he is called indiscriminately), a prominent and
notorious interloper who pressed his commercial adventures in defiance
of the Company's claims to exclusive trade, and was only too successful
in seducing from their fidelity, and involving in his own quasi-contra-
band business, a number of the Company's servants in "the Bay".

I think it well to begin by bringing together here, either in abstract
or extract, the chief passages in which Hedges takes notice of this adventurer.

On the outward voyage of Hedges and his party, on the *Defence*,
when eleven weeks from the Downs, they speak a ship proving to be the
Crown (Capt. Dorrel), which had left home some three weeks after
them, an interloper bound for Húglí, and carrying, with other passen-
gers, "Mr. Pitts" (p. 20).

On the arrival of Hedges at Balasore they see a ship in the roads:

"They told us the Ship we saw in Port was the *Crown*, Capt. DORREL, with
Mr. PITTS, who had been here 11 days before. That Mr. PITTS had hired a
great house at BALLASORE. carried divers Chests of money ashore, and was
very busy in buying of goods" (p. 31).

When Hedges visited the Court of Dacca, the Nabob asked him
various questions regarding Mr. Pitt and his trade; and he seems to have
tried to get the Nabob to arrest and bring to Dacca the latter with his
skipper, Capt. Dorrel; indeed *parwánas* to that effect, addressed to the
authorities at Húglí, were, to the Agent's great satisfaction, actually
prepared:

"If they come and appear their voyages will be lost this year. If they abscond
and go away, they will be esteemed villaines and not permitted to come again
hereafter" (p. 53).

But though the *parwánas* were sealed (p. 53, so at least Hedges was told) nothing came of them. They "were compounded with Bulchund" (the native governor of Húglí) for a good sum of money, and 5 per cent. paid by them for all their goods (p. 63). And when Hedges, on a visit to Balasore, is dining at the Bankshall on the shore there, he notes under February 2nd, 1682 (*i.e.*, N.S. 1683) :[1]

"Capt. DORREL and Mr. PITT passed by in their Sloop, with 4 Guns and about 30 ENGLISH Seamen to work the vessel and row in the *Crown's* pinnace to tow the sloop."

And on the 5th February, with " the other two interlopers", vessels apparently also belonging to Pitt's adventure, they sailed for England.

These notices of Pitt by Hedges in 1682, however, present by no means the earliest occurrence of his name in Anglo-Indian records. The following is the first mention that I have found, and shows how early the suspicions of the Court were excited against him :

From Letter of the Court to HUGLI, dated 24th December 1675 :

" We ordered you by Our Last Letter to send home RICHARD THEAD, which Wee confirme, and Wee now understand that Capt. GOODLAD in the *Lancaster* Left there One . . . . PYTTS, and that he is entertayned by Our Chief there,[2] as also the Carpenter of the said Ship did Leave the Commander, and We are informed was prevayled with so to doe by Our Chief. But whether he had a hand in it or not, Wee do require you to take Care to send them to the Fort to remaine there till next yeares Shipping, and then to be sent to England."

And in Streynsham Master's Diary in the India Office, under 15th Decr. 1676, we read :

"The Councell (*i.e.* of BALASORE) being acquainted that there was Severall ENGLISHMEN not in the Companys Service in this Towne, some that came trading Voyages from the COAST, and others that reside in the BAY, they were all sent for and acquainted with the Honble: Companys orders, that all ENGLISH-MEN not in the Companys Service are to reside at FORT ST. GEORGE or MAD-RASPATAM . . . All the English being withdrawn the Councell sent for THOMAS PITTS and read the Honble: Companys Order to send him to ENGLAND by the first Ships and required his observance thereto, who promised to comply accordingly."

About the same date (19th Decr. 1676) the Court are writing again to Húglí :

"Wee note the slight answer you give about RICHARD THEAD . . . . We doe expect that all our orders should be punctually complied with, especially of this Kinde, and would not have you think that a delay or slight excuse will serve the turn in expectation that we may forget. If he and PITTS and the Carpenter of the *Lancaster* ordered home doe not come by the next ships, wee shall esteem it to be a contumacy in you."

It appears quite certain that Pitt did not obey the order for his

---

[1] Page 66.   [2] At Balasore.

return to England, for once more the Court write to the BAY, 12th December 1677:

> "And for THO: PITT, we confirme our former order to have him sent home, for goeing out with an intent to stay in the Countrey, or running away from their ship, are courses we cannot approve, and will rather at any time send a Seaman from home to you then by our Indulgence encourage such practices . . . ."

And at the time when the letter last quoted would reach India we find Pitt still there, as appears from letters of his, and from other brief notices of him that are preserved by chance among the records, having apparently been transmitted to England with the papers of Balasore Factory. There is some mention of money to ·be paid to THOMAS PITT in a letter from MATTHIAS VINCENT at HUGLI to R. EDWARDS at BALASORE, dated February 21st, 1677-8 (O.C. 4364), and a postscript to the same letter runs as follows :

> "Now the new *Amin* is come I doe not question but you may get PITT's horses thence at twice, or at least at thrice, if you cannot at once. Pray endeavour what you can, and excuse my Silence to him and Mr. SMITH. I shall answer them both per the next, but fear I shall not have time to do it now."

We have, also, from the same to the same, March 22nd, *id.:*

> "Pray let me have an accompt what Mr. PITT has sold his horses for, that I may account to him for WAT LITTLETONS share. I heare he has agreed to goe to PERSIA upon NOROOLLA CAWN's Ship. Pray when he comes thence hitherward let somebody come with him that may give me timely notice, if he calls not in here, he being between 4000 and 5000 *Rupees* in my debt on all accompts to this day. Pray tell him I have received his letter, and expecting him up here suddenly as he promised, doe not answer it. Pray take what care you can that he escapes me not."

There is a good deal in these letters not very intelligible, owing to the fragmentary nature of the surviving correspondence, and it is not easy to understand the transaction about the horses, against which Pitt appeals so strenuously to Vincent in the letter next to be quoted :

> "*To the Worshipfull* MATTHIAS VINCENT, *Chiefe for the Affaires of the honourable Company in* BENGALL *and* ORIXA[1] *in* HUGLY."

> "Worshipful S^r: "BALLASORE, May the 11th: 1678.
>
>   "Mr. EDWARDS shewed mee the clause you writt in your last letter to him which was about the horses· S^r: I am certaine you are sensible what a losse I have and am like to sustaine by them with what I lost in your Ship and what Mr. BUGDEN gave away of mine as hee said itt was for the Companys interest and allsoe my beeing putt by (as I was) my imploy which was promised mee, and I depended on itt, not onely that butt other inconveniences attended itt, certainely noe one can thinke butt that this must bee a vast losse to a young beginner as I am. S^r: as for sending the horses to DACCA I am certaine that it will not be for my interest, the NABOB will either take them as a *piscash* or stop them there

---

[1] O.C. 4412.

till hee brings them to his prices, or this weather and the Raines will kill them goeing up, or bring them soe low in case, they will not get itt up in a yeares time. Butt what you write ' you will secure your Selfe and the Companys Interest,' S': you may doe as you please, butt I hope you will excuse mee first, being soe much interested in them, and payd soe deare for them. S': at your goeing hence you were pleased to promise mee to assist mee in the disposeing of them which I hope you will be pleased to doe. S': I have beene formerly advised and Since have perceived it that you are much my enemy, butt for what I know nott. I neuer as I can remember disoblidged you in any thing, but allwayes endeavoured as much as possible to the contrary. This of your Antipathy I suppose was caused first by a Jenerall of Mr. Rolt to you brought by mee my first Voyage from PERSIA, as to your money beeing left behind surely you cannot impute that to any fault of mine, but I suppose that was the onely Reason you were soe unwilling that I should proceed on the Ship a Second Voyage, or because that Mr. CLAVELL consigned your Concern to mee, which I wish had beene otherwise, rather then have reaped your Displeasure by it, butt of late I know there hath beene two persons as have endeavoured (and as it seemes effectually) to incense you against mee but I value them nott, but had I beene as forward to have declared what I knew to bee truth of them, as they have beene in telling things to you of mee that have beene false, happily by this time I might have had my revenge of them, and paid them in theire owne Coyne, butt I hope itt is not yett to late, and I will assure them there shall be nothing wanting in mee to complete itt.

" S': I have sent the Coppy of my accompt with Mr. BUGDEN to Mr. READE to ajust with him. I was unwilling to trouble you, supposeing that you are very busy, and knowing not how you might take itt, but I hope S': you will be pleased to make him give an accompt of the cash hee received of mee, I paying it by your order.

" S': I humbly beg your pardon for the freedom I take herein, which I thought better soe then doe as some endeavour to, hang men behind theire backs, butt speake faire to theire faces, which are like Wolves in Sheepes Cloathing, whose ends I hope will bee irrecoverable miserable. I doubt not but in time you will finde them out. Heartily wishing you may

" I Remaine Worshipfull S':
" Your most Oblidg'd and most humble Servant
" THO: PITT."

From THOMAS PITT to RICHARD EDWARDS, *the Chief of* BALASORE *Factory*[1] :

" CASSAMBAZAR, Sep'': 28th : 1678.

" Mr. RICHARD EDWARDS
" Worthy S':
" In mine to you from on board a Ship I promised to advise you farther on my arrivall in HUGLY concerning what I then gave you a hint of, butt could not thence, my stay there being so very short,—your Sloope. As I went up I saw her, and spoke with BRIGGS concerning her, who seemed to expect great matters for getting of her, and was encouraged by some of your friends, GREENHILL for one, who told mee (when that I told BRIGGS to take the Vessell into my Custody, I had your Order) that hee was a foole if that hee delivered her, the

---

[1] O.C. 4498.

vessell beeing his for Saveing her, by whose meanes and Some others shee was not come up to HUGLY before that I came thence, notwithstanding that I prefer'd BRIGGS to see him satisfyed for his care as rationall men should judge itt, but withall told him that you would not appeal to fooles, knaves, nor Sotts.

"Your Sloope hath neither cables, anchors, sayles, nor in short is there anything butt the hull. Rice I feare is damaged, and a great deale of Oyle amongst the bilge water,—if that shee bee at HUGLY when that I arrive there I will take all care imaginable of her and supply her with whatever shall want, onely desire your orders to meete mee at HUGLY. Mr. VINCENT wee expect him here every hour.

"I doe not know as yett how my business will stand, but I hope better than I expected. Here is a generall complaint against you for being soe slack with your pen, and that we drink a damnable deale of wine this yeare. And besides, that wee . . . . and worse than all that, that I was cheife in Councell when that Mr. BUGDEN'S vessell was Seiz'd on. Mr. SMITH I hope have delivered my Servant 40md. of Coire. My humble service to your selfe and thanks for all former kindnesses

" I Remain Worthy Sir
" Your most obliged and ever thankfull Servt :

" My humble service to Capt. BASSE (Basset ?)　　　" THOMAS PITT."
　　Capt. STANYARD, and Mr. SMITH.
　　My love to my horses."

The same to the same[1] :

" Hugly Octo^br: 16th, 1678.
" Honor'd S^r:

"Att my arrivall here from CASSUMBAZAR, I found your Vessell here in the hole,[2] and that you have committed her to the care of Mr. READE who I suppose will supply her with all things necessary. My stay here I hope will not bee long, pray S^r: if any opportunity presents sell my horses, lett the price bee what it will, Soe with my humble Service to your Selfe, to Capt: BASSET, Mr. SMITH, &ca., friends.

" I Remain Hono^rd: S^r:
" Your most obliged and ever . . . . Servant
"THO: PITT."

The same to the same[3] :

"From on board the Ship Speedwell in BALLASORE ROADE.

"Mr. RICHARD EDWARDS.　　　　　"Decemb^r: 25th 1678.
" Honor'd S^r:

"Pray S^r : doe us the favour to send for the Noquida and make him immediately send off the Surango,[4] with all the Ships Lascars and Ships boate ; and all things that I ordered him to provide for the Voyage especially the bolts, of which hee carried the Measures. I am now taking in the last

---

[1] O.C. 4505.

[2] This term seems to have been often applied to a frequented anchorage, as here at Húglí, and Swally Hole on the Surat shore.

[3] O.C. 4549.

[4] Noquida=Nakhudah (Pers.), a native skipper ; Surango, or Serang= Sarhang (Pers.), used for "a native boatswain".

boate of Sugar. The Ship as yett extraordinary   (1)   if the Noquida hindered not we may saile in three dayes and if the Ship continues as Shee is I will take in all that is sent to METCHEP^M: Pray, S^r: doe not forgett my Skins. I intend butt just to come ashoare to kiss your hand. I wish you all a merry Christmas, and Remain as I

"subscribe Honor'd S^r:

"Your most obliged and ever thankful servant,

"THOMAS PITT."

The departure here in view was apparently to the Persian Gulf. The letter to Vincent above, dated May 11th, 1678, shows that he had made one voyage, or perhaps two, to and from Persia before that time ; whilst the two letters quoted in the footnote,[2] if carefully considered

---

[1] I cannot make out the word ; "high in the water" seems to be meant.

[2] O.C. 4617 :

"Mr. RICHARD EDWARDS.

"Worthy Sr:

"I presumed the last yeare to trouble you with a few lines by the Shipp *Good Hope* wherein requested your reply to severall perticolers, as Your Observations on the Trade, Manufactures, and ffertillity of the Kingdome of BENGALE, together with what Antiquities it affoards, especially as to the Ruins of that ffamous Citty or be it Regall Palace near to RAJUMALE which I have heard you discourse off, as likewise the Rites, Customes and manners of those People, and the Severall Casts amongst them, with what else you might have iudged materiall and worthy the participation of my Friend in ENGLAND for whose Satisfaction I desir'd it, but I have not hitherto been favour'd with your Courteous reply, which I shall hope at receipt hereof, being assured my other letter came to your hand, in which were more perticolers than I can now call to mind.

"Wherein I may be Servicable to you in these parts, pray favour me with your Commands without any discouragements from Capt: PITT, who is greatly offended because all things answere not his unreasonable unexpectations (*sic*), with tender of due respects.

"I Remaine Sr:

"Your Most Affectionate Friend and humbble Servt:

GOMBROONE June ye: 14th: 1679.   "ISAAC LAURENCE."

"Capt: PITT and I had seuerall
bickerings here but I thanke
Heauen we parted very good
ffrds: and so shall continue.—
I.L."

Extract of letter from SURAT *Council to Court, dated* SWALLY MARINE, the 24th
of January 16$\frac{80}{81}$*

"67. Wee have beene advised by private hands of a Ship Comanded by one WM: ALLEY" (see pp. ci-ciii *supra*), "that arrived from ENGLAND at PORTO

---

* O.C. 4716.

with their dates, seem to point to two more voyages to that quarter, made respectively in the beginning of 1679, and in 1680.

The next letter appears to announce Pitt's return from the Persian voyage, and arrival off the bar of Balasore :

"Mr. RICHARD EDWARDS   "From aboard the *Recovery* 7^{br} : 25th : 79.[1]

"Honord Sr :

"I hope by this time the *Speedwell* is come up to the Dock. S^r: pray doe mee the favour whether that Shee bee or noe putt a *Pune* aboard and order Mr. CAMELL that there bee nothing taken out of any persons whatsoever till that I come up, for I want many things here, as I hope to find there. We are at the foot of the bar, and hope to come over this night the tides fall outt crosse, pray order Mr. ABERNATHY to send downe some bread, beefe, limes, 12 pottle bottles arrack, and 20 Candles, I hope that our *Purgoes* lye att the Banksall for wee have not had one of to the Ship as yet. My Service to your Selfe and the Captains I Remaine,

"Honor'd S^r:
"Your most obliged and thankfull servt:
"THO: PITT."

This letter is sealed with a somewhat roughly executed seal, which bears the shield of the Dorsetshire Pitts.

The next is a letter to Edwards from Mr. EDMUND BUGDEN of the Council at Húglí without date, and partially injured. It contains a complaint of Pitt, apparently referring to the period succeeding his return from Persia :[2]

"Mr. THOMAS PITT, after all his [? *flouri*]shing, is proved an vnworthy man. Haveing showed his and my Arbitrators all the accompts of his sixteen Baggs of

NOVA, on a particular account, the beginning of June last, but noe notice taken of her to us by your Agent and Councell at MADRASSE, soe that wee can informe you nothing further of her from hence, likewise the Commander of your EUROPE Ships (who can give you a more particular accountt hereof) acquaint us of theire meeting at JOHANNA another private Ship Commanded by one CRISPT, and sailed out with them from thence, but afterwards left them in the night pretending to bee bound for GOA, and from thence to BOMBAY, and SURRATT ; but since finde them to have first imported at MUSCAT, where meeting with one PITTS, who from BENGALLA having beene with a Cargoe of Sugars at PERSIA incouraged them for the COAST of COR-MANDEL and BAY; which hath given as a happy deliverance from them ; which otherwise would have given your affaires here great inconveniency and prejudice; and therefore it will highly concerne your Honours timely to prevent it from others for the future, as Wee on our parts shall not bee wanting to defeate all their designs against your Interest to the utmost of our Power according to his Majesties Commaud and your Honours Instructions."

[1] O.C. 4656.   [2] O.C. 4506.

A[*? tla*]sses that he . . . . into the chest at BALLASORE . . . . indiscreet man, has interlined the Invoice that I and he signed and made it seventeen, which last bagg I have by me sealed as it came from PERSIA, truth will appeare at last, in despight of all the machinations of policy,—Not else at present from

"Your assured friend and servant
"EDM^D: BUGDEN."

Another letter from Pitt to Edwards, which perhaps should precede the letter from Bugden :

"Mr. RICHARD EDWARDS,   "HUGLY October 24th : 1679.[1]
"Honor'd: S^r:
        "This morning I arrived here, and since have been advised that Mr. BUGDEN hath a desier to take part of a ship for BANTAM, pray, if you can, sell him ⅔ of the *Speedwell,* or what he please. I have referr'd him to you. You can show him the bill of sale, if he buyes lett him make good the money to you, and pray immediately advise mee of it, and for his part of the Cargo, lett him remitt the money and I will invest it. I leave you and Mr. BYAM to consult it. I doe not thinke that I shall stay longer in the Countrey ; pray dispose of her as you think fitting. I have wholely referr'd Mr. BUGDEN to you, pray Vncle doe Your Uttmost to assist the *Recovery*[2] in fitting her with all Speed, for God's sake doe not fail mee, and doe not let any but Mr. BYAM know that I doubt my longer staying in the Countrey, for if I doe not I must deliver her up ready fitted. But I will advise you more plenary very suddenly. Hold the Merchants in dispense. I have not more as yett to advise you, but that Mr. READE complains for his accompt, and he tells mee of it. My humble service to the faire lady and all the Captains. Pray assist the *Recovery*[2] in fitting [and dispose of the *Speedwell.*

"I have not to add for I will write to you again very suddenly.[3] I Remain,
"Hono^rd : S^r:
"Your most Obliged and faythfull servt :
"THO : PITT."

"S^r: Pray tell Capt. EARWIN that I will keepe his money untill that I depart hence, and then shall leave it to Mr. VINCENT for his Accompt."

"To Mr. RICHARD EDWARDS[4]   "HUGLY October 30th, 1679."
"Hono^rd: S^r:
        "Since my last to you Mr. VINCENT and I have discours'd about a PERSIA Voyage, soe that the *Bengall Merchant* is to come downe and will be profer'd to Sale. Shee is excellent well fitted with all things, and if Shee bee Sold, then Mr. VINCENT will take part of the *Recovery* for PERSIA, otherwise the *Bengall Merchant* must goe, if CHINCHAM and CHINTA-MUN[5] have a designe for MALDIVAS and ACHEENE, or ACHEENE alone, noe fitter a Ship then the *Bengall Merchant* who is ready to make any Voyage ; pray

---

[1] O.C. 4667.

[2] The ship in which he had just made the voyage to Persia ; and that in which Hedges went to the Gulf six years later.

[3] *Suddenly* means, as frequently in these documents, "soon", "speedily".

[4] O.C. 4671.

[5] These were native merchants at Balasore, often named in the Records.

assist the *Recovery* in her speedy fitting, which if afterwards sold will bee the better for the buyer. Pray let the *Recovery* want nothing, and desire Mr. WELLS to make all hast imaginable and lett him remember what it is to goe late, I did think I should have had a letter from you long ere this ; I hope that you have agreed with Mr. BUGDEN concerning the Ship, which if you have pray secure the money, and desire you would speedily advise mee.

" S^r: Pray dispose of all goods of mine as soon as possible and of the red earth for the most you can gett, pray S^r: doe not forget the *Recovery*. The news is here I have and shall I hope subdue all my enemies. I have not to add butt heartily wish and pray for your health and happiness and that you may gett money for which not doeing you are much condemned here. I Rem^a:

" Honord: S^r:

" Your most Obliged and humble servant

" VERTE."   " THO: PITT."

(On the other side.)

" S^r: Pray doe me the favour as to peruse Mr. PERRINS papers to see whether that they doe make manifest the Bulgar hides to bee WALT. LITTLETON'S who denies them now to bee his but says they are wholly Mr. PERRINS, Pray likewise advise what you have heard Mr. PERRIN declare concerning them, lett me have speedy advise concerning this and all other things and I shall ever

" Rem^a: Honord: S$^:$:

" Your ever obliged servant

" THO: PITT."

(P.S. at one side.)

" Sr: Pray tell CHIMCHAM and CHINTAMUN that I will serve them in any thing and if they buy the *Bengall Merchant* they will have a good pennyworth, and a Shipp well fitted, as for the *Recovery* lett them not know but that Shee is to be Sold. Deare Vnckle I still Rem^a:

" Your Nephew,

"THOMAS PITT."

The last letter (Oct. 30th, 1679) seems to speak of another voyage to Persia as possibly in prospect, and such a voyage (in 1680) would agree, as I have already suggested, with the indications of the date of his being met at Muscat, which are given in the Surat letter of January 1681. He might have made this second voyage to the Gulf, and still have been in England in time for that on which we next have positive intelligence of him.

In 1681-2 there took formal shape an attempt to found a rival East India Company, a project favoured by the jealousy which had long existed between the Levant (or Turkey) Company, and that of Leadenhall Street. The scheme came under consideration of the King and Privy Council in April 1682, but was rejected.[1]

Before this, however, Pitt, in the ship *Crown*, and with two or three other vessels which had been chartered by him or his principals, made the new voyage of which Hedges has spoken in the passages

---

[1] See Bruce's *Annals*, ii, 475-6.

quoted from his *Diary* at the beginning of this article, leaving England about 20th February 1682, and reaching Balasore about 8th July.

On the subject of this voyage the following entry appears in the *Court Book* under 15th February 1681-2 :

"Information being given unto this Court that THOMAS PITT and EDMOND TAYLOR who came home on the *William and John* from the bay of BENGALL are now on board the *Crown* designed for INDIA, The Court desires Mr. MOSES to procure a writt *ne exeat regnum* (*sic*) against them untill the suit depending in Chancery against them by the Company be heard and determined."

And we find in their letter to Bengal under the same date :

" We are informed that Mr. PITTS is gone for INDIA in the ship *Crowne*, and we believe will come up HUGHLY River directly, in hopes to get his passage thither before our Agent HEDGES (which we hope the Almighty will prevent). If he should appear within your Agency, we would have you Secure his person, whatever it cost to the Government or other natives, all which we recommend to the prudent management and good husbandry of our Agent and Councill. When you have got him into your Custody, be sure to secure him, he being a desperate fellow, and one that we fear will not stick in doing any mischief that lies in his power, and we have such confidence in the conduct of you our Agent and Councill in putting your authority of the Country in execution (which Mr. READ acquainted us may be done), that no Interloper shall be able to procure Water or provisions without rendring themselves to your comãnds, desiring to be received into Our service upon such terms as we have formerly directed."

The Court to Captain Wᴹ· WILDEY (*of the ship "Welfare"*).

" London, 17th February 1681(-2).

"Understanding that the ship *Crowne*, one DORRELL Comander, is already put to Sea, bound for INDIA, and that on board him is Mr. THOMAS PITTS, who lately came from the BAY in the *William and John*, We judge it highly imports the good of this Company, that you make all imaginable hast to gett before him into the BAY. In order whereunto . . . . as soon as our other 4 ships are together in the DOWNES, You are to proceed with them in Company together till you are out of danger of the ALGERINE Pirates, and then we require you to ply your Voyage all that possibly you can, and to sail directly for the BAY up the River GANGES, as near to HUGHLY as you can, without staying at BALLASORE for the Agent and Councills orders, but only to take in Pilots, that so you may answer our great designe in preventing the prejudice that may be done us by that Ship, or any other Interloper designed for that place . . ."

They also write to Fort St. George, 10th March, *id.* :

" We hear that there will be two Interlopers this year in the BAY, vizt: the *Crowne*, Capt. DORRELL, and" (blank in Records) "THOMAS PITTS, being designed supra-cargo of both, who is Mr.Vincent's cousin, and a fellow of a haughty, huffing, daring temper, and therefore by the first ship that goes downe to the BAY, we would have you send downe to Agent HEDGES a Corporall and 20 soldiers, to be at his disposall there, so long as our ships stay, or he shall think fitt to keep them there to prevent Interlopers . . . We think it may not be amiss to have them there to prevent any insolent attempt of PITTS to rescue VINCENT . . . because probably PITTS, being so well acquainted on the River of GANGES, may carry up both the ships aforesaid so high as HUGHLEY, whereas we have no ship small enough to go up, but onely the *Welfare* that is less than either of the others."

The Council of Surat again wrote to the Court, 10th April 1683:

"With advices from BENGALLA . . . Your Country servants beaten by the government, and money forced from them in such a manner that all are afraid to serve. The interlopeing Shipps neare fully laden, by the means of your false servant VINCENT . . . VINCENT intends for ENGLAND in the *Crowne ;* he and PITTS talks at a Strange rate, give out that your Honours are broke, and they chiefes for a New Company. Wee hope that they will meet with a due reward for contemning his Majestie's Charter."

The actual proceedings of Pitt and Dorrell in Bengal, so far as Hedges affords any account of them, have been indicated at the beginning of this compilation, and chronologically would come in at this point. I give a few particulars from other sources.

"*Abstract of a letter from the* ENGLISH *Councill of* y*e:* BAY *of* BENGALL *in* INDIA, *received by* y*e* Interlop*s*: *Ship Crowne, that departed* BENGALL *in* January *last,* vizt:[1] *ffirst,* that the said *Crowne* arrived 11 daies before our Agent on the *Defence* in BALLASORE road.

"PITTS entered BALLASORE in a hostile manner with guards and trumpetts, reports the EAST INDIA Company were in so low a condition that they could send forth but 2 shipps to fetch off their remaines with not 20 chests of treasure, and that there was a new Company erected and hee, the said PITTS, was their Agent. As soone as he came to the Companys late Agent VINCENT, VINCENT removed to the DUTCH Quarter, levies an armed guard of PORTUGUEZ firelocks, RASHBOOTES and Peones. The *Defence* arrived with Agent HEDGES in BENGAL the 17th of July, 1682, at BALLASORE, the 24th at HUGHLY, found all trade interdicted except the Company would pay Custome both for Goods and Treasure. . . . Under all these troubles PITTS comes with 3 shipps to Hughley and lands in great state, with 4 or 5 files of soldiers in red coats, well armed, and great attendance of Native Soldiers, with Trumpeters, and takes up his quarters with the DUTCH, by the name of the New Companys Agent, bespattering the Old Company. He treats with the Governour as Agent, as aforesaid, obtaines a *Perwanna* order, under the title of the New ENGLISH Company, to trade, and also liberty to build a ffactory with many[2]   to continue for ever, and defames the Companys servants. VINCENT, joyning with him, builds warehouses, the DUTCH everywhere assisting them, and the Companys black Merchants, by Vincents influence.

"Vpon the Agents arrivall VINCENT and LITTLETON are served with Subpœnas out of Chancery which they Slight, and a day being appointed for their Answer, they refused, saying they would answer in England."

---

[1] O.C. 4882.

[2] Blank in original abstract. Supply "privileges"?

The Court to BENGALL, " LONDON, 30th May 1683."

*　　*　　*　　*　　*　　*　　*

" We have a most acceptable accompt of the flourishing condition of all our affaires in those parts, and of the Wreck and disappointment of all the Interlopers : insomuch that if you have done your parts in reference to the *Crowne* that THO: PITTS went upon, there is no probability [that] of 7 Interloping ships that went to INDIA the same year that Our Agent did, any one Ship will ever come to ENGLAND again ; And you and all our Servants in INDIA being so incouraged with Success, and as Wee hope strongly armed with Zeal and Fidelity for our Service, Wee cannot doubt but you will in due time render Us as pleasing an Accompt of those Interlopers that went out This Year, which will certainly put an end to that kind of Robbery as long as any of this Age shall survive and remember the Misfortunes of those men who have impoverished abundance of People severall waies concerned with them in LONDON and other parts of the Kingdom.

" We understand PITTZ arrived at BALLASOAR some daies before you, but before VINCENT could have notice thereof,[1] and considering the Season of Rain at that time, the Soldiers sent you from the FORT, and those you carryed, Wee cannot think it was possible for VINCENT, LITTLETON, and PITTS, or any other wicked adhaerents to do Us any Mischief before you surprised them, so that by Capt. HEATH Wee expect you have sent them home in safe Custody according to our orders to you.

" The Wreck of the Interlopers Wee look upon as a just Judgment of GOD upon their disloyal and unjust proceedings, and that it will have such an effect upon all mens minds here as to convince the Deluded World of the Vanity and Folly of those persons that would persuade them the trade of ENGLAND in INDIA is to be preserved by any other means than the strict Rules and Discipline of an United Stock governed by a select and authorised Councell : and if you can acquit your selves as well this present year in that respect as our Servants in other places did the last year, the very name of Interloping must of necessity fall into General Reproach, Ignominy, and Contempt."

Court Book, 22nd June 1683 :

" His Majestys Counsel at Law are of Opinion that the Company do commence their suit against the commander and officers of the Ship *Crown,* and other persons interested, and it is ordered to be referred to the Committee for Lawsuits to give direction that process be taken out."

Court Book, 11th July 1683 :

" Mr. DUBOIS and Mr. CUNHAM are desired to inform themselves what the persons entertained by S[r]: JOHN WETWANG can testify touching the carriage of Mr. PITTS and Mr. DORREL, Master of the *Crown,* at their coming to HUGHLEY, and to report the same on Friday next"—

But I find nothing further as to their report.

From Court's Letter to SURATT, dated July 20th, 1683 :

" The affairs of the Interlopers we hope will be soon at an end, his Majesty

---

[1] Presumably means : "but you arrived before VINCENT could have notice of PITT's arrival."

being fully resolved to suppress them. The Methods propos'd for the effectuall doing whereof by the Kings Councell here are

" 1st. By stopping them from going out as Wee did SANDS (which lies by the Walls) ¹

" 2. By our own actions for damages.

" 3. By Information in the Crown Office in the Kings name for high Misdemeanours upon which such as are found guilty will be fined to the King at the Judges discretions.

" In the two forementioned ways Wee have begun with 25 of them, which is thought abundantly more effectuall then stopping or seizing their goods, which cannot be so well justify'd in ENGLAND by our Charter as it may be in INDIA, as Our Councell informs us.

  *   *   *   *   *   *   *

" In regard the Crimes perpetrated by VINCENT, PITTS, and DORRELL, in the BAY of BENGALL were most enormous there was a particular information against them upon which they were taken and kept some days in Custody by the King's Messengers, and then dismissed giving 40,000l. each Security to answer the King's Suit, the issue whereof (we have reason to believe) will make them Sick of that kind of Interloping trade . . . ."²

From Court to BENGAL, 5th September 1683 :

" We are satisfy'd with the Reasons you give Us for not seizing the Person of Mr. VINCENT and PITTS, but not satisfy'd with that you alledge for not sending home Mr. ROLLE, whom you say is joyn'd to LITTLETON, and that he was unconcern'd with Interlopers, in which you are mistaken, For we know that he is a Spy, and a Tool of theirs, and was a Servant of the GREGORYS here, who were the greatest Owners of the *Crown*."

The next two extracts do not name Pitt or any other individual, but they refer probably to him, among others, as one of their adversaries, the Interlopers, on whom they claimed to have inflicted such defeat.

From Court's Letter to SURAT, *of* 7th April 1684 :

" 64. The Litigation between Us and Interlopers, of the two last years goes on well according to the method of proceedings in the Laws of this Kingdome and have no doubt but the result of all our Suits wilbe to our Satisfaction, and We suppose our Adversaries are of the same opinion, the rather because We doe not know of any Interloper gone for India this year or designed to goe."

---

¹ " SANDS still continues disquieting himself and Us at law to little Purpose, while his Ship and Goods hath layn at Wrack in this River 7 or 8 months, and is never like to put you to any trouble in INDIA."—*The Court to* FORT ST. GEORGE, May 31st, 1683.

² Pitt and Dorrell had sailed from Balasore 5th February 1682-3 ; and it is a little puzzling how they could have arrived in time for this arrest to have been reported by the Court on 20th July of the same year. No doubt, however, the *Crown* must have been a fast vessel for those days. On her voyage out she left the Downs about 20th February, and arrived at Balasore 8th July 1682 (see *Diary*, pp. 20 and 31); and an equal voyage home would have brought her to port about 23rd June 1683.

From the Same to HUGLI, 3rd October 1684 :

"12. With this wee send the Printed Cargo of the Interloper *William and John*,[1] and intend to send the Print of her sale, if wee can procure it, to the intent that you may see what Kind of new goods she brought, and how they sould here, for your government in providing for us, such as you find turned to best account.

"13. Upon this occasion wee must tell you that the Interlopers have in nothing juste cause to boast than this, that notwithstanding our Councils are constantly resident upon the Place, and have alwaies our orders and mony beforehand, and time to Provide new and fine sorts of goods, and they come to the BAY but for a short time and as it were by stealth, and yet they bring home more in proportion of those new desireable goods by far then our ships, which is such an unanswerable reproach to those that mannag'd our affairs formerly that wee hope you will remove it from your doors."

I may observe here that neither I nor a legal friend, who is a member of the Council of our Society, and kindly gave his assistance in the matter, have been able to find any mention of Pitt's case in published reports. The arguments in the case of SANDYS, which is mentioned in the Court's letter of July 20th, quoted above, are given at much length in the *State Trials*, under the heading :

" The Great Case of Monopolies between the EAST INDIA COMPANY, Plaintiffs, and THOMAS SANDYS, Defendant, Whether their Patent for Trading to the EAST INDIES, exclusive of all others, is good ?

" *The Six following arguments*[2] *in this Great Case were copied from the* MSS. *of* SAMUEL PEPYS *Esqr*. . . . . *in* MAGDALEN COLLEGE, CAMBRIDGE."

Jeffries, who presided, concludes :

" Upon the whole matter, I am of the same opinion with my brothers ; and do conceive that that grant to the plaintiffs, of the sole trade to the INDIES, exclusive of others, is a good grant, and that the action is well brought.

" And therefore let the plaintiff take his judgment."—Cobbett's *State Trials*, 1811, under 36 Charles II (1684), vol. x, col. 371 to col. 454.[3]

---

[1] This ship is mentioned by Hedges, pp. 77, 94, 132.

[2] The arguments are by Holt (afterwards Lord Chief Justice), Treby (do.), Finch (afterwards Earl of Nottingham and Chancellor), Pollexfen (afterwards Lord Chief Justice), Sawyer (Attorney-General), and Williams. The judgments of Justice Holloway and Lord Chief Justice Jeffries are also given.

[3] My friend alluded to above, Mr. A. Gray, has kindly sent me notes, from which I extract the following :

" The Judges headed by JEFFRIES went for the Company.

" The Reports only notice cases which are in any way important in a legal aspect, and I imagine that SANDYS'S case settled (for the nonce) the question

Whether it was due to this course of law, and the heavy recog-
nisances ordered, I do not know for certain, but we hear almost nothing
of Captain Pitt's proceedings, and certainly nothing of voyages to India,

---

of the exclusive right of trading ; and therefore that PITT and the others
were fined without remonstrance.

* * * * * * *

" As regards the form of proceedings, which you quote from the Court's
Letter to SURAT of July 20th (*supra*), the action for damages was *an action on
the case*, as was that against SANDYS. An *information* in the King's Bench is
a criminal proceeding for a misdemeanour, and is distinguished from an *indictment*, inasmuch as it is brought directly before the King's Bench, without any
bill being found by a Grand Jury, and it was the form of procedure always
adopted to exact penalties or fines in cases when the judges and King's
Ministers were antagonistic to the people, and where, if an indictment had
been brought, the Grand Jury would probably have thrown it out. I do not
know, however, how they could proceed against the interlopers by *information*,
unless by some law the infringement of the Company's Charter was made to
be a misdemeanour, as probably it was.

" *Sandys* v. *Exton* (Hilary Term, 39 Car. II, *i.e.* 1683).

" SANDYS laded a ship and gave out that he intended for the EAST INDIES.
Upon complaint hereof to the King in Council, he ordered his advocate in the
Admiralty to arrest the said Ship, and detain her till Security was given not to
go and trade within any part of the countries contained in the patent
granted to the E. I. Company. The ship was accordingly arrested, and SANDYS
refused to give security, but prayed a prohibition in R. B. (*King's Bench*).
(The King's Bench, as the Supreme Court of Common Law, had the power to
restrain the Court of Admiralty, a Court of *Civil Law*, when it transgressed
or encroached upon the Common Law.)

" After an argument in the King's Bench with some legal technicalities, ' all
the judges' were of opinion that there should be no prohibition, as there was
no *suit* in the Admiralty Court, and they would not prohibit the King getting
a warrant there (*Skinner's Reports*, 1728, p. 91).

" The Company, having got SANDYS's ship arrested, then seems to have commenced an action against him—*an action on the case*, i.e., an ordinary action
for wrong done. Each side engaged the leading counsel of the day . . . .

" '*East India Company*. This was the great case that depended at that time
against SANDYS for interloping ; but concerned the merchants in LONDON,
who complained against the E. I. Company for being a monopoly, and began
almost to form an interloping Company. But the Judgment of Law, being
for the Company, put a stop to it. JEFFRIES espoused the matter with great
fury ; and though not much given to argue Law matters, he, in giving his
Judgment, made a prolix argument, as the Reports of the Case whereon they
appear, will show. There was somewhat extraordinary at the bottom. But I
have no ground to say what.' (North's *Life of Guildford*, ed. 1808, ii, 109.)

" . . . . The 3d year of JAMES II the King's Bench held that the King could
not give a monopoly to merchants to trade with Holland or Brabant (*Merchant*

for about ten years after this. Indeed, Sir John Goldsborough in a representation to the Nabob of Bengal regarding Pitt's reappearance there in 1693, expressly says that the great troubles which Pitt had brought on himself in England, and his detention there by the Government, would have prevented his ever returning, but for the opportunities afforded him by the wars which had recently broken out. We do not at all know how he was occupied in the interval, but as we shall find him in 1688-9 a man of landed estate and a Member of Parliament, no doubt he had found a field for his infinite activity in adventure and money-making.

The following are the only notices of Pitt in that interval that I have been able to trace :

From Court Book, 30th Nov. 1687 :

"There having been a fyne of 1000£ lately set upon Thomas Pitts of London Merchant by his Majestys Court of King's Bench upon an information against him for Interloping within the limits of the Companys Charter and other great misdemeanours committed in the East Indies, whereof he was convicted, And his Majesty taking notice that the Company has been at excessive charge in prosecution of that suit, was graciously pleased to give the said fyne unto the Company and to discharge the said Thomas Pitts thereof ; Now the Court notwithstanding all the damage the Company have sustained by means of the said Tho: Pitts and his adherents, were pleased to be so kind to him as to abate him 600£ of the said fyne, and only to receive 400£, which was payd into the Company's Treasury."

Under date 23rd Nov. 1688 we find the following somewhat surprising announcement ; but we do not know its precise bearing :

"Mr. Thomas Pitts was now admitted into the freedom of this Company gratis."

Again, under 7th January 1689(90) :

"A Motion being made that three Bales of Goods belonging to Mr. Thomas Pitts, brought home on the *Rochester*, might be delivered unto him, It is ordered that the Committee of private trade do give direction therein accordingly, he paying permission for the same according to the valuation that the Committees shall make of the said goods."

These might, seem straws indicating a more favourable air from Leadenhall Street in the direction of the Interloper. But if so this promising aspect of things underwent interruption, for at no time does the hostility between the two parties find stronger expression than during the next voyage of Pitt.

Adventurers v. *Rebow*. 3. *Modern Reports*, p. 126). The Company's case with Sandys had been decided greatly on the ground that the natives of India were infidels, and that no British subjects could, without the King's license, trade with Infidels."

For notices of Pitt's re-appearance in the Ganges Delta in the autumn of 1693 we are chiefly indebted to the official correspondence of Sir John Goldsborough, then on a visit of supervision to Bengal as the Company's " Commissary General". But earlier in that year we hear of the proposed voyage in *Luttrell's Diary* :

"On Thursday [30th March 1693] an extraordinary Councell at KENSINGTON, where was a great hearing before his Majestie, between the E. I. Company and Capt. GIFFORD and Capt. PITTS, two Interlopers ; the Company prest to have the interlopers hindered from going to sea." (iii, 68.)

They were not, however, hindered from going to sea, and perhaps Pitt had already started. The Court write on this subject to Bengal, 28th April 1693 :

"For what we can yet apprehend the Interloper *Edward* whereof Capt. WILLIAM GIFFORD is Commander, Mr. THOMAS PITTS and ALLEN CATCH-POLE Supra Cargos, will creep out to BENGALL, altho' the first and second order of Council be only to permitt them to prosecute their Voyage for MADERA, of both which orders Wee send you herewith Authentique Copyes. Wee are very much disposed to frustrate her Voyage whatever it costs, wel knowing nothing to be done in INDIA without Money.

"Mr. PITTS and CATCHPOLE will make a great huffing and swaggering if they arrive there as they did formerly, but you will have a good guard of soldiers about you, and if they prove faithfull you need not fear any great shows they will make there, not that Wee would have blood shed, but Wee would not have you outlooked or Triumphed over as PITTS did formerly over Mr. BEARD, who wanting the Language of the Country could not work so secretly with the great men in BENGALL as you may doe that have such perfect knowledge of their Language and Methods in all respects . . " [1]

They are to encourage MUTTRIDAS if he has adhered faithfully, and given help to defeat the Interlopers.

"You may give him for his expences and for the assistance of his ffriends at DACCA a present of four or ffive thousand Pounds as you shall see cause when the Business is done to your Content, in the Mean time give him a Positive assurance of it, and buy as many Goods of him as he can furnish you with, tho' they lye by you or him in Godownes Untill our next Ships arrive with you, and he have his Money for them, Alltho' Wee cant doubt he will have any Jealousy of his payment, since never any Native of INDIA lost a Penny debt by this Company from the time of the first institution thereof in Queen ELIZABETH'S dayes till this time, altho' Wee have been inform'd there is some scores of Thousand Pounds remaining Due to the Natives from the last Interlopers, and not a little from DAVIS and PITTS themselves, who were their great Champions in BENGALL, which now they will have an opportunity to secure.

"We would have no force used on our side, but all things to be done by Wisdom and Money except the Interlopers offer any force against the Natives our Allyes, and in such Case we would have you give order to our Captains and officers by force to rescue any of our Allyes, their Ships, Effects or Persons out

---

[1] Words intended no doubt for Job Charnock, no longer in life when the letter was written.

of their hands. And if there be occasion upon this Conjunction to increase the number of your Peons or Topass Souldiers We would not have you Stick at that Charge nor any other tho' not herein particularly mentioned, to prevent and defeat this Interlopers Voyage.

"This bold attempt of Mr. PITTS and CATCHPOOLE has so irritated the adventurers that they are resolved immediately to raise among themselves an additional Stock of about £400,000 to be added as a further Capitall for carrying on the Trade fully to all Intents and Purposes, which after all other Wayes is the most certain to confound and discourage all Interloping Attempts, as wee found by Experience in the late Interloping Times.

" We dyrect this Letter only to your Self that you so keep it or show it to your Councill if you think fitt, but you must conclude you have some false Breatheren, as well as Mr. BEARD had."

Mr. Henry Stanley, chief at Balasore, reported to Sir John Goldsborough Pitt's arrival at that port, 1st October 1693, in company with the Company's dismissed servant, Allen Catchpoole, on board an "Interloper" of 500 tons called the *Seymore*.[1] On this Sir John addressed a communication to the Nawáb Súbadár of Bengal, which we shall give presently, and writing also to Mr. Eyres at Dacca (dated "CHUTTANUTTE 8ber: the 9th:") says :

" By the Copy of Mr. Stanley's Letter to me of the 1st: instant you will see what is written about TOM PITT and ALLEN CATCHPOOLE being come to BALLA-SORE, who huff and Bounce, and give out Mountaines on their one Side, but this is much to be liked that they Say not one word of the Rt: Hon: Company our Masters more then Cursing of them, for if they were not Established that would be the first thing they would vent . . . ."

And on the 23rd he writes to the same correspondent :

" Since my last . . . . we have heard nothing more from Mr. STANLEY about TOM PITT and the Interlopers. However I thinck fitt to acquaint you that we, about 4 daies after my letter to you, heard that the Governour of HUGLY was fitting his boat to fetch TOM PITT from KENDUA up the River, notwithstanding what we had wrot to him about PITT, upon which we sent Captain DORRILL to him at HUGLY, with orders to lett him know that if he gave any entertainment or countenance to TOM PITT or his People, or suffered the Merchants to trade with him or them, it would bring another warr upon this place, and that we would Stop TOM PITT upon the River, from Coming up, and that if by Land he did gett to HUGLY, we would fetch him from thence.

" Upon this the Gov'r: of HUGLY seemed to be affraid, and promised he would give him noe Countenance or Entertainment, nor the Merchants should not trade with him . . . . and if TOM PITT came to Hugly he would deliver him up to us . . . . This I require you strictly to observe and follow, and not be affraid of speaking, for it is my Resolution not to stay here if they suffer him."

To this Mr. EYRES writes in reply :

" I observe what your Excellency writes as to THO: PITT and ALLEYN CETCH

---

[1] It is *Seymore* in the transcript of Sir J. Goldsborough's letter to Surat (O.C. 5886, No. 43), from which this is quoted ; but *Seymore* is the correct name, as we shall see further on.

POLES being arrived in BENGALL, having perused the Coppy of Mr. STANLEY'S letter to your Excellency, likewise I shall use my best Endeavour to frustrate their designs, and to get them turn'd out of the Countrey . . . .

"If Your Excy: thinks convenient I will acquaint the Nabob and Duan that these Strangers that Steale out of their owne Countrey in this nature are Generally those people that rob and plunder on the Seas, and onder pretence of being Merchants and comeing to trade, doe abundance of mischief to the King and his Subjects, and that 'tis more than probable this Ship may be one of those. This will soe surprise the Nabob and Duan that 'tis thought they will order their persons and effects to be seiz'd. Your Excy: may rest assured of my best endeavours in this affair."

I now give Sir John's letter to the Nabob which was recently mentioned :

"*To his Highness* IBRAHIM CAWN *Nabob of* BENGALL *and to* KAFFAIT CAWN *the Kings duan,* S: JON: GOLDSBOROUGH *Comissarie Generall, and Chief Governour of all the Rt: H: ET:* INDIA *Companys Affairs in these Eastern parts Wisheth health,* &ca:[1]

(Dated "CHUTANUTTE 8ber : ye 9th: 1693).

"May it please Your Highness it is about a Month Since I had the Honour to give your Highness an account of my arrivall in these parts, occationed by the Kings *Husbolhookem* to his duan KAFFAIT CAWN for to stop the three EUROPEAN Nations trade, upon which I gave your Highness an account of the Cause therof, that it was occationed by ill men that were ill willers to Government, and that in most kingdomes there were such, and that it was from them that Interlopers and pirots infested these seas, and your Highness Remembers the war and many differences and troubles some 4 or 5 years past which fell between your people and ours here in BENGALL, which was began and occationed by Interlopers, who are such as I have above mentioned, that contrary to our King or his Rt: H: ET: INDIA Company have come into these parts, and once or twice before were Received here by the Government and Merchants att BALLASORE and HUGLY &ca: places, which was the occation of that unhappy War.

"Now may it please your Highness I have notice from our ffactors Residing at BALLASORE that about 8 daies past arrived in that Road an Interloping Ship who without leave from our King, or his Rt. Honble: ET: INDIA Company is come thither as will appear by his not having one of the Largest Printed Passes presented some time past to your Highness by our factors, if your Highness shall think fitt to demand it of them ; further in the Ship is come one of those very men named THOS : PITT that were here formerly, upon the very same Interloping Account, whoe was one of them that Layde the foundation of the unhappy differences before mentioned and may doe the like agen if your Highness doth not prevent him, by not admitting him to trade in the Kings ports.

"I therefore doe humbly intreat your Highness to Consider the many Evills that may Ensue if such men be permitted to trade when due notice is given that they are Interlopers, which may be prevented if your Highness in great wisdome shall thinck fitt to issue forth your Commands . . . . This very THO: PITT is the man that about 11 years past did by some sinister Insinuation obtaine a *Porwana* from the Nabob SHASTAH CAUNE to build a factorie att HUGLY, and upon his returne to ENGLAND had great trouble, and hath been by the Government

----

[1] O.C. 5886, No. 32.

there detained from ever Returning hither, but EUROPE being afflicted with extream Warrs he hath now gott some Oppertunitie to Escape from thence once more with Effects and such as him selfe, and by this it will appear what little Benefit the *phirmand* granted to him hath been of to this Country, and the many Evils it hath produced, and what further may arise, if he be still incouraged, your Highness is best able to judge."

From Sir JOHN GOLDSBOROUGH *to* FORT ST. GEORGE.[1]

*   *   *   *   *   *

" CHUTTANUTTE 8ber: yᵉ 14th: 1693.

" The Governour of HUGLY hath been Extraordinary Civill to our affaires, during the Stop of trade, and I hope our Letter to him about TOM: PITT will hold him Soe.

" Itt is Reported here that TOM: Pitt sent Letters ashore att FORT ST. DAVID but this you must know best att MADRASS.

" We are now informed that the Governour of HUGLY is fitting his boate to fetch TOM: PITT from KENDUA, and have agreed upon it and sent Captain DORRELL up to give him in publique the Kings *duhoy*[2] upon it, and to lett him know that unless TOM: PITT Can produce a power from ENGLAND (such as we have) for his coming hither, we will Stop him on the river, and if he gett to HUGHLY we will fetch him out from thence, and if any Blood be Shed therein it must ly at his door, for he can have noe order from the Nabob for giving him entertainment."

From the same to

" *The Right Worshipfull* SIMON HOLCOMBE *Chiefe &ca: factors in The Rt H: C: affaires in* VIZAGAPATAM."[3]

Same date.

" Yours without date from VIZAGAPATAM I received the 8th instant . . . which was accompanied from BALLASORE with a Letter from our factors there, Copy whereof goes herewith inclosed, by which you will see that TOM: PITT and ALLEN CATCHPOLE are come agen on the (Sey)[4]*more* to try what can be made of a run hither. I have writ to the Nabob and Kings duan at DACCA and to the Governour at HUGLY about it in the best manner I can, to let them know who he is, and how he Steales hither without leave, and what did insue upon the Countenance he received here 11 yeares past, and I will doe the utmost I can to hindar his being permitted to trade."

From Sir J. GOLDSBOROUGH *to* CAPTAIN PITT :[5]

(At end) " dated in CHUTTANUTTE November the 1st. 1693."

" Sʳ:

" By Mr. WILCOKS I received yours from BALLASORE of the 22d. of 8ber on the 30th Do. in which you have written much about the H. E. INDIA Company my Masters, and twice in it threatned me with your divulging their Circumstances if you are obstructed in your way, as if I was to be frighted

---

[1] O.C. 5886, No. 34.

[2] " To give the Governor in public the King's *duhoy*", *i.e.*, to cry the Indian *Haro ; " Pádsháh ki dohái !"* invoking the Great Mogul to remedy the wrong. This is a very notable reference to the Indian practice (see *Anglo-Indian Glossary*, s v. *Doai*, pp. 248 and 792).   [3] O.C. 5886, No. 35.

[4] Bound in, and invisible.   [5] O.C. 5886, No. 36.

PLATE XI.

No. 1.

Calcutta Jary Dmo 169 7/4

Rigt Honbl

Theſe are to accompany ſome Papers
y Duplicates of wch wth ſome others I have wth me, on
Charter & Record, wth y Comiſſarys Letters wch he Requir
before y ſe Ticketts but not finiſhed. y hir left orders for
y ſp being Mr Ellis, wch y God williing att my arrivall wll
deliver you; I give you A Juſt account of y Affair in y
Curby, not ktkowing but theſe may reach yo handſ before my
arrivall, wth my humble ſerviſe to you I am

Rig t Honbl

yo moſt humble & affure ſervt

Robert Douril

therby to a Compliance with you, which if the H: C: had Seen fitt to have lett you into their intrest here, they would have ordered me to (doe) it by you, and you would have gladly been the Messinger thereof to me.

"But to come close to the matter, it is well known to you that I am the H: C: cheife Servant in all these Eastern Parts of the World, Commissioned by them under the King of ENGLANDS Charter, by which the trade of these Countreys is granted to them and their successors, exclusive to all other the Kings Subjects but whome they Reduce thertoe.

"Therefore if you have any power Either from their Majesties the King and Queen of ENGLAND, or from their EAST INDIA Company, to come and trade in these parts, shew it to me and I shall readily obey it, and that will more convince then all you can write or say, but in case you refuse and doe not give me such Authentick Sattisfaction as the Nature of the thing Requires, then you are to knowe that I must still take it for Granted that you have noe such power, but are come hither Either a piroting or at the best a Interloping, and I shall deale with you accordingly, and I doe hereby protest and declare against you and all your adherents, that you are guilty of all the Evil that shall or doth arise therby. "J. GOLDSBOROUGH."

We then have the following :

From Sir J. GOLDSBOROUGH *and the* BENGAL *Council to Capt.* ROBERT DORRILL.

Dated at end, "In CHUTTANUTTE in BENGALL, October the 20th 1693."

"You well know in BALLASORE Road lately arrived one THOS: PITT with others in a Ship which is come from ENGLAND into these parts without License of the Rt: Honble: the E. INDIA Company, upon some ill designe either as a Pirott or Interloper Contrary to the King and Queens Royal Charter to the Rt: Honble: Governour and Company of Merchants in LONDON trading to the EAST INDIES and their Successors by severall of their Royall Ancestors Kings of ENGLAND &ca: Granted, and therein Excluding all trade and commerce into these parts to any of their Majesties Subjects but such as trade hither for or under them, and by their licence and consent . . . . and you having received from themselves before your coming from thence a Commission under their Seale, Requiring you therein to make Seizure of all such ENGLISH Ships and vessells and their Lading and all ENGLISH men you shall meet with trading in those parts without their License . . . . now we the Commissary Generall with the Agent and Councell in BENGALL doe in the behalfe of our Rt: H: Masters the Governour and Company aforesaid, Require you to exercise your authority by the said Commission given you to put it in Execution in indeavouring what in you Lies, with all your power, with Ship, boates, and men, to seize the Person of Mr. THO: PITT or any under him . . . . and further, you are to use your utmost indeavours to Stop and hinder the said THOM : PITT or any under him to come into or up the River of HUGLEY or to bring or send any Ship, vessell, or boat, with or without goods into the same, and to Seize all Such, Either Ship, Vessell, or Goods . . . . Given under our hands, and the Rt: H: C's: Seale.

(Date given above.)

"J: GOLDSBOROUGH
"FRANCIS ELLIS
"ROBT: DORRILL
"JNO: BEARD."

Sir John Goldsborough died, it will be remembered, in November 1693, and Mr. C. Eyres took charge of the Agency in January 1693-4. This gentleman writes to Sir John Gayer at Bombay, in a letter dated CHUTTANUTTE, 16th April 1694 :[1]

*   *   *   *   *   *   *

" Notwithstanding all our Endeavours with the Nabob and Duân to frustrate and oppose the Interlopers in their designs, they are rather countenanced and encouraged by the whole Country in Generall, and living at HUGHLEY (24 miles higher in the Countrey then we) will have greatly the advantage of us in both buying and selling, but especially in buying all other goods for ready money, which all Merchants bring thither, being the Port Towne. They have given out Dadney[2] to Merchants who formerly dealt with us to the amount of Rups: 300 000 by the connivance of the Governour of HUGLEY to whom they have presented (as we are inform'd) Rups: 4000. But all their business must be managed in Merchants names so long as the Stop continues, As likewise must ours, which will make our goods come out extraordinary dear ."

From BENGAL, *Letter to Court, of* December 14th, 1694 :

" The 15th of August we thought it very oppertunely to putt in Execution a warrant we had received from FORT ST. GEORGE concerning one MESSENGER who had unlawfully taken possession of a house next adjoyning to the Interlopers, and in order thereunto wee sent our Sergeant with 20 men, souldiers and seamen, to HUGLEY to seize his person, and take charge of the house, for we had heard he had taken the Interlopers protection, and our main designe in sending so many men was to Interrupt their business and trade by Scaring the Government and Making them believe there was Something Intended against PITTS person, that thereby it might have been entred in the *Waacka* or Gazett to the Nabob and Duan that our Intentions were to oppose PITT by force, which in all probability would have putt a Stop to their proceedings, for neither the Nabob nor the Duan would have given them any Countenance, or permitted them to trade, had such a Story been entred in the *Waacka*[3] that Wee designed Quarrell, for this the Duan was all along afraid of, and prevented him from giving them a *Perwanna* sooner. But the only man we have reason to suspect that prevented this fair and good designe was MUTTRIDASS, who told the Governour by our Sending so many Men in Armes up was chiefly to frighten them, and that he had such an Intrest with us he could soon gett them recalled and sent away. On the Serjants first arrivall with soe many men it putt the whole Citty into a Consternation, and MESSENGER was Seiz'd and the house taken possession of without the least opposition, but as he was coming to us with a Guard in their way as they Passed by the Interloping Shipp several Musquet Balls were fired at them from said Shipp, and the boat hailed on board, and followed with their Shipps pinnace with Men in Arms (as your Honours will perceive more at large by the Guards Depositions in our Diarys, month August), on advice wherof we delivered them a protest by two of your Honours servants, and sent Mr. CORNELL up with 32 Seamen more to Joyne with the Serjant and men already at HUGLEY, in cases of any Violence that might be

---

[1] O.C. 5914.

[2] See vol. i, p. 121, *note.*

    Waḳa'a (Ar.), " news-letter".

offer'd by them in retaking the House, for they had threatned to oppose us by force, and had about 40 men in Arms in their house to Command as they'should see Occasion, and in a small time we received their Answer with a reprotest; both which are Enter'd in our Diarys for August . . . . Their business goes on but Slowly, and believe it may be the latter end of January before they can despatch their business and leave BENGALL . . . ."

From the Same to the Same, dated 15th January 1694-5.[1]

" The 25th past we received an Idle and preposterous paper dated the 15th do. from Capt. JNO: BLEWETT protesting . . . which is so erroneous nothing can be more, for wee had laden on board his Ship in CHUTTANUTTE Soe much of the Rt: Honble: Companys Estate as he declared he could take on board by the [2] November, and then offer'd him the best Pillot the Rt: Honble: Company had in health, to take charge of the ship to PIPLEY ROAD, wbich he refused, but urg'd us to speak to the Interlopers for HUSSEY, who deserted the Rt: Honble: Companys Service, which wee Refusing he sent a Compliment by his mate to Mr. PITT to send him his pillott as he was pleased to terme Mr. HUSSEY, but Mr. PITT would not grant him leave without we would signe Obligations that he should returne, which wee thought unreasonable. . . . ."

Meantime, further letters had been received from the Court having an important bearing on this matter of the Interlopers. Thus :—

In Letter to BENGAL, *of* 3rd January 1693-4.

" It is likewise fit you should know that since the passing of our new Charters under the great seale of ENGLAND we have agreed with the Principall Interlopers concerned in the two Interlopeing Ships now abroad, on which went Supra Cargoes Capt. PITTS and Mr. GEORGE WHITE, and they have written the like value into our new Stock ; and that we hope is the end of all our long quarrells and contentions."

From FORT ST. GEORGE *to Court,* 17th February 1693-4 (O.C. 5911).

" . . . 33. Allso the Coppys mentioned in our Generall Letter dated 19th January of Severall Letters written by Capt: THOS: PITT from BENGALL to the late President YALE and Mr. JOHN PITT . . . . Alsoe Coppy of Capt. THOS: PITT's letters to the Commissary Generall in BENGALL, the answer thereunto and his protest . . . . Mr. EVANS was the conveyer of the Interloper's letters to FORT ST. GEORGE."

The John Pitt here mentioned was then in the Company's service at Fort St. George, and afterwards, as we shall amply see hereafter, the New Company's President and King's Consul at Masulipatam. Mr. EVANS was the somewhat disreputable *Padre* of Húglí spoken of by Hedges (*passim, e.g.,* p. 148), and afterwards, as we now know (*quod minime reris!*) Bishop successively of Bangor and of Meath (see p. ccxcvii, *supra*). I regret to say that none of the correspondence mentioned in the last preceding extract can be found except Sir John Goldsborough's answer to Pitt, given on pp. xx-xxi.

---

[1] O.C. 5959.   [2] Blank in original.

Pitt appears to have left Bengal for England about the beginning of 1695.

Here I pause for a time in following the chain of documents concerning Thomas Pitt.

I had not grasped many of its earlier links in the Diary of Hedges, and in the correspondence existing at the India Office, before the question suggested itself to me: Was this Captain Thomas Pitt, interloping adventurer, identical with Captain Thomas Pitt, member for Old Sarum, who in the end of 1697 was appointed by the Court of the East India Company to the Government of Fort St. George, an office which he held with eminent reputation for more than eleven years; who was the owner and *eponymus* of the famous Pitt Diamond; who was the progenitor of several families holding peerages; and who (above all) was the grandfather and great-grandfather of two of the greatest of English statesmen?

At first sight it seems absurd to imagine that the man who, at intervals, for some fifteen years, and up to 1694, was a notorious interloper, defying and maligning the Company, regarded by them at times as a sort of *hostis humani generis*, at best as a swaggering desperado, more than once prosecuted by them in the Courts at home, and denounced by their Commissary-General as no better than a "Pyrott", should be, in 1697, selected by the same Company as the Governor of what was becoming their most important Presidency, and in that capacity especially instructed to direct his efforts to the suppression of the Interlopers, and to inquiry into their connection with the European corsairs who had lately been perpetrating outrages on the Indian Seas, and so fostering suspicion of the Company itself in native hearts. Trying to solve this question, I in vain sought in the peerages and in the biographies of the Pitts for information as to the early antecedents of the Governor. Though he has a place in no encyclopædia or biographical dictionary that I can discover, except Zedler's *Universal Lexicon* and a brief notice in Rose, the date of his birth and the fact of his origin at Blandford St. Mary's, with some particulars of various ramifications of his kindred (though imperfectly given) are to be found in print. But as to his personal history, it always begins with the Government of Fort St. George; nothing "back of that", as the Americans say, is anywhere to be found. At the same time this double fact becomes constantly more evident, viz., that whilst nothing is to be traced of Capt. Thomas Pitt, Governor of Fort St. George, much *earlier* than his selection for that post, neither is anything *later* to be traced of Captain Thomas Pitt, interloper. The one figure sets as the other rises. Mr. Hyde and Dr. Jekyll are never seen contemporaneously.

There would have been nothing to surprise us had Thomas Pitt, the interloper, been sent out as the representative of the New Company, which was under incubation about the time of his appointment to Madras. So indeed, a few months later, his kinsman, John Pitt, was sent as the Agent of that Company, under the title of President on the Coast of Choromandell and King's Consul, to Masulipatam. As I have repeatedly had occasion to observe, a large number of the New Company's servants and directors were men who had been dismissed by the Old Company, or had come for one reason or other into hostile relations with it. But it was by the Old, or London, Company that Thomas Pitt the Governor was commissioned.

On the other hand, the instance, assuming their identity, was not, I apprehend, solitary. We find in 1693, Captain R. Dorrell standing out as the right-hand man and colleague in Council at Calcutta, of the Company's " General", Sir John Goldsborough. And I can hardly doubt that this man, who was specially charged by his chief with measures for the suppression of Thomas Pitt's last interloping enterprise, was the same Captain Dorrell who, ten years before, had been intimately associated with the same Pitt in a like adventure. We need not say that the transformation, within four years, of the " haughty huffing" interloper into the zealous servant of the Company has plenty of analogies in history. It did not take that space of time to transform James Sharp, the trusted agent of the Scottish Presbyterian Church, into Archbishop of St. Andrew's, and malignant tool of the arbitrary Government of King Charles. And, if we could conceive that the political history of England during the last two or three years should ever become as fragmentary and imperfect, or as deeply buried in masses of partially mutilated manuscript, as that of Indian trade and service in the last quarter of the seventeenth century, there would be transformations recognised in English political life much more amazing and perplexing than that which puzzled me in these researches. Pitt's transformation was indeed for the better, and not like these for the worse.

It is a curious circumstance that Bruce, the partial annalist of the Company, in mentioning the appointment of the New Company's President and Consul in Coromandel, lately referred to, calls him " Mr. John Pitt, the Interloper, so frequently mentioned in the Annals of the London Company". But the interloper so frequently mentioned in the Annals of the London Company was most distinctly not John, but Thomas,—Tom Pitt as Sir J. Goldsborough calls him again and again in letters which I have cited, and which Mr. Bruce shows that he had read,—Tho: Pitt as he signs himself repeatedly in letters of his own, which I have transcribed in the preceding pages. I do not suppose that Mr. Bruce made this misleading statement intentionally, but rather that the idea of the identity of the interloping skipper and supercargo with the famous governor of FORT ST. GEORGE was too preposterous to have even suggested itself for a moment to that respectable annalist.

Perhaps I should apologise for these details of an inquiry now determined finally, and which may be considered thus to have lost its interest. And yet, I feel a strong temptation to recapitulate something of the course of doubts and arguments which seemed to sway the probabilities this way or that, as facts gradually presented themselves. One circumstance, which seemed to create a serious difficulty, was connected with Governor Pitt's public position at the time of his nomination to Fort St. George. He was, and is described in contemporary records as "Captain Thomas Pitt, Member for Old Sarum". And the Parliamentary History showed that " Thomas Pitt, Esq." was returned as one of the members for that ancient and distinguished (and now, for half a century, *ex*tinguished) borough, 28th October 1695. But I also found that in the election of 1689 (30th May) "Thomas Pitt, Esq.", and in that of 1689-90 (27th February) " Thomas Pitt Esq., of Stratford-under-the-Castle", was returned for (New Sarum or) Salisbury. But, no doubt, there were more Thomas Pitts than one. Was this Member for Salisbury, in the two first post-Revolution Parliaments, the same as the Thomas Pitt who represented Old Sarum in the third ? The answer is unquestionably, *Yes*. For we shall see that " Governor Pitt" purchased the manor of Stratford (and Old Sarum) from James, 3rd Earl of Salisbury, in 1690, and thus Thomas Pitt, Esq., of Stratford-under-the-Castle, who represented Salisbury in the first and second Revolution Parliaments was undoubtedly the Thomas Pitt, Esq., who represented Old Sarum in the third.

Now, is it a probable thing that a man who was Member for Salisbury in 1690-95, could be, during the currency of that Parliament, playing the part of Interloper in the Húglí? This seemed so improbable as greatly to shake for a time my confidence in the conclusion towards which I had been travelling. But probable or improbable, it is *true*. At least I can find no trace of his having vacated his seat during that Parliament.

And one piece of probable evidence that favoured the conclusion in question was contained in a Latin inscription, attached to a memorial which the ex-Governor set up to his father, the Rector of Blandford St. Mary, Dorset, in that church. The words of this seem singularly apt in application to a career which, on the assumption of identity, would embrace at once the history of the roving interloper, and that of the eminent Governor and successful diamond-merchant :

" *Hanc inscriptionem post quam*
hanc sacram aedem instauraverat,
ornavit honoratus THOMAS PITT *armiger,*
defuncti filius natu secundus,
qui post varias utriusque fortunae vices,
et multis terra marique exantlatos labores,

PLATE XII.

Autograph of T. Pitt as Interloper.

Fort S.t George Nov.r 6th 1701

60

Sir

This accompanyes the modell of a stone I have lately seen, itt weighs Mang 303 : & carr.ts 426, is of an excellent christaline water without any fowles only att one end in the flat part there is one or two little flaws w.ch will come out in cutting, they lying on the surface of the stone, the price they ask for it is prodigious being two hundred thousand pag.s tho I believe less then one would buy it, if it was designed for a single stone. I believe it would not loose above 1/4 p.t in cutting and bee a larger stone then any the Mogull has, and take itt for granted as stones goe it must be inestimable since I saw it I have been perusing of Tavernier where there is noe stone soe large as this will bee when cutt, I write this singly to you & one there desire it may bee kept private and that you'll by the first of Land & Sea conveyance give mee your opinion thereon for it being of soe great a value I believe here are few or none can buy it, I have putt the modell in a little box & marked it S: E: w.ch the Capt. will deliver you, my hearty service to you I am

Sir

Your most obliged humble servant

T Pitt

To S.r Ste: Evance K.t

Present London

demum opibus et honoribus auctus,
et in hanc sedem natalem redux,
erga Patrem Cœlestem et terrestrem,
Pietatis suae duplex erexit monumentum,
Anno Domini 1712."[1]

Another point which called for consideration in connection with the identity of the two characters was that of marriage.

According to the current genealogies (as in Hutchins' *History of Dorsetshire*, and Collins's *Peerage*), Thomas Pitt, the Governor, was married to Jane, daughter of James Innes, younger, of Reid Hall in Morayshire.[2]

On the other side, all that we gather directly as to the marriage of T. Pitt, Interloper, is contained in Hedges' incidental statement (*supra,*

---

[1] The first part of the inscription runs as follows :
H. S. E.
" Vir reverendus JOHANNES PITT
hujus ecclesiae per annos Viginti octo
Pastor fidelis
Vitae integritate, morum probitate
et doctrinae puritate
Spectabilis.
Duxit uxorem Saram
Johannis Jay generosi filiam,
ex eaque, Dei dono, suscepit liberos novem,
e quibus Johannes, Sara, Thomas,
Georgius et Dorothea
ipsi superstites.
Obiit 25°. Aprilis anno $\left\{ \begin{array}{l} \text{Dom. 1672} \\ \text{Aetatisque 62} \end{array} \right.$

Hanc inscriptionem (etc) . . ."

[2] The pedigree of this lady is given by the late Professor COSMO INNES, in his Appendix to FORBES of Culloden's *History of the Family of Innes* (Spalding Club, 1844), p. 203.

JAMES INNES of that ilk (*i.e.*, Innes of Innes), armour-bearer of King JAMES III, and sixteenth of his line, and known in the family traditions as James with the Beard, married JANET GORDON, daughter of ALEXANDER, Earl of HUNTLEY, and died 1491. He had two sons, of whom the younger was ROBERT of Cromy and Rathmakenzie.

The latter had two sons :
1. JAMES INNES of Rathmakenzie, who fell at Pinkie, 1547.
2. ALEXANDER of Blackhills.

The latter also had two sons :
1. ALEXANDER of Cotts, styled CRAIG-IN-PERIL.
2. ADAM of Reid Hall ; and JAMES, the second son of this Adam, had a daughter, JANE, who married T. PITT.

p. xlii) that Pitt had married the niece of Matthias Vincent, the unfaith-
ful Chief of the Council at Húglí, a marriage which, Hedges says, had
been the occasion of so much prejudice to the Company (presumably by
leading to Vincent's intimate alliance with Interlopers). We also know
from Pitt's own letters that R. Douglas, who was Hedges' companion
from Bengal to Persia, was a brother-in-law of Governor Pitt.

It is hardly possible that Pitt's marriage could have already taken place
in May 1678, when he wrote the letter to Vincent, wh ch has been
given at pp. iii-iv ; and we have found no clue to the time or place of
the marriage, for even of the birth of Governor Pitt's eldest child,
Robert, no date appears to be ascertained.[1]

We do find a Mr. John Innes mentioned by Hedges as one of the
society of Húglí, and apparently as accompanying himself and Douglas to
Madras (see pp. 156, 157, 183) ; whilst there is another record that one
Mr. Innes was the attorney in England of Mr. Vincent.[2] These circumstances were suggestive, at least, of the possible links of affinity
between Pitt, regarded as Interloper and nephew of Matthias Vincent,[3]
and the family of Innes.

And now having said enough as to the tentatives towards identification of the two characters, it is well (though in this I must anticipate a
little of the chronological course of documents) to furnish the keystone
of proof, after which one can deal with the subject of this biographical
sketch as a single entity.

This crucial evidence occurs in a letter written by Thomas Pitt as
Governor of Fort St. George, on behalf of the Old or London Company, to his cousin, John Pitt, who had come out from England as rival
representative of the New or English Company, and who boasted of the
title of King's Consul, as well as of those of Agent of that Company at
Masulipatam, and of their President on the Coast of Coromandel. The
letter, which is a long and remarkable one, dated Nov. 12th, 1699,
belongs to a curious correspondence, of which I shall have to speak

---

[1] We may observe that T. Pitt, in two letters given above (both of October
1679), calls Richard Edwards, Chief of the Balasore factory, his uncle. This
is no doubt a relationship by marriage, and it may indicate that the marriage
had taken place between the earlier letters and these later ones. I surmise
that Mrs. Edwards and Mrs. Vincent were both aunts of Mrs. Pitt.

[2] " We have also appointed £100 to be paid to Mr. Innis the Attorney of
Mr. MATHIAS VINCENT on account of his Sallary." *Court to the* BAY, 12th
December 1677.

[3] I find that " Mathias Vincent, Merchant, London" was knighted 20th
March 1684-5. I have no doubt that this was the former chief in the Bay.
A letter from the Court to Fort St. George, dated 6th March 1701-2, refers
to " the ground belonging to Mr. Greenhill and to Sr: Mathias Vincent's
children".

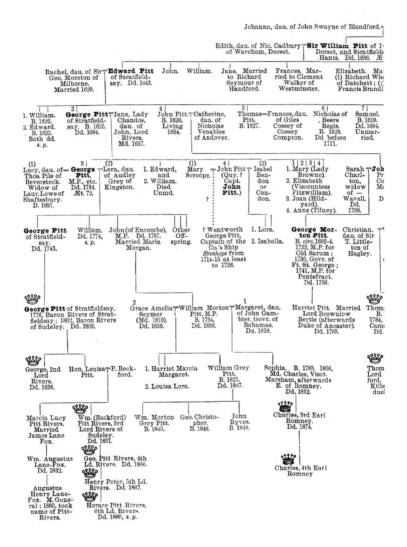

Johanna, dau. of John Swayne of Blandford.

Edith, dau. of Nic. Cadbury = **Sir William Pitt** of I
of Wareham, Dorset. | Dorset, and Stratfielde
Hants. Dd. 1636. Æ

Rachel, dau. of Sir = **Edward Pitt** | John. William. Jane. Married Frances. Mar- Elizabeth. Ma
Geo. Moreton of | of Stratfield- to Richard ried to Clement (1) Richard Wh
Milborne. | say. Dd. 1643. Seymour of Walker of of Datchett; (2
Married 1620. Handford. Westminster. Francis Brandl

1. William. | **George Pitt** = Jane, Lady | John Pitt. = Catherine, | Thomas = Frances, dau. Nicholas of Samuel.
B. 1620. | of Stratfield- Chandos, B. 1620. dau. of Pitt. of Giles Beere B. 1629.
2. Edward. | say. B. 1625. dau. of Living Nicholas B. 1627. Cossey of Regis. Dd. 1694.
B. 1622. | Dd. 1694. John, Lord 1684. Venables Cossey B. 1628. Unmar-
Both dd. | Rivers. of Andover. Compton. Dd before ried.
s. p. | Md. 1657. 1711.

(1) | **George** = Lora, dau. 1. Edward, (1) | John Pitt = Isabel 1 | 2 | 3 | 4 |
Lucy, dau. of = **Pitt**, of Audley and Mary = (Quy. ? Ben- 1. Mary (Lady Sarah = Job
Thos. Pile of | M.P., etc. Grey of 2. William. Scroope. : Capt. don Browne). Charl- Pr
Beverstock. | Dd. 1784. Kingston. Died : **John** or 2. Elizabeth ton, Co
Widow of | Æt. 72. Unmd. : **Pitt**.) Con- (Viscountess widow M
Laur. Lowe of | ? don. Fitzwilliam). of —
Shaftesbury. | 3. Joan (Hild- Wavell. D
D. 1697. | yard). Dd.
| 4. Anne (Tilney). 1706.

George Pitt William. John (of Encombe), Other ? Wentworth 1. Lora. **George Mor-** Christian, =
of Stratfield- Dd. 1774, M.P. Dd. 1787. Off- George Pitt, **ton Pitt.** dau. of Sir
say. s. p. Married Maria spring. Captain of the 2. Isabella. B. circ. 1692-4, T. Little-
Dd. 1745. Morgan. Co.'s Ship 1722, M.P. for ton of
Stanhope from Old Sarum ; Hagley.
1714-15 at least 1730, Govr. of
to 1726. Ft. St. George ;
1741, M.P. for
Pontefract.
Dd. 1756.

George Pitt of Stratfieldsay. 2 Grace Amelia = William Morton = Margaret, dau. Harriet Pitt. Married Thom
1776, Baron Rivers of Strat- Seymer Pitt, M.P. of John Gam- Lord Brownlow B.
fieldsay ; 1802, Baron Rivers (Md. 1819). B. 1754. bier, Govr. of Bertie (afterwards 1784,
of Sudeley. Dd. 1803. Dd. 1836. Dd. 1836. Bahamas. Duke of Ancaster). Cam
Dd. 1818. Dd. 1763. Dd.

George, 2nd Hon. Louisa = P. Beck- 1. Harriet Marcia William Grey Sophia. B. 1788. 1806, Thom
Lord Pitt. ford. Margaret. Pitt. Md. Charles, Visct. Lord
Rivers. B. 1821. Marsham, afterwards ford.
Dd. 1838. 2. Louisa Lora. Dd. 1867. E. of Romney. Kille
Dd. 1812. duel

Marcia Lucy Wm. (Beckford) Wm. Morton Geo. Christo- John Charles, 3rd Earl
Pitt Rivers. Pitt Rivers, 3rd Grey Pitt. pher. Ryves. Romney.
Married Lord Rivers of B. 1845. B. 1848. B. 1849. Dd. 1874.
James Lane Sudeley.
Fox. Dd. 1831.

Wm. Augustus Geo. Pitt Rivers, 4th
Lane-Fox. Ld. Rivers. Dd. 1866. Charles, 4th Earl
Dd. 1832. Romney

Augustus Henry Peter, 5th Ld.
Henry Lane- Rivers. Dd. 1867.
Fox. M. Gene-
ral ; 1880, took Horace Pitt Rivers,
name of Pitt- 6th Ld. Rivers.
Rivers. Dd. 1880, s. p.

TREE OF THE **PITTS** OF BLANDFORD ST. MARY'S AND **PITTS** OF STRA

Nicholas Pitt of Blandford and Wimborne. Living 1545.

William Pitt. Dd. before 1552.⊤Eleanour dau. of – Hartland of Poole.

rd.⊤**John Pitt**, Clerk of Exchequer to Q. Elizabeth. Thomas Pitt, Chamberlain, of Bristol. (Will dated May 1, 1618.)

of Iwerne, eldsay, Æt. 77.	John Pitt (settled in Ireland).	Qu.? a Daughter.	= – Rideout? of Blandford.	**Thomas Pitt** of Bland-⊤Priscilla, dau. of – Searle ford St. Mary's. of Hayle, Devon. Dd. 1643.
Married Wheeler ; (2) Sir ndling.	Maria. Married (1) Alex. Chape ; (2) J. Rudhall of Rudhall.	William Pitt, Mayor of Dorchester. Dd. s. p. 1687.	Rev. **John Pitt**, Rector of Blandford St. Mary's. Dd. 1672. Æt. 62.	⊤Sara, dau. of John Jay.	Edwd. Pitt. Christr. Pitt.

8		9	10	1	2	3	1 1
el. 2. B. 1630. 04. ır-	Francis. =Elizabeth, dau. of Jeffrey Jeffries of Alburnwick, Brecon.	Edward. B. 1632. Dd. unmarried.	Christopher. B. 1604. Md. Dionisia, sister of Sir W. Bassett of Charton, Somerset.	1. Edith (Sydenham). B. 1633. 2. Rachel (Kingsmill). 3. Catherine (Whitaker). 4. Elizabeth.	**THOMAS PITT**,⊤Jane Governor of Innes. Fort St. Dd. George. 1727. B. 1653. Dd. 1726.	George Pitt. B. 1654.	John Sara = Pitt. Pitt. 1649. B. 1733. Dd. Æt. 80.

John Pitt. Pres. and Consul at Masulipatam. Dd. 1703.	Harriet Villiers,⊤**Robert** Grd. dau. of Geo., 3rd Visct. Grandison. Married 1703.	**Pitt** of Boconnoc, M.P., etc. Dd. 1727.	Col. **Thomas** ⊤Lady Frances, **Pitt.** 1719 dau. and co-Baron London- heir of derry ; 1726 Ridgway, Earl of ditto Earl of (Irish Peerage). Londonderry. Dd. 1729. Æt. 41.	Col. **John Pitt**,=Hon. Mary M.P., etc., Bellasize, Lt.-Govr. of dau. of Bermuda. Thomas, Dd. 1754. Visct. Fauconberg.	General James⊤ Stanhope, 1718, Earl Stanhope. Dd. 1721.

⊤**Thomas Pitt** of Boconnoc, Steward of Duchy of Cornwall. B. 1705. Dd. 1761.	1. Harriet. B. 1704. Md. 1733, Wm. (afterwards Sir Wm.) Corbet (Bart.).	2. Catherine (Needham). 4. Elizabeth (Hunham). Dd. 1730.	3. Anne. 5. Mary. B. 1726. Dd. 1782.	**William** ⊤Hester, sis-**Pitt.** ter of B. 1708. Richd. 1766,Earl Grenville of Chat- Temple, ham. Earl Dd. 1778. Grenville. Dd. 1764.	Thomas, Ridgway. Lady Lucy Philip, 2nd E. of London- (Meyrick). 2nd Earl London- derry. Dd. 1805. Stanhope. derry. Dd. 1764, Dd. 1786. Dd. 1735, s. p. s. p.

⋆omas Pitt. B. 1737. 784, Baron amelford. Dd. 1793.	1. Amelia. B. 1732. Md. Wm. Spry, Govr. of Barbadoes. 2. Anna Maria (Murray). 3. Christian. Md. Govr. Thomas Saunders.	**John, 2nd Earl of Chatham.** K.G. B. 1756. Dd. 1835, s. p.	Hon. **William Pitt**, 1st Lord of Treasury. B. 1759. Dd. 1806.	James Charles Pitt, Capt. R.N. B. 1761. Dd. 1780.	2. Lady Harriot. 1778, Md. Edward James, eldest son of Ld. Eliot (who died before his father). Dd. 1786.	1. Lady Hester ⊤ Charle Pitt. B. 1755. Married 1774. 3rd Ea Stanho Dd. 181

⋆omas, 2nd ırd Camel-rd. B. 1775. Killed in a duel, 1804.				1. Lady **Hester Stanhope**. B. 1776. Dd. 1839.	Philip Henry, 4th Earl Stanhope. Dd. 1854.	2. Griseld 3. Lucy R

Philip Henry, 5th Earl Stanhope (Historian). Dd. 1875.

1869, Evelyn Henrietta,=Arthur Philip, dau. of R. Penne- 6th Earl Stan-father. hope. B. 1838.

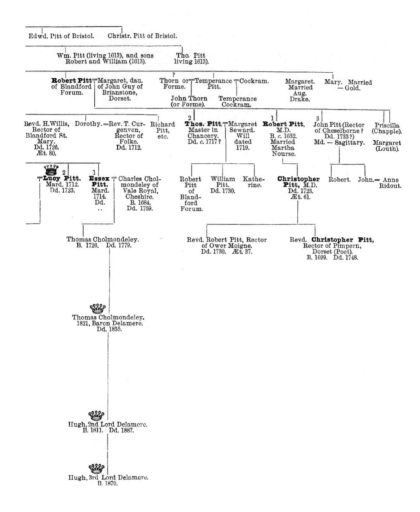

Edwd. Pitt of Bristol.   Christr. Pitt of Bristol.

Wm. Pitt (living 1613), and sons   Tho. Pitt
Robert and William (1613).   living 1613).

Robert Pitt = Margaret, dau.   Thorn or = Temperance = Cockram.   Margaret.   Mary. Married
of Blandford   of John Guy of   Forme.   Pitt.   Married   — Gold.
Forum.   Brianstone,   Aug.
     Dorset.   John Thorn   Temperance   Drake.
               (or Forme).   Cockram.

Revd. H.Willis,   Dorothy.=Rev. T. Cur-   Richard   **Thos. Pitt,** = Margaret   **Robert Pitt,**   John Pitt (Rector   Priscilla
Rector of   genven,   Pitt,   Master in   Seward.   M.D.   of Cheselborne?   (Chapple).
Blandford St.   Rector of   etc.   Chancery.   Will   B. c. 1652.   Dd. 1733?)
Mary.   Folke.   Dd. c. 1717?   dated   Married   Md. — Sagittary.   Margaret
Dd. 1726.   Dd. 1712.   1719.   Martha   (Louth).
Æt. 80.   Nourse.

  Lucy Pitt.   **Essex** = Charles Chol-   Robert   William   Kathe-   **Christopher**   Robert.   John.= Anne
Mard. 1712.   **Pitt.**   mondeley of   Pitt   Pitt.   rine.   **Pitt,** M.D.   Ridout.
Dd. 1723.   Mard.   Vale Royal,   of   Dd. 1730.   Dd. 1723.
     1714.   Cheshire.   Bland-   Æt. 61.
     Dd.   B. 1684.   ford
     ..   Dd. 1759.   Forum.

Thomas Cholmondeley.   Revd. Robert Pitt, Rector   Revd. **Christopher Pitt,**
B. 1726. Dd. 1779.   of Ower Moigne.   Rector of Pimpern,
     Dd. 1730. Æt. 37.   Dorset (Poet).
          B. 1699. Dd. 1748.

Thomas Cholmondeley.
1821, Baron Delamere.
Dd. 1855.

Hugh, 2nd Lord Delamere.
B. 1811. Dd. 1887.

Hugh, 3rd Lord Delamere.
B. 1870.

particularly hereafter. At present I only quote a clause which clinches
the question of identity :

> *"And for the Supporting my Creditt, I dont remember I was indebted, or*
> *Concern'd in anything what ever that could be Censur'd by any, unless it was*
> *interlopeing, which I never repented of to this day."*

Habemus confitentem reum!

This does not leave any room for doubt of the identity, but the
following is even more complete, for it names the vessel in which we
know the adventurer Pitt made his last interloping voyage. The letter,
dated 5th January 1699-1700, is once more addressed by the Governor
to his cousin John Pitt at Masulipatam, and refers to certain controversies that the latter had stirred, over old trading accounts between
the two :

> *"I wonder with what face you can say I carry'd the ballance of your*
> *account with me to* BENGALL *in the* Seymore . . . ."

And again, Governor Pitt writes to Sir E. Littleton, then just gone
out to the Bay as President on the part of the New Company, respecting
a house at Húglí, April 2nd, 1700:

> *" When I was in* BENGAL *last on the* Seymore . . . .", etc.

And, the day after, to the Rt. Worshipful John Beard and the Council
of the Old Company in Bengal :

> *"I am advis'd that Agent* EYRE *sold two Gunns belonging to the Ship*
> Seymore, *which I left in the hands of Mr.* GEORGE GUY", etc.

This question of identity having been settled, we may now say that
Thomas Pitt, the subject of this memoir, was the second son of the
Revd. John Pitt, Rector of Blandford St. Mary, Dorset, and was born
July 5th, 1653.

The genealogy of the family, so far as I find it recorded, and
arranged (with slight additions) so as best to serve my purpose,
is set forth in the table opposite. Of Thomas Pitt's own earliest
career I have not been able to ascertain anything. But he is
only 21 years of age when his name first occurs in a letter of
the Court of the East India Company, which has been quoted at
p. ii, *supra*, and which shows that "one Pytts" had been landed at
Balasore from the ship *Lancaster* in 1674. Probably this was his first
appearance in India. Though spoken of as "supercargo" in documents
which we have quoted on several occasions, we should suppose by the
style of "captain" which is repeatedly given to him, as well as by
expressions in his own letters, that he had been "bred to the sea" as
our fathers used to say. I have concluded above (p. ii) that, notwithstanding his promise given to Streynsham Master in 1676, he did not
then return to England, seeing that we find him in India, apparently
after more than one voyage to Persia, in May 1678.

He seems again to have made voyages to the Gulf in 1679 and 1680,
after which he returned to England on board the *William and John*,
some time in 1681. He came out again, as we know, in 1682 on board
the *Crown*, on a speculation of some magnitude, reaching Balasore
about the 8th of July, returning in February 1683. For several years
after this we hear nothing of his history. But wherever it passed we
may conclude that he was seeking that which always loomed so large an
object in his eyes—money, and was probably successful in the quest, as
we learn that he purchased from James, 3rd Earl of Salisbury, the
manor of Stratford-under-the-Castle, in Wilts—*i.e.*, of Old Sarum.
The date of this purchase is given[1] as 1690, but it was perhaps a little
earlier, for John Young and Thomas Pitt were elected for Old Sarum
to the Convention Parliament, 16th January 1688-9, though their
election was declared void. and their seats occupied by William Harvey
and John Hawles (March 25th). On the 30th May, Pitt, described as
" Thomas Pitt, Esqr., of Stratford-under-the-Castle", came in for Salisbury city (or New Sarum) *vice* Giles Eyre, Esqr., appointed a Justice of
the King's Bench. Under the same designation Pitt is returned again
as one of the members for Salisbury to the following Parliament (27th
February 1689-90) ; and once more, 28th October 1695, along with
William Harvey, for Old Sarum.

What is familiar enough to those who remember the discussions on
the Reform Bill of 1832, may not be so to all the readers (if such there
should be) of this collection ; so it may not be superfluous to say that
the borough of Old Sarum, though it had been without inhabitants, or
nearly so, for some centuries, continued, till the passing of the Bill, to
send two members to Parliament, the privilege of returning them being
in the hands of the holders of the burgage tenures.[2]

In the interval between the two last elections that we have mentioned
took place Pitt's last adventure to India as an interloper. I can find no
indication of his having vacated his seat, so it would appear that he
must have been M.P. for Salisbury whilst Sir John Goldsborough was
denouncing him—perhaps only half seriously—as a possible *Pyrott*.

We are not absolutely in the dark as to steps that partially bridged
the passage between the hostile position of the interloper, and that of

---

[1] See Benson and Hatcher's *Hist. of Salisbury*, in *Colt Hoare*, i, 603.

[2] Pitt lived at the Manor-house (Mawarden's Court). The south part of this
house was apparently added by him, bearing inscribed on the porch : *Parva
sed apta domino.*   Part of the house has been pulled down, and the rest now
forms the Stratford Vicarage. It is believed that Lord Chatham was born there,
though christened at St. James's, Piccadilly. (Information communicated by
Mr. H. F. Swayne, through the Revd. Canon Jackson.)

Pitt's name is commemorated in an inscription on the tower of the Parish
Church of Stratford : THOMAS PITT *Esqr. Benefactor*, 1711.

basking in the Company's favour as Governor designate of Fort St. George.

Even before he sailed on his last trading adventure to India in 1693, the Court, as we learn from a passage in Luttrell's Diary, had contemplated the absorption of the interlopers by the purchase of their enterprise (*op. cit.*, iii, 68).

And when the adventurers were in India, carrying matters with a high hand, the Court intimated to their Council in Bengal, under date 3rd Jany. 1693-4 :

" It is likewise fit you should know that since the passing of our new Charters under the Great Seal of England, we have agreed with the Principall Interlopers concerned in the two Interloping Ships now abroad, on which went Super Cargoes Capt. PITTS and Mr. GEORGE WHITE, and they have written the like Value into our new Stock, and *that* we hope is the end of all our long quarrells and Contentions."

The same to FORT ST. GEORGE, 2nd Feby. 1693-4 :

"The Concern in the two Ships sent out by the Interlopers called the *Edward*, Capt. WM GYFFORD, Commander, and the *Henry*, Capt. HUDSON, Commander, being now by bargain with the most of the interessed become so our own, We have thought good to give you notice thereof, and to the end that whatever remaines of their Cargoes, or may yet be left ashore, may be carefully looked after, befreinded and sent home, unto the Joynt Interessed, with whom we have a good understanding here."

Court to BENGAL, 6th March 1694-5 :

" Concerning Mr. PITT, we have no more to say, than what we writt last year, altho' the Company are now become concerned in the Ship and Cargo, and may suffer their proportion of the Disappointment he meets with, Yet the Consequence of it in deterring other Interlopers may make it equivalent to them, however if he be not yet dispatch'd give him your Assistance that he may come with our next Ships, the Company having a great Concerne in him as We formerly advised you . . . .

" We hope you will not be again troubled with Interlopers on your side of INDIA, nor hear anything more of them from other parts, since we are resolved to drive our Trade full in all places, which will be the most effectuall Check and discouragement to such licentious and unwarranted practices. But if it happen, that any should be so bold as to adventure thither, In such case we require you to put in execution our last Orders touching Mr. PITT and Mr. WHITE for defeating and disappointing their Voyage."

In reply apparently to the first of these three letters, the Bengal Council write to the Court, in a letter dated CHUTTANUTTE, 15th January 1694-5 :

" Capt. PITTS being still in BENGALL wee offered him our assistance in recovering what debts he may have made since his arrivall, and that wee would take care of any Concerns or effects he should leave behind him in the Countrey, according to your Honours Directions."

And in a later paragraph :

" Capt. PITTS to the last made a great bounceing and have carried himself very haughtily ever since his arrivall in these parts, and has not scrupled to talk very Disrespectfully and uncivilly of your Honours, and to carry home on his Shipp Mr. JNO: HILL, EDMUND HUSSEY, and WILLIAM MESSINGER, persons whome wee had warrants from MADRASS to send thither, notwithstanding the protest wee Delivered him for Damages your Honours might accrew thereby". . .

Captain T. Pitt, after his return from this last trading voyage, appears to have had some relation with Brest, which caused him to be selected for an agency in connection with two captured English vessels, respecting which the Company entered into amicable correspondence with him. From a circumstance incidentally noticed in a letter of the Court to Fort St. George (29th Feby. 1693, para. 23), viz., that T. Pitt's cousin John Pitt,—of whom we shall hear much hereafter—had been taken in the *Princess Anne* and carried prisoner to France, combined with an obscure allusion in a letter of Novr. 1699 from T. Pitt to his cousin,[1] from which we shall quote largely below, it seems probable that the introduction of Thomas Pitt to the Company, which brought on the correspondence in question, and led eventually to so important a change in the relations of the parties, was due to the said Cousin John.

From Court Book of 23rd Septr. 1695 :

" Mr. THOMAS PITTS,
" and Capt. JOHN BLUETTS
" Gentlemen,
" The EAST INDIA Company being given to understand, That some of the Owners and Proprietors of the Ship *Edward*, lately seized on, and carryed into BREST, have from thence written to Captain PITTS, to endeavour the Buying of that Ship and her goods for their use, with a liberty to advance from twenty-five to fifty per cent. on Invoice price, And the Company desiring to purchase the cargo of the *Princess Anne of Denmark*, which was taken at the same time with her ; I am directed to desire you both, to consider whether it be probable, that the Said Cargo may be bought on like termes, and upon advice of what may be done therein, You may expect further Orders touching the same ; with the usuall encouragement for your pains and care to be taken in that Business."

" EAST INDIA House, LONDON, 20th September 1695."

" The Court approved thereof, the same having been signed by the Secretary in the name of the Governour and Company."

Indications of further correspondence with Capt. Pitt in connection with this business are recorded in the Court Book, as under 25th October, and 1st Novr., but the letters are not recorded.

---

[1] " I am, I must acknowledge, beholding to you for your recommendation from BREST, I being a Stranger to the Governour and Company, and you well known to them." See below, letter to John Pitt, at p. xlviii.

The next entry shows a rapid advance of amicable feeling, in the appointment to the Company's service of a nephew of Capt. Pitt's brother-in-law, Mr. Curgenven, upon the former's recommendation.

From Court Book, 23rd December 1696 :

. . . . " Mr. THOMAS CURGENVEN, recommended by Capt. THOMAS PITTS, to be their Factor in INDIA, for five years, at the Salary of fifteen pounds per annum."

From Court Book of 11th Novr. 1696 :

" It is ordered, That the Company's Dutyes, payable on the 119 pieces of Callicoes, brought home on the *Martha*, consigned to Captain THOMAS PITT, be remitted to him, in consideration of his pains and charges, in endeavouring to buy the two ENGLISH EAST INDIA Ships, and their Cargoes, that were taken by the FRENCH the last year, and the Committee for Private Trade are desired to give direction therein accordingly."

The next extract involves what is still a leap, but no longer bears the astonishing character which, without these preparatory advances, would have attached to it.

Ext. Court Book, 24th November 1697 :

" UPON a Report this day made, by the Governour, of the proceedings of the Committees thereunto appointed, for nominating an able Person, to be President of FORT ST. GEORGE, and the Subordinate Factoryes, That they were of opinion, That Captain THOMAS PITT was a person duly qualified to take charge of that Presidency ; on consideration whereof had, The Court thought fit by the Ballot, to discharge Lieut. Generall HIGGINSON, according to his desire, from his present Employment, and by the Ballot elected the said Captain THOMAS PITT, to be President accordingly, And it is referred to the said Committee to prepare proper Instructions and Advices to be sent by the said Captain PITT, for management of the Company's Affairs, with respect to the increase of their Trade and Revenues, and retrenching the exorbitant Charges of the respective Factorys of that Presidency, and to meet *de die in diem*, for the Dispatch of the Same."[1]

From Court Book, 26th Novr. 1697 :

" Captain Thomas Pitt, now comeing into Court, was made acquainted, by the Governour, That he was unanimously elected to be President at FORT ST.

---

[1] Luttrell thus records the news in his *Diary*, under 25th November 1697 :

" The EAST INDIA Company have chose Capt. PITS, member of Parliament for OLD SARUM, to be governor of FORT ST. GEORGE in the EAST INDIES." (iv, 310.)

And under 25th December :

" Captain PITT, who is made governour of FORT ST. GEORGE in the EAST INDIES, is preparing for his departure, and will be goeing soon after the holy dayes." (*Ib.*, 323.)

GEORGE, whereupon He took the Oaths appointed by the Charter, promising to improve his utmost ability and zeal, for the Companys Service."

28th Decr. Sir JEREMY SAMBROOKE is desired to peruse and revise Capt. PITT's covenant; and 31st Decr. DANIELL SHELDON and THOMAS COULSON,[1] Esqrs., were approved as his securities in £1,000 each.

His commission to be President of and for the Company's affairs on the "COAST of CHOROMANDELL and ORIXA, etc.," is dated 5th January 1697(-8). The instructions accompanying the commission give him, for twelve months, special powers to suspend any of the Council at the Fort *ab officio et beneficio*, as he shall find just cause for so doing, and so that there shall remain at least five of the Council besides the President to transact business. Retrenchment is stringently enjoined, and the number of factors is to be reduced if possible. Of the two ministers one only is to be maintained by the Company; the other "by a voluntary contribution from the Inhabitants, as the usuall way of maintaining Lectures in our Parish Churches here";— and the two Chirurgeons to be reduced to one.

The specific direction to be given to the new President's efforts as against Interlopers, is indicated in the following extract, and is, under the circumstances, somewhat diverting.

Ext. of letter from the Court to BENGAL, 26th Jany. 1697-8:

"On the *Martha* we have sent out THOMAS PITT, Esqre. to be our President at FORT ST. GEORGE . . . . M'. HIGGINSON having . . . . desired a Dismission from his present Station by reason of the opposition he met withall from some of his Councill, and the great weight of those important affairs that lay upon him, which were too heavy for him, and therefore requested Us to send one from hence in his Stead, and to put him in a lower Station in our Councill There, wherein we have gratified him, and put him 2d. of our said Councill, under our said President, who we are all assured will now employ the utmost of his endeavours and understanding in the affairs of INDIA for our service, which we know must needs be considerable by his long Experience there, But to have no power over you in BENGALL for Suspension or alteration . . . . however we would have you correspond with the FFORT on all occasions . . . . and especially in what may relate to the defeating of Interlopers, wherein we think our Presidents advice may be helpfull to you, he having engaged to Us to signalize himself therein."

From Court Book, 12th January 1697-8:

"It is ordered that Mr. ROBERT PITT,[2] Son of the President of FORT ST. GEORGE; as also Mr. PETER WALLIS, be permitted to take their passage . . . . and to reside at FORT ST. GEORGE as free Merchants, they entering into Covenants, as is usuall in like Cases."

---

[1] A member of the Court.

[2] Thomas Pitt's eldest son, and father of the Earl of Chatham.

Under the same date is entered permission for Capt. THOMAS PITT to ship 52 chests of wine, 4 chests of Nottingham Ale, 21 Hampers, 5 Cases of Pickles, one little Box, *qt:* (?) Six Pictures.

Ditto, 2nd February 1697(-8) :

"A Question this day arising touching the Entertainment and Salary, to be given to THOMAS PITT Esqr., who is elected President at FORT ST. GEORGE ; and Mr. BEYER reporting unto the Court, that the former Presidents received only Two Hundred Pounds per Annum Salary, and One Hundred Pounds a year Gratuity ; the Court thought fit to make the same allowance unto him ; and that in his Indenture of Covenants, the time of his service to be for five years, and it is ordered that the sum of one Hundred Pounds be paid to him for fresh Provisions in his Voyage."

It need not be said that Thomas Pitt must have made some zealous friends in the Court of Committees, in order to have been nominated to such a post in the face of his antecedents. From passages in his correspondence, we gather that Sir Thomas Cooke, Mr. Coulson, Mr. Samuel Ongley, and Mr. P. Godfrey were among his strong supporters. But also that the appointment was not approved of by the stockholders of the company in general is plainly asserted by Sir Josia Child in a letter to Mr. Papillon, which appears in a work published since the present compilation has been in progress.[1] I extract the first paragraphs of this letter, dated " WANSTEAD, 22d October 1698 ":

"Honoured Sir,

"In answer to yours of the 22d I have reason to hope that you who have known me from a youth, will believe me when I tell you that in point of my own interest, now when I am going out of the world, I am neither concerned for the old Company nor for the New one ; the first has been under the saw of persecution ever since we were rid of our fears of Popery and French Government ; and I, being in the case of Mephibosheth, since the nation is safe and the King, have no anxious care for the increase of my own Estate, or my family's.

"I cannot say no member of the Company ever committed any fault, but I protest, and must do it to my death, that I do not yet know any one fault or mistake in their conduct that the Company committed during the late reigns.

" *The worst that I ever knew them to do, was lately in the sending of that roughling, immoral man, Mr. —— to* INDIA *last year, which everybody knows I was always against; and the Adventurers resented it to such a degree as to turn out eighteen of that Committee, whereas I never before knew above eight removed.*"

There can be no question that Pitt's name is that represented here in blank, whether the blank be Sir Josia's or the editor's. And turning to vol. ii, p. clxxxii, it will be found that Sir Jeremy Sambrooke, in writing to Pitt some years later, refers to this ejection of 18 members of the

---

[1] *Memoirs of* THOMAS PAPILLON, *of* LONDON, *Merchant* (1623-1702). *By* A. F. W. PAPILLON, *a Lineal Descendant.* READING, 1887.

Court at one swoop, though he does not ascribe it to their support of his correspondent, the Governor.

Pitt landed at Madras on the 7th July 1698, and at once took over charge from Mr. Higginson.

The first proceeding of the New Governor that we note is his giving "a treat" to all the Company's servants and freemen at the New Garden, on the 11th July, in honour of the reading of his commission.[1]

It is unfortunate that we do not seem to possess any of Pitt's earliest letters from India, but I give a few extracts from the Court's Letters to Madras or to the new President.

The Court extract is from a letter sent to Fort St. George by the last despatch before Pitt's appointment. If the Dacca Court was included as part of the Native Government to which the purport of this extract was to be communicated, those members of it (and they must have been many) who retained a recollection of former correspondence regarding " Capt. Tom Pitt", must have been a little perplexed.

From Letter to FORT ST. GEORGE of 16th April 1697 :

"We have reason to believe that some Interlopers are designed for the BAY, and possibly to the COAST . . . So for your own Reputation you ought not to give them the least Countenance or Assistance, but to prevent and disappoint them all in you lyes, whereby you will clear those reports which they have spread of you to the contrary here in EUROPE, and that you take all Occasions to let the Government understand, that they do no wayes belong to the Company, and thô we dont affirm they design to make any Pyraticall attempts in those Seas, yet if any Such should happen, the Company cant hinder or be answerable for it, nor for any Ship but such as do either belong to them, or have their Passes."

From Court to " Our President THO: PITT Esqre: and our Agent CHA: EYRE Esqre", dated, " 4th Feby. 1697-8" :

*   *   *   *   *   *   *

" We would have you also make an Impartiall Enquiry into the truth of a Report, We have reason to believe, Vizt: that some of our own Servants or other ENGLISH not only favour'd and assisted the Interloper Antelope to get her lading, but have themselves laden Effects on her, and adviseing what Informations you can gather, touching this Matter, that we may See who are the Secret Enemyes to our Interest and reward them accordingly."

Ext. of Letter from the Court to FORT ST. GEORGE. (15th December 1698) :

" We find our aduersaryes are not wanting to turn every Stone to carry their point, and among other things, it is whispered about, that some of them had or would advise our President, that he was not so perfectly in our favour, as might be expected. This, together with the Generall discourse of their sending Mr. JNO. PITT his kinsman and our Quondam factor to be their Agent on the COAST, at MADAPOLLAM or thereabouts, They expect will influence Affairs in their favour . . . though we need add nothing more to what we lately wrote on this

---

[1] Wheeler's *Madras in the Olden Times*, i, 338.

subject, yet to prevent the mischief they intended, and in justice to our Selves, and
our President, We do declare We have no Mistrust of nor yet the least disesteem
for our said President, but on the contrary entirely confide in and rely upon his
prudent Management and Conduct.''. .

From the Court to " Our President THOS: PITT *Esqr.*"

(21st November 1699).

* * * * * *

" We are sorry your first welcom at MADRASS should be accompanyed with
the unhappy Miscarriage at FFORT ST. DAVIDS, and you will see by our Letters
to the FFORT, and to our Deputy Governour and Councill there, We entirely
agree with your Reflections. The first Occasion of it, namely the Unaccountable
Supiness of our Deputy Governour and Councill in permitting those Souldiers to
lodge in CODOLORE Town unobserved and unregarded till the mischievous
Consequents loudly proclaimed the want of a Fit Genius to Manage so important
a Station, is too Melancholly a Theme to dwell long upon, and therefore we shall
pass to a more inviting Subject."[1]

* * * * * * *

. . . " Tho we would have you always make a figure and look big enough to
prevent Insults, yet an Ounce of Discretion well managed will go further and
cost us less then a pound of Money, to maintain downright quarrells and
hostility."

* * * * * *

" We approve of your setting so good an Example in paying the Custome of
your Goods as pr. List, as knowing Examples are the most powerfull Precepts,
and that all under you will the Less dare to disobey, when they see you strictly
observant of the Laws of the Place, and for making so good a Precedent we
have ordered a Ton of the best Sherry to be laden for your accompt on board the
King William now proceeding for CADIZ to take in her Bullion."

* * * * * *

" We . . . are well pleased to find the severall Branches of our Revenues so considerably advancing under your Management, not doubting but Time and your
further Experience will give them yet a much larger augmentation, since so able
a heart and hand are engaged therein. You will see by our former Letter, that we
had an entire Confidence in and Dependance upon you, and you may easily believe
the number of your ffriends in our Court are not at all lessen'd at this time, go
on then and prosper in your Zeal for our Service, that the World may see
MADRASS flourishing and Vyeing with BATAVIA itself, That as it appears So it
may really continue the greatest City in that Eastern Part of the World, that its
Revenues may afford an annuall September Cargo, tho yours as well as our
Enemeys believe such a promise soner said then done, We dont at all despair of
its accomplishment and shall yet hope to find the Event crowning you with the
honour, and Us with the profit of its performance.

. . . " We can't so readily fall into your design of forming the severall Casts
into the Nature of our City Common Councill, lest by advancing any of these
People to a heighth beyound there usuall wont, they become giddy with the
honour, and set up for heads of factions and mutuinous disorders, none being
more insulting when got into the Saddle, nor more perfect Slaves when out of it.

* * * * * * *

---

[1] This passage refers to an attempted surprise of Cuddalore by the Mahom-
medans. See Wheeler's *Madras*, etc., i, 325.

"We are not unsensible Grandeur and a pompous splendid Appearance dos at some times turn to our advantage, because it is an experienced and approved Maxim in all the World, Riches is Power, and therefore we are content you should Keep the Gold Bridles. But the Mischief is, we have smarted heretofore under the Management of those who made use of that pretence of appearing great, to run us out of house and home. . . . We are content you may, if you see it absolutely needfull, increase the number of our horses beyound the present Number of four, and we rest perswaded, You will take care We shall not be charged one hundred or one hundred and fifty pounds a horse, as our Auditor tells us was lately done at FFORT ST. DAVIDS."

*   *   *   *   *   *   *

The first of Pitt's correspondence after his arrival in India that I find is the conclusion of a letter addressed to the then Deputy-Governor of Fort St. Davids, Mr. William Fraser, a person with whom Pitt in after days, lasting to the end of his Indian career, was in bitter antagonism. The fragment is without date.[1]

"I am very much Surpris'd you did not write a Generall letter to the Company by the *Neptune*, nor did I hear that you had wrote any perticular, or itt may be you were loath to intrust me with yours. I assure you I cant condescend to those mean actions of intercepting letters, nor doe I vallue what people write,— this I take notice of because that everybody talks of itt, what I wrote of you in my perticular letter to the Governour I here enclose. . . .

*   *   *   *   *   *

"P.S. Sr: I inclose to you Hugonins letter which pray returne me, you should not take away their perquisites, for dead mens pay, where there is noe wife nor child, is their due all the world over, but none for runaways, you must not be extreem to mark what is done amiss, and must wink at many things espetially at this time, doe but look after the Investment well, see that their goods are well bought, well sorted, washed and pack'd, and these little things will doe our Masters noe harme, they have perquisites every where throughout the world and if you abridge 'em of it without giveing them an equivolent they will make your Government uneasy to you, this is the advice of a hearty friend."

The next extract to the same gentleman touches on a subject which in later years became an aggravation of the hostility between these correspondents.

"FORT ST. GEORGE NOVR. 26th 1699.

"This comes by the Right Hand Cast of CUDDALORE, who have been here to Sollicite mee for what neither I nor they dont know, Soe have despatched 'em with a Smile and a Nod, 2 yards of Serge, beetle and rose water, with which they Seem very well Satisfyed, and assureing them that you'le doe all things in relation to their Cast according to *Sallabade*,[2] a Small matter will please 'em Soe pray give the fools a rattle . . .

---

[1] It begins Vol. i of the Pitt *Letter-books* in the British Museum (Addl. MSS., No. 22,842), and has a note appended : "belonging to the last in the Old Book." The "Old Book", which we suppose to have contained his earliest Indian letters, is not in the collection.

[2] Old custom.

But we now turn to an episode in Pitt's history which occupies a larger part than any other in his correspondence.

Thomas Pitt had not been long established in the Government of Fort St. George, before he began to partake of the annoyances arising from the creation of the New E. I. Company, or (as it was formally styled) "The English Company trading to the East Indies". The Letters Patent constituting the Company under this name were issued by King William on the 5th September 1698, and by these the trading powers of the Old or "London Company", as it was now distinctively called, were to terminate on the 29th September 1701. Pitt had arrived in India only two months before the issue of these Letters Patent, which were followed by the appointment, on the part of the New Company, of Presidents to represent them at Surat, on the Coromandel coast, and in Bengal, whilst that Company had influence enough with the English Government to obtain, for these new officials, also the character of King's Consuls. This was a stroke from which evidently great effect was anticipated in the struggle with the New Company's long established rivals, but which in reality conduced to nothing but exhibitions of folly in those decked with such titles. From the expectation also of some like effect in the presentation of their New Company as predominant, and enjoying the special patronage of the English Crown, that body obtained from the King permission for the despatch of Sir William Norris, Member of Parliament for Liverpool, as ambassador to the Great Mogul Aurangzíb, then in failing health.

The three new Presidents were singularly ill chosen. All three were former servants of the Old Company, and all three gave their new masters ample cause to rue the day of their engagement. Of these, Littleton who went to Húglí as Sir Edward, and Waite who went to Surat as Sir Nicholas, had been dismissed by the Old Company. The history of John Pitt, a cousin of the subject of these pages, and who went to the Coast with his residence designated at Masulipatam, is not quite so easily traced. He had been in the Company's service at Fort St. George, but had quitted it a few years before.[1] Immediately on

---

[1] The relation of this John Pitt to the Governor is not indicated in the Pitt family tree, as given in Hutchins' *History of Dorset*. We learn from a letter of T. Pitt's to his kinsman, Nicholas Pitt, announcing John's death, that the latter was nephew to Nicholas, whilst another passage indicates that he bore the same relation also to George Pitt. These two must have been George Pitt of Strathfieldsay (d. 1694), and his brother Nicholas, both of whom appear in the genealogical table opposite p. xxix. But we do not know who, among the numerous brothers of George and Nicholas, was John Pitt's father. In any case John bore to the Governor the relationship of "Second Cousin once removed"; and we gather that such relations were then more

his arrival in India, clothed with his new offices, he came into collision with his kinsman the Old Company's masterful President on the Coast, and not at all to his own advantage.

The first announcement of John Pitt's arrival that we find from his own hand is contained in a letter which its indorsement in the I. O. Records describes as

"*Wrot and intended to be sent to the late President* YALE, *gon for* ENGLAND *in the* Martha, *had he bin in* FORT ST. GEORGE."

(Yale had been removed, as we have seen, in 1692, but continued to reside at Madras till 1699.)

---

frankly recognised than they now are south of the Tweed. Further notes regarding John Pitt will be found below when his death and will are mentioned.

John Pitt was nominated one of the factors for the Coast and Bay in the early part of 1684, as is shown by the Court's letter to the Bay of March 5th, 1683-4 ; but I have not been able to find the usual record of nomination and securities in the *Court Books,* The first mention of his name that I have found is in the Court's Letter to Fort, of 15th February 1688-9 :

"Mr. PITTS we hope is a good man, but his expenses at Atcheen were excessive, and more than such a poor Cargoe could bear."

Under the article TRENCHFEILD (vol. II, p. cclxxxvi) we have referred to John Pitt's employment, along with Richard Trenchfeild, on a mission to the Wazír's camp before Chenjí in 1692 ; there is also a brief notice of this mission in Wheeler's *Madras in the Olden Time* (vol. i, pp. 246-7). Kháfí Khán, in Elliot's *Mahommedan Historians* (vol. vii, 348), speaks of the Mogul army before Chenjí, but says nothing of the English Mission.

In *Court Book,* under 6th March 1694-5, we find John Pitt appointed 7th Member of Council at Fort St. George, or 9th if we include the General (Sir John Gayer), and the Lieut. General (Higginson). We do not know the exact time of his retirement from the service, but it was probably in the beginning of 1696, as a committee of gentlemen of the India House are ordered to examine his accounts under dates 23rd December 1696, and 22nd January, 1696-7.

And that no discredit attached to Mr. Pitt's quitting the service appears from an injunction to the Committee under the latter date to receive from him " an account in writing of his observations how the Company's affairs have been managed during the time he was in their service, and what he conceives may best promote their Trade and Commerce in those parts".

Moreover, a little later (18th March 1697-8) I find him elected by the Court to be Chief in Persia. But this, it must be presumed, he never took up, and the embryo New Company must already, or soon after, have enlisted him.

The last notice of him in the old *Court's Books* is under 14th April 1697, ordering a balance due on his account to be paid. At p. xxxii, *supra,* I have referred to his capture by the French in the ship *Princess Anne* of Denmark, on his way to Europe in 1695.

It is dated "*From on board the* De Grave, Capt. Wᴍ: Yᴏᴜɴɢ, *commander, in* Pᴏʀᴛᴀ Nᴏᴠᴀ *Road,* July 26: 99."

"Honble: Sʳ;[1]

"You have heard and read I presume an Act of Parliament which has Established a New Eᴀsᴛ Iɴᴅɪᴀ Cᴏᴍᴘᴀɴʏ and determined the old after 3 years, comence Michealmas last which time was allow'd them to draw in their Effects at home and abroad . . . . Sʳ: This is the Interest and Service I have engag'd in and have lookt upon't as a Lucky omen, That I have the good fortune to meet with your Honour in these parts, to own to you and the world what great obligations I have to you and from whose converse I propose to myself very great advantage in carrying on my Masters Interest, being fond to believe you to retain Still your wonted Generous temper and freedom to communicate to your Friends proper methods to bring that about which you have so often wish'd with so much Satisfaction and for efecting it if you will give me leave to see you ashore, please to propose what method you Judg may best Suit with your circumstances. I shall fancy your Garden the properest place for I would not Injure my kinsman so much as to propose the Fort, besides cou'd it be, I am so well known there, it cannot be done without a great deal of noise, loss of time, (and) some ceremony, which I hate and wou'd upon all occasions avoid.

"I bear the charecter of his Majesties Consull for the Eɴɢʟɪsʜ Nation Generall upon the Coast of Cᴏʀᴍᴀɴᴅᴇʟʟ, which will be a cheque upon your Government that they dare not affront it, if they dont pay it that respect which becomes them. I have wrote to my Kinsman the President, but can't tell how he'l relish it before I have his answer; please to favour me with yours and your Sentiments upon't by the Person who brings you this. Madam Yᴀʟᴇ and your young Ladys are well, but noe Letter, not so much as from Sʳ: Sᴛᴇᴠᴇɴ or Mr. Pᴀɢᴇ, for they beleive you on your Voyage for England . . . .
"J. P."

On arrival in Mᴀᴅʀᴀs *Roads the following note from the Port officer is delivered after usual custom by a messenger on a catamaran :*

"Sʳ:
"You are desir'd to inform the Ship's name with the Commanders, from whence you last came, and whither bound to.
"Your humble Servant
"Cʜᴀʀʟᴇs Bᴜɢᴅᴇɴ."

Reply :

"The Ship *Degraue,* Capt. Wᴍ: Yᴏᴜɴɢ Comandʳ: belonging to the Honble: Eᴀsᴛ Iɴᴅɪᴀ Cᴏᴍᴘᴀɴʏ Trading to the Eᴀsᴛ Iɴᴅɪᴇs Lately Established by Act of Parliament in 4 mos: 20 days from Eɴɢʟᴀɴᴅ, bound for Cᴏᴀsᴛ and Bᴀʏ and upon her Jᴏʜɴ Pɪᴛᴛ Esq: his Majesties Minister and Consull for the Eɴɢʟɪsʜ Nation in Generall on the whole Coast of Cᴏʀᴏᴍᴀɴᴅᴇʟʟ.

"In answ': to yᵉ: Catamaran note.
"Mᴀᴅʀᴀs Rᴏᴀᴅ July 28: 99."

From Jᴏʜɴ Pɪᴛᴛ *to President* Pɪᴛᴛ.[2]   (Same date as last.)

"Sʳ:
"I did by some of Early Shipps let you know that I had engag'd my Self in

---

[1] O.C. 6683.   [2] U.C. 6687.

the Service of the Honble : ENGLISH Company · . . . lately Settled by Act of
Parliament which determin'd yours in three years commencing last Michealmas,
and having gain'd the COAST cou'd not pass by without dropping an Anchor in
MADRASS ROAD, and wou'd Salute you, had I not the Honour to bear his
Majesties Commission which constitutes me his Minister or Consull for the
ENGLISH Nation in Generall on the whole Coast of CORMANDELL including all
your Settlements. If you think fitt to pay the respect that is due to the Cha-
racter with your fflagg Lower'd the Compliment shall be return'd you by

> " S^r: Your affect : Kinsman and Servt :

> " J. P."

Superscribed

> "*To the Honble:* THO: PITT *Esq: Pres^t: for affaires for the Governor and
> Company of Mercht^s: of* LONDON *Trading yet to the* EAST INDIES *by permis-
> sion on the Coast of* COROMANDELL."

Consul Pitt does not seem to have been quite easy as to his own
conduct on this occasion. Some weeks later he and his Council at
Masulipatam, write as follows to their masters :[1]

Dated, " METCHLEPATAM, the 19th Septr. 1699."

". . . . Came to an Anchor the 28th (July) in MADRASS road to make them
sensible to the extent of his Commission. They put abroad the Union fflagg, but
the Consull took no notice of it,—not out of any disrespect, but believing the
Priviledge of wearing it in their fforts, on this COAST, ceas'd by Virtue of the late
Act, and his Majesties Royall Charter to the ENGLISH Company, which only
Secures to them their Trade for Three Years not Military Power, and if So, he
thought the first Salute was due to him, and accordingly Sent a letter ashoar to
the President to give him notice of his arrivall and character, but he would by
no means allow the Commission to extend so far (as) to include their Settlements,
and the ENGLISH who live under them, and accordingly should give orders to
the severall chiefs not to take notice of 't, and shew him no more respect then
what his deportment might deserve, being mightily nettled at the purport and
superscription of his letter, which the Consull expects will be Sent home to be
Scan'd to the last degree, and for that reason he has sent Copys of it and the
answer, and he hopes a favourable Construction will be put upon 't and his
actions during his Stay there, by the Honble: Directors, and that they will
represent it so at Court, if he's in the wrong."

This is the rebuke he got from Cousin Thomas, temperate enough, all
things considered :[2]

Dated, " FORT ST. GEORGE, July 28: 99."

" S^r:

" I received yours the purport of which seems very odd as well as the Superscription. If you had read the Act of Parliament, and well consider'd it, you
will find that it Establishes my Masters in all their rights and priviledges in these
parts till 1701, and afterwards 'tis Secur'd to them by their Subscription, therefore you can have noe power in any place of their Settlements, nor shall I own
any till I am Soe order'd by those that intrust me.

" I am not unacquainted with what respect is due to the Kings Consull
(whether you are one I know not) but you cannot (think) or ever have heard that

---

[1] O.C. 6737.   [2] O.C. 6688.

an Ancient Fortification wearing the Kings Flagg, Shou'd lower it and Salute a reall Consull ; but I take it to be your Obligation to have Saluted the Flagg ashore at your comeing to anchor which wee Shou'd have answer'd according to custome and good manners.

"What Liquors (*sic*, but *qy*. Letters?) you have for me I desire you to send on Shore in these Boats. You must expect to find me noe less zealous for my masters interest, then you are for yours and as you act the same will be return'd you by

"S^r your affection": Kinsman
"and humble servant
"Tho: Pitt, Governour."

I find also the following, but it does not appear clearly whether it was a postscript to the last, or a separate (earlier?) communication :

"*A copy of a Parag. in a letter from President* Pitt *at* Ft: St. George (*Vzt.*)"

"S_r:

"I find you are a Young Consull by the purport and Superscription of your letter. I wish you had omitted it."

"To John Pitt Esq.
"On board the *Degrave*."

The Young Consul answers in much wrath :[1]

"I am sorry to find the zeal for your Masters has Transported you beyond Sence and Good Manners. I shall Impute it in part to the heat of the Country which has alter'd your Temper.

"The Young Consull as you term him gives you this advice to mind the main Chance and not forfeit Old Saram &ca: and expose your Self to the World to boot ; who I doe assure you will much censure and blaim this rashness of yours, and let me tell you your Masters will neither Thank you and bear you out in 't. I came later from England then your advices.

"J. P."

"I shall send your Letters from Metchlepatam and doe not question A just Accompt from you of my private Affair. You'l know in the End I am not to be taught my Duty by you.   "J. P."

"July 28. 99."

And again :

"I shall answer your Scurrilous Letter from Metchlepatam and beleive me you'l wish you had never wrote in Such a Stile. I'le take such measures to make you Sencible that my Commission reaches over all your Settlements and you your Selfe Shall be forc't to own and publish it in all your Forts and Settlements and beg pardon for the affront offer'd to the Charecter of his Majesties Consull.
"J.P."

Superscribed "*To* Tho: Pitt *Esqr:* In Madrass."

And when the Consul arrives at Masulipatam and finds the Old Company's factors take no notice of his arrival, the foolish fellow writes as follows :

---

[1] O.C. 6687.

"*To Mr.* THO: LOVELL &c. ENGLISH *in the Service of the Governour and Company of Merchants of* LONDON *Trading to the* EAST INDIES, *in their Factory or elsewhere in* METCHLEPATAM.*"*

(After stating his appointment, etc.) :

"You were not unsensible of my Arrivall and what regard and respect is due to 't. This is therefore to will and require you in the Kings Name to repair to our Factory tomorrow morning between 9 and 10 being the 8th Instant August, Upon hoisting the Flagg when I intend to open and read my Commission. I take this Course that you nor any other of the ENGLISH nation residing here may not plead Iggnorance. Therefore fail not to appear as you'l answer the contrary at your Perill.

"*Dated at the* ENGLISH *Companys Factory Trading to the* EAST INDIES *in* METCHLEPATAM Aug: 7: 99."   " J. P., Consull."

Mr. Lovell and his colleagues of course paid no attention. And the Government at the Fort, on hearing of the proceeding, issued the following proclamation :[1]

"Wee the Governour President and Council of FORT ST. GEORGE for affairs of the Right Honble: the EAST INDIA Company, being advised that Mr. JOHN PITT lately arrived at METCHLEPATAM has by a Summons wherein he Stiles himself the New Companys President and the Kings Consull for the COAST, directed to our Companys Factors there, wherein he seems to usurp an Authority over them, and to intermeddle with our Companys Affaires, the pernicious consequences of which being well Considered by us have thought fitt to Send out these our orders to all our Forts, Castles, Towns and Factorys under this Presidency for the following reasons.

"For that the Act of Parliament which erects the New EAST INDIA Company continues our Company Trade till September 1701, from whence wee Infer that they are to Enjoy all their Rights and Priviledges and there Governours, Presidents and Factorys to exercize all powers necessary for the Supports of your Governments and Trades.

"Moreover wee observe in the Act our Company are exempted from paying the five per Cent. which is for bearing the Charge of Embassadours and Consulls from which wee likewise inferr that our Companys affairs nor Servants nor any Trading under there protection in these parts are under theire direction or controul.

"Wherefore for the foregoing reasons and to prevent the great mischiefs that otherwise will undoubtedly attend our Masters affaires wee require all ENGLISH in our Companys Service as allso all that live and Trade under their protection not to obey nor regard any Summons or orders that they shall receive from Mr. JOHN PITT or any one Else under the pretence of his being a President for the New Company or a Consull.

"Wee resolve to persist in this Opinion till his most Gracious Majesties Pleasure be Signified to us, or that our Honble: Employers give us direction herein.

"In Confirmation whereof Wee have here unto Sett our hands and the Seale

---

[1] O.C. 6713.

of our Company: At FORT ST. GEORGE in the city of MADERASSE This 23 day of August 1699.

"THOMAS PITT
"FRANCIS ELLIS
"RO: BRADDYLL
"THO: WRIGHT
"M: EMPSON
"THO: MARSHALL
"RICHARD WATTS."

Our next extract is from a letter in Italian, addressed by Consul John Pitt to "Sen: NICOLAO MANUCJJ",[1] dated "MASSLAPATAM, Giulio $\frac{28}{1699}$ — Agosto $\frac{8}{1699}$."

After announcing his arrival and position as well as the expected coming of the Ambassador, the writer proceeds :

"V.S. è della mia vecchia conoscenza ed amicitia, ed huomo anchora di gran poter ed esperienza, non solamente nelle tutte cose della mercanza, ma pure nelle *Dubarti* ò Corti Degl' INDIE, i loro Languagij e condutto, e questo è che ha renduto V.S. massimamente stimata e ricomandata ai Nostri Hon: Direttori, V.S. anco stando semper apparecchiato da render i buoni officij alla nostra Nazione, ella puo adesso servir il nostro Rè, e la Compagnia Inglesa, consigliando ed assistando la S: Eccell: nella sua negotiatione, ed a questo un perfetto maestro dei Languaggij ed honesto e giusto spositore è tanto neccessario quanto un assistante" . . etc. . . . .

"Rimango il vechio Amico

"di V.S. per servirla

secondo la mia obligatione

"J. P."

An English version follows the Italian. Then :

From Consul JOHN PITT *to Mr.* BETTS *at* MADRAS :[2]

Dated, "METCHLEPATAM, August 14: 99."

"Sr: I am come to INDIA and intend to Settle in these parts : if you have a mind to ingage in the Service of the ENGLISH Company Tradeing to the EAST INDIES lately Establisht I'le make it worth your while. Your Sallary will be 60£ per Annum all paid in the country, and ile make your perquisites considerable, you know my Temper. I'le engage you'l get mony as much as you can Expect and you have a hearty wellcome from me and if you dont like public business you Shall be with me and fare as well whether you Embrace it or not if you come make hast Overland your charges Shall be allow'd dont deny me if you doe you'l be your own Enemy.

"This is the 2d I have wrot you. I am

"Yours

"P.S. Give a Speedy Answer by this *Patamar*.[3]   "J. P."
Send it to COGEE GRIGORY or NICHOLAO
MANUCHIJ."

---

[1] O.C. 6685. And see vol. II, p. cclxviii, *note.*
[2] O.C. 6702.   [3] Courier.

From CHARLES FLEETWOOD, *To the Rt: Worshipfull*
JOHN PITT *Esqr:*[1]

"FORT ST. GEORGE, July 30: 99.

" Right Worshipfull

. . . "I find our Grandees are Strangely nettled here at you(r) (as they call it) Strange carrage in the road, as likewise at your Manner of writeing which is by them lookt upon as an affront of the first rank.

" I have bin in a great dispute with my Self about given you a large account of matters, whither I should or shou'd not but 'twas carry'd on the negative, upon noe other Score (than) that soe slight a messenger was too easily rifled, therefore have resolv'd upon Silence till I have heard how Safe this conveyance, is if you write to me inclose your letter in one to MAY HEATHFIELD to CHARLES FLEETWOOD Sen': because of the Old Weomans Son.

" The WEST COAST[2] have been in Trouble ever since they turn'd me out which makes Severall of the Opinion they must be forced to Send me thither to make up the breach. Some of our People have bin cut off, and the People still continue in open hostility. I am resolv'd not to goe if it can be avoided.

"Our present Governour is really of himself a very good man and certainly very zealous to the Interest he Espouses. . . .

" Rt Worshipfull
" Your most obedt. humble Servt:
" S': If I am mistaken in your   " CHARLES FLEETWOOD.
Title please to Excuse.
" C. F."

" These are the Companys Peons therefore
I think 'twill be well to give um a
rupee or 2. For they stay at POLLE-
CATT for this."

From the same to the same; dated, August 4, 1699.

(Giving an account of an interview with President T. Pitt.)

*   *   *   *   *   *

" As soon as I came in he asked me whither I design'd to serve the New Company. I told him I thought not at present for that I were partly Ingaged in a Voyage to the RED SEA, and as yet I had noe other thoughts he asked me whether I spake really[3] and I told him yes, upon which he made me promise him that I would not leave the Shoar without leave and Soe dismissed me. But before he left me he told me that he thought the new Mannagers had bin gentlemen of more honour then to entice the Honble: Companys Servants, which was a pleasant reflection when they all knew I had bin out of their Service since 1694. I must make fair pretentions till I get my mony, and then they shall know my designs and till then I must be cautious what I doe.

" I request the favour of your advice in case the Embassader shou'd arrive in what nature 'twas best for me to apply my Self to him to get a redress of Gre-

---

[1] O.C. 6691. Fleetwood was a dismissed servant of the Old Company.
[2] Of Sumatra.
[5] *Really* in these documents generally means " sincerely".

viences, and to be clear of them. I desire you to take noe notice of me only in your private letters to MAY HEATHFIELD.

" MAY HEATHFIELD presents her Service to you and wishes you all happyness and prosperity." . . . .

From Consul JOHN PITT to CHARLES FLEETWOOD.[1]

" Mr. CHARLES FLEETWOOD.

" S:

" Your post of July 29th: which I received the 11th ultimo I answer'd, since which came to my hands two more Intimations of your Willingness to accept of the Service but that you mett with a good deal of dificulty to procure liberty from your President &ca: with whome you have accounts depending. I shall not now examine where Injustice lies, but our honble: Directors orders concerning you are provisionall that you accept of the imploy upon the terms agreed there by your friends and that you be out and clear from the Old Companys Service and that you Sign the Bond and Covenants for your Security in the discharge of your imploy. Soe that President PITTS dirty reflection upon our Honble: Directors was false and malicious, pray tell him from me they are Gentlemen of more Honour and the persons they have imploy'd, then to Intice any man in the Service of the Company of Merchants of LONDON Trading to the EAST INDIES ; I wish he and his &cas: would act soe too, and not stave off Ballanceing accounts and giving discharges on purpose to ruine those who wou'd be then at liberty to serve which Interest they pleas'd.

" Wee have taken care to mannage the affair at SICCACUL to the best advantage having more Friends then perhaps Some at MADRASS care to believe . . . . Your affec: Friend ready to serve you

"J. P."

Under the date of Nov. 12, 1699, we have a long and remarkable letter from the Governor to John Pitt, in reply to one from the latter written from Masulipatam, which does not appear to have been preserved. The letter is curious from the tone of intimacy, as to a familiar relative, combined with frank snubbing and semi-hostility, but above all that reference to the writer's old interloping days which we have already quoted.

We give some extracts :[2]

*　*　*　*　*　*　*

" 'Tis your own ill nature and uneven temper makes you Censure your relations—from me you have mett with noe disappointments ; whether I have from you, you best know, only that instance, your willfully buying the Neck': in FFRANCE, and how ready you were to draw the ruin on your own head, which I solely prevented, but I believe the Emissary at your Elbow, well nigh your own hue, distracts your thoughts.

" The fable of the froggs Suits your present temper, and the Morall and reflexion I hope will make much impression on you Soe as to prevent your having the fate of the froggs. I recommend to you allsoe the reading and practising the fables of the Lion and the Mouse, and the Wolf and the Stork.

---

[1] O.C. 6731.

[2] B. M. Addl. MSS. 22,842, No. 2.

"I find to Excuse your own miscarryage in this port, in not paying the respect due to the Kings fflagg, you seem to question our power to wear itt, and that wee are not to be esteem'd as BOMBAY, or ST. HALENA to either of which I think wee have much the preheminence, for that wee are much more Considerable in all respects. I remember BOMBAY, ST. HALENA and all other ffortifications in these parts wore ST. GEORGES fflag, and 'twas King JAMES (who I suppose you'le own once had a power) order'd that all fortifications belonging either to the AFRICAN or EAST INDIA Company should wear his fflagg . . . . don't you know they have power to raise Soldiers for these parts, which is part of the Regall power, and 'tis noe wonder the wearing his fflagg Should goe with itt—The Honour of itt has and Shall be Maintain'd during my time. . . .

"If you pass by here you must behave your Selfe very Civilly, noe Drums, fflaggs nor trumpets within our bounds, for here shall be but one Governour whilst I am here.

"Your Advice is very good, and I returne it you, mind your trade which is your Masters business, and when the MOORS have bang'd you and Stript you of what you have, upon your Submission and begging pardon for what you have done, I may Chance to protect you here. I can't but laugh at your promising us protection ; when you have neither forces, power nor Interest in the Countrey. When ours are assign'd you, you may talk at that rate. . . .

"I cant but smile when you tell me you were once near the Gown, nay and had it on too ; and I believe you would have made as good a Parson as a Consull.

"I am, I must acknowledge, beholding to you for your recommendation from BREST, I being a stranger to the Governour and Company, and you well known to them, the Same to this place, for which reason I am so belov'd, most here being my accquaintance long before you saw INDIA. And for the supporting my Creditt, I dont remember I was indebted, or Concern'd in anything what ever that could be Censur'd by any unless itt was interlopeing, which I never repented of to this day.

*   *   *   *   *   *   *

"Among the ill natur'd things you charge me with is that I would not permitt any of your ffriends to Come off to you. I must tell you there was not one Soule desired itt. After you were gone I heard you sent for Mr. TRENCHFEILD, who laughed at itt ; he went off to the Embassador. For my part I never deny'd any Man since my comeing. Then for fresh provisions, which was more then you deserv'd, Mr. HOLDEN could have told you if I order'd the Steward to send off what possible could be gott ready,—his not doeing of itt I know not the reason.

"What you want—pepper, China, raw Silk and Long cloth, you were mistaken in the Man, for he never would have serv'd you, nor I believe will any here,—if they doe I will find out a way to requite 'em.

"I have Seen your Sugar Candy how-doe-you-doe letters to Severall, all which will not doe. Itt may be with the charming way you have (that)—especially in the time of prosperity a year and a year and a halfe agoe—you might have done some thing. You say I used to raile at Mr. COULSON, if Soe 'twas for the Same reason I doe att you Now, for your bouncing and huffing.[1] But Still you see he was more my friend then yours. Hee helpt me to a Presidency, and you but (to) an Agency.[2] . . .

---

[1] The same characters are applied to the writer in letters formerly quoted (see pp. xvii, xxxi, *supra*).

[2] Presumably to the appointment of Agent in Persia (see p. xl).

"I am of the same opinion Still, and think you may Lock up your Consulls Commission till my Masters time is expir'd.

*   *   *   *   *   *   *

"I think I have now answer'd all your riff raff Stuff, which I hope will be as tiresome to you to read as 'tis to me to write.

". . . I ordered the Captain to bring me six horses, but he could not gett one. Capt. BROOK brought one which I bought of him, which proves too good for you, and only fitt for me to ride.

"I have another, an Arab, but that is small. You shall have ten chests of PERSIAN Wine sent you by the first Oppertunity . . .

"My Son is in CHINA with Mr. DOLBEN, who was Soe Kind to take him into the Commission . . .

"In May last I was Seiz'd with a Violent feavor, and Convulsions from head to foot, which gave me a kind of pallsey in my limbs, that some times I was not able to write, or hold a glass of Wine. I made a shift to put the best Side out when the Men of Warr were here, but lay by it afterwards. But since the Northerly Winds came in I find it much better, but am still troubled with a Violent heat, which Seems to be in the bones. If the hot winds next year be Soe Violent as they were this last, 'twill Sweep most of us away. The BENGALL or PERSIA ayire agrees much better with me then this . . .

"If your more weighty business will permitt I should be glad to hear what is become of our Relations, haveing not heard from one Since I came out, but Brother CURGENVEN. Is GEORGE PITT marryed or about itt ? . . . 'Tis sure now you are a great man, and have got the start of us in honour and everything, but yett I think you might Condescend to write us a little News.

"Mr. DOLBEN sent from BATAVIA a very Stately piece of Ambergreese, upwards of 800°ⁿˢ: COJA GREGORY, Mr. AFFLECK, and my Selfe have bought itt, in which I am Concern'd 1000 Pagodas . . .

"To Conclude this tedious letter I must tell you I am not unsensible how some of my Masters I now serve intended to have done basely by mee, and am not ignorant what prevented itt, yett for the sake of those that Stood my fast friends I will not doe any thing, or any wise omitt what I ought, whereby to bring any blemish on them, or my Selfe, Farewell

"Your Servt &ca.

"THO: PITT."

Extract of another long letter from the same to the same. (Addl. MSS. 22,842, No. 21.)

Dated, "Jany 5th 1698/9."

*   *   *   *   *   *   *

"What did I ennumerate the Voyages I was Concern'd in for? I thought a Man of your Sagacity and quick apprehension would have understood itt ; not that I want Partners, nor your Protection, tho' the Commodore's I expect, who told me his orders were to protect all ships belonging to the Subjects of ENGLAND, without any regard to the Old Company or New, The poor Gentleman dyed at TILLECHERRY of a *Mordasheen*"[1] . . .

Then referring to controversies with his cousin over old accounts of joint speculations, the Governor says :

"I wonder with what face you can say I carryed the ballance of your account

---

[1] *I.e.* of cholera. See *Anglo-Indian Glossary*, s.v. *Mort-de-chien.*

with me to BENGALL in the *Seymore*, and that you wrote me to remitt it to FORT ST. GEORGE, which I am Satisfy'd is a great untruth, You did desire to be Concern'd with me in the Ship to that amount, which I thought unreasonable haveing runn the Risque out; 'twas well for you I did not, and the worse for me." . . .

Governor T. PITT *to the Governor of the Company*, dated February 11th, 1699-1700. (Addl. MSS. 22,842, No. 44.)

. . . . "I shall not trouble you with much relation about the ambassador, being unwilling to committ in paper Some services I have done you, which I am forc'd to keep as Secrets here, for fear of haveing some turn Informers and come Evidence against me, he is still at METCHLEPATAM makeing great preparations for his goeing up to the King the latter end of next month, when I shall take care to have the best information I can of all the proceedings. And I hope to write you hereafter that they have not been able to doe you much harm, tho they speake very bigg and threaten hard, and 'tis said that they dont doubt but that to see us call'd to an account for all the Moneys rais'd by way of revenue in the MOGULLS Dominions ; 'tis Certain if they dont hear of a Conjunction they will endeavour your entire ruine, and 'tis as Certaine I will defend and support your cause, and doe as much as if the whole Concerne was my Owne.

. . . . "About two or three months agoe Mr. PITT (I since understand) wrote to one Mr. JOHN AFFLECK his old acquaintance, to buy him some Horses. Soe comeing to me one evening, he ask'd me whether I would Sell two Horses I had, I answer'd him I would if I Could gett my price, which upon talking of I brought 'em up to five hundred pagodas, and Sold 'em to him, which was double their value, both being old and founder'd.

"I did not know who they were for then, but Some days after heard they were for the ambassador or the Consull. This I know will be represented to you by Some, as if I favour'd the Cause. They allsoe bought five or six more in towne and gave extravagant rates. If all their Stock be invested at the same rate you won't be troubled with the noise of a New Company long. I hope you'le make no construction of this to my prejudice, for I assure you upon my word I knew not who they were for."

To Agent BEARD *at* CALCUTTA, April 2nd, 1700. (Addl. MSS. 22,842, No. 106.)

"Our kindred at METCHLEPATAM still keeps on in the same Strein, tho' he has gott nothing by it for himselfe nor masters, Wee have lately had a clash with the Ambassador (who still remains there) of which wee shall advise you in our Generall. You did very well in Standing up against Sr: Edward, and not permitt him to Concerne himselfe with our Masters affairs, which are not within his power, for I assure you lett them be Ambassador or Consulls or what-ever Characters they have, they shall not Concerne themselves within my precinct. Our Masters have not wrote us one word, in Generall nor perticular, concerning these new authoritys."

Governor PITT *to* JOHN PITT *at* METCHLEPATAM, April 30, 1700. (Same MS., No. 128.)

*   *   *   *   *   *

"You seem to be very much nettl'd that I should doubt your generosity, which you say you will not Learne from me. I remember the time when you your selfe would have own'd, I could not only instruct you in that but in every thing else, except the putting on a Cravat String, I would recommend to you the reading of your own letters to me before this Suddain and new promotion of yours, and those you wrote me upon your arrivall, and since, and doe but compare the stiles, and then you'le see the ill Effects preferment generally Carrys with it." . . . .

Governor PITT *to* " Sʳ: NICHOLAS WAITE *Merchant, and President for the New Companys affairs att* SURRATT." Dated, "May 20th, 1700." (Same MS., No. 148.)

" Sʳ:

"I received yours the 4th of Aprill with the inclos'd Letters, and Can but smile att your Superscription. Tho' you never knew me fond of titles, yet allways thought I was at least equall with any of the New Companys Servants, and above the employ of a Consull. I have been throughly inform'd of your behaviour towards our Masters Servants and what I most wonder att is that they did not doe themselves justice upon you with their own hands. For my part without direct orders from the King or from our Company I will have noe regard to your powers, nor your Persons, otherwise then as you shall deserve by your deportment. I perceive you would use your fellow subjects as some did in OLIVER's days, for which afterwards they justly and Severely Suffer'd,[1] and there is great probability that yours may be the same fate. I wish you as much health and prosperity as you doe me,

" I am Your humble Servant" etc.,

" THOS. PITT."

I have not found any copy of Waite's letter, referred to in the preceding one, but the following is from a letter of T. Pitt to Sir John Gayer,"General of India", dated June 19th, 1700. (Same MS., No. 168.)

"I received yours of the 7th of March by the *Greyhound* Sloop, and observe what past between you and the PORTUGUEZ, which is noe Strange thing, for noe other can be expected of men void of sence, honour, or honesty, and truly I can say noe better of Sʳ: NICHOLAS neither, who has wrote to me, to which I have returned him an answer which I believe your Honour will hear of, He directed his Letter to me '*As yett President and Governour of* FORT ST. GEORGE.'

"I could wish he came in the Errand to displace me without our Masters Orders. And I would make him renounce those little honours he pretends to, as well as make him senceable of the blackest of Crimes, his ingratitude to his old Masters."

Sir William Norris, nominally Ambassador of King William to the Great Mogul, but who had come out as an instrument of the New Company, and at their charges, had directed his course to Masulipatam, and landed there, apparently under the advice of John Pitt, 23rd Sept. 1699, with the idea of making his way thence to Aurangzíb's Court. The Emperor, at the great age of eighty-one, and in declining health, but still taking the field, was then encamped in the Mahratta country,

---

[1] This is probably aimed at Waite's parentage. We suppose that he was a son of Col. T. Waite, the regicide (see p. lvii, also vol. II, p. cccxix, *note*).

either before Sattara, or preparing for the siege of that place ; and it was apparently a wild project to select Masulipatam as the starting point of the march.   This, as we shall see, the Ambassador after a time discovered and resented.

Sir Wm. Norris *to the Gentlemen of the* English Company's *Factory at* Metchlepatam :[1]

> "*from on board his Majesties Shipp* Harwich *rideing att Anchor in the Roade before* Metchlipatan *on the Coast of* Cormandell the 23th. of September 1699.*"*

"Honrd: Gentlemen

"I thought it Necessary to take the first Oppertunity to Signify to you my Arrivall on the Coast, which was (with the Squadron under the Comand of Comadore Warren) on the 20th Instant about Six in the Evening.   And on Munday next I Intend to dissimbarque.

"This comes by a Shipp in the Service of the Old Company, wherefor I think itt not Expedient to say any thing further then that I am

"All possible Provision is makeing (by the Governor in Cheife of this Province vnder the Great Mogull) for my Reception, with great Grandure and all Imaginable demonstrations of ffreindshipp.   A Supply of Wine and Strong Beer will bee Necessary by the first Oppertunity."

"Honrd: Gentlemen
"Your humble Servant
"Wm: Norris.

Consul J. Pitt *to* Sir William Norris :[2]

"My Lord

*   *   *   *   *   *   *   *

"Shall get all things ready for Your Lordships reception on Monday and will advise You tomorrow what hour of the day will be best to Land.

"If your Excellency pleases in my opinion 'twill be best to have only a Cold treat and the Severall tables ready Spread Cover'd, upon Your Arrivall, for 'twill be impossible to hitt the time so exactly to have it hott and in Order besides 'twill be expected, it shou'd be done with a great deal of more Ceremony than what circumstances will admitt, for Your Excellency cannot but he Sensible Wee must be in a little hurry, not being Yet well Settled, and every body with me unacquainted with India.

"Wee had the misfortune to loose One of Our Seamen last night upon the barr.

"I am   "My Lord
"Your Excell^{cy}: most humble servant
"Metchlep^m: 23: 7br: 99."   "J. Pitt."

O.C. 6744.   2 O.C. 6743.

PLATE XIV.

Consul J. PITT to "Mr. THO: LOVELL *residing in the Factory belong-ing to the Governor and Company of Merchants of* LONDON *Trading to the* EAST INDIES. *In* METCHLEPATAM":[1]

"S^r:　　　　　　　　　Dated, "METCHLEPATAM 21 Septem' 1699."

"Thô you were so rude not to let me have your Company at my Landing, and so impudent, I will not give it a worse name, not to take notice of the Sumons I sent you to appear at our Factory when I read my Commission, 'yet I shall not omitt giving you notice of the arrivall of his Excellency S^r: WM: NORRIS Barronet Ambassador extraordinary from the King of ENGLAND to the GREAT MOGULL convey'd by 4 Men of Warr, and that he designs to come ashore in a day or two, and expects that you and the rest of the ENGLISH belonging too and resideing in your Factory doe make your appearance at his Landing, to pay your duty and attend him to his Lodgings, let me advice you as a friend not to omitt it for your neglect will be taken for contempt and greater Inconveniency's will follow upon 't then you are aware of.

"Your Father was very instrumentall in Saveing the life of an accquaintance of mine which I Shall allways own, and would not have you run your Self in a Nooze for want of a little good advice from　　　　"J. PITT."

From Mr. LOVELL "To the Honble JNO: PITT Esqr":[2]

Not dated, but should be "METCHLEPATAM, 23d. Sept. 1699."
"Honble Sr:

"Last night I received your paper bearing date the the 21st Inst. charge-ing me with Rudeness and Impudence in not obeying your former Summons. I hope the copy of the order which comes herewith will clear me of 't.

"I shall undoubtedly pay my respects to his Excellency S^r: WM: NORRIS at his Landing, if you will please to let me know the day and time he designs to come.

"I am heartily Glad my father hath Serv'd you in anything to deserve your favour and it would be an unspeakable Joy to me could I doe the same, and Shew you how much I am　　　"Honble S^r:
"To the Honble　　　　　　　"Your most humble Servt:
　　"JNO PITT Esqr:　　　　　　　　"THOS LOVELL.
　　"*Present* In METCHLEP^M;"

No doubt Mr. Thomas Lovell got a severe rap over the knuckles from Governor Pitt for his complaisance on this occasion.

"*By his Excellency* S^r: WILLIAM NORRIS Barronet *his Majesties Embassadour Extraordinary to the* GREAT MOGULL *&ca.*"[3]

"*Doll.* 500.

"You are hereby required and directed for the service of the Embassy to pay to Captain THOMAS WARREN Comander in Cheife of the Squadron the Summe of Five hundred *Dollars*, it being as a Gratuity for his Signall *Kindnesse* to Me and My Retinue, *and for his great Service and fidelity to the Company and their Intrest*,[4] and for Soe doing this Shall be Your Warrant, Given on board his

---

[1] O.C. 6741.　　　[2] O.C. 6745.　　　[3] O.C. 6746.
[4] The words in italics are interlined in the handwriting of the Ambassador.

Majesties Shipp *Harwich* riding off METCHLEPATAN this 23d day of September 1699."

" *To Mr.* THOS: HARLEWYN
  " *Treasurer to the Embassy.*"

" JOHN PITT &c².

  " *To the Victorious and Noble Navob* ZULPHER CAWNE.[1]

  " When your Excellency lay before CHINGEE I was Introduc'd into Your Presence by EMAUM COLY BEGUE and received a Grant of every thing I desir'd from Your Excellency,[2] which Goodness and Condescention shall never be forgotten and for which I have ever Since wish'd Your Excellency Success in Armes, health, prosperity, and long life. EMAUM COLY BEGUE has been so Kind to acquaint you with the Arrivall of his Excellency My Lord Ambassador Extraordinary from the King of ENGLAND &ca. and to make known to you what the Import of my Letter to him was, which was very great in your Excellency so far to comply with, and beyond all expectation to part with so Trusty a Confident and necessary a Man as EMAUM COLY is to You ; no person wou'd have done it but Your Noble Self. His Excellency My Lord Ambassadore admires your Generousity so readily to write to Court to Notifie his Arrivall, and requesting his Majesty's orders and the Great Navob ASSID CAWNS *Phirwanna*, and longs to have a Sight of your Person to tell Your Excellency how much hee's oblig'd to You. Your Excellency will find My Lord Ambassadore A Man of Honor and worth who knows how to return so great a favour with thanks, and Your Excellency may be assur'd he'l do 't, and in the mean time he'l receive EMAUM COLY BEGUE as Your Excellencys freind. My Lord gives his humble Service to Your Excellency, and desires his Gratitude may be known and humble Service given to the Great Navob.   " SALAM."

  " METCHLEPATAM the 10th Jany. 1699."

From Governor Pitt and Council " To His Excellency S[r]: WILLIAM NORRIS Barrt ; *Embassador to the Great* MOGULL, *at* METCHLEPATAM";[3]

  " S[r]:   (Dated at end, 16 Jany. 1699-1700)
  " Wee having been inform'd by Mr. THOMAS LOVELL our Companys ffactor at METCHLEPATAM, that upon the approaching of the new Nabob who is come to Govern that Country, you sent for him and deliver'd him a Paper, requireing and Commanding him in a most extraordinary manner, not to make any application to any of the MOGULLS officers (for the better carrying on our affairs) without your leave and Permission, threatening to do no less then send him home in Irons, from which we Immagine you resolve the utter ruine of our Company, hopeing thereby to promote the Interest of your Employers the new EAST INDIA Company.
  " Wee having no Orders or Instructions to Govern ourselves in this matter, but the Act of Parliament, which in Perusing wee find, that there is five per Cent. laid on all Goods for the maintaining Embassadors and Consulls, from which our Company's excepted till September 1701, which Embassadors and Consulls are to be nominated and Elected by the Directors of the New Company and sent to such Emperor or Prince in these parts as they please, and they to pay the

---

[1] O.C. 6821.   [2] See vol. II, p. cclxxxvi, and *supra*, p. xl.   [3] O.C. 6831.

Charge out of the five per Cent., and the remainder to be divided between the adventurers, and in a Subsequent Clause 'tis said, that nothing in this Act shall be Constru'd to extend, to hinder or restrain our Companys Trade, till the 29th of September 1701. Soe that they being excus'd from contributing to the Charge of Embassadors, Consulls &ca., certainly 'twas never intended that their affairs in these parts should be subjected to the direction or Controul of the new Companys Embassadors, Consulls or Agents dureing their limitted time, wee being possest as the rightfull and Lawfull Proprieters of all *Phirmaunds* and Grants necessary For Supporting the Trade, which has been procured at vast expenses, and without corresponding with the Government 'tis impossible to support our Privileges.

" S': Wee think your proceedings not only destructive to our Masters at Present, but will also prove fatall hereafter, if not entail a perpetuall ruin on the Trade. To prevent the Mischeif that may attend us, and preserve the Interest for which wee are Concern'd, we must acquaint you that we resolve to persist in Corresponding with the Government as formerly for the carrying on our Trade dureing the Time Limitted by Parliament, and Order all our Companys Cheifs and ffactors under this Presidency to do the Same untill his Majestie commands the contrary, or that we receive orders from our Company.

" As for the Injuries you have already done our Company and others of the Kings Subjects, by Embargoing their Ships (who traded here under their protection) wee doubt not but that they will represent it in such places where they may find a remedy and Justice. In Confirmation whereof, wee have hereunto sett our hands and the Seal of our Company at FORT ST. GEORGE in the City of MADRASS, this 16th day of January $\frac{1702}{03}$."

" THO: PITT
" FRANCIS ELLIS
" R: BRADDYLL
" M. EMPSON
" THOM^s: MARSHALL
" JOHN MEVERELL."

Delay after delay occurred, which seems gradually to have excited in the ambassador and his party mistrust of their adviser and resentment against him ; feelings which were not lessened by the communications they received from their President and Council at Surat on the absurdity of the course that was contemplated. And at last the ambassador took things into his own hands and decided on proceeding by sea to Surat, and commencing his march from that port.[1] His embarkation took place just eleven months after his arrival at Masulipatam. This part of

---

[1] We may here insert extract from a letter written by Sir William Norris from Masulipatam soon after his arrival, and omitted in its proper place (O.C. 6855) :

" Mr. THURGOOD thrô too great Application to the PERSIAN language has Crackt his braine, Soe as noe ways usefull to you nor capable of any business I thought it no ways advisable to take him with me to the Camp, but sent him home by the *Degrave.* He has been distracted more or less since Christmass."

the story may open with a pair of the precious compositions of Sir Nicholas Waite :

Sir N: WAITE *and Councill to the President and Council for affairs of the* ENGLISH *Company at* MASULIPATAM.[1]

Dated, "SURAT primo Julii 1700."

*   *   *   *   *   *   *

"His Excellencys landing on your Coast can never be approv'd of in ENGLAND, and the ill consequences of being detarded from reaching the Camp this Season. Shou'd the MOGULL be called to his Etarnall accompt the wisest man living will be in a Laborinth to project.

"Wee are assured that these proceedings whoever gave that advice or was Intrusted with the Management of that affair, pardon us if wee Say that they was either Ignorant or what Else you please of that Negociation which they took upon them to perform and are affraid the Company may Joyn in this opinion." . . .

The same to Mr. EDWARD NORRIS (*the Ambassador's Brother and Secretary*) :[2]

(Same date.)

" Wee very highly esteeme the favour of yours under covert of his Excellency's May the 30th[3] which came to the Consulls reception the 28th past in which are glad to find that Sympathizing virtue which is inherent to all generous minds when craftily drawne into such a Catastrophe of deceite which cant doubt being now discovered but that by the prudent and sedate genius of his Excellency shall speedily receive information of their decepation to the ignominy and over-throw of the contrivers and honour of that worthy Gentleman whose person and commands shall allways value and be ambitous to receive, in whatever may be serviceable either to his publick or private capacity."

O.C. 7101, from Waite and Council to the ambassador, of same date, goes at greater length into disparaging comment on the ignorance or interested motives of the persons who had induced the Embassy to land at Masulipatam.

From J. PITT *and Council of* ENGLISH *Company at* METCHLEPATAM *to the President* (WAITE) *and Council of the same Company at* SURAT ;[4]

Dated, " METCHLEPATAM, August 3rd 1700."

" You write Us ' Gentlemen' butt wee cant returne the Character, for under the Embassadors Covert the 1st Inst. wee received a Fying Generall from you which may very well be so termed since it soared above Sense or good Manners.

*   *   *   *   *   *   *

---

[1] O.C. 7,099.   [2] O.C. 7100.

[3] The letter in question of 31st (not 30th) May (O.C. 7079) is a very long one, and expresses the ambassador's jealousy and suspicion of artifices used to detain him at Masulipatam. In the end, he represents these suspicions as directed against VINCATADREE, John Pitt's chief *dubash* and factotum, but evidently he had misgivings as to J. Pitt himself. (See p. lvii-lix.)

[4] O.C. 7130.

"The Generall throughout is full of Reflections, and the Knight" (*i.e.* Waite) "we believe fancys himself not only Consull but Director Generall of the 3 Presidencys otherwise he cou'd not have the Impudence to Express himself as he has done in the last Paragraph but one, to which refer him and you, and the whole to the Judgment of our Honble. Masters, who are Men of honour and will not allow of such Stuff. Wee shall Conclude with the observation that none but the Son of Such a ffather[1] and his Councill durst write in such a Stile to persons who they will not pretend to so great a proportion of the Spiritt, yet thave and will Espouse the Interest and Endeavoure to discharge the Trust repos'd in them with diligence to their utmost ability and discretion and leave the Success to the Wise disposer of all things."

From letter of EDWARD NORRIS " *to the Honble. S*^r*:* NICHOLAS WAITE, *his Majesties Consull Generall of* INDIA, *etc., President and Council* . . . *at* SURATT":[2]

Dated, " METCHLEPATAM, August the 5th. 1700."

*   *   *   *   *   *   *

" The President on Saturday waited on his Excy. to Complain of some expressions in your Letter to them, and in passion was flying into very undecent words, but prevented by the Embassadours telling him you were the Kings publick Minister, and that you had said noe more but what in other words he had plainly represented to him before Causing his letter to you to be read before the President and his Councill.

" Indeed every body must expect to have their actions scan'd not only by persons Concerned but alsoe by indifferent Spectators, and what can the most unprejudiced man think, when it shall be knowne that (to say noe more) after ten months disapointment in this place, after the Governours refusall to obey the MOGULL'S orders, after the most serious resolutions taken in Councill of goeing to SURATT, and notifying the same to the MOGULL and Cheif Ministers, the Consull should not only advise his Excy: to alter his Measures and proceed by Land from this place after the Raines are over (which he Confessed would not be before the beginning of December) but alsoe desired his opinion might be inserted among the Minutes of Councill, which was grounded on noe better foundation then upon the pretended repentance of these Governours, upon the promises of a new *Vocanavis,* who lodged in the house of HAGGI MAHOMET SEDI knowne *Vakeile* for the Old Company."

Extract of Letter from Sir WM. NORRIS, *the Ambassador, to the Court of Directors of the* ENGLISH *Company :*

Dated " ffrom on board the *Summers* in METCHLEPATAM ROAD."[3]

" Augst: 19th, 1700.

*   *   *   *   *   *   *

" You may well be surprised, to find me in the Road of METCHLEPATAM, on board the *Sommers,* and may rather believe, that I have been at the Camp, and finished the Embassy, and am now on My Returne for ENGLAND, than that I am going to SURATT, in order to gett to the Camp, which as matters have been ordered, and contrived, could not be effected from this place, as well as by the

---

[1] See note at p. li ; also a remark by Pitt, vol. II, p. cccxix, *note.* The father was, I doubt not, Col. Thomas Waite, the regicide.

[2] O.C. 7133.   [3] O.C. 7147.

Delays, and Treachery of those, supposed by some, to be our best ffriends, as by
the Refusall of the Governour to obey the MOGULLS *Dusticks*.

        *   *   *   *   *   *   *

" When I wrote to you last by the *Degrave*, I was of opinion, it might be well
advised, on some Accounts, that I was directed to land here, . . . and was
promis'd then, I should have every thing in readiness to sett forward, in a little
time, but not long after, was convinc't by many circumstances (as far fatall to
the Designe of the Embassy, and my Negotiation, as Delayes could make them)
that it was very unfortunate, I was ever directed to come to this wretched place,
and much worse advised to stay here, to which add a greater misfortune than
both these, that for some Months past I could not depend upon that Advice I was
instructed to follow, in this I mean cheifly the Advice of your president, for he
alone, having had some Experience of the Country, had cheifly the management
of the Embassy left to him . . . but entrusted and put them in such hands, that
I soon found, acted more for the Old Companyes Interest, then ours, and I
doubted not had been sufficiently brib'd to doe soe." . . . . .

He goes on to name EMANCOOLI BEG and VINCATADRE, the agents
trusted by J. Pitt, as the guilty parties, and to explain how Pitt would
never admit any suspicion of them.

" Notwithstanding the Treachery of both of them is as plain to me as the
noon day, they are both still entrusted, and employed, by the Consull, and . . .
wee had noe other way left, to ridd our Selvees from this place, then by taking
the oppertunity of the first convenient Shipp to embarque with our presents,
Equipage, baggage, &ca. for SURATT, and ever since that Resolution taken,
. . . these Villanous Fellows have used all Artifices, and contrivances, and left
noe Stone unturned, to divert us from pursuing this Method, which alone was
effectuall, to break all their Measures ; the Governours themselves, who by
Briberyes, have been induced to disobey the MOGULLS orders, are Soe alarmed at
my going to SURATT, which was the only way I ever had of quitting this place,
and getting to the Camp, and informing the MOGULL of their proceedings, (that
they) have used all possible means and endeavours to divert me from it . . . but
neither their Threats nor their promises, nor fear of the Loss of their heads,
should prevaile with me to alter my Resolution . . . The Consull altred his opinion,
in few dayes after he had given it, which at his own Request was minuted down
in Councill June 21st, and the reasons he gave for soe doing, to which I refer how
valid, and has ever since persisted in the opinion of my going by Land, which I
think had been to the hazard, both of the Kings Honour and your Intrest, by
putting it into the same hands, to repeat their Villany . . .

" . . . How I have acted both for the Kings, and the Nations honour, and
Your Intrest, I leave you to judge, when you are thoroughly apprized of all
particulars, in the mean time must acquaint you, and cannot doe it but with great
concern, that I have mett with more Difficulties and Disappointments, than I
could imagin ; and have laboured under those hardshipps, it was impossible
almost to expect ; I hope now I am on board I have overcome them, and all will
end for the best, and those Designes and Artifices, that have been used for our
Delay, and practiced hitherto with Success, by the Method taken may turn to
your advantage, but I must informe you, as pressing as your President, and
Councill at SURATT, were, for my embarquing thither in order for my more
honourable, and quick dispatch to the Camp, upon advices received, how matters
were transacted, Your president here has acted as much the contrary, the other

way. I was sorry to see him, and the Governours, that had been bribed to disobey the MOGULLS Orders, still all along, pressing the same thing . . . But it is not only in this particular, but in many others, that I have suspected the Consull here, not to act for your Intrest, as far as the good Success of the Embassy, may be conducing to it . . . The Consull himself is well aware I suspect him, having spoken my mind very freely to him, as I thought it My Duty, on severall ccasions, and has acted in despight of whatever has been said to him, in relation to VINCATADRE, whom he still retains, his Merchant, cheife *Dubash*, and Councill, notwithstanding the Manifest instances I have given, of his Treachery, and long since warned him from My presence, which has given more besides me, occasion to suspect them both, involved in the Intrest they were formerly ingaged in, at FORT ST. GEORGE, and too close linked to disunite. Whether he came preingaged by the Old Company, to act as he has done, in relation to the Embassy, or whether being disappointed of putting off vast quantityes of his own Goods, brought from ENGLAND, with that Intent, and some other of his ffriends at FORT ST. GEORGE, to a vast amount, (in order to augment the presents, which I was at my first Landing given to understand were very defective) which were often prest upon me to take, and he would answer for the Advice and expence which were both Soe extraordinary, that I absolutely refused to have anything to doe with it; whether this disappointment, with some others, may have sour'd him I know not, but I must freely own, I think he has not acted with any regard to your Intrest in relation to the Embassy, whatever he has done in other matters.

. . . "This Letter I ordred to be read in presence of the Consull and Mr. TILLARD before I made it up, whereupon the Consull went out of the Cabin, and tho' twice Summoned to Councill upon urgent affairs . . . refused to come, saying that he had been Soe abused that it was neither consistent with the Kings honour nor his Commission to be present in Councill grounded upon this Letter . . .   "I am your Loving Friend

                                                            "WM: NORRIS."
From JOHN PITT *and Council, to* SURAT.

                                    "METCHLEPATAM Augst. 20th 1700.[1]
     *   *   *   *   *

"Wee are sorry My Lord Shou'd haue (given) such a loose to his pasion and Cast Such reflections upon the Consull" (*i.e.* JOHN PITT) "who wee are well Satisfied has Serv'd the Embassy well, and tho' he meets with nothing but Censures and abuses here yet wee beleive another construction will be put upon't at home, and those Censures look't upon nothing but the height of ill Nature having no other way to requite his Service then by breaking with him. Yet that usage will not in the least make him or us desist from Serving the Embassy, having more honour then to let that Suffer by an ill penn and fowler tongue." . . .

Ext. of Letter from the President and Council (for the ENGLISH *Company)
at* METCHLEPATAM *to* H. E. Sir WILLIAM NORRIS :[2]

                        "*Delivered to his Excellency, on board
                        the* Somers *in* METCHLEPATAM ROADE,
                                Augst. 22th. 1700,
"My Lord,   *by Mr.* GRAHAM *and Mr.* TILLARD."

"Wee have perused your letter to the Directors, so full of reflections and Censures on the reputation of the Consull, that upon second reading wee could

---

[1] O.C. 7148.   [2] O.C. 7149, No. 2.

hardly perswade our Selves that 'twas wrote by an Embassador. Wee are so
farr Satisfied in the Integritty of his actions, and his zeal all along for the Service
of the Embassy, that wee must be bold to tell your Excellency it does not in the
least touch him, ffor he has acted so Openly, and so like a Gentleman to your
Lordship in all respects, that it turns upon your Selfe, and clears him, and believe
us his Councill are not the onely Gentlemen (*sic*) : Wee must needs say you have
done him justice at last in Incerting his reasons for not Appearing in Councill on
board the *Somers* upon his Summons" . . . etc.

(*Signed by* JOHN PITT, JOHN GRAHAM, WM. TILLARD.) The *Somers* sailed
23rd Augst. for Surat.

Ext. Letter from President T. PITT *and Council to "the Honble Sr*:
JNO: GEYER Knt: *Generall of* INDIA &c: *Councill att* BOMBAY";
dated, FORT ST. GEORGE, 16th Septr. 1700.[1]

*   *   *   *   *   *   *

"We wonder at Sr: NICOLAS's impudence in confineing one of the Counsell of
SURATT and Capt. HUDSON, and do more the Latter did not fall on board
him with his ship and punish him for his insolence, and had the President So
contriv'd to cutt off all those that struck the fflagg it would have deterrd others
from the like undertakeing, and let him take care how he begins to turn piratt
himself in takeing any of our ships, for if he touches a ship belonging to this Pre-
cedency, wee will Certainly fit out a brisk privateer to make reprizall, and shall
be very ready to Joyn with you on the same account."

JOHN PITT *and Council to President, &ca., for* ENGLISH *Company*
at SURAT.

"MADAPOLLAM Jany. 3d. 1700 (-01).[2]

*   *   *   *   *   *   *

"Wee upon perusall of yours of ditto date" (7th of August 1700) "doe beleive
Sr: NICHOLAS was in an Extasy when he wrot it, fancying himself (to) Soare in
the Sphere of Embassy, Wondering our Directors Shou'd be so much Mistaken
in the Man, and prideing himself on the Scheme he has so neatly laid to Clout
an Ambassador, lulling him asleep with the Specious pretence that pleasure and
Ease not business was his Errand in these hott countreys and that Sr: NICHOLAS
was the fitter person of the two to goe through with it . . . In such fflights
have a Care of Coming near the Ambassador he'll beleive your in your Right
Senses, and if he has not lost his Usuall nicety will Clip your Wings and Melt
your Wax coming near a Spheare so much above your Reach." . . . etc., etc.

On the 5th of December the Ambassador had not yet reached Surat,
and one cannot be much surprised at this outburst against poor foolish
self-sufficient John Pitt :[3]

Sir WM. NORRIS *to the Directors of the* ENGLISH *Company, from*
anchorage off ST. JOHN'S, Decr. 5th, 1700 :

"I sayled from METCHLEPATAM on the 23d. of August last, and have been
forc'd to beat it hither all the way against the Wind. This ffatigue to me, and
Charge and disappointment to you, I must Impute to your President at METCH-
LEPATAM, of whom I shall say Nothing further, ffor on Perusall of the Minitts of
Councill and other letters and Papers I have sent you, His Unmannerly Carriage
to me, Pernicious Advice in your affairs, and the Embarrassing the Embassy

---

[1] O.C. 7160.   [2] O.C. 7328.   [3] O.C. 7233.

will plainly Appear; and his proceedings herein running as well Counter to the Kings Honour as Your Interest, I thought myself Obliged to write a short account thereof to the Secretary of State.". . .

Sir William Norris, when he did at last reach Surat, seems to have caught the contagion of ruffianism from his colleague there, President Waite. I quote the facts as briefly related by Bruce :

"Sir NICHOLAS WAITE, on the 22d January 1700-1, applied to the Governor to have the LONDON Company's Servants put in irons for an insult, which, he asserted, had been offered to the Ambassador: when this demand was refused Sir WILLIAM NORRIS seized Mr. WYCHE and Mr. GARNETT, two of the Council of the LONDON Company, and Mr. RICHARDSON their Secretary, put them in confinement, and then delivered them to the Governor ' with their hands tied,' who detained them, till they found security for their appearance . . . when called." (*Annals*, iii, 377-8.)

Governor Pitt, referring to this, writes savagely to Mr. Colt, President at Surat for the Old Company, (Aug. 25th, 1701) :[1]

"Have those three gentlemen no resentment, that was soe ignominiously punish'd and affronted by S': WM. NORRIS, and afterwards deliver'd up to the MOORS Government; 'tis pitty there was never a FELTON amongst them" (!).

Ambassador Norris afterwards quarrelled (as he well might) with Waite ; and died of dysentery on his way home, on board the *Scipio*, 10th October 1702.

Govr. T. PITT *to* Mr. STEPHEN FREWEN, *chief at* MADAPOLLAM.[2]

Dated, "FT. ST. GEORGE, May 30th, 1701.

"I cannot but be Concern'd at the ill treatment you meet with from Mr. JOHN PITT for I think the paper he wrote you about the diggers was more fitting to be Sent to a ffootman then to one in your post, and you ought to resent it, in yours to him you seem to cringe, and give him those Compliments which are not his due, for he Commands noe Garrison under the Kings Flagg, and tho' he has presum'd to wear it, 'tis more then he can answer, and when he writes any of his impertinent papers hither, he will not allow me to be Governour nor President of the place, thô the King of ENGLAND Confirmes both. I would have you for the future treat him as you are upon an equall foot with him, and if an oppertunity presents blow him up, mind the Companys busyness and perticularly their Investments, and have noe regard for Such as him, who does not deserve it, I refer you for news to our Generall Sent to METCHLEPATAM, Soe with my Service to your Lady and Selfe," etc.

From the Court to FORT ST. GEORGE, 6th March 1701-2 :

* * * * * * *

"We have perused your Paper contests with Mr. PITT at METCHLEPATAM, and must Say, as we have heretofore done on the like occasions, you have behaved Your Selves to Our great Satisfaction, We would also add, That we doubt not but you will persevere, however We hope the Agreements lately made between both Companyes will put a totall Stop to future Competition and paper or other Scuffles of that Kind."

Having disposed sufficiently of this episode of the appearance of the

---

[1] Addl. MSS. 22,843, No. 95.   [2] 22,843, No. 46.

New Company on the Indian arena, we may revert, in our more miscellaneous selections from the Governor's correspondence, to a somewhat earlier date.

To Mrs. PITT :[1]

" My dear   "Feby. 22d. ¹⁶⁹⁹⁄₁₇₀₀.

*   *   *   *   *   *   *

" ROBIN is not yet return'd from CHINA,[2] nor have I heard from him since May last from BATAVIA. I send you by Mr. TOPP my good Tennant's Brother Severall things as per list enclos'd, a share of which I would have you distribute among my ffriends, and by him I send ESSEX[3] a small diamond ring, and two small Stones to make LUCY something. In some of the Bales there is fine *Betteelaes* and *Chints,* if you have Occasion or desire any, Mr. GODFREY will deliver them to you.

" Here comes on this Ship the Late Governor HIGGINSON and his Lady, Capt. METCALFE and his, whome I would have you visitt if in LONDON ——, here comes allsoe Mr. PLUYMER, who will be assistant to you at all times in disposeing of any Diamonds.

" I hope you look after my plantations, Gardens &ca. as I desir'd, that I may find 'em on my returne in a good Condition. My blessing to the Children, of whose education pray take great Care. My service to all our ffriends and relations, not forgetting Mr. PHILLIPS and J. HUMPHREY, nor any of our neighbours worth remembering. My hearty love and affection to your Selfe, wishing us a happy meeting.   " Your affectionate husband," etc.

In another letter to his wife, dated 23rd *idem,*[4] he says :

" This comes by my Lord ABINGDON's Sone, who I Suppose will be Sooner at LONDON then any.[5] My   cquet comes by Capt. METCALFE, in your absence directed to Mr. PETER GODFREY, Copy of whose letter I enclose to you, by which you'le find I have sent home Considerably this year, which God Grant may arrive Safe, the produce is to be paid you. I would have you remember the poor of our Parish and ST. MARY BLANDFORD.". . .

To the Honble. the Governor of the Company for the time being :[6]

"ffeby. 11th ¹⁶⁹⁹⁄₁₇₀₀}

"I made a tryall of making some neck cloths here but coming out very dear made me desist in itt, but since I see those of FFORT ST. DAVIDS are soe very dear and Corse, I resolve to make another tryall and will send a parcell by the next Ship, which if you don't like I'le pay the loss of 'em. I have with all dilligence encouraged the painting trade, and have been at some Charge to doe

---

[1] B.M. Addl. MSS. 22,842, No. 78.

[2] Pitt's eldest son Robert, who went out with him to Madras, had gone to China on a trading speculation not long afterwards. He went a second time in June 1701.

[3] Pitt's elder daughter.   [4] B.M. as above, No. 83.

[5] . . " Here is Allsoe Mr. BARTIE My Lord ABINGDON's Son who I have in all respects oblidg'd to the Utmost of my power, knowing he has great relations, and that itt may be a means to unite 'em to your Interest, he is a very good Sort of Gentleman, and has behaved himselfe very obliging." (PITT *to the Governor of the Company,* Feby. 11th, 1699-1700.)

[6] Addl. MSS. as above, No. 44.

itt, and without any manner of partiallity I think wee farr out doe METCHLE-
PATAM, and hope by next Ship to send you a thousand peices, Such as never were
seen in the world, if I can but Keep these Cursed fellows from mixing the Southern
Chay[1] with the Northern, the latter being the best, and costs much more.

"I have delivered Capt. BROWNE . . . allsoe some *Betteelaes* and *Moores*,
which I made for tryall to see to what finess I could bring 'em, all which I have
desired him to show you. They are extravagantly dear, and have been out of
my Money ever since I came hither, all the people saying they have seen noe
such white cloth made in this Country upwards of 20 years." . . .

To the Revd. Mr. THOS: CURGENVEN. (Addl. MSS. 22,842, No. 70.)

"Feby. 20, $\frac{1699}{1700}$."

*   *   *   *   *   *   *

"Coz": JOHN PITT is att METCHLEPATAN and as I hear very much down in
the mouth for not being able to make his Masters any return this year ; he finds
by this time he has not gott the Start of me in honour nor Interest." . . .

To Sir JOHN GAYER, *Generall*, etc. (Same MS., No. 86.)

"Feby 26th $\frac{1699}{1700}$."

. . . . . "If he (Ambassador NORRIS) has Audience and any tollerable
encouragement, wee must expect all that malice or prejudice can Invent or doe
against us, for they talk of noe less then Stripping us of all our privillidges,
destroy(ing) our revenues, and be(ing) instrumental to make us Accountable
for the time wee have Collected 'em, and that at the Expiration of our Masters
time, they have a power to demand the Surrender of all fforts and Castles
belonging to our Company, which without our Masters positive Orders they'le
have none here without a Conquest.

"You'le see by the papers that past that they would have the Manageing
of our affairs with the Government, who have not as yett procured liberty to
trade for themselves." . . .

To Sir EDWARD LITTLETON in BENGAL, " Aprill 2d. 1700." (Same
MS., No. 108.)

This letter is chiefly about a house at Húglí belonging to Pitt, which
Littleton was occupying. The letter begins, " My good old friend":

"When I was in BENGALL last on the *Seymore* I expended in repairs of the
house upwards of 1600 Rupees, the condition I then found it in and left it
MUTTRA SAW can thoroughly inform you."

Also in a letter to the " *Rt. Worshipfull* JOHN BEARD *Esq. and
Councill in* BENGALL," dated April 3d. (*Ibid.*, No. 111) :

"I am lately advis'd that Agent EYRE sold two gunns belonging to the Ship
Seymore which I left in the hands of Mr. GEORGE GUY, who at your request
sent them down to you for the service of your ffactory," etc.

Then follow instructions for investment on Pitt's account of the
price of the guns, *viz.*, 972 rupees.

---

[1] *Chay, Choya*, etc., a root (*Hedyotes umbellata*, Lam.) affording a red
dye, sometimes called " Indian Madder", much used in colouring Indian
chintzes.

From Mr. JNO: FELLOWES, "LONDON 25th Novr: 1700." (Addl.
MS. 22,851, No. 42.)

"My Uncle has yours with Invoice of the great Stone &ca. you had concern'd
him in, and Approves thereof, and has accepted your bill of 1200*l*. for the same.
Said Stones are not yet in his hand, for Mr. GODFREY would not be persuaded to
runn the Risque of the Customers in having them privately. Uncle thanks you
for the pece *bettella*, and the Tea. He desires per next Ship that you send him
one of the very largest GOA Stones, that is finely guilt, Such as one you once
sent." . . .

SAMUEL ONGLEY *to* GOVR. PITT, "LONDON the 26: ffeb: 1701"(-2).
(Same MS., No. 2.)

"Madam PITTS has advised me not to concerne you in any Shipping on a double
accompt because Shipping turns to noe accompt and the greater Reason is that
She has occation for all the money in my hands to pay for Some land that she
has bought, of which I suppose She will give you an accompt. I observe you
order me to pay what Madam PITTS shall Requier of me, which order I must
obey She haveing the Same from you." . . .

From Governor PITT *to Sir* HENRY JOHNSON.[1]
"Septr: 20th 1700."

"I will not trouble you with news—only tell you that FORT ST. GEORGE is in
the same place I found it, notwithstanding the bounceing of Ambassadors and
Consulls. The former not being able to doe anything on this Coast is gone to
SURAT. They give out I am a dead man in the Eye of the Law, and they say
that one of the Kings ffrigatts is to fetch me home, and that there will be Manda-
muses and the Lord knows what, but lett them Say what they will, I am sure they
can prove nothing."

Postscript, dated October 14th : " S^r: I have sent you pr. Captn: PROWERS a
small parcell q^t: four *pces*: fine *betteelaes*, and four *pces*: fine Chints made in
MADERASS of which I intreate you to accept as part of my acknowledgment for
your noble present, for which I againe thank you." . . .

The same to the same: "October 17th: 1701."
         *   *   *   *   *   *

"Messrs. OGLETHORP and HEVENINGHAM are sons of my old acquaintance,
who I will take perticular care off, the former is under my perticular care and I
must say this of them both I thinke 'em as hopefull young men as the Company
has in their Service. I have wrote S^r: THEO: to send his Son five hundred
pounds, and if Mr. HEVENINGHAMS father has left him anything they would doe
well to send it him. I made 'em both send all they brought out to CHINA.

" S^r: Your noble present of a Chest of Wine I received, for which I returne
you my most hearty thanks and if I am not disapointed shall send a small
acknowledgment for the same by this Ship or at farthest by the *Bedford*.

         *   *   *   *   *   *

"My inclination is leaveing homeward, thô my circumstances are such that
I must come out again if anybody will imploy mee, for I have mett with hard
times and I dont see when 'twill mend.

"The ARABS now take our Ships, haveing lately taken one belonging to
this port, and of four ships gone to PERSIA and MOCO wee heare nothing of
them.

---

[1] *Johnson Papers*, B.M. Addl. MSS. 22,186, f. 186.

* * * * * * *

"Sir WM: Norris is still at the Kings Camp, endeavouring to doe you all the mischiefe hee can but I believe hee will be able to effect little or nothing" . . .

"October 31st.

Postscript. "I here inclose to you the Captains receipt for a small parcell of which I beg your acceptance, and hee will allsoe deliver to you 3 dozen Goa Arrack.

"S^r: The old proverb is that one should not looke a gift horse in the mouth, butt being told that Major Noble putt up the Chest of Wine you sent me, which came out noe more than 2 doz: 5 whole bottles, and that too had lost its colour and tast, notwithstanding which I am never the lesse oblidged to you, and heartily thanke you for it" . . .

From the Court to Govr. Pitt, dated 17th Jany. 1700-01.

"We are now come to the last part of yours, containing your assurances of firm adhering to our Interests. We are convinced of it to the last degree, and on our part give you our thanks for the zeal courage and fidelity you have shown, and do assure you That we hold our selves obliged to take such care of you as to render you Safe from any of those consequences our Enemies vainly threaten you withall."

On the 24th *idem.* the Court write to him again, referring to a rumour maliciously spread in England and in India of their intention to remove him from the Presidency ; they renew the expression of their confidence in his ability, integrity, zeal, and good conduct, and assure him of the entire untruth of the rumour.

The Revd. T. Curgenven to Governor Pitt.[1]

"Palk, Septr. 16th 1701."

"The Honble: Company is under disgrace for Using bribery in a high degree to get into the House, and the Shepherds as the Chief Managers sent to the Tower expecting their doom.

"Ridont writ to my Sister to tempt her with 600 guinnes for her Interest in Old Sarŭ for 2 honest Gentlemen that were to be nameless, and therefore no doubt of the same Kidney. My Sister was importuned by him to burn the letters, but I prevented that, and I hope they are reserved for your view.

"I am sorry my Kinsman hath neither your correspondence nor Commissions at any time, and is so far from advancing that through a groundless prejudice of the New President, he is deprived of the promis'd Subordinate, and everything else. It is common for men in the same posts to influence their brethren, and perhaps a Soft touch of your (illegible) mollify the president . . .

"The Blow in Italy is over, about the end of August, and the Germans have given a fatal Repulse to Villeroy and Catinat, who insulted their Camp. Admiral Rook is Sail'd with a Noble Navy towards the Streights, and Bembo[2] to the W. Indies with a New Governour for Jamaica, Brigadier Selwyn.

---

[1] Addl. MSS. 22,851, No. 40.

[2] Benbow, of course ! And yet what diverse associations do the two spellings suggest !

Governor PITT *to the Honble.* JOHN BEARD, Esq.[1]

"FORT ST. GEORGE March 10, 1700-01."

*   *   *   *   *   *   *

" I received your Ladies Kind present of two jarrs of Mangoes, for which I heartily thank her.

" Also yours of the 21st December wherein you mention you have sent home the Concerne of the Ship *Seymore* to Messrs. COULSON and FFALKNER on the *Chambers* ffrigott.

" Your Brother and my Kinsman PITT is still on the high roape, and expects great performances from the Ambassador.

*   *   *   *   *   *   *

" S^r: CHARLES[2] was very jolly and merry here, tho' I find him strongly inclined to be wretchedly Covetous, tho' he endeavoured here to Screan it as much as he could, Soe once taking him in a good humour wee gott a hundred pagodas out of him for the Church. I believe he will sett downe with what he has, and Concerne himselfe with neither old nor new Company.

" I am of your opinion that there is noe medling with fine *Mullmulls* or any private Trade after this Season.

" I reed. your Lady's Noble present of 4 p^{ces}. of ffloured DACCA cloth for which pray give her my humblest Service and thanks.

" To Yours of the 2d. of January, Your Son arriv'd here with S^r: CHARLES, who throve mightily in his passage hither, and in all probability this air will agree with him extraordinary well" .   .

The same to JOHN BRABOURNE, Esq., *Commodore (sic) for the Affairs of the Rt. Honble:* ENGLISH E.I. Company *at* ANJENGO.[3]

"Aprill 8th 1701."

" On the arrivall of the *Neptune*, Capt: HEATH, on whom Capt. LESLEY had his dependance, was prevailed with by him to informe the New Company what private trade in Diamonds or goods he had aboard, of which they made a Seizure upon the account of the 5 per cent. which our Company defended, and went to a tryall with them in the Exchequer, where after a long learned and Solemn pleading with 12" (figure doubtful) "Councill of a Side, Our Masters cast 'em .
By our Masters Letters they Seem to be in great confusion and hurry, and I believe since this treachery of Capt. HEATH they Seem to be fearfull that there is Some more of his gang amongst us."

---

[1] B.M. 22,843, f. 2.   [2] Eyre.

[3] Addl. MSS. 22,843, No. 21. "Commodore" is perhaps an error of the copyist. Qu. "Commissioner"?

The *English* East India Company does not here mean the *New* Company, of which that was the technical designation. Pitt for some time only speaks of the latter as the "New Company", and claims the old designation of *English* for his own. But in a letter to Mr. Woolley, Secretary at the India House, dated Sept. 27th, 1702, he writes : "I perceive now the title" (of the New Company) "must be the ENGLISH Company, which has hitherto in these parts been only ours, for they were never otherwise called then the *New Company.*" See also *note*, p. lxxix, *infra*.

From the Court to FORT ST. GEORGE, 26th June 1700.

. . . "On the *Neptune's* Arrivall here the later end of Aprill last the New Company got the King's officers to make a Seizure of the Dyamonds at the same time when the Commissioners of the Customs had sent down their Permit as usuall by one of their own officers to bring the Jewells up from the Ship, That Person joyning with two others in the Seizure thereof, and of the private Trade Goods on board, which the New Company were the rather Encouraged to do from Captain HEATHS joyning himself with them, who because he was not elected one of the Court of Committees, at the late Choice, thought himself so much disobliged thereby that he resolved to go into the New Company, and accordingly in the beginning of May was chosen one of their Directors, having thus begun, he knowing that Captain LESLEY had his dependance upon him, prevailes with him to be guilty of as great Treachery by resorting to the New Company for their protection and ffavour, which that he might the better meritt at their hands, he and his Purser villinously betray unto them what Bills of Lading he had given for any Private Goods or Dyamonds he had on board his Ship, and Shewes them wherein the Difference was between the Orders he received from the Companyes Warehouse Keeper," etc.

The affair of the diamonds referred to in these two last extracts is mentioned under the article HEATH at p. cxcvi of vol. II. Pitt refers to it several times, as in his letter to the Governor of the Company, Oct. 27th, 1701, p. **xx**, *infra*, and in the following to Mr. Thomas Woolley, Secretary at the East India House (Oct. 17th, 1701) :

"Capt. HEATH's Apostasy was a Surprise to me, Mr. BRADDYLL having told me Some time before, that Capt. HEATH was unanimously importun'd by the Committee to come Governor of this place."[1]

The same to Honble: JOHN BEARD, *Esqr. President in* BENGALL.

"May 20th, 1701."[2]

*   *   *   *   *   *   *

"I observe Sr: Edward's Slow motions, which I am sure will not answer the expectation of those fyery Sparks Concern'd with him, he has most Certainly taken some disgust at me, for I wrote him a letter last year by Capt. WESLEY and Sent him a handsome present, to which I never had any answer, I remember I rub'd[3] a little upon his Knighthood and Consullship, at which I suppose he was angry.

*   *   *   *   *   *   *

"Our Generall advises you what has happen'd at SURAT as to the MOORS Seizing Sr: JOHN GAYER and his Lady . . President COLT writes me how Shamefully they were us'd during the time of their being in the Governours house, you'll see there has been brisk doings amongst 'em ffor that Sr: WM: NORRIS Seiz'd two of the Counsell and the Secretary, ty'de 'em Neck and heels and deliver'd 'em up in Irons to the Governour, which I hope our Masters will

---

[1] Addl. MSS. 22,844, No. 18.

[2] *Id.* 22,843, No. 37.

[3] *Rub* is here used as we should use *chaff* in modern colloquial, and *chaff* = "chafe" (vide *Skeat*), which = "rub".

revenge to the last degree in ENGLAND, for our laws will not allow of it, besides those gentlemen if they have any Courage will write itt in red Letters upon his Person."

From PETER GODFREY to *Governor* PITT.[1]

"London, 23d July 1701."

*   *   *   *   *   *   *

"Unless I shculd write you what I have already done, that your Writings Signifyes little to one who will doe but what Shee will, or advise you what I hear, which I find Sowers you beyond what (is) usuall, therefore I shall only tell you I was not the author of the meanesse of your Imployment or of your Sons Trip to the Jubilee, But was as much Surprised at it as you or more, because it seemed to arrise from powers derived from you. As to my Going for DEAL I shall bee as ready If my Company may be acceptable to wait upon your Lady thither whenever shee will Imbarque for INDIA . . . althô you seem to have a mean opinion of my sincere affection to you and yours I know no reason. I am sure my actions will justifye mee. But what I have been Misrepresented it is from those to whose temper you are noe Stranger, therefore methinks you should reflect on things before you despise one you have found as a friend ; or is it that you are jealous I have an esteem for your kinsman? Consider and let me know wherein I have been wanting in respect or friendship to you. I think I cannot doe more for any then I have Endeavoured for your service. As for the Megrums, If I desir'd to enter a paper combatt you have given me handle enough, but I am for peace and soe shall say noe more, but pitty your misfortune that your, &ca. Pray what is it reignes in India that you are all upon the Quarrels ?"

A good deal of the last extract seems directed at Mrs. Pitt's peculiarities.

Govr. PITT to Sir STEPHEN EVANCE.[2]

Dated "October 15, 1701.

"I am very glad if what I have done here is to my masters satisfaction, and their bare thanks to me is of far greater value then a Barronetship, thô the gold bowle would not have been amiss, and should have esteem'd it an honour beyond my merrit, for I am sure the worst of my enemies can't say that I have left any stone unturned to promote and secure their honours Interest ; but I suppose that gold bowle mistook its way, and is gone to SURAT or Some other port where they better deserve it, for I have not heard one word of it but from you."

*   *   *   *   *   *   *

The same to Mr. ROBERT RAWORTH, *Merchant*, LONDON.[3]

"Oct. 16th: 1701.

"Your Ambassadour is at the Camp eating rice and Curry at the King's charge, and notwithstanding the vast expense he has been at wee doe not hear he has effected any thing, nor will they I believe part with him till they have suck'd him dry.

"Your people at METCHLEPATAM talk of nothing less than uniting the two Companys, and takeing possession of all, but I hope wee here whom you could

---

[1] B.M. 22,851, No. 95.   [2] B.M. 22,844, No. 7

[3] B.M. 22,844, No. 14.

never conquer, nor dare come to a battle with, shall have very honourable termes, or else wee know how to make 'em—before wee surrender, noe less then to march out with our arms, and Diamonds in our pockets, Drums beating and Colours flying, then if wee are not us'd well, wee know how to retake it, for your people will hardly know how to manage it, since they are soe much wanting in the knowledge of the economy of a little ffactory. My Kinsman and I are at as great a distance as ever, he at METCHLEPATAM, and I at FFORT ST. GEORGE, but whether it be Mellancholly or Madness occasions it, Duke TRINCOLO Swares Sometimes that he will Send for the Governour of FFORT ST. GEORGE in Irons to him, and was much of the Same humour when he came into this roade, as you say to publish his powers. Did he ever write you that he dar'd doe such a thing here, or that any body regarded his person or his power? Now why should I write this? you'le dislike it as much as when I offer'd goods to load one of your Ships home, and then at my 5 years end I am afraid, without some good fate attends me, I shall want another five years terme as much as when I first undertook this, for times are very bad in INDIA, and nothing to be gott but losses and troubles, for now the ARABS take our Ships as well as the Pyrats." . .

The same to "the Revd. Mr. THOS; CURGENVEN at FOLKE near SHERBOURNE, DORSET".[1]

" Oct. 22d. 1701.

" I observe what you write of the two boys,[2] and earnestly intreat you that you would put 'em to some eminent School where they may be most improv'd in their Learning, or else send 'em to HOLLAND to the reform'd Jesuit at ROTTERDAM where ROBIN was, whose name I have forgot, I would alsoe have 'em write excellent well and learne Arithmatick and Merchants Accompts and all languages and Accomplishments that may render 'em acceptable in the World, and able to get their livelyhood, for which I will Stand for noe charge .

*   *   *   *   *   *   *

" My Wife has writt me little or nothing to the purpose this year, nor has sent me nothing, thô I positively order'd her. She writes me God knows what that she is about purchases, but not a word of what some has cost or others will cost, I have noe manner of Accompt of what I left her, what She has received or paid since, what I have hence sent her or what it Sold for, but all railing against one or other, which has very much expos'd my busyness and done me a great deale of prejudice, Soe that I find great inconveniencies by trusting a woman with bysiness which I will avoid for the future."

The same to WM. HEWER, Esq., London.[3]

" Oct. 22, 1701.

" I Received the Honour of yours of the 23d. of December last in behalfe of Mr. HARRISON, who I immediately on his arrivall Sent 4th of Councill to METCHLEPATAM, and shall take all Oppertunities to encourage and preferr him in or any one else that your Selfe or Mr. PEPYS Shall recommend, for whome I have a very great honour and esteem, desireing you'le be pleas'd to give my most humble service to him, and accept the same your Selfe from," etc.

---

1 B.M. 22,844, No. 35. Mr. Curgenven was Rector of Folke.

2 Pitt's younger sons, Thomas and John.

3 B.M. 22,844, No. 38.

The same to the Governor of the E. I. Company.[1]

"Oct. 27th 1701."

*   *   *   *   *   *   *

"I was very much surpriz'd to heare that Capt. HEATH had deserted an interest in which hee had rays'd to himselfe so considerable a fortune, and in whome on all occasions you repos'd soe great a trust, and since I left ENGLAND I was told here by Mr. BRADDYLL that you all offer'd him to come out President and Governor of the Coast. . .

"We have now a tollerable unanimity in your Councill here, thô some who are gone made it otherwise by insencing into others that every one was equally answerable to the Company for all miscarriages and soe consequently had an equall power, which has begat in some such a stock of obstinacy and conceit back'd with ignorance, which will be difficult to remove without your sentiments of this matter, and 'twas very foolishly argued by one who I little expected it from, that I had not power to turne a writer out of his imploy for any misbehaviour without a consultation, Soe that if any young man trespasses, as they will doe sometimes, they must bee had up to Consultation, and their crimes entered on record, which has often bin to their Ruine, whereas a Reprimand or a small time of suspension or displacement reclaims 'em.

*   *   *   *   *   *   *

"The New Companys peoples menaces and threats joyn'd to their affected powers, have hitherto avayled 'em nothing, nor shall they for the future, Resolving they shall have noe more of your Interest or priviledges then they can conquer. I sent a person hence to imforme mee of Sr: WM's: proceedings at the Court, who is joyn'd there with Sr: JOHN GAYRE'S—a translate of all his letters to mee to this time I here send you, but for mine to him with instructions I keepe noe copie. Here has been various reports about his (*i.e.* NORRIS's) proceedings, Sometimes hee has gott a *Phirmaund* with wonderfull powers, and the next day 'tis contradicted, 'tis most certaine hee has endeavoured to doe you and your affaires all the mischiefe hee could, and hee had in some measure effected it, had I not secur'd an Interest in ASSID CAWNE and his Sone, who if they fullfill what they have promis'd, there must bee a considerable *peshcash* made 'em, 'tis said Sr: WM: is expected at METCHLEPATAM to embarque for ENGLAND in Jany: next, but I am of opinion they will hardly part with him soe soon unless they see hee has no more money to spend amongst 'em.

"And 'tis much admir'd at by all the great men of this country that the ENGLISH should bee at the charge of sending an Ambassadour to procure grants of priviledges of a dying King."

From Mr. ALVARO DA FONSECA.[2]

"LONDON, the 4th Novr. 1701."

*   *   *   *   *   *   *

"As for the two Companys there is great discourse of there union, but I won't believe it till I see it, and as for other news I suppose you don't want it hauing soe many friends in this place to write to you. I cannot omitt Reflecting now and then on those merry hours I use to spend with your Honour and the Rest of our friends in the Company's Garden, where wee could injoy our Bottle without

---

[1] Addl. MSS. 22,844, No. 4. A long letter copied in Pitt's holograph.
[2] Addl. MSS. 22,851, No. 51.

being disturbed with these frightfull Rumors of Warr, as here wee are every day".. . .

From Mr. JOHN PHILIPS.[1]

Dated "Stratford, Decr. the 4th, 1701."

" Much Honerd: Sr:

" Yours dated Sepr. 28th 1700 I have now before me, and am sorry the Seeds &ca: came to noething. Your Lady will now take Care to send you more from LONDON by this Bearer, and get them put in Bottels, which will save the Carrig from hence.

" As for your Plantations (I thank God) they prosper very well. Wee have planted a Row of Trees in your Meadows on the Bank of the Carrig, from my house to the upper end (most Oaks), and we have done the like on HILL PARKE side, a Walke from the Parsonage Barns to the Mills, beside what We have done on the CASTLE and several other places. We have made a double Walk of Firrs on both Sids the Long walk, from the House to the River, and Cross walks of them between the Fish ponds. The two Green plots next the Prebend is allsoe planted with them, and the two little Gardens before the Pigeon house, for 2 Groves on each Side the house, whereof some of them by the long walk are nere 20 foot high. And most of them raised in your owne Garden by a new experriment of our owne, for lesse then a Crowne charge. And have enough left to plant the top of OLD CASTLE, if you could gett it to be made levell.

. . . " Wee have had the mildest weather this last November that ever I knew in that Moneth, which still continues, and had so hott in Harvest, that when I satt still in the shade, the Sweat dropt frequently from my Head on my Clothes.

" As for your most generous offer to my Son THOM: I humbly thank you, but he is never like to embrace it, for neither he nor the Ship has bin heard off these two years, about which time they put in at ST. HELENA for fresh Water, which was there denied them, and were forced to goe off without any. Oh sad fate !

" About 10 Dayes Since, wee had an Election of Members for a New Parliament where Mr. HARVIE and Mr. MOMPESSON were Chossen, by the Old Voyces onely, except Mr. THOMPSON, who pretends to a Vote for the Eyeth[2] of the Burrow land, and has bin admitted these 3 last Elections, by the means of S^r: E: H:, who is dead, and S^r: THO: MOMPESSON dyed of the Gout at Parliment about Midsumer last

" Your most faithfull humble servant

" JOHN PHILLIPS."

From Capt. JOHN PITT " To the Honble: THOS: PITT Esqre: Governor of FORT ST. GEORGE, INDIA."[3]

" GRAVEND the 8th Jan: 1701-2.

" S^r: The honor of your oblidgeing Letter I receiv'd by Mr. PENRUDOCK

---

[1] Addl. MSS. 22,851, No. 26. Mr. Phillips seems to have been a humble neighbour at Stratford-under-the-Castle, who lent his services to the absent Governor in looking after his land and plantations there.

[2] Qu. *eighth?*

[3] Addl. MSS. 22,851, No. 99. There seem to be three John Pitts in question in this letter : (1) the writer, Captain John Pitt, a soldier ; (2) the Consul at Masulipatam ; (3) the " namesake and relation" (if the term " namesake"

and thank you for the Kind remembrance of mee and my Son, and wish I had been soe fortunate as to have wayted on you into those parts.   I am glad I was or can bee Serviceable to your good lady and selfe, there is noebody without Complyment more desierous of it.   In my way the last Sumer to my quarter I call'd at STRATFORD and stayd fower dayes with Mrs. PITT and pretty family who were all in health and learne their bookes bravely, and at my quarters at BLANFORD I met with my namesake and relation of yours who was vs'd to honour me much with his Company and wee did often in a glass remember you. S⟨r⟩: the bearer is my son who is goeing to Mr. JOHN PITT from whome I had the same kind offer as from your Selfe, and this fayer Oppertunity by my freind Capt. NEWMAN at an easy rate, was glad to accept soe kind an offer and the Dubious talke of your Staying there, and the necessity of my putting of him out, looking every day when I shall be comanded abroad, and almost now being but in a condition to begin the world agen, not receiving one penny of my Arreares since you went, but have receiv'd a Debenture for 480 od pounds, which now the war is just breaking out my Lord RANELAGH, Mr. BLATHWAITE, Mr. HILL who is now a Lord of the Treasury (three Honester Men were Hang'd last monthe) are goeing to post pone all the Debt of the Army, and send us abroad agen to Starve. Mr. HILL hath actually layd out 60,000*l.* in terra firma sence the peace, and six monthes agon I lost my good Master the Duke of WIRTEMBERG where all my prospect lay this next war, which is unavoidable, So pray forgive my dam'd Spleenatick Pen, and bee pleased to give my boy your Comands and best advise which I am sure will be of great use to him, is the Humble Request of

" S⟨r⟩: your most Obedient Humble Servant
" JOHN PITT."

" *Postscript.* I hope he brou't you newes of the Vnion, which we are very fond of heere.   My most humble Service to Mr. ROBERT, and hope hee will favour my poor boy with his friendship."

From Mr. ROBERT PITT (called in Index of Letter-Book, DR. PITT).[1]

Dated " Jany. 21. 1701"(-2).

" Dear Cosin,

" As the News of your Recovery was very wellcome to me and all your Friends, I can acquaint you that my Cosen and Miss ESSEX are both in perfect Health. But Letters from EUROPE come usually to you freighted with Business. This from me importunes your greatest Favours to our Cos. ETTRICKS Son. I am very much oblig'd to him, and must profess a great respect for the Family. I readily embrac't the opportunity of serving him and his Son, in making it my most earnest Request, that you will receive him, as you would one of my One, if I had one to send under the Torrid Zone. I doubt not your Kindness in this Affair, which shall be most gratefull acknowledged by

" Your most Affectionate Kinsman
" ROB: PITT."

---

implies that this one also was John).   The last was *perhaps* the third son of Dr. Robert Pitt of Blanford, T. Pitt's uncle.   But the very imperfect state of the Pitt genealogies prevents my being able to say anything with certainty.

[1] Addl. MSS. 22,857, No. 23.   Apparently Dr. Robert Pitt, brother of Thomas, writer of the next letter, and first cousin of the Governor.

To Governor T. Pitt *from his Cousin* Thomas Pitt.[1]

" Jany: 27th 1701"(-2) (No place).

*   *   *   *   *   *   *   *

" Your Lady was a few dayes agoe at my house and lookes as well as ever I saw her. There is no Accident has happened in our family since you went: Except that our Cousin George Pitt's Lady is dead, and he marryed again ; and that Robbin my brother John's Pitt son (*sic*) is also dead. who truly was a youth that promis'd very well. You are a great way off, and have been a great while gon. I amongst the rest of your friends could wish that you were now to Returne. You have the Satisfaction to have your Eldest Son with you. And it will be a great pleasure to you when you Return to find All your other Children so well come on. I have had two Sons since you went, who are both liveing: Robbin is grown a great fellow, and Keate thrives very well. My wife, my Selfe, and Robbin send you and Cousin Robert our best wishes . . .

" I am Dear Cousin &c:
" Tho: Pitt."

Here we may notice a new passage of arms between Pitt and his cousin at Masulipatam, which began in 1700 and lasted till John Pitt's death ; it affords a disagreeable exhibition of the violent resentments and language in which the Governor indulged. We have not the other side, which was probably not much better.

The affair arose out of the conduct of S. Woolston, who had been employed by T. Pitt as an agent for the Old Company to purchase investments at Masulipatam and Madapollam, and before he had cleared his accounts with Fort St. George had taken employment from John Pitt and the New Company, committing, according to T. Pitt, breach of trust towards the Old. The Governor considered that John Pitt had seduced away one of his servants. Here is a sample of his communications on this matter :

Dated " Fort St. George, 9th Jany. 1700-1.[2]

" Wee the Governour and Councill for affaires of the Rt: Hoble: Company in Madrass and the Coast of Chormandell &ca: did on the 2d instant receive a paper dated the 16th of last month Signed John Pitt, wherein were sundry expressions as if it had been dictated to him by the oyster wenches at Billings-

---

[1] B.M. Addl. MSS. 22,851, No. 21. This Thomas was eventually a Master in Chancery, being son of the Governor's uncle, Robert Pitt, M.D., of Blandford Forum. The said Thomas had sons, Robert and William, and a daughter Kate (Katherine). See pedigree, opp. p. xxix, and *Hutchins*, i, 226. Moreover, he bequeathed a certain property (Hemsworth East) to John, son of the Revd. John Pitt, Rector of Cheselborne (*Hutchins*, iii, 478). I cannot trace the Will, but if the fact is so this Revd. John would be the " brother John" mentioned in the letter, and we must give Thomas a brother John in the pedigree. The cousin George Pitt would be the second of the five successive Georges of Stratfieldsaye (d. 1734, whose second wife was Lora Grey).

[2] O.C. 7342. See also O.C. 7189, 7221, 7556.

GATE, besides it being Stufft with so many notorious falcities that none would or could averr but monsters of ingratitude and such as had shook hands with shame.

*   *   *   *   *   *   *

" By the information WOOLSTON gives you to 'em we Cant but take notice that he finds he has soft wax to work on, and we must be of the same opinion for your mentioning stones chested for show. Our Masters Circumstances dont want such deluding varnishes whatever yours do . . As for your summoning the Governour and Councill of this place before you is equally ridiculous with your behaviour when in this port, and know yee too that we have sufficient powers to try al manner of Delinquents, and if occasion requires can send force enough out of this Garrison to fetch you hither.

" Wee think it a trivial crime of any to disowne a Consull, considering our circumstances and yours, but are assured 'tis a Capitall Crime to disowne a King, which with some if it had so happened they had never been Consuls.

" 'Tis certain a great misfortune for any Society to have a hott brain'd president att the head of their affaires, but a farr greater to have a Crack brain'd and unexperienced President, who must undoubtedly in a little time bring all into Confusion"   . . etc., etc.

" Fort St. George 9th Jan. 1700-1."

Two years later the New Company's Consul at Metchlepatam writes to Sir E. Littleton and their Council in Bengal :

" March 25th 1703.[1]

" Do believe Mr. SAMLL. WOOLSTON is with you who took his Passage upon MATT. WALLERS Sloop, he has been under the Consulls Protection above two years ready to adjust an Accompt with the Gentlemen of MADRASS before the Consull, which they dare not do but Demand his Person, and have endeavor'd to wrest him from under his Wing to cary him in Person to the FFORT to tear him in pieces there as they pleas'd . . . and dont question but S.: EDWARD LITTLETON with your assistance will See that the Mallice and Venum of MADRASS does not reach HUGLY," etc.

Extract of a letter from Mr. WM. FRASER *to the Chairman, etc., of the English Company,*[2] *dated Jany. 31st, 1704-5.*

" As to Mr. WOOLSTON he deserted the Old Company and was by means of Embassador NORRIS taken in to the New Company's Service to bee assistant in bringing up the generall books of Accompts, but fail'd in performance. He went to BENGALL, from thence went a Passinger upon your Ship the *Union* Capt. FFRANKLIN Commander, designed for CHINA, but in their way touch'd at PULLE CANDORE, where he was detain'd, dyed there of an impostume, left his concerns to the amount of 2 or 300*l.* to Mr. LOVE Supercargo of said Ship, who was full laden thence, with a CHINA Cargo". . .

And here is T. Pitt's version of *De Mortuis*, as applied to Woolston :

---

[1] O.C. 8168.

[2] O.C. 8319. Fraser had been dismissed from the Old Company's service in 1701, but was afterwards taken into the service of the United Company.

From Letter to Mr. JOHN SHIPMAN (date about Jan. or Feb.
1704-5).

" WOOLSTON died at POLYCUNDORE, Soe there's an end of that villainous
wretch, and 'twould bee well if the Company were as well rid of more such as are
in their Service, who I see are the only people incouraged."[1]

From Sir JOHN CHARDIN *to Governor* PITT.[2]

"LONDON, Jany: the 31st: 170$\frac{4}{5}$.

'' Honble S^r:

" I give you my harty thanks for the honor of your letter Sept^{ber} 21st 1700, the
only one I had from you this Season, which I impute to your sensibleness of the
mortification it must be to me to learn from yourself the disapointment of your
care and your hope about the tuterage of that yong man which it is the grief of
my life I must call my Son, the taking him under your immediate inspection and
on your table, in order to bring him to a good conduct is a favor of a nature that
no words of mine can express the value I put upon it ; as no course of time shall
diminish the zealous resentment I'll ever have of it, but as it is so sad a Subject
to me and I dare say to you, I'll beg your leave to demur no longer on it.

" My Brother complaining of the Wine I sended him last make me send none
directly to you Sir by this Ship, although what I send to him by the same is such
choice true claret that I believe may prouve excelent. In that case I writ to him
to Supply you with Some dozens of bottles according to his goodness.

'' I must wish you joy with the union of the two Compagnies, a business of So
great moment and consequénces Since it must render your Station more easie
and quiet.   . . . '' Honble: S^r:

" Your Most humble and most obedt: Servt:
"CHARDIN."

From WADHAM WYNDHAM, Esq., *to* Govr. PITT,[3]

"LONDON, Feby. 2d. 170$\frac{1}{2}$."

" Deare S^r:
*   *   *   *   *   *   *
" Your friends makes your health still at Chappell a standing rule ; but I
am not Soe Constant there as formerly, for I have entred into Matrimony with
Coll: HEARN youngest Daughter of SARUM, and have a howss in BILLITER
SQUARE against Mr. RAWORTH, and am a father of a Shee child (but it may
turne to a Boy,) your good Lady was Soe Kind as to come and See my Spouse
this last weeke and Shee is very well. Sr: you may receive this from the hands
of Mrs. ANNE MILLER who goes to your parts to make her fortune, her father is
a Vyntner and an honest man but has many Chirildren and lives in WOOD
STREET. I have noe knowledge my Self of her, but my Wifes Midwife did
desire this favour of mee, and I wish her good Success and pray excuse my
troubling you.". . . (Pitt dockets this queer introduction—as *all* letters I
think—" answred.")

---

[1] Addl. MSS. 22,848, No. 122. In that letter-book this ferocious passage
is copied in Pitt's own handwriting.

[2] Addl. MSS. 22,851, No. 24. (Written by a clerk, except signature.)

[3] Addl. MSS. 22,851, No. 62.

From James Craggs, Esqr.[1]

"London 25th of Feby. 170½.

"In our last yeares instructions we gave you all the advises we could in respect to your conduct with the N. Company, but we find your own judgment has guided you to serve the Company better than all the advices we could pretend to give you ; for which it is not only mine, but the opinion of the generallity of our adventurers, that all the prosperity of our affairs in India is in a great manner owing to your good sense and resolution, which I am one of those that will never be wanting to acknowledge, and so I dare say will the greatest part of our people that are any ways near the knowledge of your conduct in these affairs."

From Mr. Raworth.

"London 5: March 170½".

* * * * * * *

"And as wee are thus United at home I hope you there will be friends as becomes Englishmen and Christians, that all these Animositys Created betwixt you and your Kinsman will be Reconciled, and you'l Take such Courses both at Court and Country to secure the Trade at as little charge as possible. This is what will Consist with your and our Interest, as well as with your affinity in Blood. Lett there bee no further Contest, But a True friendship Betweene You."

J. Styleman says (London, Jany. 31st, 170½) :[2]

"I must tell your Honour as you have many freinds here Soe you have some potent Enimys."

From Sir Stephen Evance.[3]

"August 1st, 1702.

"The Two Companies have joyned and the New Charter passed to all our content. Old Stock that was at 75l. is upon the Union at 105l. and the new risen proportionable. There is great harmony between us both,—Wee have chosen 12 out of our Committee and the New 12 out of theirs, to make a Committee of the United Stock, the names of each are inclosed . . . there arose a discourse when the old and new Company Cheifs mett how they should sitt, perticularly as to yourself, the new proposed Mr. Jno: Pitt should come up and wait on you att Fort St. George, and that you should take the Chair one day and Mr. Jno: Pitt the next, but it was at last agreed Hee should Sitt at your left hand, the old Court was very hearty to your Interest, and most of the New spoke with great respect of you, soe by this I see you are safe in with both sides. . . .

"Mr. Rich: Gough with some of the new Companys men have a notion of sending out a Generall Superviser all over India, and the man desired, as I find, is Mr. Roger Bradyll who they have lately perswaded to buy some new East India Stock. This is Kept very private with them, but I am in with both sides, soe they doe nothing but I presently heare of itt. Mr. Gough and Mr. Bradyll have whispered about that you have sent 60,000Pa: of the Companys money to China in the *Hampshire* on your own account, which is whispered about to doe You a prejudice. I spoke to Mr. Gough about itt. Hee said he heard itt.

---

[1] The elder of that name ; father of Queen Anne's Secretary of State. Addl. MSS. 22,851, No. 64.

[2] *Ibid.*, No. 84.   [3] *Ibid.*, 22,852, No. 5.

I desired to know who told him but he would not tell mee, I am satisfied there is noe such thing, but take it to be in order to promote Mr. BRADYLLS interest. . . ."

GOVR. PITT to Sir CHARLES EYRE.[1]

"FT. ST. GEORGE, Sept. 29, 1702."

*　　*　　*　　*　　*　　*　　*

" I am advis'd of your delivery of the bulses of diamonds upon account of the Unfortunate Contract I made with you,[2] which if honourably complied with I hope was to your Satisfaction, thô no thanks to Mr. COULSON for the same.

" I know you are a generous man and never design'd to raise your fortune by the ruining of your brother INDIANS, so that if after abundance of pains no male heirs come I hope you will remember and give us a plentifull Legacy in your Will, and if you please make my Son, the bearer hereof, your Heir, whose ffather has suffer'd most by you.

" I cant but take notice your letter is very short, at which I cant be much concern'd when I am told you are so deeply engag'd dayly at the Play house with our ffriend ROGER and BOWRIDGE, to both whom give my service, and tell 'Em 'tis reported here that now being thoroughly accomplish'd they are coming out for the top employs of INDIA, so pray bespeak a small one for me under them and JNO: MEVERILL to be their jeweller. . . ."[3]

Govr. PITT *to Mr.* JNO: PHILLIPS *at* STRATFORD.[4]

" Sept. 30: 1702.

" I received yours of the 4th December last, and desire you'l continue to give me the like account yearly of those affairs. I received noe Seeds this year, and when you send any it must be in bottles, and the Captain must be desir'd to keep them in the Coolest part of the Ship.

" I heartily intreat the Continuance of your care of my plantations, and that you'l yearly encrease them and see that my Gard'ner keeps large nurseries of all sorts of Trees by him, that so I may have sufficient to transplant as I shall see occasion when I come home ; I wish you could send some ffirr tree seed hither with some advice and directions of what you have newly discover'd in that matter.

" I am heartily sorry for poor TOM's misfortune, which Ship I fear mett with some unusuall Accident, for they could not want water having been just before at the CAPE.

" This comes by my Son to whom I refer you for the news of these parts, and if there should happen a new Election of Parliament men whilst he is there I expect he should stand, and desire your assistance to him therein. I have order'd him to stand upon the old voices, and no other, and to that Purport was the Determination in Parliament, all Papers relating thereto are in my wife's

---

[1] B.M. Addl. MSS. 22,845, No. 64.

[2] This matter of a speculative transaction in diamonds with Sir Charles Eyre, when he went home, is often referred to by Pitt as having caused him heavy loss.

[3] In various letters he casts the blame of his loss by the bargain with Eyre on Mr. J. Meverill, of the Madras Council, as having greatly contributed thereto by his ill-judged selection of diamonds.

[4] Addl. MS. 22,845, No. 78.

hands, and Mr. COULSON wrote me out that Sr: E: HARVEY declar'd that when
I return'd Sr: E: would quit his pretensions in the Borough, and it being my Son
'tis one and the same as if I came myself, besides Mr. MOMPESSON can't in point
of gratitude but join with my Son, he standing upon my Interest, which had been
null'd butt for the favour I did his Father in adding his life, who always gratefully
acknowledg'd it and declar'd his Interest should never be separate from mine.
I desire you also to preserve the priviledge of the Bayliwick, but how
Mr. TOMPSON came to have a Vote I cant tell, and if he has not an undoubted
right to it, by no means suffer it.[1]

    " I have not heard from HUMPHREY this year, so I know nothing of the price
of Wheat, Barley, Oats, &ca ; nor do I know how it fares with the Old Castle, nor
what crop it had last; the levelling the upper Ring of the Castle as I design'd
will be best done when I come home, so with my hearty service to yourself, your
wife, and all your family, neighbours, and frends,

" I am your most assured ffriend and

" Obliged humble servent

" THO PITT":

To Sir H. JOHNSON.[2]

" October 3rd 1702."

*   *   *   *   *   *   *

    " For the news of the Country I refer you to the bearer hereof my Son,[3] whome
I recommend to your favour, and have sent you by him two peices of *Betteelas*,
hearing that once or twice a year you are oblidg'd to goe into mourning for relations that leave you two or three thousand pounds a year, of which I wish you
a long enjoyment.   . ."

To Mr. PETER GODFREY.[4]

" October 8th, 1702."

*   *   *   *   *   *   *

    " I always esteem'd old friends as old gold, and in these matters I am not
given to change. Those that have known mee longest must say that 'twas never
my temper to bee quarrelling and jangling, nor to purchase any ones friendship
upon dishonourable termes. . . "

    The following is a striking example of the President's composition
when writing on an occasion which led him to throw off his usual free
and easy style; as such it is exceptional, and yet characteristic. He is
addressing the New Company, when their union with the Old had been
arranged, and when their consent to Pitt's continuance in office under
the United régime had been announced. It is perhaps the first time in
which he uses the style "English East India Company" as distinctively
that of the New Company. In previous letters, and, indeed, in a later

---

    [1] All this refers to the representation of Old Sarum.

    [2] Addl. MSS. 22,845, No. 87.

    [3] Robert Pitt went home on the ship *Loyall Cooke*, 9th October 1702,
carrying with him the great Diamond, and very numerous letters of commendation from his father, which are in the B. M. letter books.

    [4] Addl. MSS. 22,845, No. 116.

one below (Feby. 9th, 1702-3), we find him persistent in the use of this appellation as belonging to his own masters.[1]

" To the Honble The Directors for affairs of the ENGLISH EAST INDIA *Company."*

Dated " FORT ST. GEORGE, October the 3rd, 1702."

" Sr:

"Whereas my gratitude as an ENGLISHMAN obliges mee to pay all Defference to the Blessed Memory of King WILLIAM, So allso on this occasion I can't butt remember that Great Saying of his to the FRENCH Kings Plenipotentiarys att RYSWICK upon concluding the Peace, which furnishes mee with apt words for this address to You.

" ' 'Twas my Fate and nott my choice that made mee Your Enemy', and Since You and My Masters are united, Itt Shall bee my utmost Endeavours to purchase Your Good Opinion and deserve your Friendship.

" The Bearer is my Son whome I recommend to Your favour as You shall find him meritt the Same ; My Service to you all.

"I am Srs:

" Your most obedient Humble Servant

" THO: PITT."

From T. PITT " *to Sir* E. LITTLETON, President for the New E. I. Co.'s affairs in Bengall."[2]

" Nov: 8th: 1702."

*   *   *   *   *   *   *

" When the Generall you mean Sat down before this Citty,[3] his demands were as Exorbitant as you mention, which were answered with equal Scorn to his impudence and injustice, and we were soe far from truckling to him that wee bid him defiance, and to this day gave him not one Rupee, and this you may Credit, whatever Relation you might have had from others, and how little soever this Settlement and the Welch ffort[4] may be in your esteem, you See your Masters have allow'd 350,000*l.*, and our Masters for your land in the moon 70,000 (which is not worth 7 ff.).

" We are pretty well Satisfy'd who has been the occasion of our troubles, and doubtless those whose ffronts are cas'd with Corinthian brass will stick at nothing to excuse it, when they see they are to be brought to judgment for it, which will Certainly be seen in a little time.

*   *   *   *   *   *   *

"I hear our old ffriend Doctor EVANS is made Bishop of BANGOR (alias BENGALL), and 'tis said by your means. I am glad you are Soe much in love

---

[1] In a letter to Pitt from Mr. Woolley, Secy. to the Old Company, dated 16th March 1701-2 (Addl. MSS. 22,851, No. 61), we find it intimated that it had been found expedient to make use of the style ENGLISH Company in all public documents, covenants, etc., as applicable to the New Company. " We did for a long time controvert that matter, till finding there was a danger if wee did not allow it, as to our Intent in Generall in the Lawyers opinion, and then we acquiesced." (*Vide supra,* p. lxvi.)

[2] The Nawáb Dáúd khán, who blockaded Madras, February to May 1702.

[3] Addl. MSS. 22,846, No. 95.   [4] *I.e.,* Fort St. David.

with Bishopps that you contribute to the makeing of 'em, Soe hope you'le Send him home a Super fine peice of Muslin to make him Sleeves.

" You call me your Antient ffriend, but you are kinder to any new one, for is it not hard that you don't allow me something towards the extraordinary repairs I gave your house, which amount I am sure was between 16 and 1800 *rups.*, or you had found it flatt Smooth ? I allways esteem'd you a man of Conscience ; pray retaine a little of it for me, and think of this matter.[1]

"My Son is gone home on the *Loyall Cooke* who Sail'd a rich Ship home for England the 9th of past month, and the *Hampsheir* with about 600 bales to the WEST COAST[2] to fill up with Pepper.

*   *   *   *   *   *   *

" 'Tis Strange that you Don't know the Governor and FORT WILLIAM, having been soe great a thorne in your side, I hear your Copper is detain'd for Outrages you have committed, and for infringing the Liberty and property of the Honble: JOHN BEARD Esqr., and rather then you'de want a billiard table, 'tis said, you have seiz'd another mans house to set it up in. I hope the matter is Compos'd and that by this time you are in quiet possession of your Copper.

" I want 3 or 4 hours discourse with you to set you right in your old honest principles, till when I conclude this, and am

" Sr:

" Your antient ffriend and humble servant

" THOS PITT."

" *To the Governour, &c., of the Rt. Honble: the* ENGLISH *E. I. Company*[3]
LEADENHALL St: LONDON."

" Feby the 9th: 1702-3."

*   *   *   *   *   *

" . . . . you'le See they (the Mahomedan Government) have a great minde to quarrell with us againe, and 'tis most Certain that the MOORS will never let your trade runn on quietly as formerly till they are well beaten, for the Contests here has made 'em put noe Small value upon their Trade, besides your having Suffer'd your servants to be treated after that most ignominious manner at SURAT for many years past, has encouraj'd 'em to attempt the like in all your Settlements, and I hear in BENGALL that they chawbuck English men in their publick Durbars, which formerly they never presum'd to doe, and the *Junkaneers*[4] all over the Countrey are very insolent, only those within our reach I keep in pretty good order, by now and then giving 'em a pretty good banging.

*   *   *   *   *   *   *

" Whereas the New Companys people have on all occasions spoke slightly and undervalued this Settlement, let 'em take their measures for the future from the account that comes inclos'd, which is an Account of what I have coin'd from the time I came hither to *ultimo* of December last, which one year with an other is near as much as is Coin'd in ENGLAND yearly, excepting those times when the Nation recoin'd all their money, besides 'tis (to) be Consider'd that our Silver

---

[1] This refers to Pitt's house at Húglí (see p. lxiii, and John Pitt's letter, p. xcii, *infra*).

[2] *I.e.*, of Sumatra.

[3] Addl. MSS. 22,847, No. 42. This is here the Old Company. See remarks in notes at pp. lxvi and lxxix.

[4] Collectors of transit duties. See *Anglo-Indian Gloss.*, pp. 361 and 812.

generally is carry'd for CHINA, and a great deale of that gold which returns is Carry'd up into the Countrey for the makeing of Jewells, and coining it in their own Mints, where by makeing it of a lower *Matt*[1] they reap more advantages.

* * * * * * *

"You are pleas'd to give your reasons in your last letter for the reducing of your Trade, and yet at the same time you very much increase your charge, by sending out Soe great a number of ffactors and writers, haveing here at this time three times as many as you have occasion for, besides Some of 'em so refractory that I Should as willingly see 'em return to their ffriends as I believe their ffriends were glad to be rid of 'em, more particularly one Person, the *most* incorrigiblest wrech as ever I knew,[2] who has lately been guilty of such a piece of insolence as is not to be parrellel'd, whom I have at this time under confinement, and will severely punish him, tho' here is an Imbib'd Notion in Some who ought to know better, that noe Servant of yours Ought to have Corporall punishment, which has been the Ruine of many a Youth in this place. Some others I could name who I hope are reclaim'd, and will make you good Servants."

From SAMUEL PEPYS *Esq': to* GOVERNOR PITT.[3]

"CLAPHAM, Wednesday, March 3d, 170$\frac{2}{3}$."

"S^r:

"I could not lett the present opportunity slipp, of returning you my most thankefull Acknowledgements of the most convincing Instances of your Respects, shewen mee, in your letter to my friend Mr. HEWER: by whiche I understand the earely markes of your Favour express'd to Mr. HARRISON, and therein to my small part of the Recommendations hee attended you with from ENGLAND, which as I shall allways inculcate to him the weight of his Obligations to your Selfe for, and the reasonablenesse of his endeavouring by all methods of Obedience and Service to the Company and you, to merit the same, Soe should I bee most glad if any Comands from you, by which I might have opportunity of expressing my Esteeme of your Favours soe bestow'd and continued in him there, by the effects of my ready Services on all occasions to you here; Whose Prosperity and Health I am heartily a well-wisher to, and rest

"Your most obliged and most faythfull
"humble Servant   "S: PEPYS."

The letter to Littleton regarding Woolston, from the New Company's Council at Masulipatam, quoted at p. lxxiv, is followed by another from the same body to the same address, of 20th May, 1703, reporting the death of poor foolish John Pitt :[4]

"Our last was the 25th March by the *Hugliana* Ketch; this is principally to acquaint you of the great Loss we have Lately received by the Death of Consull PITT, who departed this Life the 8th Inst. at night, being taken about 6 hours before with an Appoplectick fitt; this mallancolly accident befell us at DAURUM PARR to which place we went in Persuit of the Wreck, but after 5 weeks Search to no purpose, the Consull had resolved to return to this place on the 9th Inst: but unfortunately was taken with an Appopletticall fitt about 4 the day before;

---

[1] *Matt, i.e.,* "touch", as applied to gold. See *Anglo-Indian Gloss.*, p. 430.
[2] Insomuch as to carry the President out of all grammar and spelling !
[3] Add. MSS. 22,852, No. 72.   [4] O.C. 8168.

it was the more Surprizeing because he never Complain'd of any Sickness before the fitt came upon him ; God prepare us all for our Latter End."

The wreck which John Pitt was in search of was that of the *Norris*, a ship which had sailed from the Downs 9th March 1701-2, in the employment of the New Company. Thomas Pitt, in a letter to Sir John Gayer, dated Sept. 4th, 1702, says that she

"Arrived near METCHLEPATAM 2d. past, when she mett with the misfortune of being sett on fire by a cask of brandy about 7 in the morning, and blew up about 4 in the afternoon, when was saved in the pinnace about 30 men and two women, the captain and about 90 men destroy'd in her, 130 chests of treasure lost, besides Cloth, Anchors, Guns, &ca. to a considerable amount, and nothing of the wreck can be since discovered." (O.C. 8010.)

"Daurum Parr" was probably *Devaram* in the Kistna delta. We find in a Memo. of concessions to be asked of the Emperor by Sir W. Norris (O.C. 7141) "a grant for the town of DAVREMPORT and ELAGEE BUNDER, with river adjoining, for renting of both which we have the *Fousdar* of METCHLEPATAM'S *Cowle.*"

To Sir JOHN FLEET.[1]

"Sept: the 11th, 1703.

"I am extremely concern'd at the ill news wrote us from the CAPE and MAURITIUS of the *Bedford*, but trust in God 'tis not true ; hope that she gott about the CAPE, or Winter'd at ST: LAURENCE,[2] for that Ship's Cargoe is the flower of our good services, which would leave the greatest impression upon me immagineable should she doe otherwise then well, nor can I be at rest within my Selfe till I hear she is Soe.   . .

"Mr. JOHN PITT the New Companys President, dy'd the 8th of May, at DURRUMPAUT whither he went contrary to all Sence and Reason to look for the *Norris's* wreck, which is not yet heard of, Soe intend the next fair season to trye what luck I can have att itt, for certainly it must be found."

To his Son ROBERT PITT.[3]

"Sept. 17th, 1703."

*   *   *   *   *   *   *

"I advis'd you Overland that Mr. JOHN PITT was dead, upon which I wrote a Complement to his Lady who answer'd it, and some months after She wrote me about interring her husband here, which I did not refuse her, but would pay noe respects to his Corps. The copies of the Letters past between us are here inclos'd, which doe you show to the Members of both Companies to prevent mis-representation of that matter. When he came out of ENGLAND his Will was in favour of your Brother JOHN, but since he came into INDIA he has made a new one and left him out, and every relation he had except his Uncle NICK from whome he had expectations. .   . Mrs. PITT 'tis said is here in town, but gave not the least notice of it to me. .   .

*   *   *   *   *   *   *

"My love to your Mother, to whome I charge you all to be very Dutyfull, and my blessing to you all, and I hope you'le follow my Advices to you of

---

[1] Addl. MSS. 22,847, No. 52.   [2] *I.e.*, Madagascar.   [3] *Ibid.*, No. 53.

Sticking close to your Studies, and take those good Courses I have Soe often recommended to you, which will be advantageous to your Selfe and a comfort to me. My service to Brother CURGENVEN, whose Nephew came up and marry'd Mrs. DOBYNS, and Carry'd her to BENGALL. I hope you remember the Advice likewise which I gave you in such affairs, for I am afraid he will repent it att leasure. . . "

To the same.[1]

"Nov. 8th, 1703.

" I strictly injoyn you to be Dutyfull to your Mother and Loving to your Brothers and Sisters, and follow the good advices I have always given you, and if nothing presents which may be advantageous to you, I should advise you since your Years will admit of it, to enter your Selfe in the Inns of Court, and goe to OXFORD for 3 or 4 years, and Stick Close to your Studies, which I would Cheifely have to be Civill Law, and if possible too make Your Selfe Master of fortyfication and Gunnery, and I hope the little experience you have allready had in the World will not only render these accomplishments necessary, but desireable by you.—Let me alsoe desire you to take great Care of what Company you keep, and let it ever be a Rule never to lend any money but where you have unquestionable Security, for generally by asking for it you loose your ffriend and that too. I assure you 'tis noe small care that I am hourly under for your Welfare, and whereas I have and ever shall doe my part I hope you will yours.—Give my Love to your Mother, my blessing to your Selfe, Brothers and Sisters, and Service to all ffriends particularly S[r]: STE. EVANCE, Mr. ALVARES, Mr. RAWORTH, Mr. COULSON, Mr. CRAGGS, and all that are soe."

To Mr. JNO: PHILLIPS, SARUM.[2]

"Decr: 26th: 1703."

*　　*　　*　　*　　*　　*　　*

"I was heartily concern'd at the hard fate of poor Tom, and I fear the Same has attended the *Bedford*, where the Poor Captain and all his familly is lost with one of the richest Ships that ever went from INDIA. . .

"I think you were in the wrong in not attending the election and vindicating my right, which pray doe for the future, let the charge be what it will.

*　　*　　*　　*　　*　　*

" I am glad to hear that OLD SARUM continues soe faithfull, and wonder that my Wife do's not all that can Contribute thereunto, and Levelling any of the places or anything else."

To W. HEWER, *Esqr.*, LONDON.[3]

"Decr. 30th, 1703."

*　　*　　*　　*　　*　　*　　*

" The United Company as well as our Old Masters have been very breife in their orders Instructions and advices this year, but by what I can inferr from the former I find they are leaning to a Commonwealth Government throughout their Settlements, which I beleive will noe way Suite the Companys Interest where our trade and disputes are with such absolute Monarchs ; for my part I never desir'd power for any other Reason then to make me the more Capable to Serve my employers, for I am sure I never made use of it but for their advantage, for unless there be a power lodg'd in Some Single person 'twill be here as 'twas formerly, their time spent wholy in jangling and quarrelling, to the endangering

---

[1] Addl. MSS. 22,874, No. 58.　　[2] *Ibid.*, No. 59.　　[3] *Ibid.*, No. 68.

the ruine of the place. For my part if the next Shipping do's not bring such Instructions and Orders, as that I can serve 'em with reputation, I resolve home upon the *Tavistock*, or Man of Warr.

* * * * * * *

" I am glad to hear of a good understanding between the United Companies Consisting of 12 of each, tho' our letters Generally Say 'tis Superficiall, and am sorry to hear that some of 'em in their debates Should urge the necessity of having Spyes and Checks in their Councills abroad, and bring in such who are branded with infamy to such a degree that noe body would have Sat with 'em, and others who are Soe impertinent and troublesome, besides soe insipid, that they were never capable by their advice or otherwise of making any advantage to their Masters or themselves, but have rather been the Occasion of the loss of vast Sums, and this must be Said and for a truth too, that where the EAST INDIA Company have Suffer'd here abroad by Knavery in their Servants 1000*l.*, they Suffer'd at least 10,000*l.* by employing of ffools ; and how can it be expected that any by their advice otherwise, shall contribute towards getting an estate for their Employers, when they think themselves uncapable of managing what little they have of their own, by leaving it to others ?"

* * * * * * *

" . . . You are a good judge and have the right sentiment of this matter, but I know from whome this project comes, who made Confusion wherever he resided and Sacrafic'd the Companys Interest allways to his own, and as I hear wants now to come out in a post to disturb your whole affairs that he may make the advantage of fishing in troubled waters.[1]

"I esteem you my ffriend and therefore have imparted my mind freely to you. . "

* * * * * * *

To Mr. JOHN STYLEMAN, LONDON.[2]

* * * * * * *

" Jany: the 2d: 170$\frac{3}{4}$.

" They have putt Mr. FRASIER and Mr. DU BOIS into the Councill here as able Spyes and Checks, and 'tis said next year being throughly inform'd of the ability of the One and integrity of the other, they intend to make 'em equall in power with the Governor, the latter,[3] without doubt you hear is dead, but 'tis easy to find one of the same Stamp to putt in his room, JO: HILLER or some such person, Soe that he who Stays here with the name of a Governor may expect Halcyon days. The BAY is Settled and (with) as they Call it a Rotation, and if they doe the same here, 'twill give an Oppertunity for every man to Show his parts, and puzle DOWD CAWNE and all his Government to know who he shall apply himselfe to for mercy, Soe that he must think of getting all or none, I wish it be n't the former."

To the Honble: Sir JOHN FLEET.[4]

* * * * * * *

" Jany: 3d: 1703(4).

" We have wrote fully to our old and new masters, Soe knowing you have a veiuw thereof need not trouble you here with any relations of their affairs,

---

[1] Viz , Roger Braddyll.   [2] Addl. MSS. 22,847, No. 76.
[3] Viz., Dubois.   [4] *Ibid.*, No. 81.

which certainly cannot but doe well when you have added two so considerable persons to the Councill of this place, one being famous for his ability and the other for his integrity. I perceive those methods are takeing that will not only tend to the ruine of your Interest but honour in these parts, Soe resolve to waite upon you *per* next Shipping. . . . "

To Capt. EDWARD HARRISON.[1]

" Jany: 6th: 1703-4.

" 'Tis easy to guess what ROGER means by proclaiming my Riches, and what must be the naturall question thereon from those that are my enemies ; ' where a plague did he get it ? ', and then comes a nod and a Shrugg, and some doglike reflection or other, for which it may chance he may be accountable sooner then he is aware of. Wee all know him and shall take care to value him accordingly.

*   *   *   *   *   *   *

" You may remember the Condition you left us in, which held till the third of May, when upon the importunity of all the Councill and inhabitants, wee agreed matters with DOWD CAWNE, which was to withdrawe his forces and returne all which he had seiz'd of our Merchants or the Companys and set at liberty their ffactors in the Countrey whome he had imprison'd, and then wee were to pay him 25,000*rups.*, all which was not Comply'd with till August, when he was paid the Same, but all this my Son will acquaint you by word of mouth.

*   *   *   *   *   *   *

" In May last JNO: PITT dy'd at DURUM PAUT, going thither to look after the *Norris's* wreck, which he suppos'd was drove thither against the wind and Current ; the Generall report is he dy'd very Rich. . . . Had he liv'd there would have been Strange Rotation worke between him and me, for 'twas impossible wee could ever be reconcil'd, for I think him the ungratefullest wretch that ever was borne. He is dead and there's an end."

To Sir STEPHEN EVANCE.[2]

" Jany: 7th: 1703-4.

" I thank you for the ample account you give me of the proceedings of both Companies ; and 'tis a matter of Ridicule with us that they talk of ROGER BRADDYLL for a Supervisor, for I beleive few or none in INDIA will regard him : for my part I will not.

" If Mr. GOUGH and Mr. BRADDYLL have had the Impudence to report that of my sending 60,000 *pagodas* of the Companys money to CHINA, or as much as one *fanam*, I hope if my Son hears 'em he will tell 'em they lye, and I wont faile to confirme it whenever I see 'em, and 'tis a true Signe of BRADDYLL'S worth, when his interest must be promoted by such a villainous mean."

To Mr. ROBERT RAWORTH, LONDON.[3]

" Jany: 11th: 1703-4.

" . . We must alsoe have a Rotation Government, or a Government without any power ; if votes are even it must be decided by lotts. . . . that Jack Straw who cares not what becomes of the Companys affairs, nor never broke a minnet of his rest to preserve their honour or interest, he must be upon equal termes with the Governor or any in the Rotation. Then besides 'tis generally reported

---

[1] Addl. MSS. 22,847, No. 99.   [2] *Ibid.*, No. 101.
[3] *Ibid.*, No. 103.

that 'twas urged there was a necessity of adding two to the Councill, for Spyes and Checks upon the President; one of which[1] that has neither a Graine of Sence nor Manners, nor ever any way contributed to getting a penny for his employers, but by his uncontroulable nonsensicall obstinacy has lost 'em many a thousand pounds, and for the other[2] I shall say noe more of, for the respect I bear his Brother,[3] tho' I must Say this that he .had not a dram of Integrity, and had he been living I could never have condescended to have sat with him in Councill, for it would have made your Government Scandalous and Infamous, and neither white nor black would have regarded it.   For my part if I find your next letters in the Same Strein, I resolve home on the Mann of Warr or on the *Tavistock*, tho my Circumstances doe require my Staying here Seven Years longer, if I could serve with Reputation, or any way promote my interest.   I cant tell who is your Pilot, but let him be who he will I doe averr that he Shapes you ill Courses. . . .

*   *   *   *   *   *   *

"I having said before that the difference between my Couzen PITT and Selfe were irreconcileable, may be 'twould Seem odd, if I gave you noe reasons for the same.   My Couzen PITT when I came from INDIA in the *Crown*, I found him in a deplorable condition, cast wholy off by his Uncle GEORGE who had Supported him from his infancy, with whome I interceded to reinstate him in his favour, but found 'twas to noe purpose.   I then advis'd him to come out to INDIA, and not only Supply'd him with money for his outset, but likewise an adventure, whereby he appear'd handsomely abroad, and from that time Supply'd him in such manner as I may say without vanity I was, under God, his only Support, yet you see in what manner he came into this Road, what an Impudent Letter he Sent me, and many others since, which I still keep by me, and permitted his wife to treat me at his table with the worst of Language, tho he at the same time would be drinking my health; and giving his Service, if there was anybody present that was coming hither, and when he came out first he wrote me that he was Godfather to my Son borne after my departure, on whome in case of failure of Issue male he had Settl'd what he had in the world, and I had done the Same by him at my comeing out of ENGLAND, but Since his death here's a Will produc'd made two years agoe at MADAPOLLAM, in which he has left him out, and not mention'd any Relation he had in the world, except his Uncle from whome he had expectations, and this the Woman brags of that she had the directing of the Will, Since which I have cancell'd mine, and made a new one, in which I have given you the trouble of a Trustee, and begg you would accept of the Same.   'Tis not my busyness to Censure the management of my Kinsman, who was very great and wise in his own thoughts, but this I'le write to you, that there are noe Generall books kept, noe consultations, and I believe your Company indebted at METCHLEPATAM a farr greater Sum then they think of; and if he be dead rich, I believe your Son will write you, that *he* has liv'd poor, and I fear can hardly make his principall.   I hope 'twill be better with him for the future.   The Woman sometime after her husband's death desir'd to remove his Corps hither, and that I would complement him, as he had bore the Kings Commission, which I refus'd, upon account that he did not Salute the Kings fflagg when he came into this Road.   The Copies of her and my letter I here inclose.

---

[1] Braddyll, to wit.   [2] Dubois.
[3] Charles Dubois, a member of the Court of the Old Company.

She came hither the latter end of August, without taking any notice to me, or I of her. . . .

"You'le see wee have wrote the Managers about Sr: EDWARD LITTLETON, who has us'd us very Scurrillously and unworthyly upon the account of WOOLSTON, who has been a villian to everybody he has been concern'd with, and know you'le have the Perusall of the Letters. I cant think of any thing that has been the Occasion of it unless that Sr: EDWARD is a little distemper'd in his braine, tho' I must add this, that all the feather-men you sent out have had a Strange picque against this place. . . ."

" To THOS. PITT, Esqr., Master in Chancery, near LINCOLNS INN, LONDON."[1]

"Jany. 28th: 1703-4."

*   *   *   *   *   *   *

" I doubt not but you'le have heard of the death of our good Kindred Mr. JNO: PITT, which was in May last, who thought him Selfe noe less then a ROMAN Consul, which made him grow soe proud and Soe ungratefull as not to be parrallel'd. I had Reason to expect to have found a ffriend in him, but it prov'd otherwise, yet never in his power to doe me any prejudice, thô he has not been wanting to attempt it." . .

He then speaks, as in other letters, of the testamentary change made by their late cousin, and goes on:

" I have had a Cursory view of it (the Will), and I think the will is very odly penn'd, therefore would desire you to peruse it, and See if it be not authentick, that the Will he left in ENGLAND with his Uncle NICK or Mr. GODFREY be produc'd, which entitles my Son to the Reversion. I suppose if Cozen NICK should Scruple Showing you the Will made here you can gett the Copy of it out of DOCTORS COMMONS. I would have Sent it you but She has not prov'd it here in our Court, nor have I seen her thô She came hither in August last, She is said to be very rich, and as Vertuous as ever.

*   *   *   *   *   *   *

" I should have been very glad to have heard how it was with Cozen GEORGE PITT, and that part of our ffamilly, for that I hear 'twas a Common Saying by the Deceased JNO: and his Lady that they did not doubt but to live to have the possession of STRATFEILD SEA, but She says now all her hopes are for her Son, who if he be noe better then the ffather 'tis noe great matter if there be ever any more of the breed of him . . .

"I am Sr your most affect':

" Kinsman and humble servant

" THOS: PITT."

To Mr. JNO: RIDOUT.[2]

" At the Nun near the MONUMENT, Jany. 29th, 1703-4,

" London."

" Cozn Ridout

" Sr:

*   *   *   *   *   *   *

" You will have heard of the Death of Cozn: JOHN PITT which was the 8th of May last, who by his Suddain preferments, was become one of the haughtyest

---

[1] Addl. MSS. 22,847, No. 130.

[2] Ibid., 22,848, No. 3.

Proudest ungratefullest wretches that ever was borne, he forgott all fformer kindnesses from me, insomuch that he deny'd I ever did him any, and that he was allways upon an equall foot with me, . .   his vertuous mellancholly Relict came hither in August, whome I never saw nor ever desire to See. In case that his Son dyes he has given the reversion of PRESTON, if it is in his power— to Cornet JOHN PITT's Son, to whome[1] pray give my Service, and tell him that the Ship on which his Son came out went direct to BENGALL, where noe opportunity presenting to goe for METCHLEPATAM, President BEARD sent him up hither to me, then I took charge of him, and kept him under my eye   . in the Secretary's Office, and I believe would have prov'd a pritty lad, but Mr. PITT to his death, and since his wife, tooke him off from me, and from that time has been rambling about the streets .   now at last they have bound him prentice to the Chiefe mate of the *Tavistock*, pray tell his father that had he consign'd him to me, I would have provided for him in an other guess manner. . . "

To NICHOLAS PITT, *Esqr.*, *at his Lodgings in the* TEMPLE, LONDON.[2]

"S^r: " ffeby. 1st: 1703-4.

"It has not been for want of Respect that I never before troubled you with a Letter but for want of busyness to write, well knowing that you are noe admirer of Complements, nor am I Stor'd therewith ; this is Cheifly to acquaint you with the Death of your Nephew Mr. JOHN PITT the 8th of May last, of which and all matters relating to his affairs, I know you'le have a more full account from others then I can give. I have seen his Will that was made in these parts, which I hear differs very much from that he left in ENGLAND, for that he has given away PRESTON to Cornet JOHN PITT's children in Case of the death of his Son, and none but your Selfe, for Reasons you may easily guess at, of all his Relations mention'd in his Will. Preferment had most strangely alter'd him, and made him forget his greatest obligations. He acquainted all people that he and I was allways upon equall termes, and that I never did him any kindness. He was Soe ignorant as to phancy that his diminutive title of Consul made him equall with the Governor of FFORT ST. GEORGE, but he found it otherwise. I doubt not but you'le have a great Complaint about my denying his Corps buryall here with the Complement as his Wife desir'd, the Reason of which was the manner of his comeing in this Road without paying any Respect to the Kings fflagg. His Wife came here in August last, who thought it not worth her While to take any notice of me, nor I of her, Soe that I have never seen her. 'Tis very unhappy that these differences Should be between relations, but I appeal to all mankind who has been the egressor. The Company did enjoyn us to Unanimity, in which I should have obey'd 'em as far as related to their affairs, but on noe other account would I ever have had to doe with him. My hnmble service to you and all our relations at STRATFEILD SEA and elsewhere. Wishing you all health and prosperity, I am

" Dear Cozen
" Your most Affectionate, etc., etc."

---

[1] *I.e.*, to Cornet John Pitt, who is apparently the same as Captain John, from whom we have letters to his cousin the Governor, and from the latter to him (see pp. lxxi and xcix).

[2] B.M. Addl. MSS. 22,848, No. 6.

Also 22,848, No. 11, a letter to "GEORGE PITT, *Esqr.*, *Att* STRAT-FEILD SEA, HAMPSHEIR":

"I believe you are not fond of the trouble of letters, Soe would not have Sent you this but to advise you of the death of Soe near a relation as Mr. JOHN PITT, which was on the 8th of May last of a Suddain appoplectick fitt, without any warning. I have seen his Will, in which there is not a relation he has in the world mention'd but your Uncle NICK as Trustee, which I suppose is for the expectations he had from him in behalf of his Son . . . Our kindreds preferments had most strangely alter'd him insoemuch that he utterly forgot his relations, freinds, and all obligations. . . ."

The will of Consul John Pitt, referred to in several of the Governor's letters which have recently been placed before the reader, is to be seen in Somerset House, under date of Feby. 1706 (*i.e.*, 1705-6). The following is an abstract of its contents :

The will was made at "MADAPOLLAM in the COAST of CHORMANDELL in the EAST INDIES," the 7th of January 1701, and the Testator describes himself as "Consul General of the ENGLISH Nation on the COAST of CHORMANDELL."

1. After payment of debts and funeral expenses, one third of all his personal estate is to be laid out in land for his eldest son GEORGE MORETON PITT, when he shall attain the age of 21 years.

2. Another third is to be equally divided between his other children (if any), but no such child's portion is to exceed 2000*l.* If there is any surplus it is to go to GEORGE MORETON PITT.

3. As regards the remaining third, his wife SARAH PITT is to have the interest for life; but if she marries again one half is to go to GEORGE MORETON PITT.

4. GEORGE MORETON PITT is besides to have a yearly income of 200*l.*, as soon as he reaches the age of 18. This was to come from the real estate.

5. A bequest to MARY WAVELL, daughter of his wife by a former husband, of 1500*l.*, payable to her on her marriage. Till then she is to have the interest.

6. To his wife a rent charge of 60*l.* issuing out of his manors, farms, etc., at TARRANT PRESTON, LITTLE PRESTON, KEINSTON, or elsewhere in the Co. of DORSET.

7. Subject to this rent-charge all the real estate is to go to the said GEORGE MORETON PITT and his heirs ; failing these to the Testator's other children if any ; failing these, to his wife for her life ; then to his Uncle NICHOLAS PITT of BEERE REGIS in the Co. of DORSET, for his life ; then to WENTWORTH PITT a lieutenant in Colonel WOOD's Regiment of Horse.

8. He then bequeaths to Mrs. ANN CHARLTON of STOKE in the Co. of SALOP the sum of 40*l.* "which I formerly lent her".

9. He appoints his wife SARAH PITT, his Uncle NICHOLAS PITT, and ANTHONY KECK, to be his executors. And he appoints the Revd. JOHN EVANS, D.D., and Mr. PETER GODFREY of LONDON, Merchant, to be (along with his executors) the guardians of his children.

10. He appoints SARAH PITT and JNO. AFFLECK of MADRAS to be his lawful attorneys to collect and receive all the estate of what kind soever which he may die possessed of in the E. INDIES, and to give a just and true account of the same to his executors.

Finally there is a legacy of 50*l.* to JNO. AFFLECK to buy mourning.

The witnesses are WILLIAM TILLARD, ROBERT RAWORTH, and ORL. NICOLLS. (The two former names are familiar in the India Records as those of two servants of the New Company at MASULIPATAM.)

The will is accompanied by two other documents.

I. A Letter from "Mrs. SARAH PITT and Mr. JOHN AFFLECK to Mr. NICHOLAS PITT Esqʳ: and Mr. ANTHONY KECK :"

" Gentlemen,
    " It pleased God of the eighth May last to take unto himselfe our dear husband and friend Mr. JOHN PITT, who haveing by his last Will (copy of which we now send you) appointed us attorneys for the getting in his estate in these parts, We have accordingly entered upon it, an account of which we cannott now send you by reason we found all his accounts upon loose papers which takes up more time to bring into methode than we are at present masters of, but by our next you shall not fail of them, and in the meantime for the good of the estate we shall endeavour to let att interest what money we can with good security. We are not much surprized that we found noe methodicall Bookes of accounts considering the little Respite he had from Companies business, which for want of all assistance employed his whole time ; however we doubt not but from his papers to take such an abstract that the estate will not in the least suffer.
                    " We are
                        " Your most humble servants
                                    " SARAH PITT
                                    " JNO: AFFLECK."
" FORT ST. GEORGE, Feb. 13, 1703-4."

II. There follows an affidavit by NICHOLAS PITT of the INNER TEMPLE, dated 10th Feb. 1705, in which he swears " that some time in last summer, the time particularly he remembers not, PETER GODFREY of LONDON, merchant, a member of the EAST INDIA Company came to his chambers in the TEMPLE and brought a packet", containing *inter alia* the above will, and he goes on to swear that to the best of his belief it is the will of JOHN PITT, and that it has not been tampered with while in his possession.

The *Probatum* shows that the will was proved on the 12th Feb. 1705, by the said NICHOLAS PITT, power being reserved to the other executors, SARAH PITT and ANTHONY KECK, to come in and prove afterwards.

There is a marginal note, dated 1711, in which it seems that PETER GODFREY took some oath as guardian, and that GEORGE MORETON PITT was then still a minor, and it seems to imply that George Moreton was the only child surviving.

A copy of the will of the widow SARAH PITT (without date) is in the B. M. (*Egerton MSS.* 1971). It seems to have been made in India. GULSTON ADDISON is named trustee, with a legacy of 3000 *pagodas*. Her estate is bequeathed to her son GEORGE MORETON PITT, but not to be delivered into his hands till he attains the age of thirty years. If he dies earlier *sine prole*, the estate to go to her daughter, MARY WAVELL.

There are substantial legacies to two sisters, and to a nephew and
niece, etc. We gather that her own maiden name was CHARLTON, and
that she was the widow of a WAVELL when John Pitt married her.

Here we may make a few further tentative remarks regarding the
Consul John Pitt's probable immediate relatives.

In the current pedigree, as given in *Hutchins*, iv, p. 90, we find
" GEORGE MORTON PITT, who was M.P. for Pontefract, etc., and had
been Governor of Fort St. George (1730-1735), and who died in 1756."
He is there represented as the son of JOHN PITT, next *brother* to the
first George Pitt of Stratfieldsay. But we know that Consul John
Pitt was *nephew* to the said George Pitt, and as we see by this will that
Consul John Pitt's only surviving son and heir was GEORGE MORETON
PITT, I think we may reasonably conclude that the latter is identical
with the Madras Governor of 1730-1735, and that the current pedigree
is wrong. Consul John Pitt himself may have been son of the John
Pitt, brother of first George of Stratfieldsay ; but there were other
married brothers of that large family (Thomas and Francis), and we
have no evidence determining the point.

"Cornet" or Captain John Pitt was, as we gather from the Governor's letters, father of Lt. Wentworth Pitt, who was named as contin-
gent heir to the Consul's real estate. We can only conjecture that he
may have been the John Pitt who appears in the pedigree as fourth
son of the first George Pitt of Stratfieldsay, and first cousin of John
Pitt the Consul.

The Will of George Moreton Pitt, proved 20th Feby. 1756, is in
Somerset House, but I have derived no light from it. Failing his
daughter and her heirs he leaves his residence to John Pitt of Encombe,
who appears in the pedigree as George Moreton Pitt's second cousin.

The following letter, which I have just met with in the India
Records, written by John Pitt on his *first* arrival as a young man in
India, goes far to justify T. Pitt's view of his cousin's ingratitude,
though not the savage bitterness of his resentment :[1]

From JOHN PITT " *For* Capt. THOMAS PITT *in* LONDON, ENGLAND."

"Pr. *Eagle*   METCHLEPATAM, Febry. 4th 168$\frac{4}{5}$."

"After a long and tedious voyage the 30th of the last month we got safe to
anchor in this rode, where the Captain was forc'd to touch, our provisions being
almost all spent. Mr. TREMAN the Chief has shew'd me a great deal of civility ;
as soon as I came ashore I acquainted him with my circumstances, and 'tis his
opinion (as well as others) that 'twill not be for my advantage to go down to the
BAY, by reason the season being over I shall not be able to get up to the FORT
in six months time. He acquainted me too that the Companys affairs are in a
very ill posture there, the Governments demanding the arrears of custom for

---

[1] O.C. 5323.

severall years back will amount to a vast Sum̃. Mr. DOWGLASS is gon for
ENGLAND overland with Mr. HEDGES. He sent his wife up to the FORT and
she returns in one of the Companys Ships; by relation he has got a very good
Estate. I made bold to open your letter to him, and finding there was no
bussiness in't I burnt it. I have given Mr. FREEKE your letters to Mr. LITTLETON
and he has promised to deliver them very safely, and in case he is not there
(for there is a discourse that he is gon home too) I have ordered him to burn them.
I have sent him too your paper of instructions about your house and other
affairs there. The jarr of Mangoes my Kinsman will take care to procure for
you. They are like to lie there a long time unless they are Sent a voyage up
(. . . ¹ . .) ye country, for 'tis a hard matter to get loading at BENGAL,
the affairs are in that ill posture there. I thought it not best to send Down
Mdme GRE(GORYS) ventor because 'tis so uncertain whether Mr. LITTLETON
be there or not. I'le take Mr. YALES advises in when I come to the FORT
and send it home invested to the best advantage I can. Mr. BIGRIG the 2d. of
the Fort being lately dead Mr. YALE is put in his place, he is capable of doing
me great Kindness (¹. . . . . .) This comes to your hands to give my
Service to my relations and friends in Citty and Country, and let them know
pray that I got well into these parts. As soon as I am Settled in my station I'le
write to them all, and try my Uncle GEORGE PITT whether he'l be as good as
his word to send me out something to set up with; in the mean time my Service
to him, and do me the Kindness pray to put him in mind of it and use your
interest with him. My humble Service to your Lady and give her my thanks for
all the civility I have received from her, and be pleased to accept the same
yourself. I'le assure you S: I shall allways gratefully acknowledg them, and
study to demean my selfe so that I may not by any miscarriage forfeit them; be
so kind to stand my friend in my absence to those of your acquaintance that are
in power, that my interest may be secured at home whilst I am abroad. Pray
S: let me have letters from you as frequent as you can conveniently that I may
hear how affaires go in England, of yours and your familys health, and the rest
of my relations and friends, which will be the greatest Satisfaction imaginable.

"I am Sr: for all your Kindness

"Sr: your most Obliged Kinsman

"Pray write a word to my Father and give my   "and humble Servant
  humble duty to him my Service particularly   "J. PITT.
  to my Uncle NICHOLAS PITT, and to my
  friends in FRYDAY STREET. I'le write
  to them all by the first."

To Capt. EDWARD HARRISON, *in* CHINA.²

"Aprill the 23d, 1704."

*   *   *   *   *   *

"Yours of the 21st May I received via ANJENGO the 8th inst. I heartily
thank you for it, and all the news contain'd therein unless it be that part
relating to my disobedient Son, who has not follow'd any one direction or order
of mine, or had any regard to the advice I gave him before he parted with me.
His Sudden Captivation must certainly have render'd him a light and incon-
siderate fellow in the eyes of all men of busyness and thought.³

---

¹ Mutilated.   ² Addl. MSS. 22,848, Nᵒ 38.

³ Robert Pitt, very soon after his arrival in England, had married
Harriet Villiers, daughter of the Hon. Edward Villiers (d. in 1693), eldest son
of George, third Viscount Grandison.

"The Lady I'me a Stranger to, and I believe shall allways be Soe, if her Caracter answers what you write, I wish she have not the worst of it, thô with her fortune and what he has of his own, with the advantages I have given him in his Education are very good working tools, and all that he must ever expect from me. thô he him Selfe not only Sets a value upon the Lady and her fortune but alsoe upon the interest of the ffamilly which I have little regard to, since that I can remember I never heard you say that you had any advantage thereby.

"You write me that you had noe hand in this matter therefore I'me oblidg'd to Credit it, yet I wish you had given him ffriendly advice to have desisted from Soe ffoolish and Suddaine an undertaking. I have received a letter from him which gives me little or noe Satisfaction in my own busyness, nor does he mention as much (as) when he arriv'd at MILFORD HAVEN or LONDON, or (that he) has a Brother or Sister, or had deliver'd a Letter of mine Sent by him."

To Sir HENRY JOHNSON, dated Febry. 8th, 1703-4.[1]

"We are expecting here the *Severne*, Capt. RICHARDS. If he comes I think 'twill be a fair oppertunity for me to come home, for by these last years letters, I find they are resolv'd to give me noe incouragement to Stay longer."

To Sir STEPHEN EVANCE *and* Mr. ROBERT PITT.[2]

"Septr: 12th: 1704.

"The Gloves and Shoes are much too little for me, and that my Son could not but know, who should send me every thing according to the list I gave him. . ."

To Sir STEPHEN EVANCE.[3]

(Same date.)

"The *Bedford* is doubtless lost, whose Cargoe was the flower of our service for our Old Masters, for whose loss I'me more concern'd then my own, and should be was mine ten times as much. I believe she Run ashore upon the Island DEGRAISE[4] or somewhere there abouts, and beleiving that some persons may be Sav'd wee are considering here of sending a vessell in search of 'em.
          *   *   *   *   *   *   *
"You may permitt my Wife to receive the income of my land at OLD SARUM and ST. MARY BLANDFORD in DORSETSHIRE to maintaine her, her two Daughters and three Sons, two of the latter I believe may be come away, if Soe I desire you to disburse their maintainance in which pray be thrifty, and Charge them Soe too, or I'le put 'em to short allowance when I come home, and if my Wife draws any bills upon you, I order 'em to be return'd, and not a penny paid, for I will not allow it in my account.
          *   *   *   *   *   *   *
"I can say little to my Son's Marryage Since 'tis done. What money he carryed with him hence including my note, with his Wife's fortune, will be near about ten thousand pounds, which is a very good beginning for a young man who have been brought up to busyness, for that at present I have no money to share, nor shall any of mine be fool'd away by my Wife or Children whilst I am liveing nor afterwards neither if I can provide against it. . . .

. . . As to what you write of my Wife, if she can't live upon the income of my land, let her Starve, and all her Chilldren with her, therefore pay not one penny that she draws upon you.

---

[1] Johnson Papers in Addl. MSS. No. 22,186.   [2] *Ibid.*, 22,848, No. 39.

[3] *Ibid.*, No. 40.   [4] Probably "Diego Rais"

"I hereby inclose a bill of Exchange upon my Son ROBERT PITT for three hundred Dollars, being So much paid to discharge his bill from the CAPE, which he is to make Good to my Cash, as allsoe the thousand pound his mother gave him, She not having power to dispose of a penny of mine nor never shall. . . ."

To ELIHU YALE, *Esqr.*[1]

"Sept: 15th: 1704."

* * * * * * *

"To conclude this letter I have comfortable news to write you. Here was one PASQUALE DE GRAVE fell very sick and dy'd in May last, who had formerly been a Supercargo of yours in the *George* to MANILHA, who whilst he lay Sick was conscious to him selfe he had injur'd you of two thousand dollars, and S^r: STREYNSHAM MASTER nine hundred. I had a hint of this, soe sent him word that I was both your attornys, and bid 'em tell him 'twas a maxim in our religion that if any dy'd without restitution they were certainly damn'd, and made his Confessor give him an hourly memento of the same ; and truely JOHN CAROON was very active in it, soe that at the last gasp, he began to make a will, and order'd the payment of the two aforesaid Sums at 16 Dollars per 10 *pagodas*, but before he had Compleated it he dy'd, which I gott into our Court and had the witness that wrot it, and those that were bye, to be witnesses to it, Soe recover'd the Money and have gott it into my posseassion, which shall send you as soon as anything presents at *respondentia*, or good and cheap Diamonds."

He writes to like effect to Sir S. Master.

To Mr. JOHN STYLEMAN, *Merchant in* LONDON.[2]

"Decr. 7th: 1704."

* * * * * * *

"I hear there are a great many candidates for this Employ, soe that next shipping I expect some new faces, since that you must have heard by last ship the death of Mr. JOHN PITT and Mr. ELLIS, soe FFRASIER is here a second who is likewise the ridicule and Buffoon of the Town, and if it were not for Mr. HUNT, wee should have bad noe books, who he has almost made mad with his impertinences."

To ROBERT DOUGLAS, *Esqr.*[3]

"Decr: 8th: 1704.

"Dear Brother,

"I received both yours of the 10th and 31st of January last ; I can't but resent the negligence of my Sone in not sending your letter, and I believe many others that I sent by him had the same fate. I am heartily sorry for the indisposition of my Sister,[4] and I pray God restore her health.

"My Sone I perceive was very hasty to marry, before hardly he knew the woman's name. The ill or good consequences that may attend it must be wholly attributed to himselfe, for as I hear he took noe ffriends consent (counsell ?) therein.

"What indisposition I have been under since my arrival here, has arose cheifly

---

[1] Addl. MSS. 22,848, No. 53.   [2] *Ibid.*, No. 70.
[3] *Ibid.*, No. 73.   [4] Mrs. Douglas.

ELIHU YALE.

GOVERNOR OF MADRAS 1687—1690.

From a picture in Yale College, Connecticut.

from the land Winds, which sometimes are intolerable, otherwise I thank God I have had a great share of health.

*   *   *   *   *   *   *

" I, finding that I am like to have no encouragement from the Managers, who employ FFRAZIER and such for Spyes, I have Resolv'd to leave this place in September next, or at farthest in January, and for their encouragement to employ such men as before mentioned, I doe aver it is my opinion, and that too upon good grounds, that where the Old Company Suffer'd One thousand pound by a knavish action of their Servants they have Suffer'd ten times as much by employing fools, and I think those the greatest knaves who eat their bread and are incapable of doing their duty, of which there are many in these parts. . . . "

To Sir W. LANGHORNE.[1]

" Decr: 11th: 1704.

" I should have own'd my Selfe very much obliged to the Managers, who write that they unanimously chose me in their Service, thô private letters Say that I was ellected by balletting, and carry'd it but by one from Mr. JOHN PITT, which has been industriously spread here, and in BENGALL, and doubtless all other parts of INDIA. But I cannot but resent the blemish they put upon me, when they came to fill up the Councill here, first in putting in Mr. FFRAZIER, and secondly the reasons they gave for it, which I heard our old Masters oppos'd, who represented his temper and deportment intolerable, and his ignorance in all affairs unspeakable, soe that he could not be in any way serviceable to them, all which 'tis writ the New Companys people confess'd, but still insisted on his being one of the Councill, for that he would be a good Spye.   .

" What must become of that Government, when such as FFRAZIER are in the Councill, who runs about boasting of a letter he has received from the New Company, promising him great matters, and inculcating after his foolish method into the people that the power now of this place is in the Councill, and the Governor *nothing*, of which I have convinc'd some of his under Spies with a Chawbuck, and doe and will bear him accordingly, for whilst I am here I'le govern according to the power given me in the Commission I brought out, which is never yet superseded.

" 'Tis said here too, which I have reason to Creditt, that the vile good for nothing wretch, with some others, have underhand perswaded the merchants who have been in prison soe long, not to pay their debt to the Old Company, for that a new Governour would come out, and then they might get clear of it for little or nothing. . . .

" I have heard the great success of the King of FRANCE is attributed to his choosing his ministers, and not his ministers choose him. And soe if ever the Company thrives, they must elect such men as are most capable of serving them, and not such as are put upon 'em by importunities, and for relation sake. For 'tis to be considered your servants are at a great distance, not under your eye, to be controul'd and advis'd by you. . . ."

Here he mentions a few men of capacity such as HOLCOMBE at VIZAGAPATAM, BRABOURNE at ANJENGO, LANGHORNE'S cousin JAMES, etc.

. . " Seniority certainly is the best and justest Rule for preferring your

---

[1] Addl. MSS. 22,848, No. 82.

Servants, but then 'tis very necessary that merrit should goe with it, but those you make judges of it are generally such as have noe share in it, thô soe much cunning as to assist each other with their vote. . . . ."

. . . . " S^r: NICHOLAS and S^r: JOHN are Striveing who shall be Generall, if the latter[1] prevails our Old Company's interest will be ruin'd.

The two following short extracts allude to persons whose books are more or less well known, the second especially so :

To JOHN HUNGERFORD, Esqr., Decr. 19th, 1704.[2]

" Mr. CHARLES LOCKYER here wants noe recommendation from me, for that I have been his ffriend from his ffirst arrivall, and his behaviour has deserv'd itt, and for his advantage, I permitted him to lay down the Companys service, to goe to CHINA on the *Stretham* with Mr. BREWSTER, where I hope he will doe extraordinary well, and get considerable thereby, and if be returns hither, he shall never in the least want my assistance."[3]

To Capt. HARRISON, Feby. 23d, 1704-5.[4]

" I'll be sure to represent HAMILTONS affairs to the Gentleman of SURATT as you desire."[5]

To the Rev. Mr. CURGENVEN.[6]

" Decr: 19th: 1704.

" Dear Brother . . . I did not find my wife had done much towards Settling my Accounts, while for want of understanding, as well as some perverseness, She has not put them in a little confusion, for which Reason I resolve to hasten home. . . "

To NICHOLAS PITT, Esqr.[7]

Same date.

" Dear Cozen

"Yours of the 10th of June 1703 I did not receive till the 3rd of September last, and am sorry I should lye under soe severe a Censure from you, as to think time or distance could make me forget Soe old a ffreind as your Selfe, for whome I ever had and shall retaine an honourable esteem.

"In ffebruary last . . . I gave you an account of the death of your nephew JOHN, whose behaviour to me was perfect antipodes to what you expected and mention in your letter, ungratefull as well as disrespectfull, but he is dead, and there's an end of the matter. And 'twould be noe great loss if his Wife was soe too, who will never be a Creditt to our name ; She is still here but I never saw her. . . ."

---

[1] We must surely read " former " here, considering Pitt's often expressed contempt for Sir Nicholas Waite, and the latter's hostility to the Old Company.

[2] Addl. MSS. 22,848, No. 94.

[3] LOCKYER was author of *An Account of the Trade in India*, etc., etc., etc., LONDON .1711.

[4] *Ibid.*, No. 152.

[5] Capt. ALEXANDER HAMILTON, author of *A New Account of the East Indies*, etc., etc. In two volumes, EDINBURGH, 1727 (and LONDON, 1744).

[6] *Ibid.*, No. 96.   [7] *Ibid.*, No. 100.

To his cousin GEORGE PITT.[1]

"January 2d. 1704-(5)."

Tells him he has made him an executor.

* * * * * * *

"I wish my Son had been so fortunate as to have fallen into your acquaintance before he had engaged in Matrimony, and then, had itt been with your approbation, itt would have been much more to my Satisfaction, but of that I shall say little, till I arrive in ENGLAND, when may have better grounds to give my Judgement thereon, then at this distance. And as you say he was very likely to tread in his father's steps, I wish too he had taken his father's advice, and then he would not have been so hasty in a matter of that consequence. . ."

"Sr: I would willingly send you some Curiosities from these parts, but that all ffriends write me of the great trouble of getting 'em out of the Companys warehouses more than they are worth. . . ."

In a letter dated January 25th, 1704-5 (Addl. MSS. 22,848, No. 112), the Governor commends to the continued kindness of Mr. Poirier, Governor of St. Helena, his kinsman Mr. Hastings Pitt. I have not been able to trace the relationship.

To Capt. EDWARD HARRISON, *Commander of the* Kent.[2]

"Jany: 29th: 1704-5.

"I find as I am now us'd by those I serve, who make me pay ffreight as much as for my Wine, and put spyes into their Councill, and other little sneaking tricks, that I shall neither be able to get Credit or money in their service, and not expecting it better by the next Ships, I believe I shall stick to my resolution of Comeing away."

In a letter of Feby. 1st, 1704-5, to the "Honble: Sir THOMAS COOKE",[3] Pitt expresses obligations to him which "time nor distance shall never make him forget."

To the Governor and Deputy Governor (of the Old Company) *for the time being.*[4]

"Feby: 2d: 1704-5.

". . . Amongst the many things I have often thought on, and some of 'em done, for your Service, there has been one which should have been put in execution at the first Setling of this place. . .

"Nothing in these parts have made the DUTCH so formidable as the bringing up all *Mustees*[5] in their Religion, about which I have been discoursing our Ministers severall times, and desir'd their opinion how the matter might be best effected, which they gave me lately in writeing, and I now send it inclos'd. For now all our *Mustez* are Roman Catholics. Soe consequently more under the command of their Padres then (of) our Government, thô of late I have taken occasion to make those Churchmen know that they are under an ENGLISH Government. . . "

---

[1] Addl. MSS. 22,848, No. 104.   [2] *Ibid.*, No. 118.
[3] *Ibid.*, No. 124.   [4] *Ibid.*, No. 127.
[5] Half-castes. Corrn. of Portuguese *Mestiço.* See *Anglo-Indian Gloss.*, p. 462.

To Sir STEPHEN EVANCE *and* R. PITT, *Esqr.*[1]

"ffeby: the 5th: 1704-5.

"I have sent you Some effects on these Ships, and principally in bills of exchange on the New Company which I hope they will honourably comply with, in regard that the loan of the money here has very much contributed to their honour as well as interest, for that they were indebted very considerably at METCH-LEPATAM whose Merchants followed their President hither, and have been very clamorous and troublesome till wee rais'd money to pay off good part thereof, which was rais'd by a great many people of this place, I am concern'd my Selfe thirty nine thousand pagodas, but have sent a bill in my own name for noe more then ten thousand five hundred, which is made payable to you two, and the other twenty eight thousand five hundred as hereafter mention'd is made payable to S^r: STEPHEN EVANCE, thô I consigne it to you both, and letters are sent by each person to S^r: STEPHEN to Countenance it, and I have here taken Declarations of trust from each person, soe pray let it be conceal'd, as I intend it, and if the Company can't pay you in money, and you see noe reason to the contrary, take their bonds at interest, and if they pay you money, I doe empower you, *if you meet with an advantagious purchase* in WILTSHEIR or DORSETSHEIR, *to lay it out* all or any part of it, and if it should exceed the sum you may take it up at interest till I send more effects or come my Selfe, but let it be bought in S^r: STEPHEN'S name with the advice of Mr. DOBYNS, Cozen ETTRICK, and Cozen TOM PITT, and *if noe such thing offers, then put it at secure interest,* or where it may make some advantage towards the bearing the charges of my ffamily."

*   *   *   *   *   *   *

"Since writeing the foregoing I have been considering how to arme you to dispute with the New Company, if they should refuse the paying of these bills, the loan of which money has been at the earnest request of their President Mr. TILLARD who comes on the *Dutchess*, who I take to be a very honest man, and I am sure will give you all assistance that lyes in his power, whome I would not have to come into any trouble if possible to be avoided, what he has done in this matter has been by the advice of the President and Councill, all which Relating thereto I send you Copy thereof, which must be only for your own direction, and not publish'd by any means."

*   *   *   *   *   *   *

To Sir STEPHEN EVANCE (sole).[2]

*   *   *   *   *   *   *

"I have sent my Sone some Arrack and Jarrs of Mangoes to be distributed amongst my friends, amongst whom I have ranck'd you, and hope I am not mistaken.

"I observe what you write of my Sone talking of comeing out in a Sepperate Stock Ship and going into a Mann of Warr. I hope 'tis but talk, and that he will remaine at home till my arrivall ; he has wrote me to inlarge his fortune, which I take to be considerable, as mention'd to you in a former letter, not less than ten thousand pound, besides he is qualify'd for any manner of employ, but if you see him streighten'd and that I am in Cash, Scruple not the leting him have five hundred or a thousand pound, but let him give a receipt to repay the same

---

[1] Addl. MSS. 22,848, No. 134.   [2] *Ibid.,* 22,848, No. 136.

to my Cash, and when I come home I shall not be wanting to doe what becomes an Indulgent ffather, if he deserves it. . . ."

To Sir STREYNSHAM MASTER.[1]

*   *   *   *   *   *

"Feby: the 10th: 1704-5.

" . . . . There is noe hopes of recovering anything of your old debts, nor is itt reasonable to believe there should, for that there is noe paper nor witnesses to prove anything, nor hardly any of the people alive, and those few that are are dead in law, and are not worth a groat. . . ."

However, he sends him a bill for £337 10s., at 30 days' sight, being a debt recovered from Mr. CHUDSLEY, supercargo.

To Capt. HARRISON of the Kent.[2]

"Feby: 23d: 1704-5.

" I could wish that S,: STE: and my Son had been soe much my ffriends, as to have concern'd me with you, and Mr. PETTY too, and not to have left me in the blackboy, without any manner of order of mine, but rather contrary thereto, 'tis a great Loss, and wish itt may be the onely one I meet with, from their left handed management. The Knight I doubt not, but 'tis very careful of *number one*, and looks no further. . . ."

It is unexpected to meet with this common modern phrase so early ! To Sir Stephen himself also he writes (Feby. 24th) :

" Pray take care of my Kettle of Fish, and in the usuall oath you administer with the ffinger in the hole, let 'em promise not onely to be true to the black-boy, but alsoe to remember *number two*, whereas I hear present 'twas but *number one*."[3]

To " Mr. THOS: CRADOCK in BLANDFORD, DORSETT."

"July 24th 1704-5.

" I cant but remember the poor condition of Cozn: JOHN FORME (?) and his sister, TEMPERAUNCE COCKRAM, her name since married I have forgott, to each of which I have advis'd your son RICHARD to pay 'em tenn pounds out of the produce of some small concernes I have consign'd him. . . "

" Your most affectionate kinsman and humble servant."

In the next letter, which is to RICHARD CRADOCK above-named, the cousin is called John THORNE in Blandford.

In the Family Tree, it will be seen that an aunt (father's sister) of T. Pitt's is registered as Temperance (Cockram), so this cousin Temperance would be the daughter of that lady ; but it is a puzzle how the brother should be JOHN FORME (or THORNE).[4]

---

[1] Addl. MSS. 22,848, No. 145. See vol. II, pp. ccli-lii.

[2] *Ibid.*, No. 152.

[3] There is some slang allusion in the mention of the "black-boy", which I cannot explain.

[4] In a letter to his brother-in-law, the Rev. Mr. Willis, of Jany. 24th, 1708-9 (B.M. 22,850, No. 174), Pitt writes: "I am glad to hear Cozen THORNE'S children are so well provided for."

To Capt. John Pitt, Westminster.[1]

" Sept. the 3rd, 1705.

" S^r:

"I Received yours of the 28th of December last, and heartily congratulate
your safe returne to your Countrey, after haveing a Share in soe glorious a
victory,[2] and I wish the Duke the same success for the future, who I hope will
contribute to the raiseing your Fortune, in which I am glad to hear our
Relations have been assisting.

"I wrote Mr. RIDOUT your Son was disposed of, without my knowledge or
advice, and much to his disadvantage of what I intended to have done for him,
but as it is I hope he will make the best on't, and he may depend on my
assistance, whatever is in my power, for that foolish Action of our kinsman that
is dead never effected me, nor worth my thinking of. . ."

Under Sept. 7th, 1705, we have another letter from Pitt to Mr. John
Phillips[3] (v. *supra*, pp. lxxi, lxxvii), thanking him "for the care and
trouble you have taken in planting, &ca., on my Estate". It goes on :

" To say noe worse of the Churchmen I think they have been hard with me ;
and before I would have paid 'em a penny, I would have had the opinion of all
the Courts of Justice in ENGLAND, for doubtless the Value of the Timber blown
down could not repair the dammage of the building, and other Losses on my
Estate, that happened by that Storme, soe that if the Church are to grow rich
by such disasters, they are likelyer to pray for 'em often, then to God Almighty
to divert such Judgments.   ."

" 'Twill be very hard if my Son should meet with any Opposition att the next
election for Parliament men, when soe much of the Interest is in my own hands,
and I hope Mr. MOMPESSON will understand it soe, and Join with him."

To William Hewer, Esqr., London.[4]

" Sept: ye 8th: 1705."

" S^r:

" I Received the honour of your 15th of Jan^{ry}: last by the *ffleett* ffrigott who
arrived here the 27th of June, and am sorry for the death of that Honble: and
worthy Gentleman Mr. PEPYS, and for Mr: HARRISON he shall never want my
Freindship, who is now att FFORT ST. DAVIDS in a post to his own Satisfaction
and as he desired.

" The Mannagers might well expect me home, after such usage, and as I dare
adventure to write plain to you, I assure you S^r: that nothing has kept me here,
but the great regard I have for preserving the Old Companys Interest, which
you'll hear, is much lessened in all other parts, since the Union, and wou'd have
been the same here, had I not prevented itt, for people of little honour and less
honesty, soon forgett those that gave 'em their first bread, and fall to adoreing
the Riseing Sunn, I pray God direct 'em, in choosing a Successour for this
place, tho' I don't know, but that itt may be as great a prejudice to their
officers, as an Injustice to Mr. ROBERTS, if they putt him by. I am firme in my
opinion, that if they ever send out R. B.,[5] from the day of his Landing,

---

[1] Addl. MSS. 22,849, No. 39.   [2] Blenheim, no doubt.

[3] *Ibid.*, 22,849, No. 42.   [4] *Ibid.*, No. 46.

[5] Roger Braddyll, of course.

I shall date the Ruine of this place, and all who thoroughly know him, I am sure, will be of my opinion, for this is a more difficult Government to mannage, as times now are, then the Company are aware off, more espetially since they have putt itt under such a ticklish scheme, which has not onely allready tyred me, but frequently putts me under great Concerne, to see their Affairs runn to ruine, and thô hearty in my will, yett not in my power to prevent itt. I would give many Instances of itt, but that I resolve to leave the place, in Jan" next, or att ffarthest in September following, if any unforeseen Accident or Encouragement don't prevent me.   For the latter I am under noe apprehension of, I perceive they are come to believe that Fortifications are usefull, and in a little time they will find 'em much more, when they invest the Governours thereof with power to serve 'em, the want of which, 'tis said, very much contributed to that sad catastrophe of PULOCONDORE,[1] and the confusion in all other parts of INDIA."

From this point onward the copy in the letter-book is in the Governor's own handwriting :

"I am loathe to trouble you with instances that to some may seeme very frivolous, as many times it does without doors when they have long debates in the House of Commons about their Orders, such as Candles, &ca., thô the consequences that attend it are considerable.

" Here was an Old custome, and I thinke a very good one too, which I industriously observ'd, but since the Union it has dwindl'd, which was that the Councill every Sunday Morning mett, and accompany'd the Governour to Church, which some of late have neglected, upon which as my duty I have putt 'em in mind of itt in consultation, when some have answer'd, that thô they allow'd the custome to bee good, yett they thought the Governour had not a power to injoyne 'em to it ; by this you may guess the rest, and You'll see in your Generall that many of our men were pressing to be discharged as having serv'd their time, which not being granted 'em, some deliver'd in sawcy petitions, which I would not permitt to be read, upon which my right hand man[2] ask'd where the liberty and propriety of the Subject was, it being a petition of his countryman, a SCOTCH drummer, and all these malecontents have Run up and downe to the Councill, who tell 'em that they are for their goeing home, and only the Governour against.

" S': Soe you may judge what time I have of it, yett nevertheless I have quitt 'em and most of 'em by faire meanes.   I am forc'd to Rupee the gentry here sometimes of which I wish the Company were Spectators and they would not thinke it their interest to allow 'em equall Votes with their Governour nor any, for few or none of 'em understand anything of good government or management, and are too proud to learne, tho' often putt in mind of their excessive Sloth and ignorance.   All matters here are very quiet and I doubt not but to Keepe 'em Soe dureing my stay and I must hint this observation I have made here, that if the person at the head of your affaires setts good example as hee ought, it is of as great moment to you to preserve your honour and interest as anything else whatever can be nam'd.   And thô I my selfe have not bin soe strict as I ought, I hope

---

[1] The massacre there (see vol. II, p. cccxxxvii, *seqq.*) had occurred in the spring of this year.

[2] William Fraser, doubtless.

you'l heare of noe complaints. I believe by this I have tired you, so conclude with my very best humble Service to you and thanks for all favours.

" I am S^r: your oblidg'd and

" obedt. humble servant

" THO: PITT."

To Mr. WOOLLEY (22,849, No. 72).

" October 5, 1705.

"   . That vile fellow WOOLSTON is dead, and his bloody pen'd protectors as quiet as lambs. . ."

From the Court of the Old Company to Governor PITT (near the time of closing that Company's separate affairs).

" 12th Feby: 1705(-6).

" We assure you that we have a particular relyance on your self, to see the whole compleated. We are sensible your active genius and hearty espousing our Interest has been the main Spring that has set all the other wheels in motion, and as we have experimentally found the benefitt which has accrued to us by your being at the head of our Affairs on the COAST in many Instances from your first arrivall at MADRASS, during the whole Struggle and Competition with the New Company and their servants, Soe we own to you that we perceive the same Zeal inspires you hitherto in looking after our Separate Affairs, and doubt not but it will run through the whole of your Management till all our depending affairs are perfectly adjusted and the last penny of our Separate Estate is remitted to ENGLAND."

To the Honble: Sir THOMAS COOKE, LONDON (22,849, No. 155).

" Septr: the 11th: 1706."

*   *   *   *   *   *   *

" . . Unless you get abler men, to manage your affairs here abroad, you must unavoidably be ruin'd, for 'tis a rule amongst 'em that they must have employs according to their seniority, let this qualification be what it will, by which you don't suffer a little, now as here in your councill the greatest place of trust is your warehouse Keeper, Sea Customer, and Paymaster, now when any Ignorant, dishonest, or raw young fellow in busyness (that his own ffather wou'd not trust with a hundred pounds) comes into these employs must not you of course suffer by it ? 'tis true 'tis an ungratefull office for one to Characterize men, thô necessary, and I wonder that you don't pick out some sober and discreet man that comes from these parts and knows your servants, and take him to your Selves and conjure him by all that is Sacred, that he will impartially tell their character to the best of what he has heard or seen.

" . . . I would beg of you to take a view of your Councill here, and consider that if Mr. ROBERTS and I should dye, into whose hands the management of your affairs must fall. . ."[1]

To Sir GILBERT DOLBEN, Bart., WESTMINSTER.[2]

" Septr: 13th: 1706.

" . . . My Sone sent me noe manner of the proceedings of the Parliament tho' I had it from others. I am glad to see the character you give of him, and I hope

---

[1] A little later than this, Pitt writes that though there were two chairs then vacant in his council, these were just as useful as the persons who had lately filled them (see *Bruce*, iii, 659). This is from one of his letters to the Managers of the United Company, a series which I have not found.

[2] Addl. MSS. 22,849, No. 162.

be deserves it; and he would much more if he accorded with his Brothers and Sisters, between whome I hear there is hellish distraction, For God Sake advise him in that matter, and to be a good husband,[1] as alsoe against his prateing in Parliament till he is Master of the orders of the house, and knows who and who is together, and that he can speak to the purpose. He is none of my Sone, if he is otherwise then for the honest, fair, and true Interest of England."

To Sir EDMUND HARRISON, Knt., LONDON.[2]

"Sept: 14th: 1706."

* * * * * * *

" . . Honesty and ability are certainly the only qualifications that should recommend persons to your service, but if I was under a necessity to take a Servant that wanted either of 'em it should be the former; for I could call him to an Account, and oblige him to satisfaction; but fools that want ability can give none. For my particular affairs I employ the cursedest villain that ever was in the world, and see him cheat me before my face, but then he is a most dextrous indefatigable fellow in busyness, which makes me such amends that I can afford to bear with it. 'Tis very true what I formerly wrote you that the old Company lost ten times as much by employing fools as they did by Knaves, and honest WM:" (SHELDON apparently) " with many others I could name, may be in the list for both."

Governor PITT to the Court of the Old Company.[3]

" Septr: the 19th: 1706.

" Surely will there never be a Turne of Times againe, that you will be able to wrest this Trade out of the Hands of those that did the same with you, who I believe have got but little by their project? for my part I will throw in my Poor Mite to help itt forward, and if you succeed in itt I'll come abroade againe to serve you too.[4] 'Twas very unfortunate your being soe hasty in the Union; for if your Servants here abroade had all alike stood their Ground, there had not by this been a New Companys man in the Land of the Liveing in these parts. Att this time my Intentions are to come upon the Tankerville, and if I stay till this time twelvemonth, 'tis purely on your account, by which time your Bottome will be wound up on this COAST; but how I am to serve you at the WEST COAST[5] God Knows, but when any Person goes over, that I look upon him fitt to be employ'd, I shall give him orders to inspect your affairs. . "

Both in Pitt's Letter-books in the B.M. and in the fragmentary correspondence (O.C.) in the India Office, much space is occupied by disputatious letters concerning liabilities which had been incurred on behalf of the New Company during John Pitt's management of their affairs at Masulipatam. Heavy debt had been incurred by his extravagant and losing contracts, and the loss of the Norris, with the large treasure on board, had greatly aggravated the disastrous state of the affairs of that

---

[1] I.e. a good economist.   [2] 22,849, No. 166.   [3] O.C. 8460.
[4] Pitt, in his letters, for some years before this, frequently speaks of his desire and need to come back to India after going home for a time.
[5] This always (I think) meant, as still with the Dutch, the West Coast of Sumatra

plaĉe. After his death the native merchants came to Fort St. George clamouring for payment, and a large sum had been raised by bills drawn on the English Company to pay them, at least in part. We have seen in a letter of Pitt's, already quoted (Feby. 5th, 1704-5, p. xcviii *supra*), that Pitt himself had shared largely in the speculative purchase of the bills—to the amount indeed of 39,000 pagodas,—whilst the letter referred to shows that he was conscious that his action might probably be looked on as very questionable. The Directors of the English Company, in fact, professed to regard the whole proceeding as unjustifiable ; they objected to the amount of the debt as admitted in India by their representatives, to the interest allowed on it, to the exchange at which the bills had been drawn, and in short they refused to honour them. The correspondence was hot and protracted. In the end the Company gave way, but we give some passages in illustration of the episode :

From T. PITT *and Council of* FORT ST. GEORGE *to the Court of Directors for the Separate Affairs of the* ENGLISH *or New Company.*

" 21st: Septr: 1706.

" You say likewise you think it not reasonable that you should pay more money then was paid to the Black Merchants, and that at Nine Shillings a Pagoda. Where is the obligation, or Custom for anybody to Lend you money on those termes ? don't you yourselves when you Lend money to subsist Ships abroad make them pay Fifty Pr. cent. ? and the same Profit upon all Damaged Goods ? We are here Merchants too, and make it our care to turne our money to the best advantage. What sort of Idiot must that be to Lend you a Pagoda at Nine Shillings, when at Bottomry at that time could have had Thirteen and Sixpence, and Diamonds Security ? or to have bought them, would have made from Sixteen Shillings to Twenty Shillings a Pagoda ? The Governour beleives all of you have been concerned, as he has, in buying of Tallys, Exchequer Notes, Bank Bills, and East India Bonds, and did you ever hear that the Persons who bought them were question'd for it, and thô never so cheap anything deducted when Payment made ? and then for the security of the two former there was the faith of the Nation, not to be mentioned with that of a Company ; so then are your Bonds so sacred as not to be bought or sold, or of so little value that we should not have regarded them ?. . ."

From a very long letter of PITT'S *to* JOHN DOLBEN, *Esqr.,* LONDON, dated Septr. 11th, 1707.[1]

*   *   *   *   *   *   *

" I wrote you by the *Loyall Cooke* how matters stood as to the New Companys debt, what scurrilous and impertenant letters they wrote hither, and the answer we gave 'em ; but this year to my great amazement they have thrown that matter wholely into my hands, but with an IF they owe any more, for me to clear it and draw bills upon 'em for the same, which bills if there was money to be taken up makes me lyable for payment if they should be protested."

*   *   *   *   *   *   *

---

[1] Addl. MSS. 22,850, No. 75.

From T. PITT *and Council to Court of Directors of the English Company.*[1]

"December the 19th, 1707."

*　　*　　*　　*　　*　　*

"You are advis'd in a letter apart from THOMAS PITT of the receipt of yours of the 7th of ffeby: and that he had taken ROBERT RAWORTH to his assistance in your METCHLEPATAM affairs, as haveing been conversant therein.

"We observe your resentment of the actions of your METCHLEPATAM President, with whom T. PITT held no manner of correspondence, or had to doe with him for a *fanam*, after he came into your Service, soe is wholely a stranger to any frauds committed by him, or any *pishcashes* he received, yet cant but think you had hard usage in some respects, but know not whether it may be justly imputed to his infidelity, Ignorance, or carelessness, and Mr. R. RAWORTH he was then very young, and the top of his preferment was a little while the Secretary, soe was never let into the *arcana imperia*. As to the *Dustore*, Mr. TILLARD, wee suppose, informs you, that was shared between the Chiefe *Dubash* and some *Conocoplies*, for that you have noe credit for it in any of your accounts, but the Merchants paid it. How well satisfy'd the proprietors of your bills are with the payment, is fully answer'd in other letters, only we must advise you this as a great truth, that your paying those bills in the manner you did, and wee not paying the WEST COAST, has so impaired the credit of Companys that black nor white will not lend anything considerable to 'em, unless your Governour gives his single bond, instances of which is few days past."

Sir N. WAITE writes in a letter to the Directors (of the English Company), dated "BOMBAY CASTLE, 26th November 1707",[2] in his usual confused and almost unintelligible style :

"I have not received copie of your consultation Books from Messrs. PROREY and BONNELL, as told you by the *Albemarle* I expected to enable my fully examining their last Books F two years jumbled together, am apt to believe may not now come upon the Publick news wrote from the other Coast that certain alterations that will be made on this side, the SURATT gentlemen writes are confirm'd by the great President's directions, RUSTUMJEE being Broaker to all their private Ships, thereby setting up an oposite Interest to the United Trade, the prejudice of which the Managers may read in our Consultations was wrote the governor and Councill of MADRASS, and this Year they appointed the Old Companys Broaker VENWALLIDASS with RUSTUMJEE to be their Broakers."[3]

---

[1] O.C. 8529.　　　　　　　　　　[2] O.C. 8525.

[3] Sir JOHN GAYER and his Council at Surat, under date April 25th, 1706, say of this Rustumjee (from his name a PARSEE—O.C. 8451):

"Thô the Union affairs be at such a full stop, yet by means of RUSTUMS bribery and one of his assistants . . there hath been more goods stript off, of late for account of private Shipping, who undoubtedly must bear the charge one way or other, but by such bribery he keeps all the officers fast to his Interest, and perhaps is master of so much vanity as to think that he shall at last by such means bring the Company to truckle to him ; he sticks at no cost, and whatsoever the Governor bids him do, he ffrankly doth it,

He also refers to the Managers having " compounded for the bills drawn by Mr. TILLARD"[1]—*i.e.*, the Metchlepatam bills of which we have heard so much :

" . . . Which has been spread in SURATT as well as in this Island, that the New Company, who valued so much their Honour has comenc't a method for the Old Company, which otherwise they should not have mentioned, may at first view apear a trifle when you have so great a Stock, still with your Servants in SURATT without one Rupee debt that I know, yett am sorry to tell you what reproachfull reflections are made upon you whose Creditt in every part was Honorable to the day I left SURATT, will not become me to reflect upon what I never expected to have seen, but you are the proper Judges, Authorizing and directing what best pleaseth you in the court of Managers, where I'le leave all such matters."

From T. PITT *and Council to Court of the* ENGLISH *Company.*[2]

" 20th Decr: 1707.

" Honble: S^r:

" We received yours of the 26th April 1706 by the INDIAN Frigatt who arrived here the 24th April last, in which you advise you are come to an Agreement on the Bills of Exchange drawn on your Company by Mr. TILLARD, and that you shall pay them to the satisfaction of the bearers thereof, but by the last Ships, the *Howland* and *Dutchess*, those concerned here have received an Account on what terms you have pay'd them, which is Nine Shillings and Sixpence a Pagoda, instead of Ten Shillings and Sixpence, Three per cent. discount, noe Interest from the time they were due, and half pr. cent charg'd for recovering what they did of you, with which the Proprietors here are greatly dissatisfyed, and think they have unparallel'd injustice done them.

(Sd. by)   " THO: PITT,   M. EMPSON,
              " W. MARTIN,   ROB: RAWORTH,
              " THO: FREDERICK, and RICH. HUNT."

From Governor Pitt (alone) *to the same.*[3]

" 19th Decr. 1707.

" S^r:

" 'Twas with no small surprise to me to see that you honour'd me with your Commands, which I will be sure to execute with the nicest honour and care immaginable, and the best judgment I am capable of . . .

" I did conceive I had done you an eminent piece of Service (and believe time has or will confirm it) in assisting as I did Mr. TILLARD, in paying soe considerable a part of your METCHLEPATAM debt, for having not only been an eye witness, but likewise concern'd in ENGLAND, in buying EAST INDIA bonds, Tallies, banck notes, &ca., which I never heard was censur'd as unfair or illegall, encourag'd me to buy yours here, which was then a demonstrable

---

however prejudicial to the Public, which secures him from his Creditors ; but certainly it can never be for the Companys interest to constitute such a broker, thô he be a useful tool at present for the private interest."

[1] There is in the India office a petition from the native merchants at Metchlepatam, giving their account of the affair, but not dated (O.C. 8458).

[2] O.C. 8531.   [3] O.C. 8530.

advantage to your selves, and no less than preserving the Merchants from ruine, but you who are the fountaine of Justice have convince'd me of my error in making soe considerable abatement as a shilling upon each pagoda—three pr. cent. prompt payment, as if the bills of exchange had been put up to Sale, and a whole years interest, besides put us to a charge of ½ pr. cent. recovering it, all which amounts not to less then between 18 and 20 pr. cent.; but hope when you have consider'd it, you'll find it more just and reasonable to repay it, then at first you did to deduct it; for I assure you I came not into that undertaking wholely for my own Interest, for that I could have invested my money to as much or more advantage, and nothing induc'd me to it, Soe much as the consideration that I then serv'd my friends as well as my Selfe, but let some Sycophants Suggest to you what they please, had not that money been paid, the merchants would not have had reason to have been ten times more angry with us, then you happen'd to be upon paying it. At present I shall say no more on this Interest, not doubting but you have, or will do us justice therein, my Service to you all.

"I am Honble. S^r,

"Your most obed. humble Servt.

"THO: PITT."

O.C. No. 8457 in the India Records is a letter from the New Company's servants at Masulipatam, Messrs. Faunce and Baker, full of insinuations against Governor Pitt in connection with this affair.

Leaving that subject I go on to other selections.

From letter to Mr. DOLBEN, *of Feby. 5th,* 170$\frac{6}{7}$.[1]

"There are three Pyrats abroad from MADAGASCAR, one of which took poor PENRUDDOCK in the *Dorothy*, as he was comeing out of the RED SEA in August last, otherwise he had made a great voyage, wherein you have lost Rups: 6000 principall and I the same. The same tooke STACEY belonging to BOMBAY, and three or four Saile more belonging to the MALLABAR Coast. I wish the *Mary* may escape 'em, who Sail'd from the COAST in November last. An other Pyrat took two vessells from BENGALL bound for ACHEEN and JUNK CEILONE off NEGRAISE, the other wee don't hear of yet, but are in paine for our CHINA Ships."

*   *   *   *   *   *   *

To Mr. THOMAS MARSHALL, LONDON.[2]

"Febby. 6th 170⁶⁄₇."

*   *   *   *   *   *   *

"You'le hear of the Death of your old friend Mrs. PITT,[3] from Mr. ADDISON, to whome she has given a Legacy of three thousand *pagodas*, and in her will made him sole ,Trustee, 'tis said that her private estate may amount to about *Pas.* 15,000, but of this he will advise you the particulars. . . ."

---

[1] Addl. MSS. 22,850, No. 19.

[2] *Ibid.*, 22,850, No. 23.

[3] Widow of John Pitt, the Consul.

To Mr. EDWARD ETTRICK, LONDON.[1]

"Febby. 12th 170⅞.

". . I must advise you that your Sone ANTHONY is marry'd which I would have disswaded him but could not prevaile, and thought it not convenient rigorously to oppose it, for as I intend home speedily I was apprehensive that he might make a worse choice after I am gone, as once he was like to doe. The young Woman he has marry'd is Capt. SEATON'S Daughter, whose ffather is Captain of one of the Companys of Souldiers in this Garrison. He has about a thousand pound with her, but what is most valuable is that She is a vertuous, modest, good humour'd, comely young woman, and I dont doubt but will make him a good Wife, since he was resolv'd to marry in these parts, for She justly deserves the Charecter I give her. Soe to contribute to their happyness, I should advise you to send him out a couple of thousand pounds, or what you can conveniently give him to enable him to trade, and something to your other Sone to begin the world with, for a mans youth is the only time to drudge in busyness, and that which would chiefly contribute towards makeing it a pleasure is to have good working tools, and that generally begets good success. You are my old friend, acquaintance, and kinsman, who I advise to nothing but what I would doe my Selfe. For is it not much better to give our Children something in our life time, to see how they manage it and improve it, then to keep it like Curmudgeons, and leave it them at our Death because we cant help it? Soe with my Service to your Selfe, Lady, and all friends,

"I am S^r: your affecte: kinsman

"and obliged humble Servant

"THOS: PITT."

To Captain RICHARD BOLTON, *Commander of the* LOYALL COOKE, LONDON.[2]

"Augst: the 30th: 1707."

*   *   *   *   *   *   *

"ffew days past, wee have had a great deale of trouble between the Right and Left hand Cast ; and who should be at the bottome of it but honest FFRASIER, for which wee have expell'd him the service ; and wish wee dont find matters soe villianously lay'd as to oblige us to proceed further against him." . . .

From Letter to JOHN DOLBEN, Esqre., already quoted (p. civ).

"I own 'tis my failing to be angry, thô not revengefull. I never did my kinsman, his widdow, or children, any prejudice, and when ever any of their affaires have been discours'd before me I alsoe chose Rather to be Neutre then Judge or party, and shall ever doe soe."

The following letter, like a short extract of one to Captain Bolton just given, and many others in Pitt's letter-book, is much taken up with an affair between the factions at Madras called the Right and Left Hand Castes, which gave the President much disturbance, and brought him into open conflict with his old adversary, William Fraser. The action of the latter gave Pitt an opportunity, as he judged, or (as perhaps I should say) which he snatched at in his anger, of aiming a

---

[1] Addl. MSS., 22850, No. 32.   [2] *Ibid.*, No. 56.

blow at this enemy, and dismissing him from the Council. But he reckoned in this without his host; for this rash measure gave the Directors at home *their* opportunity in turn of striking at the strong but impatient man, who had, as we see from his own letters, long ceased to be *persona grata* to the majority of the Court, and led to his removal from the government.

Governor T. PITT *to Mr.* THOS: WRIGHT, *Merchant in* LONDON.[1]

"Augst. the 30th: 1707."

*　　*　　*　　*　　*　　*　　*

" There was in June last, two or three hundred men of the Right hand Cast[2] arm'd, rose at Midnight upon the Left hand, who were making a Wedding in

---

[1] Addl. MSS. 22,850, No. 57.

[2] There are a right-hand and a left-hand worship connected with the obscene and degraded Tantrik or Saktí mysteries of Northern Hinduism. M. Barth, speaking of the *Mahámayá*, or "Great Illusion", which is worshipped as the (female) apex of this system, under a multitude of forms, says : " These forms correspond, for the most part, to one of the aspects of her two-fold nature, *black* or *white*, benevolent or cruel ; and they constitute, in this way, two series of manifestations of the infinite energy. . To both a two-fold cultus is addressed : the confessed public cultus, the *Dakshindcára*, or ' cultus of the right hand', which . observes essentially the general usages of Hinduism ; and the *Vámácára*, ' the cultus of the left hand', the observances of which have always been kept more or less secret. Incantations, imprecations, magic, and common sorcery play a prominent part in this last. " (*Religions of India*, Eng. Transl., pp. 202-203.)

But the connection, whatever it be, between these Tantrik mysteries, and the extraordinary cleavage of the castes of the Tamil country into " Right hand" and " Left hand" (in Tamil, *valan-kai, idan-kai*), if there be such, must be referred back to a remote period : and these latter are absolutely obscure in their origin and meaning, though the parties have been habitually as bitter in their antagonism, and in their readiness to break into violent faction-fights, as the Catholic and Orange Societies in Ireland, or in Glasgow. The castes of the Right Hand fraternity claim certain privileges which they jealously deny to those of the Left Hand. For instance, the former claim as prerogatives the riding on horseback in processions, the carrying standards bearing certain devices, the using for their marriage *pendals*, or pavilions, twelve pillars, etc. These faction-fights have given trouble from the beginning of the English rule at Madras, or at least since 1652, and frequently in last century. But the existence of the division is noticed by the historian Diogo de Couto in the Vth Decade of his history, published in 1612 (Bk. VI, cap. iv). Speaking of the four great castes of Hinduism (which he enumerates as—1, of the *Rayas, i.e.,* Princes and Warriors ; 2, of the *Brahmans ;* 3, of the *Chatins, i.e.,* Chetties or great merchants ; 4, of the *Balalas, i.e., Villálan,* the most respected of the agricultural tribes) he says : " From these four castes are derived one hundred and ninety-six, and these

their own Street, and until'd Some of their houses, but by the PEDDENAIGVE[1] were dispers'd, soe complaints came to mee next morning, when I found the Right hand notorious Egressors, soe punish'd the Ringleaders, and in Consultation wee order'd that NARRAN and SURAPA for the Right hand, and COLLOWAY and VINCATTY for the Left, to whome wee joyn'd the paymaster and Gunner, (should) Survey their Streets and report what could be convenientest appropriated to the Left hand Cast to keep their Weddings in, and prevent future disputes, Soe accordingly they mett at the very place severall times, when the beginning of this month they all were before us in Consultation, and Reported unanimously that the Left hand should have two Streets where all their houses were, Soe 'twas order'd that the Paymaster should put up Stones at the Charge of the Right hand, with a Suitable Inscription to Stint the limitts, which accordingly was done and all well, but few days after, wee selling the Broadcloth, and

---

again are divided into two parties, which they call *Valanga* and *Elange*, as much as to say, those of the Right Hand and those of the Left Hand."

Mr. F. Ellis, in commenting on his translation of the *Kurral*, says :

"Though various manufactures existed in the provinces to which the dominion of the ancient Tamil Princes extended, the several castes by which these were conducted were, by the ancient institutions of the country, in absolute subjection to the cultivating tribes . . . . circumstances have in latter times materially altered the manners of the olden time, and infringed the privileges of the landed proprietors, but they have not been able to prevent a lively tradition of them remaining, and this has given origin to the dissentions between the factions denominated *Valang-caiyár* and *Idang-caiyár*, or, as commonly, though improperly called, *the right hand and left hand castes ;* the former including the whole of the agricultural tribes, who endeavour, under a different order of things, to maintain their ancient preeminence ; the latter including chiefly the trading and manufacturing tribes, who endeavour, and in modern times generally with success, to evade it" (pp. 43-44).

It looks, however, as if the violent antagonism which breaks out between these factions must have a foundation in some (so-called) religious element. And the late Sir Walter Elliot was of opinion that this rancour was in reality the occasional outbreak of the smouldering antagonism between Brahminism and Buddhism, although in the lapse of ages both parties have lost sight of the fact.

It is curious that though the Right Hand party occupy for the most part the higher social position, the *Pariahs* side with them, and bear the designation of *Valangai mattar*, or "friends" of the Right hand. Also the *women* of the leather-workers take the side of the Right Hand, the *men* that of the Left Hand.

(See, besides the works quoted above, Sherring's *Hindu Tribes and Castes*, iii, 98, *seqq.* ; *Indian Antiquary*, v, 353-4 ; *Sir W. Elliot* in *J.Ethnol. Soc.*, N. S., 1869, p. 112 ; and Talboys Wheeler's *Madras in the Olden Time*, ii, 80, *seqq.*, which contains many curious particulars on the subject, from the Madras Records.

[1] *Pedda-nayakan*, Head Police-officer.

makeing the Contract with the Left hand Cast, COLLOWAY and VINCATTY, the
PARRIARS, made a wedding, or the pretence of it, and Went thrô the Street
order'd for the Left hand, upon which I sent out a party and seiz'd about 20 of
'em, and about two days after at a Consultation acquainted 'em with it, which
as soon as I had done FRASIER, who had joyn'd with us in every little that was
done, nay, I may say, forwarder than my Selfe, begun a long Speach, which you
may remember I seldome hearken to, but as providence would have it I did to
this, and as soon as he had done it wee were told that the Right hand Cast was
at the door with a petition, who were presently call'd in, and as usuall 'twas
read, which prov'd to be the purport of FRASIERS speach, Soe I that minet
charg'd him with having made it or read it, which he deny'd with Confusion;
and the purport of it was against all our proceedings, to which we gave 'em a
flatt denial as became us; when two days after the boatmen, washermen,
Barbers, Cooleys, PARRIARS, &ca., deserted us, this made us not a little jealous
that FFRAZIER betray'd our Councills, upon which wee Suspended him the
Service, and looking further into it found that SURAPA, SUNCA RAMA, and
others of the Right hand was deep in this plott, and that they had intimidated
NARRAN, Soe as to make him passive. The PARRIARS refus'd to desert us
unless they would Send one of their Cast with 'em with a thousand *pagodas*, and
the boatmen, washermen, and others would not goe till they gave 'em a paper
to pay 'em *pro rato* for what they gott in MADRASS for the days they should be
absent. And I am told by one of their own party, I mean the Right Hand, that
two thousand *pagodas* was promised to Somebody if they could procure the
Stones to be pull'd down, which must be FRASIER, for 'twas Put the Consultation that the Governor would never consent to it, to which 'twas answer'd he
had but one vote, and that CHINNA CAPTAINE was of their side, who could
bring over the Majority of the rest, and as much as Cooleys and *bratty*[1] women
talke up and down that CHINNA CAPTAIN *tene no's bandos*, and I believe it in
my conscience, and that the designe was noe less then to extirpate the Left hand
cast, to prevent them any more makeing the Companys Investment; for he was
very Strennous in Consultation for SUNCA RAMA and JAPA CHITTY buying the
Companys broad cloth and making their Investment: you know how (the) one is
involv'd with the Government, and the other not worth a Groat. Soe wee must
have had brave doings. I beleive I have broke the neck of their designe, for
that some of the handycrafts are return'd and noe other went out of the Town.
You must impart this news to all our MADRASS ffriends, for I have not time to
write it to any more of 'em . . . Soe with my Service to your selfe, lady, Madm.
TRENCHFEILD, and all our ffriends," etc.

To JOHN DOLBEN, *Esqr.*[2]

A very long letter from which passages have been already given, and
which relates the Caste business much as before.

"Sept. 11th, 1707.

". . . I must say this much, I never mett with Soe knotty a villany in my
life, nor ever with anything that gave me Soe much trouble and perplexity, for
upwards of twenty days past, as this has done."

---

[1] "Bratty", Tam. *varaṭṭi*, a cake of cow-dung fuel. The women pat them
into shape.

[2] Addl. MSS. 22,880, No. 75.

Mr. ROBERT RAWORTH, *Merchant*, LONDON.[1]

"Sept. 13th, 1707."

*   *   *   *   *   *   *

"I perceive my Sone is remov'd into the Countrey, which he just gives me a hint of, and 'tis Strange for me To hear, that he is become Soe considerable as to be disgusted at the proceedings of the House, and therefore not give his Attendance. S^r: STE: EVANCE in a postscript of a letter writes me the Same as you doe that my Younger Sone is Captain of Horse in IRELAND, which Cost £1200. But he nor his Brother Says not one word. And I am of opinion with you that is too much for that employ ; they may if they please beggar themselves, but I'le take care it shall not effect me . . . . I never did intend that my Younger children should depend upon their Elder Brother, and the Lord have mercy upon who do's.

*   *   *   *   *   *   *

" 'Tis certaine your affairs have suffer'd in BENGALL for want of a President. Mr. HEDGES has been or is now with you. I had allways an Esteem for him ; but to deale impartiall in the matter, and have no other in my eye than the good of the trade, I must be for Mr. SHELDON, for there is noe comparison to be made between 'em for that employ. . "

"Your Sone has received the box of books, and I have read part of My Lord CLARENDONS works, which are very diverting, being as I beleive nothing but the truth ; which I hope will divert our age from falling into the like misfortunes from their intestine divisions."[2]

Then referring to the Right and Left Hand Caste affair :

" . . In which villany your Worthy SCOTCH Second has had a hand, which you'le see fully prov'd in our letter to the Company, and I must say I think there is not such a Wretch in the world for mischeife and Compassing Confusion ; and this is a Saint of the New Companys.

"I believe I may be gone before there can be an answer to this, and if I am not, Should they reinstate him he should never sit with me, let their orders be what it will, therefore I beg of you and all other of my ffriends that if they insist upon restoreing him, that you'le all vote to turne me out, for noe power whatever Shall ever enjoyne me to act with him againe."

To Sir ST. EVANCE.[3]

"Septr. the 15th, 1707."

*   *   *   *   *   *   *

"My Sone nor ffamily gives me noe manner of Satisfaction but quite contrary

"I cant but think the busyness of the Black boy was a great hardship upon me, and as I am told you Suffer'd little or nothing by it. . "

To Mr. JNO: DOLBEN.[4]

"Septr. the 25th, 1707.

"   Captain SOUTH has told me, which I impart to you as a Secret, and I desire it may remaine with you, that my Lord ARUNDELL of WARDER in WILTSHEIR designes to dispose of that Seat, which I beleive is capable of great

---

[1] 22,850, No. 83.   [2] Clarendon's History, first issued at Oxford, 1702-4.
[3] *Ibid.*, No. 84.   [4] *Ibid.*, No. 87.

PLATE XV.

'Tis thought necessary that Jreturne how & whereforw'd wth all expedition, to hasten a conclusion of our Durbar Businefs there, least mr. Hallsy, the Old Company, the Reef at (Shim Bazar, lately gon up, Dce (according to custum) endeavour to Interrupt us, the, I thank God, it seemes Out of his power, & hope his, and all our Enemys endeavours to Injure us, will be vaine, and only serve (as heitherto) to manifest their own Spite & folly.

I need do no more, becaufe the gen'll. Letters, Are long and very pticuler: to wch I referr you, and Remain

Most Hon'd Sirs.

Your faithfull and most. Obedient servt

Rob Hedges

Hugly. 16. March 1699/1700.

improvement. If Soe, I wish you may have money to buy it for me, and I doubt not you'le manage it to my best advantage, and an indifferency therein may contribute thereto. You are the only ffriend that I confide in, in any matters of concerne. Dont forget to sue my Sone and S^r: STEPHEN for the £160, as mention'd in the Generall Letter."

To Sir EDMUND HARRISON, LONDON.[1]

" Decr. the 8th, 1707.

*   *   *   *   *   *   *

" You will see the troubles we have had between 2 sects of our Inhabitants distinguished by the names of Right and Left hand Casts. The former had layd a design deep and black, utterly to extirpatt the other out of this City, and that they might the more effectually compass their ends some of the heads of the Left hand Cast were to be murder'd, which would have put such a consternation upon the rest, that not one would have remain'd with us. The grounds of these dissentions, and what lead the Right hand Cast into this hellish combination I find to be that it had firmly been pracktis'd among 'em that the Left hand Cast could not make any bargains or buy any goods unless one of the Right hand were Join'd with 'em to direct their Shairs, so that they govern'd the trade as they thought fit, and the Companys Investment fell generally under their management, who would never enter upon any contracts of providing goods without advancing money to 'em—to break the neck of which (sometime before the Company had order'd us the method wee now took) I put up papers upon the sea-gate and other publick places, to encourage all merchants indifferently to bring in goods to be Sorted by the Companys *musters*, and wou'd agree the Price and pay 'em ready mony for 'em, but this tryall had not the effect I desir'd. The Left hand Cast (who are the only merchants that can serve you in this method) being intimidated by the threats of the Right, and overaw'd by 'em, and upon receiving your order to advance no mony or payment upon Investments I took care to publish it among 'em, and that we could not recede from the directions you had given us, upon which some of the most eminent Merchants of the Left, prevail'd upon by the assurance of our protecting and defending 'em against the insults of the other, undertook the providing goods in the manner you direct (and indeed none else could have done it), upon which the Right hand seeing their designs defeated, and that the reigns of trade was no longer in their hands, fell upon this barbarous attempt to regain it, industriously spreading false rumours amongst the poor and ignorant people to cause 'em to desert us. I have discover'd the heads of the faction, and shall reward 'em according to their deserts.

" Your Second Mr. FRASER was made use of as a tool to promote this vile designe, whom wee found to (have) betrayed our Councill, so expell'd him the Companys Service *ex officio et beneficio*, which not being sufficient to quiet his turbulent humour, and having intelligence of his combining with the Rebells, we confin'd him to his lodgings in the FORT under a guard, for that the clamours of the mobb were so great, and their messages from ST. THOMA Soe Sawcy, we could find no other expedient to quell 'em then by clapping up the Person who countenanc'd their villainy, they themselves loudly proclaiming thron' the streets that they knew him to be their friend, and that they would adhere to no terms but such as shou'd be proposed by him, nor wou'd they return to their duty unless

<hr/>

[1] Addl. MSS. 22,850, No. 90.

he was reinstated. . . . I must say that he is the vilest wretch I ever knew, utterly incapable of any business, and eminent for nothing but mischief, which is his whole study and delight . . . ."

At a Consultation in FORT ST. GEORGE, January 8th, 17C8-9.[1]

" This day the ARMENIANS, MOORS, and GENTUE Inhabitants of this place, hearing that the Governour design'd home upon the *Litchfeild*, deliver'd in a Petition (as entered after this Consultation) requesting that he would Stay till the bussiness of a *Phirman* was negotiated with the GRAND MOGULL, And all the Councill urged the same, which the Governour cou'd nor wou'd not promise to comply therewith, but take some days to consider thereof, haveing disposed all his affairs for goeing home on the *Litchfeild*."

PITT to JOSEPH MARTIN, Esq., LONDON.

"Jany. the 18th, 1708-9.

*   *   *   *   *   *   *

" I observe you have laid S[r]: NICHOLAS WAITE aside, and wish they had done so by me too, thô not for the same reasons, and then I could have come home as I intended on the *Litchfeild*, having all things prepared for it, but by the first Ship in September, nothing but death shall prevent, having laid aside all trade, and stay till then for no other reason but to finish your grand affair with the Emperour. If you pitch upon men suitable for such an undertaking, I think it not difficult to bring your trade at SURATT to BOMBAY, for where the carrion is the Eagles will resort. ."

To Colonel WINDHAM.[2]

" Jany. 19th, 170⅘.

*   *   *   *   *   *   *

" *I cant but stand amaz'd to see so many ingenious men made tools of to contrive the ruin of their country,—Surely in the end they must be cloath'd with more shame than many figg leaves will cover.*[3]

*   *   *   *   *   *   *

" My daughters are my greatest concern, and heartily wish they were well disposed of, which I have left entirely to my Cozen GEORGE PITT. I have appointed the Sum (£6000 each) for their fortunes, which should not be unwilling to augment, if they were match'd into such an honourable family of (*sic*) yours or those you mention. . . ."

PITT to Sir THOMAS COOKE.[4]

" Feby. 7th, 1708-9.

*   *   *   *   *   *   *

" You shall find in October that I am firm in my Resolution of coming home, and nothing but death shall prevent, for as you hinted their service now is fitt for none but their Scoundrel favourites, and I doubt not but in very little time they'll find the effect of itt, and God alone knows the care and trouble I have

[1] *India Records*, Range ccxxxix, No. 85.
[2] Addl. MSS. 22,850, No. 148.
[3] I need hardly say that the Italicizing is the editor's, in 1887.
[4] Addl. MSS. 22,850, No. 222.

had upon me to preserve the peace and tranquility of this place. For had I let loose the reins of Government as your letters from time to time have directed, long before this I doe firmly believe it had been in such confusion as irretrievable, whereas now, I may speak it as a truth and without vanity, 'tis the jewell of all European settlements, but how long 'twill continue so I cant say.

"S^r: I would begg you to observe the behaviour of Mr. FREDERICK, who is so prevented by the villainous caball he is in, that he is become pernicious to the Companys honour and interest. . . . Now I am writing of this poor mischievous wretch I must not omitt to let you know that when we had th trouble about the Cast, and that the right hand left us, amongst 'em was those that clean the Streets, which was omitted during that trouble, so when the Scavenger came to collect the duty many of the inhabitants refus'd to pay for that time, which the Scavenger acquainted me of, which at first I made light of and order'd him to send his servant again, but afterwards he came, and told me, that they were resolv'd not to pay itt, when I order'd him to bring me a list of such persons, which he did, and who should be in the head of 'em, but this choice servant of yours, FREDERICK, who I imediately sent for and lock'd the door of the Consultation, and laid the Key upon the table, and very freely told him how I would use mutineers, and begin with him, then showed him the list, when he let fall a few penitential tears, and promised amendment. And by what I found afterwards it was an agreement amongst many of 'em, but I cool'd their courage. . . ."

PITT *to his son* ROBERT.

"March 11th, 1708-9.

*   *   *   *   *   *   *

" Son ROBIN

" On the 12th past month here arriv'd the *Stretham* from BENGALL, from whom I received the severall Stores per bill of Loading, the condition of 'em as follows :—

" The FLORENCE wine very good, but not above 4 or 5 dozen in each, Mr. Shepherds servants being such villains that it purely run out for want of good corks, which I suppose they bought for cheapness. The Companys the same, as also Capt. GOUGHS.

" The CANARY is excellent good, well cork'd and pack'd, and that which you call FRENCH wine most of it is port, and for the ale and beer, all spoilt, not one dropp fitt for any use, and there being no mention in any of your letters nor the bill of loading, nor any receipt appear for my wearable stores, I did beleive you had sent none, but about 25 days after the Captain arriv'd here he sent me a box found in his *Godown*, which by (a) little direction wrote upon itt, 'twas guessed it was for me, so when open'd it found in it a note of your writing and the contents as mention'd therein,

3 doz^n: of Towells
2 doz^n: of Cambrick Hankercheifs
1 doz^n: of Gloves
4 p^r: Silk Stockings,

but can find no box or chest of the hatts, perewigs &ca. you usually sent me. So beleive it lost or spoilt. This is the effect of your great care of my necessarys, which are not a little valuable when wanted. I here write you a little but think the more."

i 2

"FORT ST. GEORGE, *Wedensday*, Augst. 3d, 1709.

"At a Consultation. Present : THOS: PITT, *Esq., Governour and President ;* WM: MARTIN, ROBT: RAWORTH, THO: FREDERICK, GULSTON ADDISON, RICHD: HUNT, HEN: DAVENPORT.

" The Governour this day acquainted the Councill that he having lately heard of some Villanous and Scandalous reflections that had been made upon him by the Late Leiutenant SEATON, who he yesterday sent for from the MOUNT and Examined thereon, who with his usuall impudence everred to him the (most) Notorious falsitys, that ever could be thought or imagined, upon which, he said he had confin'd him to the Ensign's room, and had desired that he might be sent for up and Examined thereto, which accordingly was done ; and when he came into the Consultation room before us, without first hearing what the Governour had to charge him with, and the reason of his confinement, he immediately addressed himself to the Councill, Saying, Gentlemen of Councill, I am come here to accuse the Governour for buying a great Diamond to the Companys prejudice, when the Governour answered and told him we would discourse of that by and by, and demanded of him whether he had said that he had received of PAUPA, to make him chief *Dubash,* five hundred *Pagodas,* and that RAMAPA offered Seaven hundred to be continued, which was refused, this he accknowledged to have said, but being commanded to prove the same, he answered he had it from a black fellow, but could not remember who he was, after which the two *Dubashes* before mentioned declared they never gave the Governour a *Pagoda,* or that ever he asked or hinted to them of any such thing, and to this they took the most Solemnest Oath in the Pagoda, then the Governour demanded of him what he knew of his buying a Diamond, he answered in Generall terms that he knew every perticular of it, when he was commanded to accquaint the Councill with it, which he said he would then do, knowing their would be a change of Goverment this month, and therefore what this Governour said to him did not signifie a farthing, with many such Insolent and Villianous expressions, he further said that to his knowledge the Governour was betrayed by all his black Servants about him, insomuch that he knows everything that was done and said, nay as much as in his counting house, and to give an Instance thereof said that the great Diamond he had bought was entered in his Books Fol. 64, he farther told us, that one ROGERS that went hence in October last for BOMBAY had carried papers along with him, signed by black people, that would do the Governours buissness, the which Sʳ: NICHOLAS WAIT had got translated, and carried home with him.

" The Governour also accquainted the Councill that he had very good reason to suspect that this SEATON was turned Informer to the Government and held a Correspondence with them, and promised in few days to prove the same, in Expectation of which, and what the Governour Charged him with, and he confessed before us, we now unanimously confirm his confinement, till other means can be considered of, and for what discourse passed between the Governour and him yesterday in his Consultation room, after his coming from the MOUNT is as Entered after this Consultation, the truth of which he shall be always ready to justify by Oath or otherwise."

(Signed by T. PITT, WM. MARTIN, ROBT. RAWORTH, THOS. FREDERICK, GULSTON ADDISON, and RICHD. HUNT.)

" This Evening being the Second of August about 5 a clock I discoursed Capt. SEATON in the Consultation Room, when haveing charged him with his haveing said that I had 500 *Pagodas* given me to make POPPA Cheif *Dubash,* which he owned and told me I was betrayed in whatever I did, or Spoak, by all my Servants about me, and that I had not a friend upon the Place, whatever I thought.

"Then I asked how he durst presume to talk up and down of what I bought or sold, and how it was possible for him to know anything of it, to which he answered that he had so good Intelligence that their was not the least thing done or said by me but that he knew, and to convince me desired leave to ask me some questions which I permitted him to do, and were as follows, whether Mr. ROBERTS did not write me to request that he might be concerned in a great Diamond which I had bought? Answered 'false'. Whether a person did not come and wish me joy, of its being sold for 500,000 Dollars? 'false'. Whether two persons did not come from the DUAN to demand a great Diamond, and that I gave one of them, at coming 11. Rupees, and the other at going away 150? 'all false', only that one man came. Upon which I told him I found him a Villain, and as I found he had been endeavouring to betray me, doubtless he would do the same to the Garrison, so ordered the Captain of the guard to confine him to the Ensigns roome, none to come to him but the Councill."

(Consultation, 11th August 1709.)

"This day Lewtenant SEATON was brought up again before us when the Governour told him that since their was yet no changed Government It was high time to make him know their was some, and read to him what he had said to him on the 2d Instant in the Consultation room, and what he said the next day there, before the Governour and Councill, and demanded of him to prove the same, instead thereof he impudently denyed all he had said in private to the Governour and Councill, with strange imprecations and asservations of Gods Vengeance upon him if ever he had said it, this from any other man in the world would have amazed us all, but by the many years Experience of him, we are entirely satisfied that he is a person capable of perpetrating any villiany that can be named, the Governour also produced two Letters, one from Mr. RAWORTH, and the other from Mr. COPPIN, but proving what (by) the Governour in private and before the Councill SEATON was charged with and a great deal more, which Letters were now read, and the persons present that wrote them, who was ready to tender their oaths to the truth, yet nevertheless he denyed all as before mentioned, both which Letters likewise prove his haveing been tampering and corresponding with the Government, and may other vile Actions, which Letters remain in the Governours hands to prove the same when ever there is an occasion, so we demanded him whether he had anything more to say, to which he answered that he had not, and as he withdrew denyed again all he was charged with   .   . there is no ill action can be named but what we beleive he has been Guilty of, as well as what now charged with, and that he has been many years the Plague, Pest, and Disturber of the Peace of the Place, and now to compleat his Villainy aims at nothing (else) than the betraying of the Governour and trade of the place . . . 'tis unanimously agreed that he be confined till the first Ship goes for ENGLAND and in her to be sent home a Prisoner to the Company. . ." (*India Records*, as at p. cxiv, Note 1.)

PITT *to his son* ROBERT.[1]

"Sept'. the 16th, 1709.

*   *   *   *   *   *   *

"Here has lately been discover'd an unpareleld villany of SEATONS, who has been tampering with the MOORS, to informe 'em that I bought great Diamonds,

---

[1] Addl. MSS. 22,850, No. 226.

thó he knows nothing of it, when I call'd him before the Councill and charg'd him with what I had been inform'd of, he owned it all in the most insolent manner as ever was heard of, and the next Consultation day disown'd all he had said before, with the strongest execrations and assevrations as the Wickedest man could be guilty of. He is confin'd in the FFORT, and shall be sent home a Prisoner on *Peacock*. FREDERICK, WRIGHT, and ETTRICK have marry'd into a Blessed family. . . ."

Pitt probably, in writing to Mr. Raworth as he did, on the subject of Fraser's conduct and possible reinstatement, evidently still calculated on being supported at home; for the account, such as we have it, of his reception of the reply, and of his own supercession, hardly suggests that this was really expected by him. That he had maintained his post for nearly twelve years, and that in the face of all the changes at home, was marvel enough, considering the history of past governors and their rapid failure in favour; but the length of his tenure had perhaps brought him to regard it as a freehold.

The Court's letter, in reply to the "general" one from the Council at Fort St. George, in regard to Fraser's conduct in the business of the Castes, is dated 4th February 1708(-9).

In several long paragraphs the letter animadverts on the mismanagement which the Court judged to have taken place in respect to the quarrel of the Castes. The tenor of their remarks may be gathered from a few short passages which I extract :

"Nor can we think that the Right hand Cast would have carry'd Things to that extremity on the Single quarrel of the left hand Cast making a Wedding in their own Street. It seems to us that the Seeds of discord lay deeper, and that things growing ripe for a Rupture, this handle was taken to begin the quarrell and set fire to the fuell that was before preparing for it. We should have esteem'd it a praise worthy mannagement in our President and Council to have foreseen and prevented this Mutinous disposition before it broke out, or at least to have quenched it when it first began to flame.

"Nothing sure do's better bespeak the Ability and Diligence of Governours than Keeping their Subjects and dependants in quiet, and they can never do that without an impartial Administration of Justice to all under them . . It was very Surprising to us to read that so many of the Handicrafts and other usefull hands went away on this quarrell, and gave us but ordinary apprehensions of the Conduct of the then Administration. Surely they were too valuable to be parted with without the last extremity. All Nations and times have agreed in this that usefull People are the Riches as well as the Strength of a City or Countrey.

*   *   *   *   *   *   *

"On the whole matter we heartily recommend to you all to endeavour in your Stations to prevent such like quarrells in future.

*   *   *   *   *   *   *

"The charge against Mr. FFRAZER in Severall parts of the History of this difference we have consider'd, and would hope no ENGLISH man, especially none of our Servants, would be guilty of such pernicious practices which Strike at the root of the well being of the Place, and are the more enclin'd to this Opinion because we find in the Consultation of the 22d August that the Council were generally unwilling to suspend him, which we cant think they would be if they apprehended he was justly taxed, and that it was Mr. PITT's solemn averring he would sitt no more with him that prevail'd with them. We have therefore reinstated him, as thinking it not fitt to give so much Countenance to any Governour whatsoever as to approve his Single opinion against all the rest of the Council in a Case of this nature, which if it was true do's not fully appear to us to be prov'd. . . ."

The letter just quoted from was accompanied by the following from the Court of Managers to the President individually :

(Dated "28th January 1708-9".)

" Sr :

" You having for some time past intimated to us your desire to return to ENGLAND we have granted your request, and have appointed Mr. GULSTON ADDISON to be President and Governour of FORT ST. GEORGE, and in Case of his death or absence, that Mr. JOHN BRABORNE succeed thereto, and settled the Council as appears by our generall Letter and Comission now sent by these Ships, and by said Letter have directed that you do imediately Surrender the Government to the Succeeding President, and all Books, Papers, Effects, and other things belonging to us. . . That when you desire to take passage on any of our Ships who shall be bound for ENGLAND, the President and Council are order'd to direct the Commander to receive you on board with your necessaryes, To allow you the Great Cabbin, and give you respect in the voyage Suitable to the Character you have born in our Service.

" All which we acquaint you with in order to your Complyance, we are

"Your Loving Friends, &c."

FORT ST. GEORGE, September 17th, 1709.

" AT a Consultation. Present: THOMAS PITT, Esqr., Governour and President ; WM. MARTIN, ROBERT RAWORTH, THOS. FREDERICK, GULSTON ADDISON, RICHARD HUNT, HEN. DAVENPORT.

"Yesterday Evening appeared a Ship to the Northward of this Port, and about Nine at Night Came ashoar Capt. TOLSON, who acquainted the Governour that he was Commander of Ship *Heathcote* come directly from ENGLAND, and that he brought the Companys Packett, which he produced Directed as follows :

" ' To the Honble: GULSTON ADDISON, Esqr., President, Messrs: FRASER, MOUNTAGUE, MARTIN, RAWORTH, FREDREICK, HUNT, BULKLEY, and JENNINGS at FORT ST. GEORGE.' And withall told him their was great alterations hear, and that he was dismist the Service, therefore prayed that the Council might be immediately called, the Governour told him that it was impossible to be done, not only for the lateness of the Night, but that severall of them were at the MOUNT, so desired the Captain to strictly observe in what condition he delivered the Packett, and be hear tomorrow Morning by eight a Clock, against when the Councill should be summon'd, that so he might see it in the Like Condition he deliver'd it, and this morning accordingly all the Late Councill mett, when the Governour refus'd to surrender the Goverment by virtue of the Superscription on the Packett, but demanded a Superceedent to his Commission by Vertue of which he had been Governour of this Place upwards of Eleven years, so after some hesitation the Packet was opened, wherein their was a Commission that

Superceeded his; he also demanded the reading of the Generall letter, which was refused him, but in the Packet their being a Letter from the Managers to him, wherein 'twas fully expressed his dismission from their Service, and the Constituteing GULSTON ADDISON Esqr: in his room, he immediately read the Cash and tendered the Ballance thereof, being one thousand nine hundred and thirty five *Rupees*, twenty *fanams* and three *Cash*, but the New Governour desired the payment for that time might be deferr'd for that he was very much indispos'd, so the Governour Just as he left the Chair challenged the whole board, or any upon the place to charge him with an unjust action dureing the whole time of his Goverment, or that he had ever refused a kindness to any one that asked it, and that it lay in his power, or that ever he acted arbitrary in any one matter, notwithstanding some villians of this place have had the Impudence to represent him otherwise, so rose out of the Chair, and placed the New Governour in it." (*India Records*, as at pp. cxiv, cxvii).

To his son ROBERT.[1]

" Sept. the 21st, 1709.

" . .   On the 17th in the night here arriv'd the *Heathcot*, which brought me as true a relish of the managers gratitude as I have had of their justice, and on the 18th in the morning I surrender'd the Government to Mr. ADDISON, and would at that time have deliver'd in my Cash and all Accounts, but he was Soe indispos'd that he could not receive 'em, Soe deferr'd it till the next day. I think they have made a very good choice in him for Governor, but God deliver us from such a Scandalous Councill unless it be two or three that are in it, and for that fellow FRASIER, they had done the adventurers justice if they had sent him to a galley, but I suppose he is kept in to serve the turn of some of the Managers as infamous as him Selfe.   . "

A curious reference to Pitt's supercession occurs in the *Wentworth Papers*, in a letter from Peter Wentworth to Lord Strafford :

" Jan. 28th, 1709.

" P.S.—Since I wrote this I am told a great Peice of News that Mr. ADDISON is really a very great man with the juncto, and that he has got his elder brother, who has been a factor abroad in those parts to be Governor of FORT ST. GEORGE, and the great PITS is turn out; his son here has a great while constantly voted with the Toryes, which has been a great help to Mr. ADDISON. It seems Mr. ADDISON'S friends can do what they please with the chief of the EAST INDIA Company, who I think have the liberty of naming their Governor, and by management with them the place is got, which they say some years are worth 20,000 pound." (*Op. cit.*, p. 75.)

To Mr. HENRY RAWORTH, *Merchant*, LONDON.[2]

" October 17th, 1709.

*   *   *   *   *   *   *

" By last Shipping I desir'd my Will might continue in your hands, but upon receipt of this letter I desire you to burn it in the presence of my Son ROBERT PITT, I having made a new Will, and sign'd to three of one and the same tenor

---

[1] Addl. MSS. 22,850, No. 227.   [2] *Ibid.*, No. 228.

and date. One, I bring with me, another will come by the January Ships, and the other remains here in FORT ST. GEORGE. I hope to be with you before this can reach you. . ."

There are several more business letters of 21st October, announcing his immediate embarkation by the *Heathcote*. In one, to SAMUEL BRADSHAW, Esq., he says:

" Governour ADDISON (who is since dead) joyn'd with me in making you this remittance," &ca.

Pitt quitted Madras on the *Heathcote* about the 25th October ; the exact date I have not found. By the following entries in the Court Books we learn that at the Cape he had quitted the *Heathcote*, and taken his passage by a Danish vessel, which landed him at Bergen in Norway.

From Court Book, 5th of July 1710.

*   *   *   *   *   *   *

"Letter from Governour PITT, Dated 30th May 1710, near BERGEN in NORWAY, was read."

From Court to FORT ST. GEORGE.

"7th July 1710.

" Since writing our Generall Letter of the 5th Instant we have advice from Mr. PITT, who came from the CAPE on board a DANE, and arrived at BERGEN in NORWAY the 31st May, That Mr. SHELDON of BENGALL is dead, and also our President Mr. ADDISON.[1] That the troubles at MADRASS were renewing again on account of the Casts, all which greatly concerns us. . . "

" FORT ST. GEORGE, Consultation, *primo* June 1710. Present : WM. FRASER, Esqre: Governour and President," etc.

"THE President produces a Letter from the DUAN received by a Brammeny attended with Six horse, intimating something of a great Dyamond, but soe intricate and obscure wee cant perfectly tell his meaning. Translate of which is entered after this Consultation. . "

"(*Translate*)

"*From Duan* SADATULA CAWNE, received 30th May 1710.

" ALL HEALTH ! I formerly wrote you about the *Hosbull hookum* I received from Court seal'd with the Kings Jewellers JEVOYHEE CAWNES Seal; that RAMA CHUNDRA VOGGEE had given a bond in the Court about the Diamond that was brought, so I hope you will observe it, and I received a Strict order from said Jeweller to send up that Diamond to the King with all Speed, therefore I have sent MOORO Pundit to you, and as soone as you receive this send up said Diamond with all care under your seal, being there is still a friendship between Us, soe don't delay sending said Diamond, for this is Extraordinary busines belonging to the King. What can I write more ?"

From Court Book, 20th December 1710.

" The Court being informed that the late President of FORT ST. GEORGE, Mr. PITT, had Some things to acquaint the Company withall for their Service, if any Gentlemen were appointed to meet him,

---

[1] Mr. Addison died 17th October 1709, whilst Pitt was still at Madras.

" Ordered

"THAT the Chairman, Mr: NATHANIEL HERNE, Mr: COULSON, Mr: LYELL, Mr: SHEPHEARD, Mr: Aldⁿ: WARD, Mr: DAWSONNE, and Mr: PAGE, or any Three of them, be desired to discourse Mr: PITT thereupon, and to make Report, And that Mr: President HARRISON be present thereat."

From Ditto, 9th May 1711.

"LETTER from the President and Councill of Fort St. George, Dated the 22d June 1710, received by the *Abingdon,* being read together with the Translate of a Letter received therewith from the said President and Councill, which Letter was sent to them by the DUAN SAUDATULLA CAWN, relating to a great Diamond, which he demands should be sent to the MOGULL:

"AND THOMAS PITT Esqr: late Governour of FORT ST. GEORGE comeing into Court, and being acquainted with the said Letter of DUAN SAUDATULLA CAWN and the Clause in the Generall Letter, and having discoursed with the Court thereupon, and of other matters relating to their Affairs at FORT ST. GEORGE,

" Ordered

" That it be referred to the Committee of Correspondence, to draw up a Letter, to be sent to FORT ST. GEORGE, on the Debate of the Court, in answer to the aforesaid Generall Letter, and the Letter from the DUAN."

From Court to FORT ST. GEORGE, 28th December 1711.

*   *   *   *   *   *   *

". . . . Your 15th Paragraph of the *Abingdon* Letter mentions the Letter from the Duan SADATULLA CAWN, and that it is very ambiguous and intricate, relating to a great Diamond belonging to the King which you know not what to make of, perhaps some of the Persons who signed that Letter do not, but wee apprehend those who have Supported Captain SEATON are let further into the Secrett. What is incumbent on you is to prevent every handle the MOORS may take to embarrass us, of which such a Report as this might be made a very great one; how far and wide the mischievous consequences of it may Spread the wisest of you all cant foresee, and by the late mannagement Show you want Tallents to Stop, Wherefore it is all your Dutys to prevent it, and whatever has a tendency that way. It dos not appear what answer was returned to that Letter, by anything in your Packett. This wee mention as to your Carriage towards the MOORS. But with relation to our Selves wee say wee expect you to send us the best account you can on your Enquirys how that Dyamond was come by, whether the buying it or bringing it to ENGLAND has been to our prejudice, and wherein and how much, and anything else you think proper for our notice, that if wee should Suffer thereby wee may endeavour a Remedy. Enquire also who they were that first Sett on foot the discourse about it, and how it came to pass that when the Dyamond had been in ENGLAND severall years before, the Natives, if that Letter was genuine, never mentioned anything about it till after the late President was come to ENGLAND."

*   *   *   *   *   *   *

" Wee dont at all like the Account given us in your 50th and 51st Paragraphs about RAJAH SYRRUP SING's detaining Lievtenant HUGONIN and Ensign RAY, and a present of Two Hundred *Pagodas* given for their releasement, which thô taken the men are where they were. *Had the like case happen'd in the late Pre-*

sidents time he would have recover'd them both at a tenth part of the Money, or rather the RAJAH *would not have dared to attempt the Surprizing of them."*

*   *   *   *   *   *   *

It would seem from this that the Court already had begun to regret the recall of Pitt. And in Mr. T. Wheeler's work we find another example in one of the Court's letters, in which, congratulating the Government of Fort St. George on their success in obtaining certain valuable concessions from the Nabob, they go on :

"This we take to be the effect of your good conduct and President PITT' interest with the great men ; and shall be glad you, our present President and Council, will follow in the same steps, which is now so much the easier because the path is ready trodden."

The political events, so to speak, of Pitt's long government were few ; in fact, the politics of Anglo-Indian history were only nascent in his time. But they were hardly so insignificant as might be deduced from Mill's History. That writer, to the best of my knowledge, never deigns even to name this notable person.

The most prominent circumstance in his government, apart from the internal history of the Companies, was the blockade of Madras by the Nawáb of the Carnatic, Dáúd Khán, threatened in 1701, and carried out more seriously in 1702. There is little reference to it in Pitt's letters : the only example that I have quoted is at p. lxxix. But it was met by the President with great tact and firmness. He organised defence with a bold face, whilst treating the Nawáb at once with resolution and with courtesy. And eventually Dáúd Khán, after all his threats, retired, contented with a payment of 25,000 *Rs.* between himself and his Dewán.[1] In the latter years of his government, too, and after the death of Aurangzeb, Pitt got into direct communication with his son and successor, and negotiated for a confirmation of the Company's privileges. Pitt's removal cut this short, and the *firmán* did not come till 1717.

---

[1] Mr. T. Wheeler (*Madras in the Olden Time*) is the only writer who has given any account of Dáúd Khán's blockade, or other details of Pitt's government. The following passage of his is perhaps too strongly expressed, but it is well-founded :

"The reader will perceive that the germs of that lofty pride, untiring energy, and stern consciousness of power which formed the great characteristics of two of England's greatest war ministers, are discernible in the proceedings of their more humble progenitor, who from the little Fort of St. George defied the threats of the grasping Nabob, and proved more than a match for the low cunning and courtly dissimulation of the Oriental" (i, 359-60).

That Pitt's reputation was great during his rule at Madras, and had spread not only over the coasts of India, but to England, may be gathered from the words of Sir Nicholas Waite, whom Pitt so scorned, but who speaks of him (p. cv) as "the great President", and from those of Peter Wentworth (p. cxx): "the great Pits is turn out." It was his general force of character, his fidelity to the cause of his employers (in spite of his master-fault of keenness in money-making), his decision in dealing with difficulties, that won his reputation. He was always ready; always, till that last burst which brought his recall, cool in action, however bitter in language; he always saw what to do, and did it. He maintained the cause of his masters, the Old Company, unflinchingly and triumphantly, when every wind seemed to be against them; he was indefatigable and successful in recovering their debts, and in winding up their affairs. The New Company, once his enemies, gladly put the winding up of their affairs also into his hand; whilst the United Company, largely composed of those whom he had defied, maintained him as their President. And though his growing impatience gave them a chance to strike at him which they could not forego, we see that they had no sooner done so than they repented.

Having reached this point in Pitt's history, when he is safely returned to England, and when questions regarding his great diamond are mooted, both at Madras and in Leadenhall Street, we now take up episodically the history of that famous stone, and the correspondence connected therewith.

THE PITT DIAMOND.

Some incidental allusions to this famous stone have occurred in the correspondence or consultations already quoted, but I have kept back most of the letters connected with its history, in order to present the narrative, so far as I can trace it, in something of a continuous form.

In the British Museum are preserved three thin folios of transcripts of invoices of merchandise shipped from Madras by Thomas Pitt, during his government there (Addl. MSS. Nos. 22, 854-56) .They extend from the latter part of 1698 to January 1708-9, after which probably (as may be gathered from his own words, *supra* p. cxiv) he gave up trade. But even for that period there is a large gap in the record, extending over several years. These invoices embrace goods to very considerable amounts, shipped chiefly to Europe, but also occasionally to Bengal, Pegu, China, etc., both on his own account and on commission from friends at home. These shipments consist of diamonds (and a few other stones), piece-goods, China-goods, opium, brass and tutenague,[1] cotton, chank-shells, beaver hats (to Pegu and Achin), and minor sundries, in amounts ranging roughly in the order here set down. Diamonds seem to have constituted one of the most usual means of remittance to Europe, and by far the largest part of Pitt's shipments on account of other parties consists of diamonds.

The first extract which leads up to the subject of the great diamond is the following from a letter addressed to Sir Stephen Evance, his most usual London agent and constant correspondent, and it seems to suggest that Sir Stephen had put him cn the search for a particular great stone.

Extract of a letter from PITT *to* Sir STEPHEN EVANCE, dated
" Oct. 18th, 1701".[2]

"I have alsoe heard that there are two or three large stones up in the Countrey which I beleive had been here, but that the troubles of the Countrey have prevented it, besides they ask soe excessive Dear for such Stones that 'tis Dangerous medling with 'em, but if that Stone comes hither shall as near as I can follow your advice and orders therein, and should I meet with it here is little money to be taken up, besides you have given your orders to Soe many in this matter that wee shall interfere one with another."

---

[1] *Tutenaga,* an Indo-Portuguese term applied to two metals, viz.: (1) the Chinese alloy, sometimes called " white copper"; (2) zinc.

[2] Addl. MSS. 22,844, No. 7.

In the next letter we have *the* historic stone appearing.

To Sir STEPHEN EVANCE, Knt., "FORT ST. GEORGE, Novr. 6th, 1701".[1]

" Sr: This accompanyes the modell of a Stone I have lately seene ; itt weighs *Mang.* 303[2]: and *car*[tts]: 426. It is of an excellent christaline water without any fowles, onely att one end in the flat part there is one or two little flaws which will come out in cutting, they lying on the surface of the Stone, the price they ask for it is prodigious being two hundred thousand *pag*[s]: thô I believe less then one (hundred thousand) would buy it. If it was design'd for a Single Stone, I believe it would not loose above ¼ part in cutting, and bee a larger Stone then any the MOGULL has, I take it. *Pro rata* as Stones goe I thinke 'tis inestimable. Since I saw itt I have bin perusing of TAVERNIER, where there is noe Stone Soe large as this will bee when cutt. I write this singly to you, and noe one else, and desire it may bee Kept private, and that you'l by the first of land and sea conveighance give mee your opinion thereon, for itt being of Soe great a vallue I believe here are few or none can buy it. I have put it (*i.e.*, the model) up Inclos'd in a little box and mark'd it S: E: which the Capt: will deliver you, my hearty service to you, I am

" Sr: Your most oblidged humble Servant

" T. PITT."

From Sir STEPHEN EVANCE *to* T. PITT.[3]

"London August 1st, 1702.

*   *   *   *   *   *   *

" I have received yours with a modell of a great diamond weighing 426 *Car.* therein you give an account of itts water and goodness, certainly there was never such a Stone heard of before, and as for Price, they asked 200,000 *Pas.*, though you beleive less than 100,000 would buy. Wee are now gott in a Warr, the FRENCH King has his hands and heart full, soe he cant buy such a Stone, There is noe Prince in EUROPE can buy itt, soe would advise You not to meddle in itt, for the Interest Yearly would come to a great sum of Money to be dead, as for the Diamonds received per *Dutchess*[4] cant Sell them for 8s. a Pagoda. Mr. ALVARES tells mee he received some diamonds from Mr. MEVERELL that he sold for 6s. a pagoda, soe there is noe encouragement to send for diamonds."

*   *   *   *   *   *   *

The stone was purchased by Pitt under the circumstances which we shall afterwards relate in his own words, and was sent home by him in charge of his son Robert on board the *Loyal Cooke*, which left Madras 9th Oct. 1702.

---

[1] Addl. MSS. 22,844, No. 90.

[2] The *Mangelin* is a small weight used for precious stones in South India, and varies in standard from 1¼ to 1¾ *carat*, or thereabouts.

[3] Addl. MSS. 22,852, No. 5.

[4] The invoice of goods by the *Dutchess* is not among those preserved in the volumes mentioned above.

To Mr. ALVARO DE FFONSECA, LONDON.[1]

"Jany. 27th, 1702-3.

*   *   *   *   *   *   *

"The Consignment I made Sr: STEPHEN EVANCE, Your Selfe and My Son I hope came Safe to your hands, and that 'twill answer in goodness to the full as I represented it, the Satisfaction I have of your abilities, as well as integrity in Such matters gives me great hopes 'twill answer my expectations, 'tis most Certain there is not the fellow of it in the world, there has been Some Smattering of it in the Countrey for which severall were sent for up to the King, who I hear of late are come off with Impunity but great Charge, the King of FFRANCE or SPAINE will in all probability be the likelyest Chapmen for it, unless our Parliament, upon good Success in some noble undertaking, will be Soe Generous as to buy it for the Crown of ENGLAND. I have left it to your discretion whether you'le make a Single or two Stones of it, but remember don't part with it without its full value, which must be very Considerable Computing it as those of an inferior magnitude are Sold."

To Sir ST. EVANCE.[2]

"ffeby. the 3d, 170¾.

*   *   *   *   *   *   *

"I hope my Concerne on the *Loyall Cooke*, will come Safe to your hand, and doubt not but you'le doe all you can to Contribute to the well disposall thereof, 'tis a very good Water, ffree from all foules and noe flaws but what will be worked out, and the Shape is not bad, and upon the best enquiry I can make 'tis Certainly the finest Jewell in the World, and worth an immense Sum, and I hope you'le never part with it but for its reall value, which it may be you'le not be able to get dureing the Warr, to which God send a happy and Speedy conclusion, when I doubt not but you'le have Chapmen enough for it, for Princes generally covet Such Jewells as cannot be parellel'd, and I am sure that cannot, for its excellency and magnitude, and 'tis my opinion 'tis best to keep it in one Stone, which I leave wholy to you and the rest consign'd to."

To Sir ST. EVANCE *and* Mr. ROBERT PITT.[3]

"febby. 10th, 170¾.

"I hope my Son will be Safe arriv'd and that that great Concern of mine will come safe to your hands, which I doubt not but you'le dispose of to my most advantage, or lett it lye bye till you are offer'd the full value thereof.

"'Tis my opinion to Continue it a Single Stone, which I am sure is not to be parrellel'd in the world, which must Certainly be Coveted by the richest of Princes when 'tis a peace, and by the Calculate I make when I am by my Selfe, Computeing it as large Stones have been Sold, and this in proportion to 'em, when 'tis Cutt it must be worth £1500 a *Carrat* if not more. I would never have it trusted out of your hands upon noe account whatever, and if you are in treaty with any fforreign Prince about it, I beleive my Son may be a proper Person to Send with the Modell or what directions you Shall think fitt, but take care he receives noe money on that account in a fforreign Countrey for fear they Strip him of it before he gets out of it . . . ."

---

[1] Addl. MSS. 22,847, No. 28.   [2] *Ibid.*, No. 33.   [3] *Ibid.*, No. 46.

To Mr. ROBERT PITT, *Merchant*, LONDON.[1]

"April 29th, 1703.

"Son ROBIN

*   *   *   *   *   *   *

"My last to you was per Ship *Phœnix* who sail'd hence the 13th ffebby: when I wrote you fully about all my Affairs, and hope in God by this time you are safely arriv'd in ENGLAND to look after the same, more particularly the grand Concern you carry'd with you."

And again to the same, Nov. 8th, 1703 :[2]

"Thô I abated something of the true value, could wish that the Crown would buy it, for the like will never be to be had againe in these parts."

To Capt. EDWARD HARRISON, Jany. 6th, 1703-4.

"I sent Sʳ: STE: the Modell of the Philosopher's Stone by the *Dutchess,* unto which he gives a very imperfect answer, and to my great amazement I have not a line from Mr. YALE."

From letter to Sir STEPHEN EVANCE, *dated* Jan. 7th, 1703-4.

"Upon veiw of the Modell of that great Stone you give little encouragement[3] which I hope long before this is safe with you, and let it be warre or what it will, pray never part with it but for its full value, and what will contribute most thereto will be the concealing of it.

*   *   *   *   *   *

"That great Stone by the *Dutchess*[4] was esteemed here very Cheap and good, and what flaws in it look'd as if they would come out in cutting, 'twas never yet known here that the Braminies greas'd a Stone to hide the foules, but wee all know they are Rogues enough and studdy nothing else but cheating."

To Sir STEPHEN EVANCE *and* Mr. ROBERT PITT.[5]

"FORT ST. GEORGE, Sept. 12th, 1704.

*   *   *   *   *   *   *

"'Twas Well come news to hear of the Safe arrivall of that concerne of mine, and observe the progress you have made in Cutting it, of which you should have wrote me fully in your joynt Letter, of which there is Smattering thereof in both your particular, 'tis very fortunate that it proves soe good, and 'tis my desire that it be made one Brillion which I would not have sold (unless it be for a trifle) less then fifteen hundred pound a *carrat,* tho by all Computations that I can make from Presidents of that nature, 'tis worth much more. 'Tis my whole dependance, and therefore it must be Sold to the best advantage, for which reason I have trusted it in the hands of a ffriend and a Sone, whose care I doubt not, but will likewise preserve it from Any accident of ffire or any other event, and I approve of your locking it up, and defer the Sale till after the Warr."

---

[1] Addl. MSS. No. 50.   [2] *Ibid.,* No. 58.

[3] See above ; letter from Sir St. Evance at p. cxxvi.

[4] See same letter.

[5] Addl. MSS. 22,848, No. 39.

To Sir Stephen Evance.[1]

Same date.

" . . . . 'Tis not a little unkind that Mr. Alvares refuses me his assistance in the matter, for which I wish I knew his reasons, for what trouble can accrew since you have enter'd it and paid the Customs, and I thanke you for the care you resolve to take of it, and I take notice what progress you have made in it and the prospect you have of its being most excellent, of which I assure you there is not the fellow in the world at present. Of this I have wrote fully in my letter to you and my Sone, which I desire you'le observe."

To the same and Robert Pitt *jointly.*

"Feby. 5th, 1704(-5).

" I againe confirme what I wrote about that great concerne and will not have it sold under fifteen hundred pounds a *Carrat*, or a trifle less. You write that the peices Saw'd off will yeild about 1500*l.* which I hope was a mistake, and that there was a Cypher wanting to make it thousands, for certainly the peices must be extraordinarily well spread, which makes it most valuable, and those that judge of it here by the modell make it very considerable. But of that I doubt not but you'le take care that he that cuts it do's not abuse me. Let it be Kept a Secret, and not any one person whatever to see it, unless it be to the advantage of the Sale of it. My Wife, Mr. Yale, and Capt. Harrison have given me hints of it, but I have wrote 'em there is noe such thing. Here has been and is at this time great inquiry after it, by orders from the King. The greatest man that had a hand in the Sale is dead, and another is sent up for him ; how he'll come off I dont know, therefore it as much imports me to have it a secret in England as here, for Reasons I shall give you when I see you."

Governor Pitt to Mr. Alvaro da Ffonseca (London).[2]

"Feby. 12th, 1704-5.

" . . . . In the mean time I doe most earnestly reiterate my former request to you for your care in that grand Concerne of mine, the good success of which Crowns all my labours, which have not been a little fateaguing insoemuch that a little ease and retirement is very desirable by me, therefore pray as a ffriend give your advice and assistance in that matter, and direct my Sone how he shall act in it. . . . ."

To Mr. Alvares da Ffonseca, *Merchant,* London.

"Sept: ye 13th: 1706.

"Dear S^r: and good ffriend

" I reed: yours of the 24th: of December and 8th of March per the *Tanker-ville,* in which I have a more particular account of that grand affair of mine then from my Sone or S^r: Stephen, and I assure you I think your favours to me in that matter are as inestimable as the thing it Selfe ; and I shall be gready of an oppertunity to acknowledge it otherwise then by words, for with the account you give I'me intirely Satisfyed, thô very much Chagrin'd last year, when I was writ, that the magnitude would not be above halfe as much as was formerly writ, without giveing any reasons for it. If we are soe lucky to put Charles on the throne of Spaine, I know nothing he can purchase to make his acknowledgments

---

[1] Addl. MSS. 22,848, No. 40.   [2] *Ibid.,* No. 147.

VOL. III.   *k*

to our Queen soe acceptable as that matter. I never will part with it without I meet with its value, and the least I can think of is fifteen hundred pounds a Carrat."

To JOHN DOLBEN, Esq., LONDON.

"Feby. the 5th: 170⅞."

*   *   *·   *   *   *   *

" Here is nothing as yet done in the New Companys Merchants busyness, those that were here I stopt their mouths, by employing 'em in a small Investment of the Old Companys, but those that are at METCHLEPATAM make a fearfull roaring against 'em, and I once intended to have concern'd you and Mr. AFFLECK and my Selfe in that affair, of which I have consider'd and resolv'd not to meddle with it more. I hear nothing of the Younger Brother,[1] for he that has it has often wrote that he was comeing hither but do's not yet appear. If I get that or anything else which I think advantagious for you, I will most certainly concerne you in it, for my dependence is very much upon your care of the Eldest, and would have lodg'd such a paper as you mention was I sure it would meet you at home. I am resolv'd not to part with it under the Sum formerly fixed on, and pray be so kind as not to let it be expos'd to view, more than what is absolutely necessary for the disposall of it.

*   *   *   *   *   *   *

" Did I not think it uncertain whether this will come to you, I should write you more than I doe, but I must not omitt one thing, which is that there are some that is come upon these last years Ships that have thrown a Slurr upon S.ᵣ: STE: Credit, such as was formerly when I came, in which I hope there is more malice then truth as was then, for God sake be carefull, for you know my all is at Stake in his hands, and if you dispose not of the Grand affair, I believe 'twill lye securest in an Iron Chest at the Bank, each of you a different Key, or if you think that not the securest place, pray agree upon some other amongst your Selves, and as I have any money come in let it be put into publick funds or mortgages, as desir'd in my Letter. . . ."

From a letter to the same.[2]

"Septr. 11th, 1707.

" I observe what you wrote to my Sone, who I perceive minds very little of my busyness, in which I wish he do's not neglect his own. He has wrote me about the grand affair, as alsoe Mr. ALVAREZ, Mr. COPE, and S.ᵣ: STE: in which I am fully Satisfy'd.

*   *   *   *   *   *   *

" With concern I read what you write of the Lieut: Generall. My Sone had noe Commission to impart my affairs to him[3] ; and for God sake prevent any misfortune that may attend me from anything that shall befall S.ᵣ: STE: of which

---

[1] This is doubtless a reference to another of the large stones spoken of in the first letter in this section that I have quoted ; *the* diamond already sent home being the " Eldest Brother".

[2] Addl. MSS. 22,850, No. 75.

[3] "The Lieutenant-General" was, perhaps, Lieut.-General William Stewart, who had married Robert Pitt's wife's mother, and was some years later (1711) appointed Commander-in-Chief during the absence of the Duke of Ormond (see Lodge and Archdale, *Peerage of Ireland*, 1789, iv, 91).

I gave you a hint in my last; and I am not a little Jealous too of my Sone, who has allready made too bold with me on severall occasions, therefore pray take care now that he do's not strip me. I am of your opinion of these two gentlemens charecters, and wish that My Sone may deserve a better. I wish it was bought for that small sum the Generall mentions, and for that use. I heard from Lisbon, that upon the Union with SCOTLAND passing our Parliament, 'twas intended to present the Queen with the Royall title of Empress. I am sure no thing is soe proper to accompany it, being the best and the biggest in the world. In this matter I rely wholely on your kindness and management, and I hope on your arrivall you tooke effectual care to Secure it from either of the Sharpers.

To Mr. ALVARO DA FFONSECA, *Merchant in* LONDON.[1]

"Sept: 12th: 1707."

*   *   *   *   *   *   *

"I shall say no more as to the great concerne but that I am entirely satisfy'd . . . . and I confirme what I formerly wrote my Attorney that I will not part with it under £1500: a Carrat, which I am sure is as cheap as Neck beef, and let any Potentate buy it, the next day 'tis worth a Million of pounds Sterling. I could wish it may be contriv'd Soe that it may be bought by the Crown of ENGLAND, for the honour of me and my posterity; and if wee have been successful this last Campaigne as before, I doubt not there will be mony enough to buy it, and the parliament have a heart great and gratefull enough to present it to her Majesty.[2] I am alsoe Satisfy'd as to the peices that are cutt off, and I hope when Mr. DOLBEN is arriv'd, Mr. COPE will hearken to reason as to the polishing of it. . . . In the midst of my trouble and concern that I was in for my great affair, I allways comforted my Selfe with the assurance that you would take care of it, and I agree with you intirely as to the Judgment of ABENDANA in the pieces cutt off, and I had the same thought when he represented it to me to be worth £16,000—without being assur'd the goodness in any Respect, 'tis like the valuation of that at 5000 which was not worth one.[3]

That scandalous stories as to the means by which the diamond had been acquired were afloat in India before Pitt left the Coast, we have already seen, and probably they had been long prevalent there, and had reached England before him. Hints of these we shall see in the extracts which I shall now give from various sources, before proceeding to transcribe Pitt's own solemn declaration of the history of his purchase.

---

[1] Addl. MSS. 22,850, No. 82.

[2] So also Lady Wentworth writes, Dec. 15, 1710 : "My dearest and best children, for all the great Scairsety of mony, yett hear will be a gloryous show one the Queens birth day, wonderful rich cloaths ar preparing for it ; thear was one that see Mr. PITS great dyomont that I writ you word of, and they say its as big as a great eg ; I would have the Sety of LONDON bye it and mak a present of it to put in the Queens Crown" (*Wentworth Papers*, pp. 164-5).

[3] Mr. Abendana was a diamond dealer at Madras, who is often mentioned in Pitt's letters.

This solemn declaration has been several times printed. Its first publication, so far as I can discover, occurred in the *Daily Post* (of London), No. 7540, of Nov. 3rd, 1743, with the following editorial preface, which I transcribe from the original newspaper in the British Museum :

" The Publick will no doubt expect some Reasons for inserting at this Time of Day, anything on so old an affair as the Manner in which the late Governor PITT purchas'd the large Diamond which he sold to the FRENCH King : All we can say is, that we have done it by Desire, and hope the following Piece will give Satisfaction to all those who may still suspect that Gentleman did not fairly come by the said Stone."

At the end we read :

" On the Back of this Declaration the following Words are written :—In case of the Death of me, THO: PITT, I direct that this Paper, seal'd as it is, be deliver'd to my son ROBERT PITT."

In the *Gentleman's Magazine*, vol. xlvi, 1776, occurs the following letter (p. 64) :

" Mr. URBAN,

" In the *Journal des Sçavans* for July, 1774, p. 553, is an extract from a letter of a French missionary,[1] with the following singular passage :

" —— That one of the principal diamonds of the crown of FRANCE, and which was purchased of an ENGLISHMAN, was one of the eyes of the god JAGRENAT, a famous idol, placed at a pagoda at CHANDERNAGOR, in BENGAL ; that this god JAGRENAT has since continued with only one eye ; and that the FRENCH have done all they could to blind him entirely, but have not succeeded because he is better guarded.

" This account differs, I think, from the common one of that diamond, which is, that it was brought from its native bed, concealed in a gash which a slave had made in his leg. In what condition was it when it first came into Mr. PITT's hands ? If rough and unpolished, I should not doubt of the supposed sacrilege; for I imagine, a diamond in its natural roughness would not have made a more brilliant figure in JAGRENAT's head than a piece of alum.

" If any of your correspondents will give some account of this remarkable gem, it will probably be an entertainment to several of your readers.
                                                                      " J. C."

Again, at p. 105 :

" Mr. URBAN,

" In your last Magazine, p. 64, a FRENCH missionary's account of the King of FRANCE's great diamond, introduces a very unexpected conjecture, viz., that ' it was a fitter ornament for the head of an INDIAN idol, while it had no more brilliancy than a piece of alum, than when cut and polished.'

" The writer of this remembers that opinion being rejected, on account of its

---

[1] The reference to the *Journal* is incorrect, for no such passage occurs at the place indicated, nor have I, after diligent search, been able to find the communication in question.

absurdity, soon after the diamond became the common subject of discourse in Queen ANNE'S reign.

" Perhaps the following account may be worth some notice.

" The stone was brought over rough by Governor PITT, and bought by the Duke of ORLEANS, Regent of FRANCE (in LOUIS XV's minority), for which reason it is called *The Regent*, and we sometimes have heard it mentioned by that name in the papers, as worn by the FRENCH king for a button to his hat, on extraordinary occasions.

" The following particulars are copied from a memorandum made before it was disposed of.

" Mr. PITT's great diamond, when raw, weighed . . 410 carats.
" —— when brilliant cut 135
" It was bid for by a private person . . . . . 80,000*l.*
" It cost 5000*l.* cutting in brilliant.
" The clips (chips) yielded . . . . . . 8000*l.*
" The diamond dust to cut it cost 1400*l.*

" It is about an inch and a quarter in diameter. Weighs about an ounce and the eighth part of an ounce.

                                        " W. G."

In the *Museum Britannicum* of John and Andrew van Rymsdyk, folio, 1778, which contains representations of the diamond and the models, of which we shall give an illustration, we find (p. 71) the following note :

" In showing the draught of the Model of PITT's Brilliant, and mentioning its history to many People, it became the common discourse of the Town. One Gentleman in particular, advertised for a true history of the said Diamond :

" To which we answer thus : Sir, it was THOMAS PITT Esqr. (of a Noble family, which were anciently of BLANDFORD in the County of DORSET) who in the Reign of Queen ANNE[1] was made Governor of FORT ST. GEORGE in the EAST INDIES, where he resided many Years, and there purchased the above Diamond, which he sold to the King of FRANCE for one hundred and thirty-five thousand pounds. The following true account of his purchasing the Diamond, and to vindicate the Governor's Character, was printed some years ago in the *Daily Post*, Nov. 3, 1743."

Here follows Pitt's Bergen narrative, given further on. At the end of it the writer of the note proceeds :

" Mr. SALMON, Author of the *Universal Traveller*, says (p. 166), vol. i, That he was upon the Spot at the Time of the Transaction, and is able to refute the Scandalous Stories raised on the Governor about it.[2]

---

[1] KING WILLIAM.

[2] The following is the passage from the book in question, where the diamond mines of GOLCONDA are spoken of :

" These Diamond Mines are walled round, and have a garrison for their Defence ; and these Stones may be purchased, either of the Merchants who reside near them, or a Man may hire a Piece of Ground and take his Chance. Sometimes they have a good Bargain . . . . and if they happen to meet with

"The above account agrees in every respect with that which I had from the Right Hon. Lord RIVERS's own Mouth. This Diamond was consigned by Governor PITT to Sir STEPHEN EVANCE of LONDON, Kt. It appears by an original Bill of Lading, that it was sent in the Ship *Bedford*, Captain JOHN HUDSON Commander, March 8th, 1701-2, and charged to the Captain at 6500 *Pagodas* only. The date of this bill of lading agrees with the Time, the Governor mentions, of his purchasing the Diamond in INDIA.[1]

"I have since been informed that the Workmanship of this Stone did cost 4000*l*. D. JEFFRIES will have it that it was sold for 135,000*l*., but 5000*l*. thereof was given and spent in negotiating the Sale of it."

The *European Magazine* of Sept. 1791 (vol. xx, pp. 245-6) prints, for the third time, Pitt's declaration about the purchase, from the communication of an anonymous correspondent, who writes :

"The following account of his purchasing the diamond was written by himself, and appeared in the Daily Papers of the time."

The last words are certainly erroneous. This communication also repeats Rymsdyk's mistaken statement about the shipment of the diamond by the *Bedford*.

I conceive the mistake to have arisen from a cursory inspection of those books of Pitt's invoices in the British Museum to which I have already referred. In those we see that Pitt did ship by the *Bedford*, Capt. Hudson, on the date named, one large diamond valued at 6,500

---

a Diamond of an extraordinary Size the MOGULL's agent will have the refusal of it ; though if a large Diamond happens to be carried out of the Mine without the officer's knowledge, nobody questions the Proprietor how he came by it ; he may sell it in any Fair or Market. The greatest market for Diamonds .   is in the MOGULL's Camp in the dry season. For all at that time . . . . all Tradesmen and Artificers forsake the Towns and follow him into the field. And it was a rich Black Merchant in the MOGULL's Camp that sold the great Diamond to Mr. PITT about the Year 1700, which he afterwards sold to the FRENCH King for about 100,000*l*., but I could never learn the exact sum. And this was so far from being a great Bargain, that Mr. PITT declared he lost Money by it : He gave 24,000*l*. for that Diamond, and considering he was Governor of FORT ST. GEORGE for ten years, he might have made more money by trading with that Sum, than he did by the Diamond. I mention this Passage because I was upon the Spot and thoroughly acquainted with the Transaction in INDIA, and am able to refute the scandalous Stories, that have been raised of the Means whereby the Governor acquired this Jewel. It lay some Months at FORT ST. GEORGE, in the hands of the Merchant's Agent that sold it, in order to find a Chapman for it, and Governor PITT was the best Bidder ; no Manner of Compulsion was used to obtain it."—*The Universal Traveller*, by Mr. SALMON, i, 164-5. LONDON, 1752.

[1] This statement about the despatch of *the* great diamond by the *Bedford* is mistaken. As may be seen above (p. lxxviii, *note*), the stone came home with Robert Pitt on the *Loyal Cooke*.

pagodas. But the weight of this diamond is also stated in the invoice at 41½ *mangelins*, or 58½ *carats*, which is little more than one-eighth of the weight in the rough of the Pitt diamond.

I see by Pitt's letters some time afterwards that he repeatedly expresses his apprehensions that the *Bedford* had been lost on this voyage; fears eventually confirmed.[1]

The writer in the *European Magazine* proceeds :

"It was reckoned the largest jewel in Europe, and weighed 127 *carats*. The cuttings amounted to 8 or 10,000*l*. . . It appears that the acquisition of this diamond occasioned many reflections injurious to the honour of Governor PITT, and Mr. POPE has been thought to have had the insinuation then floating in the world, in his mind when he wrote the following lines" (in his episode of the history of " Sir Balaam", *Moral Essays*, Ep. iii) :

> "Asleep and naked as an INDIAN lay
> An honest factor stole a gem away :
> He pledged it to the Knight, the Knight had wit,
> So kept the diamond, and the rogue was bit."

There could have been little doubt indeed that the stories floating about the world as to Pitt's having fraudulently acquired the diamond were in Pope's mind, however vaguely, when he penned these lines. And we now learn from Mr. Courthope's notes that in the Chauncy MS., which is (as we gather) in the poet's own handwriting, the last line runs

> "So robbed the robber and was rich as P——".

This allusion has been developed, in accordance with the fashion of a certain class of readers, into the suggestion that the whole story of *Sir Balaam* is founded upon the character and history of Pitt, the absurdity of which idea is manifest on the most cursory perusal of Pope's lines.[2]

---

[1] He writes to Sir W. Langhorne, September 18th, 1705 : "The loss of the *Bedford* is never to be forgotten. God send I may never heare the like."

[2] A notable example of such treatment may be seen in *Notes and Queries*, Ser. IV, vol. iv, pp. 235-6. A correspondent, "BEZONIAN", asks "whether the Sir BALAAM who lived near the Monument, was impeached by the House, harangued by Coningsby, deserted by the Court, and finally hanged, has been ever supposed to be a portrait ; and if so, of whom ?"

The reply is given in a long editorial note, too long for me to extract, especially as it would be necessary to accompany it by the complete episode from Pope (62 lines). In this the writer declares himself decidedly as "disposed to adopt the opinion in the matter which very generally prevailed in the last century, and to consider the vituperative passages as aimed primarily and specially at Governor THOMAS PITT of 'Diamond' notoriety", etc.

Here is an example of the kind of accuracy and knowledge displayed :

"In the main the particulars accord very well with what is known of the

The Bergen declaration was printed for the fourth time in the *Gentleman's Magazine* for 1825 (vol. xcv, pp. 105 *seqq*.), to which it was communicated by the Revd. W. Meyrick, a descendant of the Governor through the Cholmondeleys. This gentleman must have been under the impression that the document had never before been published, for his introductory letter runs as follows:—

"I have much pleasure in communicating to you Governor PITT'S own account of his purchase of the celebrated Diamond, both from the personal interest I feel in vindicating his character, and as I shall be glad to see his candid and plain statement of the fact recorded in your valuable Magazine."

Even this fourth publication seems to have been in vain as regards later compilers. For we read the following gossip in STREETER'S *Precious Stones and Gems*, LONDON, 1877, p. 118:

"It was said PITT had obtained the Stone in GOLCONDA in the year 1702. It came from the mines of PARKAL, 45 leagues South of GOLCONDA. It was found by a slave, who in order to hide it, wounded himself in the thigh, and hid the stone beneath the bandage. He at length acknowledged this to a sailor, and promised him the stone, if only he would secure him his freedom. The sailor enticed the slave on board, took from him his Diamond, and then threw the slave into the Sea. The murderer sold the Diamond to PITT for £1000, spent the money quickly in excesses of all kinds, and from a murderer became a suicide.

"Another story is that PITT bought the stone in 1701 of the far famed JAMCHUND, the greatest Diamond merchant in INDIA, for £12,500. A commission, consisting of all the most experienced French jewellers, valued it at £480,000," etc.

The story of the slave with a wounded thigh has been referred to already, and must be told in some work of the earlier half of last century, but I have not been able to find it. Nor do I know where, in his second version, Mr. Streeter, or his historian, got hold of the name Jamchund (borrowed and corrupted from Pitt's declaration), or why he has halved the price paid for the diamond in that version. The latter circumstance must have originated in some misvaluation of the pagoda, for the same sum is named in the *Grand Dictionnaire Universel* of M. Pierre Larousse (vol. xiii, p. 846, Paris, 1875). After telling us that the diamond " was found at MALACCA in the Kingdom of GOL-

---

sudden elevation and prosperous career of the Governor of FORT ST. GEORGE, in the East. According to GILBERT, 'THOMAS PITT, although remotely descended from a good family, is said to have been the son of a person concerned in trade at Brentford' (*Parochial Hist. of Cornwall*, p. 68). He was a man therefore of somewhat obscure origin." And so forth.

Beyond the love of riches, which was too conspicuous in Pitt, and the dragging in of the diamond-scandal in the crudest of shapes, there is nothing in the character or history of Sir Balaam to suggest the Governor.

CONDA" (which seems rather mixed geography) this work proceeds to say :

"The *Régent* (*i.e.*, the diamond) was the cause of calumnious reports affecting THOMAS PITT. It was alleged that he had acquired it in a dishonourable way. Some asserted that he had caused it to be violently extracted from the leg of a slave, who, having found it in the mine, had wounded himself in order to hide it." (The article then refers to a letter in the *J. des Sçavans* for July 1774, a reference which we have already seen to be erroneous, and which was therefore borrowed directly or indirectly from the *Gentleman's Magazine* (vide *supra*, p. cxxxii) and proceeds) :

"These statements were quite unfounded. Pitt, as he himself relates in a letter which has been published, had bought the precious stone from a merchant for the sum of £12,500 (312,500 *francs*)," etc.

I now proceed to transcribe Pitt's own declaration, so often referred to.

At what place called BERGEN it was written, and how Pitt came to be there, remained quite without explanation till the compilation of these sheets (see above, p. cxxi).

"Since my coming into this melancholy place of BERGEN, I have been often thinking of the most unparalleled villainy of WILLIAM FRASER,[1] THOMAS FREDERICK, and SURAPA,[2] a black merchant, who brought a paper before Governor ADDISON in Council, insinuating that I had unfairly got possession of a large Diamond, which tended so much to the prejudice of my reputation and ruin of my estate, that I thought it necessary to keep by me the true relation how I purchased it in all respects, that so, in case of sudden mortality, my children and friends may be apprised of the whole matter, and so enabled thereby to put to silence, and confound those, and all other villains in their base attempts against either. Not having got my books by me at present, I cannot be positive as to the time, but for the manner of purchasing it I do here declare and assert, under my hand, in the presence of GOD ALMIGHTY, as I hope for salvation through the merits and intercession of our Saviour JESUS CHRIST, that this is the truth, and if it be not, let GOD deny it to me to my children for ever, which I would be so far from saying, much less leave it under my hand, that I would not be guilty of the least untruth in the relation of it for the riches and honour of the whole world. "About two or three years after my arrival at MADRAS, which was in July 1698, I heard there were large Diamonds in the country to be sold, which I encouraged to be brought down, promising to be their chapman, if they would be reasonable therein ; upon which JAURCHUND, one of the most eminent diamond merchants in those parts, came down about December 1701, and brought with

---

[1] Of WILLIAM FRASER, one of Pitt's colleagues in the Council of Fort St. George, we have heard repeatedly above.

[2] In all the repetitions printed *Smapa*, which I have ventured to correct as above. SURAPA was a well-known merchant, and an ally of Fraser's. See II, cclii, cclxxxii; *supra*, cx, cxi.

him a large rough stone, about 305 mangelins,[1] and some small ones, which myself and others bought; but he asking a very extravagant price for the great one, I did not think of meddling with it when he left me for some days, and then came and took it away again; and did so several times, not insisting upon less than 200,000 pagodas; and, as I best remember, I did not bid him above 30,000, and had little thoughts of buying it for that. I considered there were many and great risques to be run, not only in cutting it, but also whether it would prove pale or clear, or the water good; besides I thought it too great an amount to be adventured home in one bottom. But JAURCHUND resolved to return speedily to his own country; so that (as) I best remember it was in February following he came again to me (with VINCATEE CHITTEE, who was always with him) when I discoursed with him about it, and pressed me to know, whether I resolved to buy it, when he came down to 100,000 pagodas and something under before we parted, when wee agreed upon a day to meet and make a final end thereof one way or other, which I believe was the latter end of the foresaid month, or the beginning of March; when we accordingly met in the Consultation Room, where after a great deal of talk I brought him down to 55,000 *pagodas*, and advanced to 45,000, resolving to give no more, and he likewise resolving not to abate, I delivered him up the stone, and wee took a friendly leave of one another. Mr. BENYON was then writing in my closet, with whom I discoursed on what had passed, and told him now I was clear of it: when about an hour after, my servant brought me word that JAURCHUND and VINCATEE CHITTEE were at the door, who being called in, they used a great many expressions in praise of the stone, and told me he had rather I should buy it than anybody, and to give an instance thereof, offered it for 50,000; so believing it must be a pennyworth, if it proved good, I offer'd to part the 5000 pagodas that was then between us, which he would not hearken to, and was going out of the room again, when he turned back and told me that I should have it for 49,000, but I still adhered to what I had before offered him, when presently he came to 48,000, and made a solemn vow he would not part with it a pagoda under, when I went again into the closet to Mr. BENYON, and told him what had passed, saying that if it was worth 47,500, it was worth 48,000; so I closed with him for that sum, when he deliver'd me the stone, for which I paid very honourably, as by my books appear. And thereby farther call GOD to witness, that I never used the least threatening word at any of our meetings to induce him to sell it to me; and GOD himself knows it was never so much as in my thoughts so to do, Since which I have had frequent and considerable dealings with this man, and trusted him with several sums of mony, and balanced several accounts with him, and left upwards of 2000 pagodas in his hands at my coming away. So had I used the least indirect means to have got it from him, would not he have made himself satisfaction when he has had mony so often in his hands? Or would I have trusted him afterwards, as I did, preferable to all other diamond merchants? As this is the truth, so I hope for GOD's blessing upon this and all my other affairs in this world, and eternal happiness hereafter. Written and signed by me, in BERGEN, July 29th 1710: THOMAS PITT."

The diamond remained in Pitt's possession till 1717, when it was sold to the Regent Duke of Orleans, as a jewel of the French Crown. The following particulars regarding this transaction are noted in a memo. in

---

[1] Always in the copies *mangelius*.

the handwriting of Philip, second Earl Stanhope, Pitt's grandson,[1] and which may, I presume, be regarded as the most authentic account of the transaction :

"Diamond sold in 1717 for 2,000,000 *livres*.[2] Before it was sent over to FRANCE £40,000 (sterling) was deposited in ENGLAND, to be taken in part payment of the diamond. When carried to FRANCE, should be agreed to be bought, but otherwise £5000 of the deposit money was to be allowed to my Grandfather for his expense and risk.

"It was cut by HARRIS, and not by VAN HUFLIN. The expense of cutting was £6000. The chips were valued at £10,000, though not all sold. It was carried over to Calais by my Grandfather himself, accompanied by his two sons, Lord LONDONDERRY and Mr. JOHN PITT, and by his son-in-law Mr. CHOL-MONDELEY, who were there met by a Jeweller of the FRENCH Kings appointed to inspect and receive the Diamond, and to deliver in return some (I think three) boxes of Jewels belonging to the Crown of FRANCE, as a security for the payment of the overplus of the purchase money above £40,000 before deposited, which payment was agreed to be made at three several times fixed upon by the Parties concerned.

"The Diamond after it was cut weighed 128 *Carats*.

"My Grandfather's letter, dated at BERGEN, July 29th, 1710, about his purchasing the diamond in the EAST INDIES, was copied from the Original after his death at SWALLOWFIELD by Mr. CHOLMONDELEY'S Chaplain, and the Original was sent to Mr. ROBERT PITT my Grandfather's eldest Son."

"The 'overplus of the purchase money' was never paid," adds Lady Stanhope, "and when it was claimed from the French Government by the children of Governor PITT, the debt was fully admitted, but it was pronounced impossible to enter into the past transactions of the Regent."

This being so, the price really received by Pitt must have depended on the value of the three boxes of jewels pledged as security, respecting which there seems to be no evidence forthcoming.

The following anecdote regarding the transfer of the stone is given by the editor of the *European Magazine*, after the letter of W. G., quoted *supra*, p. cxxxii :

"Gov. PITT having engaged to deliver his diamond at CALAIS, determined to convey it thither in person, and in his way, dining at the CROWN Inn at CANTERBURY, where his son, Lord LONDONDERRY, was then quartered with his regiment of dragoons, he called up the landlord, Mr. LACY, a man of address, who had been consul at LISBON, and told him that when he travelled he ⹁ ways carried his own wine, not being able to meet with such on the road, and desired him to taste it and give his opinion. LACY did so, and gave it due commendation, wishing politely that he could have treated his guest with as good. Upon this Mr. PITT made him repeat his draught, and at length was so pleased with his frankness as to tell him that he liked him much, and wished it was in his

---

[1] For this memo., hitherto (I believe) unpublished, I am indebted to the favour of the present Countess Stanhope, communicated through my kind friend Mr. George Scharf, C.B.

[2] The value of the *livre* at that date may be taken at 1s. 4d. sterling.

power to serve him. To this the landlord innocently replied that he (PITT) had a pebble in his possession, which might indeed do him the utmost service. At this the Governor, thinking the secret of his having it with him was betrayed and known, flew into a violent range, abusing poor LACY in the grossest terms (so that he ran frightened out of the room) and saying he should be waylaid, murdered, &c. In vain did his son and the officers endeavour to pacify him, telling him that if he himself did not make the discovery, no one would know it. He insisted on having a guard mounted directly: Lord LONDONDERRY told him there was one already, with the standard. He then would have a guard to DOVER; and at length, as a compromise, accepted of the escort of the officers and their servants, giving them a second dinner there. Two of them he took with him to CALAIS (one of whom gave the above account); and, after getting rid of the incumbrance of his *pebble, en gaieté du cœur,* he franked his companions to PARIS and back again."

There is a curious passage in the *Memoirs of St. Simon* which connects with the purchase of the diamond both that famous personage, and another, perhaps still more famous, our own countryman, John Law. I give it at length in translation.[1] The passage begins by alleging that a person employed at the Great Mogul's diamond-mines (whether European or native is not specified) had succeeded in secreting a stone of prodigious size, and in escaping the usual processes of examination, and all suspicion :

"To complete his good fortune he arrived in EUROPE with his diamond, and had it exhibited to several princes, but it was beyond the means of any of them, and at last he carried it to ENGLAND, where the King admired it, but could not make up his mind to be the purchaser. A crystal model of the stone was made in ENGLAND, and (eventually) the man, the diamond, and the model, which was a perfect fac-simile, were despatched to LAW, who proposed to the Regent to buy it for the King.

"LAW, who on many occasions had large ideas, came in search of me in a state of excitement, bringing the model to show me. I thought, like him, that it was not becoming the greatness of the King of FRANCE to refuse, on account of its price, a gem like this, unique in all the world and past valuation, and that the more in number the potentates were who had been debarred from thinking of it the less we should be disposed to let such an acquisition slip us. LAW, delighted to find I had such ideas, begged me to speak to the Duke of Orleans on the subject. The state of the finances constituted an obstacle on which the Regent dwelt with insistence. He feared the blame that would attach to him for making so considerable a purchase at a time when there was so much effort required to meet the most pressing demands, and when so many people were of necessity abandoned to privation. I said these sentiments did him credit; but at the same time that when the greatest King in EUROPE was in question, we ought not to act as in the case of a private individual. In such an one it would doubtless be highly censurable were he to throw away 100,000 *francs* to treat himself to a fine diamond, when his debts were heavy, and he was unable to meet them. But now the honour of the Crown had to be thought of, and this one chance of acquiring a diamond of priceless value, one which eclipsed all existing in EUROPE,

---

[1] Edn. of Ste. Beuve, Hachette, 1857; tome xiv, pp. 416 *seqq.*

should not be allowed to escape.   It would be a perpetual glory for his regency, and, whatever might be our financial straits, the parsimony of such a refusal would not do much to help them, whilst the additional charge involved in the purchase would make little perceptible difference.   In short I did not leave the Duke of ORLEANS till I had obtained his assent to the diamond's being bought.

"LAW, before speaking to me, had represented in such strong terms to the dealer the impossibility of effecting a sale of the diamond at the price demanded, as well as the pity it would be to cut it up, and the loss which he would suffer by such a proceeding, that he brought him down at last to 2,000,000, including the chips which would come off in cutting.[1] The bargain was struck on these terms, and interest was to be paid on the two millions until the principal should be made good, and meanwhile two millions worth of jewels were to be pledged to him until the whole payment of two millions was completed.

"The Duke of ORLEANS was agreeably disappointed by the expression of public applause bestowed on such a splendid and unique acquisition. The diamond got the name of the *Regent*. It is of the size of a *Reine Claude* plumb, nearly circular in form, and of a depth proportioned to its magnitude. It is perfectly colourless and exempt from every kind of speck, shade, or flaw, of an admirable water, and weighs more than 500 grains. I take great credit to myself for having counselled the Regent to make such a memorable purchase."

It is curious that the name of Pitt never once occurs in this passage ; whilst it certainly contains some inaccuracies besides those as to the original acquisition of the diamond. The allusion to the chips implies that it was uncut, or imperfectly cut, when offered for sale, which we know to be contrary to the fact. Probably these forgetfulnesses are explained by the circumstance mentioned by M. Bapst (whose article in the *Revue des Deux Mondes* has indicated to me the passage in *St. Simon*) that the narrative was not written at the time, but nearly thirty years afterwards.

The first prominent place occupied by the *Regent*, as the diamond was now called, was in the circlet of the crown made by Ronde[2] for the coronation of Louis XV in 1722.[3] Beside the *Regent* were others of the

---

[1] LAW . . . avoit tant representé au marchand l'impossibilité de vendre son diamant au prix qu'il l'avoit espéré . . . . qu'il le fît venir en fin à deux millions avec les rognures en outre qui sortiroient necessairement de la taille."
The *Grand Dict. de Larousse* (xiii, p. 846, see below) calls the price 3,375,000 *francs*. But this, I fancy, has been due to a reconversion of £135,000, the price generally stated in English books as that for which Pitt sold the stone, at the present par of 25 *fr.*

[2] Laurent Ronde, from 1689 jeweller to the King, was succeeded by his son Claude Dominique, who made a famous crown for the coronation of Lewis XV.

[3] Most of the particulars of the succeeding history are derived from M. Germain Bapst's article in the *Revue des Deux Mondes*, 15 Février 1886, corrected and supplemented by additional information from documents since discovered by that gentleman, which he has communicated with generous courtesy to me.

diamonds known as the *Mazarins,* including the *Mirror of Portugal;* whilst the middle point of the fleur-de-lis, which formed the apex of the crown, was the famous *Sancy.*[1]

In 1791, by votes of the 26th and 27th May and the 22nd June, the National Assembly decreed that a complete inventory of all the jewels of the Crown then existing should be drawn up for publication, in presence of commissioners and experts named for the duty. This report consists of not less than 300 pages, of which 100 are devoted to the diamonds.[2] At the head of these figures the *Pitt,* with this description:

"Un superbe diamant brillant, blanc, appelé le *régent,* forme carrée, les coins arrondis, ayant une petite glace dans les filets et une autre à un coin dans le dessous, pesant 136 *carats* $\frac{13}{16}$ (environ 29 gr. .617), estimé 12 millions de livres."

The inventory was drawn up in August 1792, whilst the treasure was deposited at the *Garde-Meuble,* where the jewels were shown on Mondays to the public.

The Legislative Assembly ordered the sale of the diamonds, but meantime the bulk of them, to an estimated value of a million sterling, including the *Regent* and the *Sancy,* disappeared.

The history, which follows, of this audacious burglary, is condensed from the communications of M. Bapst:

Paris was in the utter demoralisation and anarchy which followed the September massacres; and lay open to any violent enterprise. The municipality had set an example of pillage; and though many real criminals had been murdered in the prisons, many roamed the city without restraint, and the police was reduced to nullity. Meanwhile practised thieves had made good use of the Monday exhibitions to reconnoitre the interior of the Garde-Meuble.

Under these circumstances, during six days in succession, beginning from the 11th September, a band composed (at least on the last of those days) of some 30 or 40 individuals, made their way every evening into the halls of the first floor of the Garde-Meuble, by help of the rusticated joints of the masonry and the ropes of the lantern at the corner of the Rue St. FLORENTIN. After breaking open a window—whilst leaving intact and securing from inside the sealed doors of the

---

[1] The *Sancy* diamond belonged to Nicholas Harlay de Sancy, Colonel-General of the Swiss, and Supt. of Finances, who raised an army of Swiss for the service of Henri III in 1589. It is not known where he got it. In 1604 he sold it to our James I, and during the Civil War Queen Henrietta Maria carried it to France and pledged it, with another famous diamond called the *Mirror of Portugal,* to the Duke of Epernon for 460,000 *livres.* In 1657 Mazarin paid off the Duke, and with the Queen's consent took possession of the diamonds. He bequeathed them with other fine stones to Lewis XIV.

[2] These particulars as to the report of 1791 are derived from *Larousse, Grand Dict.,* tome vi, p. 718. I have not seen the report itself. Mr. Franks of the B. M. possesses the copy which was Robespierre's, and which bears marks from his hand.

halls—they forced the presses one after another, and gradually made off with nearly the whole of the treasure. The police were quite unconscious of the robbery until it was accomplished.

During the night of 16th-17th September[1] certain men of the National Guard thought they saw a movement of the street-lantern attached to the colonnade, and on coming near saw a man clinging to the rope, and called out that unless he came down at once they would shoot. He made haste to come down, and they took him to their post.

Another man sliding down in a fright fell on the pavement, and came likewise into the hands of the National Guard. These two thieves had diamonds in their pockets, besides carrying other portable valuables, such as a child's coral set with diamonds, which had been a gift of the Empress Catharine, and pieces of jewellery sent to Lewis XVI by Tippoo Sultan in 1790. Thus the captors became aware of the robbery, which had in fact been going on without disturbance since the 11th. Next day ROLAND, then Minister of the Interior, related from the tribune of the Assembly what had occurred, and declared that out of 25(30) millions worth of valuables scarcely half a million remained.

Whilst the operation was going on, no regular patrol had been made; the police in their rounds had discovered nothing; and yet the thieves had lights in the rooms of the *Garde-Meuble;* they must have taken supplies of food, and passed successive nights there. For when an entrance was eventually made after them, fragments of victuals, empty bottles, and candle-ends were found lying about, as well as burglars' tools, and diamonds!

Nothing could illustrate the demoralization of Paris at that time more thoroughly than the manner in which the news of this burglary was received by the various parties in antagonism, unless it was the way in which the trial of the captured criminals concerned was conducted.

Madame ROLAND roundly ascribes the robbery to DANTON and his secretary FABRE D'EGLANTINE. Her husband took, or professed, the same view, and declared that his repeated demand for a proper guard over the valuables had always been treated with neglect. FABRE D'EGLANTINE on the other hand accused ROLAND of the crime; and MARAT, in the *Ami du Peuple*, ascribed it to "the aristocrats", who had hired a gang of brigands to pillage the *Garde-Meuble*, in order to discredit the Municipality and the Committee of Public Security. LULLIER, the Public Prosecutor, in a violent and atrocious harangue, such as was the fashion of the day, denounced *une femme orgueilleuse, lascive et cruelle*, to wit poor MARIE ANTOINETTE, as the author of the whole affair. One popular story ran that it was an act of the existing government in order to obtain means for purchasing the retreat of the DUKE OF BRUNSWICK. And this has found an echo in the *Memorial of St. Helena*.[2]

The two thieves taken on the night of 16th-17th September were condemned but respited; and it is believed they died in prison. At least three other persons were then condemned and executed. But the crime with which all were

---

[1] "Les tapisseries qui tendaient les murs, et les armures de nos rois de France, éclairées par des chandelles, devaient former un cadre saisissant à cette orgie de brigands, qui fêtaient ainsi la réussite du plus beau coup que les temps modernes devaient enrégistrer." (*Narrative by M. Bapst.*)

[2] I take this from M. Bapst. I cannot find the passage.

charged, and for which the last were executed, was *un complot à main armée, ayant pour but de renverser le gouvernement nouvellement constitué!* And the President (PEPIN) tried hard to make the accused admit that they had entertained relations with princes or other great personages attached to the late Court, who had set them upon this robbery. One of the executed was an unhappy Jew against whom nothing was proved but his having sold to another Jew *un certain nombre de bijoux dont la provenance n'a pu être justifiée!* He also was put to death under the article of the penal code directed against *conspirations ou complots tendant à troubler l'Etat par une guerre civile!*

Others, and leaders of the enterprise, who had succeeded in obtaining an appeal to the Court of Beauvais on the inapplicability of the article to their crime, whilst they admitted the burglary, obtained either release or commutation to imprisonment.

A certain number of diamonds also were presently recovered, but the most important—the *Regent* and the *Sancy*—escaped the earlier endeavours to trace them. A man of the name of COTTET had stolen the *Sancy;* he passed it on to a comrade who made off. As for the *Regent,* it was not found till twelve months later, and then in a *cabaret* of the Faubourg ST. GERMAIN. Other diamonds were recovered in the following years, and were carried to the credit of the *Caisse de l'Extraordinaire.*

On the 20th Frimaire, An. II (*i.e.,* 10th Decr. 1793), VOULLAND, in the name of the Committee of Public Security, appeared before the Convention and reported the recovery of the *Regent* in these words :

" Your Committee of Public Security continues its search for the authors and accomplices of the robbers of the Garde-Meuble ; and yesterday discovered the most valuable of the stolen property ; viz., the diamond know as the *Pitt* or *Regent,* which in the last inventory of 1791 was valued at 12 millions. To hide it they had made a hole of an inch and a half diameter in the timberwork of a garret. Both the thief and the receiver have been taken ; and the diamond, which has been brought to the Committee of Public Security, will serve as a *pièce de conviction* in bringing them to justice. I move, in the name of the Committee, to decree that the diamond be carried to the General Treasury, and that the Commissioners of that establishment be directed to come and receive it during our sitting."

The *Procès Verbal* proceeds :

" The National Convention after having heard the Report of its Committee of Public Security decrees that two Commissioners of the National Treasury shall come during the present sitting to the presence of the Convention, to receive and deposit in the National Treasury the diamond known as the *Regent,* discovered through the inquiries of the Committee of Public Security, and which shall be available at need as a *pièce de conviction* during the proceedings against the persons charged with the theft or the receipt of the property at the Garde-Meuble."

Another decree of the same date directed that two members of the Committee of P.S. should proceed to the National Treasury and deposit there, in a box with three locks, the diamond called the *Regent*. A *Procès Verbal* should be recorded, and one of the three keys should be placed among the National Archives.

Three months later (1st Germinal, *i.e.,* 21st March 1794), among a number of stones seized in the possession of one TAVENEL and his wife were recovered the *Sancy* and another important diamond known as *de la Maison de* GUISE.

In 1796 the *Regent* was pledged to German bankers, through the mediation of a cavalry officer,—Adjutant-General DE PARSEVAL,—as security for the cost of horse-furniture, which had been advanced by TRESKOW. In 1797, TRESKOW having been paid off, DE PARSEVAL recovered the *Regent* and brought it back to Paris. But in 1798 the diamond was again pawned, through the same officer, for another supply of horse-furniture needed for the Army of Italy, this time in the hands of VANDENBERG, a banker of AMSTERDAM. The First Consul BONAPARTE released it in 1802.

These details, including the *Procès Verbal* of VOULLAND, have been hitherto entirely unpublished.

M. FAYE, ex-minister of Public Instruction and Member of the Institute, has told M. BAPST that he often heard his father relate how VANDENBERG the Banker, when he had the *Regent* in his possession, put it in a glass case that all the world might admire it ; and a considerable crowd came to his office to do so. His friends remonstrated with him on the danger of exposing before people, some of whom might be capable of evil designs, an article at once so valuable and so easily carried off. But the Banker answered with a twinkle in his eye : " The *Regent* that is in the glass case is a worthless sham ; the real Regent is in my wife's stays."

At the coronation of Napoleon in 1804 the Crown jewels once more appeared in public ; the *Regent* being set in the pommel of the Emperor's sword.[1]

In 1814 the jewels were carried off to Blois by Marie Louise, but her father the Emperor Francis claimed them from her, and sent them to Louis XVIII, who on the night of March 20th, 1815, took them on his flight to Ghent, and brought them back at the second Restoration.

On the accession of Charles X all the stones were reset for his coronation, and thenceforward remained unused till 1854, never having been worn by Louis Philippe or his Queen Marie Amélie. Between 1854 and 1870 they were several times remounted, and in August 1870

---

[1] " Napoleon had it placed between the teeth of a crocodile, forming the handle of his sword, unaware perhaps how much this gem had contributed towards raising up the most formidable opponent to his ambition and ultimate aggrandisement". (Davies Gilbert, *Parochial Hist. of Cornwall*, under BOCONNOC, vol. i, p. 69.)

Some curious misconception gives rise to a statement by the late Mr. E. B, Eastwick, that " among the rings" (in the Shah's Jewel-House at Teheran) " is one in which is set the famous Pitt diamond, sent by George IV to Fath Ali Shah." (*Journal of a Diplomate*, II, 119.) The diamond alluded to is, from what Mr. Eastwick adds, evidently that which was taken to the Shah by Sir Harford Jones Brydges on his mission of 1807-11. It had nothing whatever to do with *Pitt*, though (oddly enough) it had been bought by a governor of *Bombay* (Hornby), and for almost exactly the price that Pitt paid for his great stone— £21,000. See *Brydges' Account of his Mission*, 1834, I, pp. 13 *seqq.*, 144, 172, 186.

they were put up in a sealed box, and deposited with M. Rouland, Governor of the Bank of France. In 1875 they were verified by an extra-parliamentary commission, which declared the record to have been kept with perfect regularity.

In October 1886 the Chamber resolved that such of the Crown jewels as had no artistic value should be sold.[1] They were then valued at twenty-one millions of *francs*, but out of this the *Regent* was still reckoned at twelve millions. The diamonds which have been sold, in consequence of the resolution of the Chamber, are stated to have realised £289,000. There seems to be no present intention of selling the *Regent*,[2] which, in spite of two small flaws or internal cracks, commencing from the *filetis*,[3] remains the finest diamond in the world.[4] The Crown diamonds which have not been sold have been distributed between the Louvre Museum, the School of Mines, and the Natural History Institution. It is intended that eventually a quadrangular receptacle of thick glass shall be placed in the Louvre, in which the Diamond which has occupied so many of our pages, the Watch of the Dey of Algiers,

---

[1] See *Times,* Oct. 27th, 1886.

[2] There is hardly a market now for stones of approximate calibre. The *Sancy,* in the inventory of 1792, was priced at 1,000,000 *livres,* and that value was regarded as a minimum. In 1867 it was offered for sale at an upset price of 700,000 *fr.*, and was shown at the Exhibition in the Champ-de-Mars. All the foreign sovereigns came to look at it, but there were no offers, and the *Sancy* is still in the market. (*Article of M. Germain Bapst.*)

The history of the *Sancy,* since the robbery of 1792, seems to be somewhat obscure. After its recovery by the national depository, it was (as M. Bapst states) apparently disposed of with other portions of the rescued spoil, to meet expenses of the great campaign of 1796, and since then has not been among the national jewels. It made its appearance in Spain in 1809, and passed into the possession of the Demidoff family, with whose representatives it is believed still to remain.

One of the crown treasures which was never recovered, was the jewel of the Golden Fleece, valued in 1791-2 at 3,394,000 *livres.* In the middle of it was set a famous blue diamond which Lewis XIV bought from Tavernier. The jewel was broken up in England, according to M. Bapst, and the blue diamond cut in two. The largest piece came into the late Mr. Beresford Hope's collection, and (I think) was recently sold.

[3] *Filetis* I do not find in *Littré* or any other French dictionary. M. Bapst explains it to me as *la ligne extérieure de la table qui forme le centre de la partie supérieure du diamant.*

[4] The *Koh-i-Núr,* equal in quality, would have excelled the Regent in magnitude, but for its disastrous treatment.

THE PITT DIAMOND.

From Models in Natural History Museum, South Kensington.

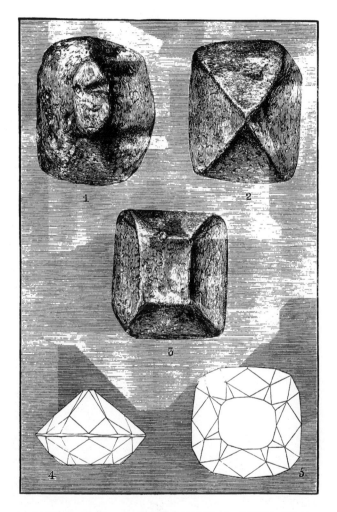

1. The Rough Stone, from Model sent home by Governor Pitt to
   Sir Stephen Evance.
2 & 3. The Diamond in different stages of cutting.
4 & 5. The Brilliant as cut.

the Dragon Ruby,[1] and other similar precious objects, shall be exhibited to the public.[2] The *Regent* awaits this eventual destination in the cellars of the Treasury.

Of Pitt—Governor Pitt, as he continued to be called apparently to the end of his days—after his return to England, there is not a great deal to say. It is evident that his name was well known to the public, and that a certain interest attached to him as a man of great wealth and force of character, as may be gathered from occasional allusions in the correspondence and fugitive literature of that and the succeeding age, though my acquaintance with these is not sufficient to indicate this fully, and my search for such notices has had little success. But the fact may also be collected even from the slanderous stories that were current as to his acquisition of the diamond. The slang term had not then come into use, but Pitt was evidently a kind of prototype of the *Nabob* of half a century later. There does not appear to be any surviving depository of his papers and correspondence subsequent to his return from India. None is to be traced in the Reports of the Historical MSS. Commission, so far as these have been issued, and none is known (as I am informed) to his descendants in the Stanhope family.

For years after his return from the East the Court Books of the Company show traces of his still occasionally importing Indian wares, and on one occasion (22nd December 1714) of his sending, through them and the President at Fort St. George, a present for " Zoudee Caun".

The same Books (27th Feb. 1712-13) note that Mr. Pitt was requested to lay before the Court the letter mentioned in the Fort Consultation of 11th August 1709, or any other papers or facts relating to the charge against Capt. Seaton (*vide supra*, pp. cxvi-xvii).

A few meagre facts may be set down as to the landed property which he acquired, and as to the. seats in Parliament occupied by Pitt and his immediate relatives, and other incidents of his public life.

We have seen that Stratford-under-the-Castle (Old Sarum) was in his possession some years before he went out to Madras as Governor. Mawarden Court, there, appears to have continued to be one of his residences, but he had also a residence at the Down, near Blandford

---

[1] The Dragon Ruby, formerly known as the *Côte de Bretagne*, was bequeathed by Anne of Brittany to Queen Claude, and had been placed by Francis I in the Crown Treasury in 1530. After being worn by Mary Stuart, and going through many vicissitudes, it was brought into the Treasury again by Colbert in 1661, and the artist Gay cut it into the dragon form which it now has (*Bapst*).

[2] *St. James's Gazette*, Sept. 9th, 1887.

St. Mary's, and another at Kynaston in the same county. Boconnoc, in Cornwall, along with all the estates in Cornwall and Devonshire left by Lord Mohun (who in 1712 was killed in a duel with the Duke of Hamilton, when the latter also fell), was purchased from the widow in 1717 for £54,000. Boconnoc is styled by Davies Gilbert the finest seat in Cornwall. Pitt is stated to have remodelled the house, but it seems to have been usually occupied by his son Robert.[1] Other manors, mentioned as purchased by the Governor, were Broadoak, or Bradock, near Lostwithiel; Treskillard in the parish of Illogan, ten miles west of Truro ; Brannell, seven miles north-east of the same town ; Tarent Kynaston in Dorset ; Woodyates and Gussech in the same county, near the borders of Wilts and Hants, etc.[2] Also Abbots-Ann in Hampshire ; Swallowfield in Berks.

During Pitt's absence in India his son Robert had, in 1705, become member for the proprietary borough of Old Sarum. On the election for the third Parliament of Great Britain (which met Nov. 25th, 1710) the Governor took up his old seat, his colleague being William Harvey, whilst Charles Fox and Robert Pitt became members for Salisbury.

22nd April 1713, Thomas Pitt, Esq., was elected a burgess of Wilton, sworn, and paid 13s. 4d. (*Wilton Corporation Ledger*).[3] This was apparently Pitt's second son, who appears as elected M.P. for Wilton, along with John London, Esq., in the Parliament of 1714-15, and as "the Hon. Thomas Pitt, jun.", was sworn Mayor of Wilton, 4th October 1716.

In the fourth Parliament of Great Britain (met Feb. 16th, 1714-15) Pitt and his son Robert are returned for Old Sarum.

March 18th, 1714. Thomas Pitt, senior, voted against the expulsion of Sir Richard Steele.

April 23rd, 1714, Peter Wentworth writes to Lord Strafford :

"Governor Pitts declared himself against every part of the address. . . . The Peace had left us in such a miserable condition that they ought to be thinking of another sort of an Address, how to reduce the King of France in a condition, and to be the Arbitrator of Europe ; therefore he mov'd that an humble Address be presented to her Majesty that her present Ministry shou'd be sent to France to be his Ministry for three years." (*Wentworth Papers*, p. 379.)

---

[1] Boconnoc had been the headquarters of King Charles in 1644, when the Parliamentary force recently commanded by Lord Essex capitulated at Fowey.

[2] Lysons, *Magna Britannia* (1814), iii, 29, 46, 144, 172, 183, 286 ; Davies Gilbert, *Parochial Hist. of Cornwall*, i, 67-68 ; Hutchins's *Dorset*, 3rd edition, i, 164, 165, 322 ; iii, 608, etc.

[3] For these notes from local records I am indebted to Mr. H. F. Swayne, through the kindness of Canon Jackson.

It would be hardly fair, perhaps, to judge of Pitt's wit by the report of this blundering Wentworth.

1715. Fifth Parliament of Great Britain (met March 17th). Thomas Pitt and Robert Pitt again chosen members for Old Sarum. In this year also Pitt was named one of the Commissioners for building fifty new churches.

April 24th, 1716, we find the Governor and his son Thomas (member for Wilton, and afterwards Earl of Londonderry) voting for the repeal of the Triennial Act (*Parly. History*, vol. vii, col. 371).

August 3rd, 1716, Governor Pitt, having been appointed to the Government of Jamaica, vacated his seat in Parliament, and was replaced by Sir W. Strickland. Of this appointment I shall speak presently. But having resigned the Government of Jamaica, he was chosen for Thirsk at a bye-election, 30th July 1717.

August 7th, 1717. "The Hon. (*sic*) THOMAS PITT, of OLD SARUM, sub Castro", and John Pitt his (youngest) son are elected Burgesses of Wilton (*Corporation Ledger*).

On the same date, at a Common Council (at Wilton), "it is agreed and ordered that the £200 lately given by the Honble: Coll[u]: THOMAS PITT for the benefit of the Poor of WILTON aforesaid, shall be (with all convenient speed) laid out in erecting and building of a house in WILTON aforesaid", etc.

"*Memo. Jany.* 8th, 1717(-18). Mr. ELIAS CHALKE the elder, paid into the Chamber of WILTON, pursuant to an order of the Common Council, nine-score and six guineas and one shilling, being £200, at the rate of £1 : 1 . 6 pr. guinea, and which £200 was lodged in the hands of the said ELIAS CHALKE by the Hon: COL: PITT, for the use of the Poor of the Parish of Wilton."

(The house thus built was called LONDONDERRY HOUSE. It was sold at the time of the introduction of the new Poor Law, and pulled down soon after.)[1]

"*Memo.* Likewise, that by the sudden fall of guineas £4 : 3 : 10 is sunk in the said sum of £200. . ."

October 3rd, 1717. THOMAS PITT, junr., Mayor, records the gift of his "scarlett gowne to be worne by the succeeding Mayors."

Parliament of 1722 (met Oct. 9th). THOMAS PITT (the Governor) and ROBERT PITT (his son) chosen for OLD SARUM; but the latter elected to sit for OAKHAMPTON, and his seat for Old Sarum fell to GEORGE MORTON PITT, of TARRANT PRESTON.

This last must have been the son of our old acquaintance JOHN PITT, Consul and President at METCHLEPATAM ; and it is a pleasant indication that the Governor had not extended his old resentment against the father to the next generation.

---

[1] Mr. H. F. Swayne.

GEORGE MORTON PITT was appointed to an office of profit under the Crown (Registrar of Revenue of Excise), and was replaced, 20th Jany. 1723-4, by "JOHN PITT", apparently the Governor's youngest son.

May 30th, 1726, G. PITT, Esqre., of STRATFIELDSAYE, elected for Old Sarum v. THOMAS PITT, Esqre., deceased (our Governor).

I turn back to 1716 and Pitt's nomination to the Government of Jamaica.

For many years, and under a succession of Governors, there had been constant collisions between these latter and the Assembly, on such constitutional subjects as the settlement of a permanent revenue; a provision for the maintenance of the troops garrisoning the island; the length of currency of laws passed; the Assembly's right of adjournment for longer periods than *de die in diem;* and other matters, such as may be gathered from papers that will be quoted presently.

Lord Archibald Hamilton became Governor in June or July 1710, there having then been eight assemblies and fifteen sessions within nine years. After Lord Archibald's assumption of the Government, disturbance was at first allayed, but speedily recommenced with virulence, and proceeded to great extremity. In the beginning of 1716 an address was framed and submitted for presentation to the King, upon the report of a Committee appointed to inquire into the state of the Island. It was little better than an impeachment of the Governor and his Council, and brought the session to an end before the exigencies of the colony had been provided for. After a most ungracious dismissal the angry members met again in ten days; but it was only to renew the struggle, and to receive messages from the Governor to the effect that he would receive no further communications from them. An abrupt dissolution succeeded, followed by Lord Archibald's removal from the Government, and his return home in arrest, as a state prisoner.[1]

The Ministers of the day were probably induced by the reputation for strength and tact which Mr. Pitt had acquired during his eleven years' Government in India, and his successful contest with difficult circumstances there, to turn to him as a resource, when in perplexity about this West India Island. In this they set an example which was followed (though probably in ignorance of this bit of history) several generations later, when Sir Charles Metcalfe was sent to Jamaica, and, still later, Sir John Peter Grant, each to contend with a state of things probably even more difficult than awaited Pitt in that Island, which (as a matter of fact) he never visited. But of all this I find no information. A fragmentary series of documents, regarding the discussions which followed his nomination to the Government, is to be found, divided between the Record Office and the MS. Department of the British Museum; and some of the most apposite of these I here transcribe.

---

[1] See B.M. Addl. MSS. 12,403 (*Long Papers*).

The first document has no date. This should probably be some day in September 1716.

" *To His Royal Highness* GEORGE, PRINCE OF WALES, &c. &c. *The humble Memorial of* THOMAS PITT, *Esqr:*[1]

" *Sheweth*

" That his Majesty having been Graciously pleas'd to Appoint the said THOMAS PITT Governour of the Island of JAMAICA in AMERICA, he has endeavour'd to gain the best account he is able of the present State and Condition of that Island.

" And the Right Honble: the Lords Commissioners for Trade and Plantations having favour'd him with the perusal of the several papers transmitted for some time past from thence, by reading the same, and also from the information of persons interested in and well acquainted with that Island the said Governour is inclin'd to believe that the affairs of that Country are in great disorder and confusion.

" That the Island is also in a most dangerous State and almost defenceless, as well from the want of a greater number of white people to prevent any Insurrection of the Negroes, as (of) Ships of war to secure the Coasts, Trade and Navigation, and to put an end to the Robberyes and disorder in those parts.

" That as the said Governour of JAMAICA is preparing to go and take upon him the Government of the said island, he is desireous to discharge his duty in his Post, for his Majesty's Service and the good of the Country, which he shall not be able effectually to doe without Such Instructions and powers as may be thought necessary in the present circumstances of the said Island. On consideration thereof

" It is humbly pray'd that before the departure of the said Governour, the present State and Condition of JAMAICA may be taken into Consideration, whereby such Dispositions may be made, as on a Report thereof may be found most safe and beneficial, for the Island, and his Majesty's service."

From the Secretary of State to the Council of Trade.[2]

" My Lords and Gentlemen,

" The inclosed Memorial from Mr. PITTS having been laid before his Royal Highness, I am commanded to transmit the same to you, and to signify to you H. R. H.'s Pleasure that you consider what is represented in it, in relation to the present State and Condition of JAMAICA, and report your Opinion of what you shall judge may be most effectual for retrieving the bad condition of that Island. And as this is a service of Importance I shall be ready to concur with you in your Deliberations on this Head, and to meet you when you shall let me know that it is convenient for you.

" I am, My Lords and Gentlemen,
" Your most humble and obedient servant,
" P. METHUEN."

---

[1] Record Office, B. T. No. 16. Jamaica O. 53.

The Prince of Wales was from 6th July 1716 administering as Guardian of the Realm, during the absence of George I in Hanover.

[2] Record Office, as above.

We find also :[1]

"*Memorandum from Mr.* PITT *relating to the Disorders at* JAMAICA, *and the Dangerous State of the Island, with Proposals for remedy thereof.*
                    "*Communicated to the Board by Mr. Secretary* METHUEN."

"Recd. }
"Read } 16th October 1716."

The next paper seems to be a Minute of the Secretary of State's office, containing remarks by the Board of Trade on Mr. Pitt's Memorial and Memorandum. This is without date.[2] It says :

" The Memorial was Imediately referred to the Consideration of the Lords for Trade and Plantations by Mr. METHUEN, into whose hands Mr. PITT afterwards put a Paper containing heads of matter necessary to be determined he had drawn from reading the Representation and Memorial of the Council of JAMAICA and other papers he had been favoured with by the Board of Trade, which having been taken into Consideration by that Board, it may be necessary to make some observations thereon, which may further clear or enforce those points."

(The following are the chief points put forward by Mr. Pitt, with the request for instructions as to each, as quoted in the Minute.)

" 1st. Upon the Assemblies declaring they have a Power to adjourn them Selves, without Leave of the Gòvernor, for what time they think fitt.

" 2nd. Mr. PITT desires to be instructed in relation to the Assembly's declaring the Council have no right to mend Money Bills.

" 3rd. Mr. PITT desires to be instructed upon the Assembly's appointing other Persons than the Receiver-General to collect Public Money.

" 4th . . Concerning the better Subsistence of the Soldiers in case the Assembly do not provide for them.

          *   *   *   *   *   *   *

" 6th. Concerning other debts of the Government unprovided for.

          *   *   *   *   *   *   *

" 7th. That the Treasury be duly Supplyed with money for the Support and Honour of the Government, or that a Revenue be Settled, Equal to the Annual Charge of the Government, which is computed to be £6000 per annum, and the present Settled Revenue do not amount to £4000 per annum.

" 8th. Mr. PITT desires to be instructed relating to the encouragement to be given to white People to go and settle in that Island.

" 9th. Mr. PITT proposes that Lands and Houses may be extended to the payment of Debts.

" 10th. He further desires that neither Councillor nor Assembly Man be allow'd any Protection (unless in his Person) from Suites of Law.

" 11th. Mr. PITT desires directions concerning the raising of money by Subscriptions in the Island to manage the affairs of that Country in this Kingdom.

" 12th. Mr. PITT proposes that Ships of Warr may be sent to JAMAICA, and to be under the direction of the Governor during their stay in those parts, and that care be taken that they be relieved by others when recalled.

" 13th. Mr. PITT further desired that the Governor be Impower'd to appoint the Clerk or other officers attending the Assembly."

---

[1] Record Office, B.T. No. 54,   [2] Addl. MSS. No. 12,426.

There follow observations of the Lords of Trade, etc., on each of the points raised, and then

Conclusion.

" By the whole Tenour of the Report the London Trade &ca. are of opinion and show the necessity from the present circumstances of JAMAICA that Mr. PITT should be instructed as his several kinds of matter require. Wherefore if it should be found necessary to give Mr. PITT instructions on these heads for the better Government and security of the Island, a Letter from his Majestie to the Governor to be communicated to the Council and Assembly on the present Circumstances of JAMAICA, recommending more especially the providing for the Soldiers, paying the Publick debts, settling the necessary revenues, and Encouraging the Resort and Settlement of White people in the Countrey, may perhaps very much conduce to Exacting or Enforcing whatever Instructions Mr. PITT may receive hereon."

We have also in the Record Office :

Letter of Mr. PITT *to the Lords Commissioners for Trade, dated "* PALL MALL, 7th Nov. 1716."

" My Lords,

" By your Lordships command I received a Letter from Mr. POPPLE of the 3 instant, in answer to which I beg leave to say that were I not able to assign Particular instances in a Strict Literal Sence of the Assemblys assuming the Executive part of the Government the whole course of their Proceedings might well justifie that Expression, and whether in particular their Order to muster the Soldiers, and visit Fortifications by their own authority ;

" Their appointing of Officers to collect the money raised by them, and making large appointments out of it ;

" Their refusing to admit the Council to mend money Bills, or confer with them ;

" Their Soliciting Bill, in which the whole busyness of the Government is put into the hands of a few of themselves, to be transacted without the Privity of the Governour and Council ;

" Their Raising money by Subscriptions to Support that Power here, with Extraordinary acts of oppression, which appear upon the minutes ;

" are not some instances which amount to an assuming in good measure the Executive part of the Government, I submit to your Lordships.

   *   *   *   *   *   *   *

" My Lords, as these memorandums were drawn out from the Papers relating to JAMAICA which I was favoured with from your board, and such other information as I obtain'd from Persons I beleiv'd to be the best versed and most knowing in the affairs of that Island, and were not delivered as a Publick Paper, I hope your Lordships will not consider it as such, nor have any other regard to it then as you find it supported by the Papers transmitted to you, it having been my only aim by my memorial to be instructed in such manner as might Enable me to do his Majesty Service by Providing for the Welfare of JAMAICA, and not to give a handle to any Person to foment or continue the divisions there.   I am with the greatest Esteem

     " My Lords, &ca :   " THO : PITT."

And, again, the following *Report to* Mr. Secretary METHUEN *from the Lords Commissioners of Trade and Plantations, dated* December 19th, 1716.[1]

" S^r : —

     Mr. PITT, appointed by his Majestie Governor of JAMAICA, having desired to be instructed upon several heads, whereof he delivered some Memorandums to you, we Immediately took the same into consideration, and finding that the matters therein relate principally to the Powers and Privileges of Assemblies, we thought it necessary to look back into our Books, as far as to the first settlement of Assemblies in that Island, for such precedents as were to be found upon these several heads in the Minutes of the Councils, Journals of Assembly, and other Papers received from thence.

     " As this our search into the several Books and papers relating to the Government of JAMAICA, has required much time and application, So it has necessarily occasion'd the Enclosed Extracts to be so voluminous, for we have rather chosen to swell this collection to an unusual length than to omitt the least transaction that might give light to the points that have been laid before us.

     " We do not presume to give an opinion of our own upon matters which so nearly concern the Prerogative of the Crown, and are so Essential to the Constitution and Government of that Island, Humbly conceiving they may deserve his Majesties more immediate consideration.

     " We think it proper to acquaint you, on this occasion, that disputes of the like nature have lately arisen in other of his Majesties Governments in AMERICA.

" We are S^r: Yours &ca :

" J. MOLESWORTH	P. DOCHMINIQUE	JA : ASTLEY
" Jo : COCKBURNE	J. CHETWIND	J. ADDISON."

I find no further information as to what passed in reference to Pitt's appointment except the following in the Record Office portfolio :

" *To the Rt. Hon. Lords Commissioners for Trade.*

" Whitehall, 21st June 1717.

" My Lords,

     " His Majesty having been pleased to appoint NICHOLAS LAWES Esqre. to be Governor of Jamaica, I desire that you will please to direct the Draughts of his Commission and Instructions to be prepared, that the same may be laid before his Majesty for his approbation.

" I am My Lords &ca.
" J. ADDISON."

I also find in the B.M. " Long Collection" regarding Jamaica :[2]

" 1716. THOMAS PITT, Governor of FORT ST. GEORGE, E. INDIES, was appointed Governor, and Col. (Otway) Lieut. Governor. He resigned in favour of Mr. LAWES, a planter, afterwards S^r: NICHOLAS ; Col. DUBOURGAY, Lieut. Governor. S^r: NICHOLAS embarked in his Majesty's Ship *Ludlow Castle* March 18, and arrived at JAMAICA the 26th Aprill 1718."

---

[1] Addl. MSS. 12,426.

[2] *Ibid.*, 27,698, f. 179.

It is evident therefore that Pitt never took up his Jamaica Government. But whether the Ministers thought he made too many difficulties, or he, as is probable enough, at 64 years of age, hesitated to occupy so thorny a cushion as the Government of Jamaica, I have found no evidence.

The only other circumstances in Pitt's remaining life, that I have found to record, are his sale of the diamond, and purchase of the Mohun estates, both already spoken of.

His death took place at his manor of Swallowfield, in Berks, April 28th, 1726 ; but under what circumstances I have not found. He was buried at Blandford St. Mary's, as were his wife, his eldest son Robert, and his second son, Lord Londonderry. Governor Pitt had restored the church in the style of his age, and added on the north side a chapel intended for his burial-place. But in 1861-62 the church was again restored, in different style, and I believe the tower is the only part which remains at all as Pitt looked upon it ; and that, too, is now entirely clothed in ivy. He had also given some communion plate to the church, but of a style deemed in later days so ugly and cumbrous that, at the time of the more recent restoration of the church, it was melted down and refashioned, except a silver alms-dish, which still retains the Pitt arms on its underside.[1] At the time of the restoration, also, a vault was found, under the present vestry, containing three coffins. One of them, having a metal coronet, must have been that of Lord Londonderry ; a second was believed to be the Governor's.

The following inscription (which we may hope and believe was composed and set up after the Governor's death) formerly was to be read on the wall over the entrance to the aisle, but is there no longer, having apparently been removed at the time the church was restored in 1861-62 :

" To the Glory of God.

" THOMAS PITT of this place in the year of our Lord 1711 very much repaired and beautified this Church, dedicating his substance to his Maker in that place where he himself was dedicated to his service. In this pious action he is alone, his own example and copy ; this being a specimen of many of like nature. Thus by building GOD'S house, he has most wisely laid a sure foundation for his own. And by honouring the name of the Almighty has transmitted himself to posterity by such actions as deserve not only this perishing register, but also to be had in everlasting remembrance."

The only other instances of church restoration by the Governor that I have found notice of, to justify this extravagant laudation, are at Stratford (already mentioned, p. xxx *supra*), and at Abbot's-Ann, Hampshire, where, says Murray's *Handbook to Surrey, Hants, etc.*,

---

[1] Information from the Rev. J. Mansfield, formerly Rector of St. Mary's, through my friend Lieut.-Gen. F. C. Cotton, C.S.I., R.E.

"the present brick church was built in 1716, in the debased classic style, by Governor (or ' Diamond') Pitt" (p. 330).

Two portraits of Pitt, by Kneller, exist ; one at Chevening ; the other I cannot say where at present, but probably at Boconnoc. They look as if they were the result of the same sitting, differing only in accessories. No engraving of him has ever been published, but I have been enabled, by the favour of Lord Stanhope, and through the kind intervention of my friend Mr. George Scharf, C.B., Keeper of the National Portrait Gallery, to present as frontispiece to this volume an autotype reproduction of a photograph from the Chevening portrait. The other picture was shown at the second of the three loan exhibitions of British National Portraits at S. Kensington, viz., that which took place in 1867. It was lent by the (late) Honble. G. M. Fortescue, who had inherited Boconnoc, Pitt's old seat, from his aunt, Lady Grenville.

At Pitt's funeral a sermon was preached by the Rev. Richard Eyre, Canon of Sarum, which was published, and of which a copy exists in the B.M. library.[1] I extract from it the following passages :

" . . I believe few men pass through the world without some share in these sufferings, which we may allow to be called unjust, if we look no further than the hand of the Oppressor, who do's the wrong, or the tongue of the Slanderer, which *this* PERSON, whose Prosperity was so wonderfull, could not escape ; that he should have enemies, is no wonder, when Envy will make them, and, when their malice could reach him no other way, 'tis as little to be wondered at, that they should make such attempt upon his Credit by an abusive Story, as if it had been by some stretch of his power, that he got that *Diamond*, which was of too great value for any Subject to purchase ; an Ornament more fitly becoming an *Imperial Crown*, which, if it be consider'd, may be one reason, why it was brought to the GOVERNOR by the *Merchant*, who sold it in the INDIES ; and it was brought to him more than *once* or *twice*, before he could be persuaded to part with so great a sum of money for it as it cost him, of which (if I may be allow'd in this place to take so much notice of it), I have seen an authentick and clear account, such, as, I will venture to say, will intirely satisfie every good or reasonable man, that *that story* could have no foundation, but in the malice of him who invented it.

" And, if, when such a *Viper fasten'd* on an innocent person, any of you were prompted too hastily to think the worse of him, when You see it *shaken off*, it must change your opinion, and may well raise your thoughts of him, who bore so horrid an abuse with so much patience, as, for his more effectual vindication, to wait the time of his going to appear before God, to whom he makes his appeal in the most solemn manner for the truth of that account, which he left to be open'd at his death.

"This abuse, I am inclin'd to believe, might occasion his taking more par-

[1] *A Sermon Preached at* BLANDFORD ST. MARY *In the County of* DORSET *On May* 21 1726 *At the Funeral of* THOMAS PITT *Esqre. By* RICHARD EYRE M A. *Canon Residentiary of the Cathedral Church of* SARUM. OXFORD, *Printed at the Theater.* MDCCXXVI.

ticular value of a short admonition, which, with others he had collected for his use, was found in his own hand with the paper I mention'd before ; it was in these words only—*Learn to suffer.*   The first of those monitory maxims (which had, as it deserv'd, the first place in his thoughts), was *Trust in God*, and that which followed next, *Pray to Him often* (and accordingly he was known to retire very constantly to his Closet for that purpose), *Oppress not the Poor* was another ; and the last was to remember the last thing he had to do, *Remember to dye.*

" And it may be reckon'd among the felicities of his life, that he, who had pass'd through so much business, should have so many years of Retirement and Leisure before his death, to draw off his thoughts from the world so long before he left it.   And, as great as his Concerns were in it, he consider'd, he had much greater relating to another life, and towards the last (for the last two or three years especially) he took little notice of any other. . . ."   (*Sermon*, pp. 18-20.)

The eulogies of a funeral sermon are proverbially untrustworthy, but in these passages there is no straining for praise ; and little as we have been able to gather of the Governor's later life, the facts they disclose as to the retirement and serious thoughts of his last years are interesting, and show that he had ceased to drive hard after the world, as he seemed to do in the years when we had ampler revelations of his thoughts.

Taking him throughout his active life he is hardly, as painted by himself, an attractive character, though a most forcible one.   Bold, decided, and shrewd himself, he held in utter contempt those who failed in such qualities ; and in the frank, unrestrained expression of his sentiments, whether in seriousness or in merciless and rasping chaff, he must often have given offence to friend as well as foe.   Foes he must have had in plenty, being such as he was, and among other things so eminently that character which Samuel Johnson *said* he loved, " a good hater."   Of his character as a servant of the Company I have before spoken, and I have already indicated that he was by no means delicately scrupulous : how should a man have been so, whose early life had been passed like Pitt's, struggling to maintain trade in the teeth of a Company that claimed a monopoly, and that looked on him as an enemy with whom no terms were to be kept, in a country open to every kind of intrigue and corruption ?   Nevertheless he *had* a standard of duty and honour, if not a high one, and I believe he kept to it.

Sir Josia Child, at the time of Pitt's nomination to Fort St. George, calls him " that roughling and immoral man"   What particular ground he had for the latter epithet I know not.   " Ruffling", if that implies great freedom of speech and little tenderness for the susceptible toes of other people, or for the minor ethics of life, I can well believe he was. In any case, these pages for the first time give any means of judging what manner of man was this immediate ancestor of two such illustrious personages as the elder and the younger William Pitt.   And we can

but regret that the last fifteen years of his life have sent down to us
such blank canvas.

Of his wife Jane, too, we know nothing since the earlier years of her
husband's government, during which, we have seen, he often blamed
her ill judgment in the conduct of his family, and of his affairs, so far as
they were in her hands. Pitt's will seems to make no mention of her,
beyond alluding to an annuity of £200 a year charged in her favour
upon his landed estates, which was "to be in bar of her rights of
dower", an expression which seems to imply that it was all the provision made for her; though we may hope this was not so. In any
case, she survived him only some ten months, dying 10th January
1726-7. I may note that the period 1726-1729 was very fatal to the
family.[1]

The offspring of Thomas and Jane Pitt were as follows :

I. ROBERT, the date of whose birth has not been ascertained. He
sat in seven Parliaments continuously, from 1705 to his death in 1727,
viz., four times for Old Sarum, once for Salisbury, and twice for
Oakhampton. He had married immediately after his return from
India (see *note*, p. xcii).

His eldest son, THOMAS, was father of the first Lord Camelford
(cr. 1784), a title which became extinct with the death of the second
lord, in a duel (1804).

Robert's second son was the illustrious WILLIAM, Earl of Chatham
(1766), whose title became extinct with the death of the great man's
son, JOHN, Earl of Chatham, K.G., in 1835.

II. THOMAS, born *c.* 1688 (as he is stated to have died, aged 41, in
1729). A colonel of horse. He sat for Wilton in the Parliaments of
1713, 1714-15, and 1722 ; and was sworn Mayor of Wilton in 1716. He
married Frances, daughter and coheir of Robert Ridgeway, Earl of
Londonderry ; and was himself in 1719 created Baron Londonderry in
the Irish Peerage, and in 1726 Earl of the same. In 1727 he was
appointed Captain-General and Commander-in-Chief of the Leeward
Islands ; and died at St. Kitt's, September 12, 1729. His title passed
successively to his two sons, becoming extinct with the death of the
second in 1764. A daughter, Lady Lucy (Meyrick), survived to 1802.

III. JOHN, who was Colonel of the 1st Regiment of Guards, and
Lieut.-Governor of Bermuda. He sat for Hindon (1714-15), Old Sarum
(1722), Camelford (1728). Married Mary, eldest daughter of Thomas,
Viscount Fauconberg, and died *s.p.* in 1754[2] (see *Gent. Mag.*, xxiv, p. 95).

---

[1] The Governor died in April 1726 ; Mrs. Pitt, January 1727 ; their eldest
son Robert, May 1727 ; their second son Thomas (Lord Londonderry),
September 1729.

[2] It is worthy of remark that of the seven boroughs for which T. Pitt and
his sons sat in various Parliaments, viz., *Hindon, Old Sarum, Oakhampton,*

MRS. THOMAS PITT
(Née JANE JNNES.)
Drawn by G. Scharf Esq. C.B.
From a Picture at Chevening.

IV. Essex (eldest daughter) married in 1714 Charles Cholmondely, of Vale-Royal in Cheshire.

In the peerage-books, etc. (including Burke's *Dormant and Extinct Peerages*, ed. 1883), Essex is represented as the younger daughter, and I was misled by this (at p. cxxviii of vol. II, *note*); but it is certainly a mistake. Allusions in the correspondence (*e.g. supra*, p. lxii, p. lxxii, and at the place just quoted from vol. II) indicate plainly that Essex was the elder.

"L^d. Angelsey was marry'd last Satterday, Mrs. Pit to Mr. Chomley, ye ware at St. James Church a Sunday very fine" (Letter of Selina, Countess Ferrers, dated July 27th, 1714; in XIth Report of Hist. MSS. Commission, App., pt. iv, p. 224).

V. Lucy, married (1712) to General James Stanhope, created in 1718 Earl Stanhope. She died in 1723, and was buried at Chevening.

"Governor Pitt will no doubt prove a rough character, but from the little known of his gentle daughter Lucy Lady Stanhope, he must always be an object of interest to her descendants at Chevening." (*Note by the present* Countess Stanhope.)

The descendants of Pitt, or at least the most important of them, are shown in the genealogical table opposite p. xxix. The basis of that table has been the " Pedigree Pitt and Pitt-Rivers of the county of Dorset, etc.", presented in the third edition of *Hutchins's Hist. of Dorset* (IV, pp. 90-92); but I have enlarged it, and in some instances corrected it, from knowledge acquired in the course of the present compilation.

I am quitting Governor Pitt with some regret, after tracking his career diligently during such hours as I could bestow on the subject, during many months. Before quite parting from him I will gather up in a kind of *catalogue raisonné*, and at the risk of occasional repetition, notes regarding such of his relations as are mentioned in the correspondence ; and I will add an abstract of his Will, as it is to be seen at Somerset House.

(1.) John Pitt (*a*), President for the New Company at Masulipatam, and King's Consul (see pp. xxxix, *seqq.*, and lxxxix, *seqq.*, etc.). His father was certainly one of the sons of Edward Pitt of Stratfieldsaye (who d. 1643), and was alive in 1684 (see P.S. to letter at p. xcii). But till this sheet was just going to press I was unable to say which of Edward Pitt's sons he was. A Pitt pedigree in the College of Arms, kindly shown me by Mr. Alfred Gatty, York Herald, determined that he was (as I had suspected) George Pitt's next brother, John, married to Catherine Venables.

Camelford, Salisbury, Wilton, and Thirsk, the last three only survived what (north of Tweed) a venerable Tory relative of the present writer used, in 1832, to call *Skiddle Aw, i.e.*, the disfranchising schedule A of the first Reform Act.

(2.) GEORGE PITT (*a*) of Stratfieldsaye (the first of that Christian name), uncle of the last; mentioned pp. lxxxvi and xcii; d. 1694.

(3.) GEORGE PITT (*b*) of ditto (the second of that name); see pp. lxxxix, xcvii; d. 1734.

(4.) NICHOLAS PITT, of Beere Regis, Dorset, and of the Inner Temple; see pp. lxxxvi, lxxxviii, lxxxix, xc, xcvi. Brother of No. 3.

(5.) THOMAS PITT, Master in Chancery (1694). See pp. lxxiii, lxxvii, etc. A son of the Governor's uncle, Robert Pitt (*a*), M.D., of Blandford Forum. I have not been able to ascertain the date of his death; but he was succeeded in his Mastership, in 1712, by Henry Lovibond,[1] and his estate was administered to in 1717.

(6.) Dr. ROBERT PITT (*b*), see p. lxxii. Apparently brother of No. 5, and grandfather of the Rev. Christ. Pitt, "the Poet" (see *Johnson's Lives*).

(7.) JOHN PITT (*b*). Another brother of 5 and 6. See p. lxxiii. If Hutchins is correct (*ibid. note*) he was Rector of Cheselborne, and died 1753; but this date is certainly a mistake for 1733.

(8.) ROBERT PITT (*c*). Son of Thomas Pitt (No. 5), mentioned as the second "Robbin" in No. 5's letter at p. lxxiii.

(9.) KATHERINE PITT. Daughter of No. 5; the "Keate" of p. lxxiii.

(10.) ROBERT PITT (*d*). Son of No. 7, mentioned as the first "Robbin" in same letter.

(11.) JOHN PITT (*c*). Captain in the Army, and served at Blenheim (see pp. lxxiii, c); called by the Governor "Cornet John Pitt" (pp. lxxxviii, xci). I conjecture that he may be the John Pitt who appears in the Genealogical Table as a son of No. 2, and therefore a first cousin of John Pitt the consul (No. 1).

(12.) WENTWORTH PITT. Named (Jan. 1702) in the will of John Pitt (*a*) (No. 1), as a lieut. in "Colonel Wood's regiment of horse", and to have the reversion of the testator's landed property (pp. lxxxix, xci). From what the Governor says (twice) at p. lxxxviii, this must have been a son of Capt. John Pitt (*c*) (No. 11). We gather from what is said by the latter, at p. lxxii, and by the Governor at p. lxxxviii, that a son of the captain's went to seek his fortune in India in 1702, and that the Governor was willing to befriend the lad, but Consul John (No. 1) took him on his own hands, and after the consul's death, the young man, being left unprovided for, was bound apprentice on board the *Tavistock*.

Again, I find in the *Court Book* of Feb. 4th, 1714(-15), that Capt. WENTWORTH GEORGE PITT was elected to command the *Stanhope*, and, from other notices, continued to serve the Company in that command for many years. We might easily suppose this to be the same as the young man who was apprenticed to the sea on the *Tavistock*

---

[1] Haydn's *Book of Dignities*, p. 240.

twenty years before; but it is not so easy to see how he is to be identified with a "lieutenant in Wood's regiment of horse".

(13.) HASTINGS PITT. Employed at St. Helena in 1704, and called "kinsman" by the Governor (see p. xcvii). But the relationship is not known.

(14.) GEORGE MORTON (or MORETON) PITT. This name involves some perplexing questions of identity. We have the following mentions of the name :

(a) GEORGE MORETON PITT, son of the Consul (No. 1), appears in the latter's Will (p. lxxxix), and in the Will of his widow (as GEORGE MORTON, p. xc). It also appears, on the page last quoted, that in 1711 this G. M. Pitt was still a minor.

(b) In 1722, as we have seen (p. cxlix), GEORGE MORETON PITT "of TARRANT PRESTON", therefore certainly the son of No. 1 (compare p. lxxxix), was chosen M.P. for Old Sarum, as colleague to Governor Pitt. But in January 1723-4 a new writ is issued for Old Sarum, in consequence of the said G. M. Pitt having been appointed "Register of the Revenue of Excise" (*Parliamentary History*, vol. viii, col. 15).

(c) In the *Court Book* of 31st Oct. 1712, GEORGE MORTON PITT is, on his petition, permitted to go as a "Free Merchant" to Fort St. George. He appears not then to have acted on it, as the grant of his like petition is again recorded under 24th Nov. 1714. And in the list of Company's servants and European residents at Fort St. George for 1716 (*India Office Records*) George Morton Pitt appears in the number of "Free Merchants"; and again in the list for 1717 in the number of "Sea-faring Men not constant Residents".

(d) In the India Company's *Court Book*, under 5th July 1723, we find that a petition of GEORGE MORTON PITT was read, setting forth that having been bred a merchant, and by his residence at Fort St. George and his having been employed on several voyages to other parts of India, he had acquired a competent knowledge of affairs there, and prayed to be employed by the Company in such station as he should be thought qualified for.

The Court (10th July 1723) resolve that Mr. George Morton Pitt be appointed Deputy-Governor of Fort St. David, when Capt. Macrae should succeed to the government of Fort St. George, and in the meantime should be Second at Fort St. George. And on 15th November the same G. M. P. is appointed to have the chief direction of the ship *Macclesfield* and her cargo, bound for China and Fort St. George. *8th Decr.*: Securities for this G. M. P. as "Chief of the Council for managing the Company's affairs in China", to the amount of £4,000, are rendered by John Freeman of Fowley Court, near Henley-upon

Thames, Esq., and John Raworth of Bedford Row, gentleman ; and by the same two to the same amount on account of the same G. M. P., as Second of Fort St. George. *20th December:* Permission granted to said G. M. P. to carry out on the *Macclesfield* £10,000 in foreign bullion ; and (*24th December*) to carry in the same Christopher Cradock as a menial servant.

> (*e*) In the lists from Fort St. George, GEORGE MORTON PITT is returned as having arrived in India 26th December 1724, with the position of Deputy-Governor of Fort St. David. In the list of 1730 he appears as President of Fort St. George ; and so continues till 1735.

Again, in the *Gentleman's Magazine* for 1756, vol. xxvi, p. 91, we find :

"Deaths of the year 1756 . . . Feb. 5, GEO. MORTON PITT, Esq., Member for Pontefract, Yorkshire, and formerly Governor of Fort St. George, East Indies."

Tracing back in the lists of the House, we find that GEORGE MORTON PITT represented Pontefract in the Parliaments of 1741 and 1747.

The Pitt pedigree in *Hutchins* (iv, 92) has no hesitation in identifying the member for Old Sarum in 1722, and "Register to the Revenue of Excise" of 1724, with the member for Pontefract of 1741 and 1747, who died in 1756. Though the pedigree errs as to the identity of this G. M. Pitt's father, I have little doubt the other identification is right. But there is a difficulty as to the identity of (*a*) and (*b*), though there need be no doubt as to the identity of (*c*), (*d*), and (*e*). The difficulty is this : George Morton Pitt of Tarrant Preston, M.P. for Old Sarum (*a* and *b*), vacates his seat on account of being appointed "Register of the Excise Revenue", and the new writ is issued Jan. 1723-24.

But in July 1723, George Morton Pitt (*c, d, e*) applies to the Court of Directors for employment in India, which he obtains *per saltum* in a high post on the Coast, and sails for India about the beginning of 1724. How can this be the same with the M.P. appointed "Register of the Excise Revenue"? The explanation may yet be found. Possibly the latter office was a sinecure.

(15.) Rev. HENRY WILLIS (p. xcix, *note*). Pitt and this correspondent always write to each other as "Dear Brother". Mr. Willis was married to Sara, the elder of the Governor's two sisters, and was Rector of Blandford St. Mary from 1674. The advowson had belonged to her father, the preceding rector, and came to her, and continued with her descendants.

The epitaphs of Henry Willis and Sara Pitt his wife are given in *Hutchins*, i, 168. Mr. Willis died in 1726 and his wife in 1733, each at the age of eighty. There are several letters in B. M. from and to Mr. Willis, but I seem not to have transcribed any.

(16.) Rev. THOS. CURGENVEN. This frequent correspondent also always exchanges " Dear Brother" with the Governor. It seemed to me pretty certain that he must have been married to Pitt's other sister, DOROTHY, born 1656, and this I have found confirmed in the Heralds' office. Mr. Curgenven was instituted (1694) as Rector of Folke near Sherburne (see p. lxix, *supra*, and *Hutchins*, iv, 185), having been at an earlier date Master of Blandford Free School, and then head master of Sherburne School. He died 1712. (See pp. lxiii, lxv, lxix, lxxxiii, xcvi.)

(17.) WILLIAM, EDWARD, and ANTHONY ETTRICKE are styled " Cousins" and " Kinsmen". The relation is unknown. The Ettrickes, in spite of their apparently north-country name, were a county family, of Holt near Wimborne (*Hutchins*, iii, 219 and 245). (See pp. lxxii, cviii, cxviii, etc.)

(18.) ROBERT DOUGLAS. Also a brother-in-law of the Governor's. Almost certainly his wife must have been a sister of Mrs. Pitt's. His son Charles was Pitt's godson, and was regarded by him with favour. (See vol I., *passim;* vol. II., pp. cxxv, *seqq.*; vol. III., pp. xcii, xciv.)

(19.) JOHN RIDOUT. Called " Cousin" and " Kinsman", p. lxxxvi.

(20.) THOMAS and RICHARD CRADOCK, in Blandford, p. xcix. Relationship unknown.

(21.) TEMPERANCE COCKRAM, and JOHN THORNE or FORME; cousins. See tabular pedigree and p. xcix.

(22.) (Sir) MATTHIAS VINCENT, called " Uncle" (see vol. I., p. xlii, where Hedges says Pitt had married Vincent's niece) ; also see vol. II., pp. ccxc, *seqq.*, and vol. III., pp. iii-viii. It is probable that Vincent had married an aunt of Jane Innes.

(23.) RICHARD EDWARDS, Chief at Balasore. In letters at pp. viii, ix, *supra*, Pitt calls Edwards " Uncle" and " Dear Uncle", and signs himself " Your Nephew". This also was probably a connexion through Mrs. Pitt.

ABSTRACT OF WILL OF THOMAS PITT.[1]

WILL dated 18 July, 1721.

Trustees and executors : EARL OF PEMBROKE, GEORGE PITT of STRAT-FIELDSAY, CHARLES CHOLMONDELEY of VALE ROYAL, and W. CHAPPLE of the MIDDLE TEMPLE.

1. Leaves certain lands at OLD SARUM to his trustees until his grandson, THOMAS PITT, son of LD. LONDONDERRY, shall attain 21.

---

[1] I am indebted for this abstract from the will at Somerset House (which fills more than 20 large folio pages) to my friend Mr. ALBERT GRAY, barrister.

Remainder to other sons of LD. LONDONDERRY in succession.

    ,,   ,, ROBERT PITT, elder son of testator.
    ,,   ,, WILLIAM PITT,[1] (second)[2] son of ROBERT.
    ,,   ,, other sons of ROBERT (successively).
    ,,   ,, ESSEX, his daughter, wife of CHAS. CHOLMONDELEY.
    ,,   ,, her eldest and other sons successively.
    ,,   ,, his daughter LUCY, COUNTESS STANHOPE.
    ,,   then to his grandson PHILIP, EARL STANHOPE.
    ,,   then to GEORGE STANHOPE, son of LUCY.
    ,,   then to daughters of ROBERT PITT.
    ,,   then to daughters of CHAS. CHOLMONDELEY.
    ,,   then to daughters of LD. STANHOPE.
    ,,   then to testator's own heirs.
    ,,   then to his godson, THOMAS PITT, son of GEO. PITT of
         STRATFIELDSAY.

2. The manor of BRANWELL or BRANNELL, and that of TRETHANSA, in
   CORNWALL, lately belonging to JOHN TANNER, and land in parishes of
   CROOD CUBY and borough of TREGONY, in CORNWALL, and certain
   lands in parish of STRATFORD, OLD SARUM, to his grandson, THOMAS
   PITT, and remainders as before.

3. "In case LD. LONDONDERRY shall be living in my house in PALL MALL at
   the time of my death," he is to have it for one whole year thereafter.
   It was a leasehold house. Then it is to go to "my son ROBERT PITT"
   for the remainder of the term, with use of linen, plate, pictures, etc.
   If he dies before end of term, then to THOS. PITT (son of ROBERT) [" and
   after his decease to his son THOS. PITT." This is repeated twice, and I
   think may be only an error of the copyist, and that only one Thomas
   Pitt is meant.—A. G.]. After death of THOMAS, then to the said
   WILLIAM PITT [second son of Robert]. In case the lease determines in
   the lifetime of these "the said ROB. PITT, THOS. PITT, and WILLIAM
   PITT" [seems to show that only one Thomas Pitt was meant[3]], then the
   linen, plate, pictures, etc., to go with residuary estates.

4. Ground rents in DEAN STREET, parish of ST. ANNE, WESTMINSTER [i.e.,
   Soho], to go to his son ROBERT PITT.

5. As to his leases of Crown lands in said parish of ST. ANNE, and "all my
   messuages and hereditaments in or near DEAN STREET"—then to his
   trustees, in trust ; the rents and profits to go to ROBERT PITT, "till my
   grandson THOS. PITT shall attain the age of 21 or die."

6. He recites that by a settlement previously made he settled manor of ABBOTS
   AUNT, or ABBAS AUNT [Abbots Ann], in Co. SOUTHAMPTON, and
   advowson thereof, on himself and his heirs. He now confirms that
   settlement.

7. All my manors at BLANDFORD ST. MARY, and KAINSTON or elsewhere in
   Co. DORSET, ABBOTS AUNT in Co. SOUTHAMPTON, STRATFORD in
   Co. WILTS, and other lands in Counties of DEVON and CORNWALL

---

[1] Viz., afterwards Earl of Chatham.

[2] The abstract says "eldest". But THOMAS was the eldest son of Robert.

[3] There *was* a second Thomas, grandson of Robert, but he was not born till
1737, long after the Governor's death.

lately bought or to be bought from Lady MOHUN, also manor of
SWALLOWFIELD in Co. BERKS: to my eldest son ROBERT PITT for
life; then to his said son THOS. PITT for his life; then [hiatus]; and
then as before to grandsons, and then granddaughters.

8. All these lands are charged with annuity of £200 to testator's wife, which
is to be in bar of the rights of dower.

9. Certain leaseholds at OLD SARUM to his son ROBERT PITT.

10. The residuary estate to be laid out in lands.

11. Annuities:

    (a) £200 a year to MARY, wife of my son JOHN PITT.

    (b) £200 a year to my grandson THOS. PITT, son of ROBERT PITT, from
        the age of 21 to 25.

    (c) £200 a year to my grandson WM. PITT from age of 21 during his
        life.

    (d) £100 a year to each of my granddaughters HARRIOT PITT, CATHE-
        RINE PITT, ANN PITT and ELIZABETH PITT, from age of 16
        till marriage or death.

12. Legacies:

    (a) £5000 to HARRIOT, on day of marriage.

    (b) £2000 to CATHERINE, ANN and ELIZABETH, each, on marriage.

    (c) £1000 each to my grandson THOS. PITT; son of Lord LONDONDERRY.

,,	,,		LUCY PITT, daughter of L^d: LONDONDERRY.
,,	,,		granddaughters ESSEX CHOLMONDELEY.
,,	,,	,,	JANE CHOLMONDELEY.
,,	,,	,,	MARY CHOLMONDELEY.
,,	,,	,,	ELIZABETH CHOLMONDELEY.
,,	,,	PHILIP Earl STANHOPE.	
,,	,,	GEORGE STANHOPE.	
,,	,,	Lady GERTRUDE STANHOPE.	
,,	,,	Lady JANE STANHOPE, on day of marriage or on	
		attaining 21.	

    (d) £5000 to Lady LUCY STANHOPE on day of her marriage.

13. Household goods at SWALLOWFIELD, OLD SARUM, BLANDFORD, KAIN-
STON, and BOCONNOCK, to son ROBERT PITT.

14. £100 to each of his executors for a ring.

15. £50 to my sister WILLIS for mourning.

16. £100 to ROBT. PITT and L^d. LONDONDERRY and to each of my daughters for
mourning.

17. £100 to my kinsman JOHN SUTTON.

18. £50 to my servant JAMES ABBIS.

19. Various legacies to the poor of the various parishes.

First Codicil, dated 13 March 1722.

    Revokes annuity to MARY PITT wife of my son JOHN PITT, and gives £400
a year to his trustees in trust to pay same to MARY.

    £200 a year to be raised out of his CORNWALL estates for the benefit of
the eldest son of MARY and JOHN PITT.

    If there shall be children of MARY and JOHN, then the trustees are to raise
£4000 out of s^d lands for portions to such younger children.

    He refers to certain other lands lately bought by him in CORNWALL from
one ROBERT NICHOLLS; these he leaves in trust for his grandson
RIDGEWAY PITT;

then to other sons of Lord LONDONDERRY ;
then to "my own heirs".

He recites that he had received the fortune of s^d. MARY PITT on condition
that he would make a settlement in her favour, this is it.

Second Codicil, dated 24 Nov. 1723.

Recites will and then goes on :

"Whereas I have sustained very great losses by the late SOUTH SEA Scheme
and otherwise, and therefore find myself obliged to retrench some of the
legacys given in and by my said will, and am also desirous to show some
token of my affection unto such of my grandchildren as have been born
since the making of my said will"—

for such reasons

he reduces HARRIOT PITT
        and Lady LUCY STANHOPE } from £5000 to £3000 ;

and bequeaths to grandsons RIDGEWAY PITT
        ,,   JAMES STANHOPE   } each £1000,
gr^d.daughters Lady CATHERINE STANHOPE   at 21 or
        ,,   CHARLOTT ANN CHOLMONDELEY } marriage ;

also to THOS. PITT son of ROBT. PITT, £500 (a year?) from his age
of 25 during the joint lives of his father and himself.

Reduces JAMES ABBIS to £30 ;

and also reduces the legacies of the poor of the several parishes.

The will was proved 7 May 1726 by Lord LONDONDERRY and CHAS. CHOL-
MONDELEY ; Power being reserved to the others to prove thereafter.

Marginal note in the Probate Copy states that :

On 15 Oct. 1756 letters of administration (with the will annexed) of the
estate left unadministered, were granted to THOS. PITT, grandson of
the deceased, residuary legatee named in the will ; CHAS. CHOLMON-
DELEY, having survived L^d. LONDONDERRY, and died intestate ; and
CHAPPLE not having proved and being dead.

Another marginal note states that :

On 8 Feb. 1762, letters of administration of estate left unadministered were
granted to THOMAS PITT, son and administrator of THOS. PITT now
deceased.

EARLY HISTORY OF THE COMPANY'S SETTLEMENT IN BENGAL.

THE early history of the Company's trade and settlements in the Bay of Bengal cannot, so far as I have been able to discover, be traced with satisfactory precision. It belongs to the decades between 1630 and 1650, during which the surviving correspondence from India is more imperfect even than in the latter half of the century, whilst the regular series of the Company's *Letter-books*, containing the communications of the Court to their agents in India, and to their ship-captains, as preserved in the India Office, does not commence till April 1653, and among these the first letter that I have found addressed direct to Bengal is dated no earlier than 27th February 1657(-8).[1] The first from Bengal direct to the Company appears to be that from Francis Day, dated "BALLASARA, Novr. 3d. 1642", which is quoted on p. clxxxi; and the next that I have found is one dated 12th December 1650, from Wm. Netlam, at the same place, defending himself against certain charges.[2]

The story of the beginning of English trade in Bengal is generally told in the manner that I am about to quote from Stewart's *History of Bengal*:

"In the year of the Higira 1046" [*i.e.*, A.D. 1636-7], "a daughter of the Emperor SHAH JEHAN, having been dreadfully burnt, by her clothes catching fire, an express was sent to SURAT, through the recommendation of the vizier ASSAD KHAN, to desire the assistance of a EUROPEAN surgeon. For this service the Council at SURAT nominated Mr. GABRIEL BOUGHTON, surgeon of the ship *Hopewell*, who immediately proceeded to the Emperor's Camp, then in the DEKKAN, and had the good fortune to cure the young Princess of the effects of her accident. Mr. BOUGHTON, in consequence, became a great favourite at Court ; and having been desired to name his reward, he, with that liberality which characterizes BRITONS, sought not for any private emolument ; but solicited that his nation might have liberty to trade, free of all duties, to BENGAL, and to establish factories in that country. His request was complied with, and he was furnished with the means of travelling across the country to BENGAL. Upon his arrival in that province he proceeded to PIPLEY ; and in the year 1048" [*i.e.*, A.D. 1638-9] "an ENGLISH ship happening to arrive in that

---

[1] "*To Our Agent and Factors at* HUGHLY."   [2] O.C. 2185.

port, he, in virtue of the Emperor's firman,[1] and the privileges granted to him, negociated the whole of the concerns of that vessel without the payment of any duties.

"In the following year, the Prince SHUJAA, having taken possession of the government, Mr. BOUGHTON proceeded to RAJEMAHEL, to pay his respects to his Royal Highness : he was most graciously received ; and one of the ladies of the haram being then indisposed with a complaint in her side, the English surgeon was again employed, and had the good fortune to accelerate her recovery. Owing to this event, Mr. BOUGHTON was held in high estimation at the Court of RAJEMAHEL ; and by his influence with the Prince, was enabled to carry into effect the order of the Emperor, which might otherwise have been cavilled at, or by some underhand method, rendered nugatory.

"In the year 1050" [i.e., A.D. 1640-41] "the same ship returned from ENGLAND, and brought out a Mr. BRIDGMAN, and some other persons, for the purpose of establishing factories in BENGAL. Mr. BOUGHTON, having represented the circumstances to the Prince, was ordered to send for Mr. BRIDGMAN ; that gentleman, in consequence, went to RAJEMAHEL, was introduced to the Prince, and obtained an order to establish, in addition to that at PIPLEY, factories at BALLASORE and HOOGLEY.[2] Some time after this event Mr. BOUGHTON died ; but the Prince still continued his liberality to the English."

This extract from Stewart (pp. 251-2) furnishes the earliest version that I have been able to find of this story in its completeness, and it has become the staple of the popular historians, but I cannot trace it to any accessible authority. The extract certainly makes some confusion of authentic dates and circumstances, which will be noticed presently. But apart from that confusion, and though we shall see that Gabriel Boughton was a real person, who acquired the favour of Sháh Jahán and members of his family, I know not where to find the authority for the particulars given in the extract as to Mr. Boughton's treatment of a daughter of the Emperor, suffering from an accident by fire, or as to the patriotic direction given by that gentleman to the Great Mogul's proposed remuneration of his skill, anticipating so closely the conduct more authentically related of a brother of his noble craft, three-quarters of a century later, Mr. William Hamilton. I have already noted (vol. II, p. xcviii) how such a jumble has certainly occurred in the legend of Job Charnock, as recounted by an anonymous Mussulman writer in one of Orme's *Fragments*. But see extract from "J. B.s" MS. at p. clxxxiii.

---

[1] "I was not able to find a copy of this firman among the *Indian Records ;* but Mr. Bruce mentions that it is in the State Paper Office, and is dated Feb. 2, 1633-4." (*Stewart.*)

There is no such firman now in the Record Office. I cannot help thinking there is some misapprehension in the statement. "2nd February 1633-4" is the date of the arrival of the *firmán* at Surat. See O.C. 1519, extracted below.

[2] See *East India Records*, vol. xiv, p. 22

Major Stewart was, as far as I can see, a conscientious and diligent writer ; but it was not the fashion of his day to give any amplitude of reference, and his references are not clear. It is possible that an examination of certain of the native authorities, used by him in the composition of his history, would disclose the foundation of his story.[1]

It will be seen from our extracts, a little further on, that the dispatch of Boughton from Surat took place not in 1636, but in the beginning of 1645, and that he was sent to Agra, and not to " the Emperor's camp, then in the Dekkan" (as Stewart relates), a circumstance that seems to have been imagined in order to render less impossible the intervention of so vast a distance, to be twice travelled over, between the demand for a European surgeon, and his arrival in time to treat successfully the injuries received by the princess.

The first concession of trading privileges in Bengal is sometimes ascribed to the negotiations of Sir Thomas Roe, when ambassador from King James to the Great Mogul Jahángír. This is not correct, for it will be seen by the extracts following, that though the Company's servants at Surat had been very desirous to obtain such concessions, and had urged the matter repeatedly on the ambassador, the latter had not obtained them, and was not indeed disposed to press for them keenly.

---

[1] There is authority apparently for the fire-accident, though Boughton's connexion with the cure is, I suspect, imaginary. The following passage occurs in *Dow's Hist. of Hindostan*, which is, I believe, a loose and glossed translation from Mussulman writers :

" The Emperor's alarm for DARA was scarce subsided, when a dreadful accident happened to his eldest daughter, whom he loved above all his children. Returning one night from visiting her father to her own apartments in the haram, she unfortunately brushed with her clothes one of the lamps which stood in the passage. Her clothes caught fire ; and as her modesty, being within hearing of men, would not permit her to call for assistance, she was scorched in a terrible manner. She rushed into the haram in flames ; and there was no hope of her life. The Emperor was much affected . . . . he for once became devout, to bribe heaven for the recovery of his favourite child. He however did not in the meantime neglect the common means. ANIT-ALLA, the most famous physician of the age, was brought express from Lahore, and the Sultana, though by slow degrees, was restored to health." (*Op. cit.*, 1772, vol. iii, p. 179.)

This is approximately put under the marginal date A.D. 1643, A.H. 1053, which would indeed almost correspond to Boughton's actual mission to the Court (see extract at p. clxxxii).

If it be allowable to form a conjecture, mine would be that one of Stewart's native authorities may have " combined the information'' as to the lady's accident and Boughton's mission (the latter derived from some European source), and that Stewart had adopted this without sufficient inquiry.

Extract of Letter from Sir THOMAS ROE " *to my loving frends* Mr. LUCAS ANDRINUS *or to the Principall of the* ENGLISH *Merchants resident at* MESOLAPATAN *for the East India Company these be delivered.*"[1]

Dated at end, " ADSMERE the 23 : of July 1616."

*   *   *   *   *   *   *

" I daylie expect a concession of new articles and priviledges, propounded in the name of my Master to the MOGUL, wherof I have newly obteyned grant, wherin I haue prouided for all inconveniences, so farr, as the faith of this King can secure vs : I was requested to procure a *firmaen*, or command for BENGALA : it beeing supposed that some Shipping would be this yeare diverted thither, but fynding them by experience, to be ordinary warrants, and lightly regarded, I haue resolued as a firmer course, to send a Copye of the Articles vnder the Seale of the King, (which are more effectuall, and conteyne in them lardger priviledges and Stricter commands then any *firmaen*) vnto your factorye : that they may lye ready to bee deliuered to any ENGLISH commander, that shall goe for BENGALA, supposing that hee will first visitt your residence, being in his way, which hee may take a longe with him and make vse of in all parts, and when he hath resolued to settle a factorie in any certaine place, If I may receive advise, I will accordingly procure any further command to the particular Gouernor, that shalbe requisite, and so Soone as I haue receiued and countersealed them, I will despatch them vnto you, desiring such vse may be made thereof, as the Companies busines shall require."

Extract of a Letter from the same " *to my Honored friends the Governor and Committees for the* EAST INDIA *Company.*"[2]

Dated at end, " De Cember: 1: 1616."

*   *   *   *   *   *

" Whereas you write for new factoryes, except the silkes of BENGALA require yt, which yet in my opinion is had cheeper at AGRA, then you will fynd it there, to mainteyne a factory for yt, beeing this People trauell, and liue hardlyer then yours can, I am of opinion your residences are sufficient, and best chosen, as they are, and the disposure of them I have mentioned in my last to the Consultation at SURATT, but what Creditt it will carry I know not. But I will lay this as a rule, you will sooner want Stock to employ in these places, then new residences to buy in."

Sir Thomas goes on to urge the Surat Agency to buy all they can in

---

[1] O.C. 382. *Andrinus* must have been a misreading of the signature of LUCAS ANTHEUNISS, a Dutchman in the service of the English Company.

In Purchas's *Pilgrimage*, ed. 1626 (not the *Pilgrimes*, though it is sometimes bound as vol. v of that work), this Antheuniss is mentioned by Wm. Methold as Lucas Anthonison, along with Pieter Willemson Floris, as two Dutchmen in the English Company's service, who first set up their English business at Masulipatam some thirteen years before.

This was actually in 1611. There are other letters written by Antheuniss, or jointly with colleagues, in the India Records (O.C. 76, 80, 291). He seems to have oscillated between Masulipatam on one hand and Siam and Patani (Gulf of Siam) on the other. He is mentioned occasionally in Richard Cocks's *Diary* (HAK. Soc., 1883).   [2] O.C. 411.

Western India, not at distant places like Agra, except silk and "small goods"—not indigo, even if they give a higher price at Surat. Also to send their purchases from Agra by carts, and not by camels. He goes on :

"It is in vayne for mee to talke to your factors of these matters, they eyther loue not that I should vnderstand yt, or els crosse yt, because I doe. But I would saue you So much yearly, by disposition only of your busynes, if you durst creditt mee, as would buy you 500 chuorles[1] of Indico: when I come home I will discourse it lardgely, in the meane tyme I pray only compare the chardge of way of this Caravan of 170 Camells, with others farr lesse, and you shall fynd it is in the husbandry of your servants to ease many expenses. My freedome in your busines I desier you to take in good part, and for your priviledges, I will so watch, you shall Susteyne no wrong in silence, nor I hope without redresse. The past yeare is a good example, and what I write, when you haue considered it, make it not publique. Soe in hast on the way I Committ you to God."

Extract of Letter from THOMAS KERRIDGE *and* THOMAS RASTELL *at* SURATT *" To the right Honble: and right Worshipfull Company tradinge the* EAST INDIES" :

Dated, " the 26 february 1616."[2]

"There is not now fitt shipping for the discovery of PORTO PEQUENIA nor doe wee hould itt a fitt place ffor your trade, parte of the Ryuer GANGES beeing Comanded by the PORTING(ALLS). Wee haue heard of other places thereaboutes more Comodious which to the next ffleete (if Shipping convenient) may be propounded ffor discovery."

Extract of Letter from LUCAS ANTHEUNISS *"To the Honoble:* Sr. THOMAS ROE, *Knight, Lord Embassador for the King's Majestie of* ENGLAND, *in the Court of the* GT. MOGULL *in* ADSMERE."[3]

(In reply to O.C. 384, and another of 23rd August):

Dated, " MUSULPATAM the 21: March: A. 1616."

*　　　*　　　*　　　*　　　*　　　*　　　*

" Whereas Your Honour makes Mention, to provide for the Coast of BENGALA the same priviledges procured here, or according to the Nature and Custome of

---

[1] In the old books we find Indigo reckoned by the *churl.* I have failed to discover the origin of the word, but I suspect, like *farazola*, it really denoted the hamper, wrapper, or what not, in which the indigo was packed. The *churle* of *Neel* (or Indigo) is stated by Master Newberie (Modern ed. of *Hakluyt*, II, 378) as 27½ *rottles* of Aleppo. And W. Barrett (p. 408) says that 20½ *rotoloes* of Aleppo = 123 *lbs.* English. Hence the *churl* = 138 *lbs.* English. Also the old Portuguese work *Lembranças* says that at Cambaya a *fardo*, or load, of *Anyll* (or Indigo) was equal to 3½ maunds ; 3½ maunds of Cambay or Surat would be 140 *lbs.* So these values are in good agreement, and we may say the *churl* = about 140 *lbs. avoirdupois.*

[2] O.C. 450.　　　　　　　　　　[3] O.C. 461.

such places where for a proofe we might leaue some one. Itt were good for all occasions to send the same thither with the first, although itt were but a *Coule*[1] to a further foundation. Vntill by experience and more ample Information therein, order might be taken as shalbe needfull, for the establishing and setling of factoreyes yf they shall be found proffitable, and then with lardger letters of more force then *Coules* to confirme the same."

From Sir T. ROE to the Council at SURATT :[2]

Dated, "MANDOA 21: October: 1617."

*   *   *   *   *   *   *

" ASAPH-CHANS[3] denialls are all turned into Sollicitations in my behalfe: Soe that I hope to effect that of BENGALA as in my last."

From ditto to ditto :

"LESKAR 6 *course* from MANDOA :[4]

"November 8: 1617.

*   *   *   *   *   *   *

" You may try GOGA, SINDU, BENGALA, but no Port so fitt as SURATT, if you practise to send our goods vp, by our owne Pinnace."

*   *   *   *   *   *   *

Dated, " The Woods 30 *course* short of AMAD(AVAT):

" Decemb: 6: 1617.[5]

" A *firmaen* for BENGALA cannot be had while the Prince hath SURATT, vnles wee should quitt it, and rely on the other only, he pretends that all our fine goods shall come thither and his Port beare the burthen of trash and hinder others, but of this and new changes at Court at the end of my letter."

*   *   *   *   *   *   *

(Sir T. R. *to the Company*):

Dated, " AMADAVAT ffeb: 14: 1617."[6]

*   *   *   *   *   *   *

" BENGALA hath not Ports but such as the PORTUGALLS possesse for smalle Shipping, it will vent nothing of yours : the people are vnwilling in respect of the warr, as they suppose like to ensue in their Seas : and the Prince hath crossed it, thincking we desire to remooue thither wholy : and that, yf wee stay in INDIA, hee takes to bee an affront. But now I may obteyne one Ship to come and goe, vpon hope of Rubies, from ARACAN and PEGU, but I know not what profitt you can make by any residence there, and I speak vpon searching the bottome of all the Secretts of INDIA. If you will haue patience to trye one yeare you shall see one thing effectually done is worth 20 by fragments, you will find it is not many factories here that gett you a penny ; I will forecast your case, and by gods grace settle not only your priviledges, but your Profitt. This two yeare the Prince hath beene my enemie, and if I had yielded, I must haue beene his

---

[1] Ar. *Ḳaul*, a word, a promise ; generally used in India for a written engagement.   [2] O.C. 552.

[3] "Āṣaf Khán" was a title often conferred, taken from the name of Solomon's Wazír. This one was Mírza Abul Hasan, Yamínuddaulah, the father of the "Táj Bíbí", the lady who has the most splendid tomb in the world. He was a man of enormous wealth and influence ; died 1641.

[4] O.C. 558.   [5] O.C. 575.   [6] O.C 610.

Slave; this last year I haue stood out to the last and adventured the feircenes of his wrath, it hath succeeded better then I expected, wee are soe reconciled, that hee is now my effectuall mediator, and will procure mee content; indeed hee only can giue it, his father growes dull, and suffers him to write all commands and to gouerne all his kingdomes. . . ."

Here is a marginal note by Sir T. Roe :

" *When I wrote this I had words enough But such delayes in effect that I am weary of flatteries as of ill usadge.*"

The paper from which the next extract is made is endorsed :

"*A copie of the Articles of Agreement betwixt the* ENGLISH *and the* GUZERATTS,"

(and added in another hand, also old) :

" Vpon the seizure of their Junckes, A°. 1623." [1]

There is no date to the document, but a modern pencilled one of "[12 Nov. 1623]."

This is, as far as I have found, the first document in which there is an express concession or recognition of the English Company's privilege to trade in Bengal. But what powers the Governor of Surat, and other local dignitaries there, who sign the document, had to grant such recognition, does not appear.

" ffor the better conservation of Amitie peace and free comerce of trade with the ENGLISH whoe haue justlie complained of Sundrie abuses and hindrances therevnto in the passed, it is agreed and granted vnto THO: RASTELL president with his Councell, for and in the behalfe of that nation, that they shall freelie for ever hereafter enjoye they the (*sic*) benefitt of these graunts and privileges here vnder written.

" They shall bee permitted free trade as well in the ports of SURATT, CAM-BAYA, GOGA, SINDA and BENGALA, as in all other cities and places within the dominions of JANGERE PAUDSHAH, without prohibition of any Comoditie to bee brought in or exported out of the Kingdome, neither limitation confininge them vnto places times or quantities, where when or how much of any Marchandize gould or Rialls they shall So bringe in or carrie away or transporte from place within or without the aforesaid dominions."

* * * * * * *

There is a second version of this agreement which I now give below to a larger extent. The two agree in substance, but not with precision, looking like two different translations, one or both loose, of the same Persian document, loosely read.

---

[1] O.C. 1179. This appears to refer to the circumstances mentioned in Bruce's *Annals*, i, 236. The Dutch had made prize of several Mogul ships from the ports of Guzerat ; and the Governors, not being well acquainted with the distinctive flags, etc., of European nations resorting to the Indian seas, considered the whole of them to have been acting in concert, and ordered the English agents, etc., to be imprisoned. But I cannot find in Bruce any notice of the present agreement.

"A Contract of Peace made with Mr. RASTELL, *Captain of the* ENGLISH *Nation, which we for the future do oblige ourselves exactly to observe.*[1]

" 1. It is agreed that the ENGLISH shall freely trade at their pleasure in the Ports of SURAT, CAMBAYA, BAROCH, GOGA, BENGALA, SCYNDA, and in other of the Cities the Kings Dominions, and that they shall have liberty to import and Export all sorts of goods excepting Currall[2] for 1 year, promising not to question them either touching the quantity or time, be it Silver or Gold or any other Goods whatsoever they shall export from HINDUSTAN for their own Country, Excepting as (to) the said Currall for one year, which being Expired the import of that also shall not be prohibited.

" 2. That it shall not be lawfull for either the Governour, the officers or *Droga* of the Custome house, upon the pretence of the King or Princes Occasion to require the same of any goods unto them intended for their own proffitt, onely what shall be indeed necessary for the Kings use may be taken.

" 3. That the house belonging to COJA HOSSAN ALLEE wherein they formerly lived paying rent shall be continued unto them.

" 4. That what ever Carts shall be needfull to the ENGLISH for bringing of their goods from the maryne of the towne SWALLY and for transport of Goods from the River TAPPEE and other places, as also water and Provisions for their Ships Expences they shall be furnished of them without molestation or prohibition by the Governours of WOORPAR either present or to come.[3]

" 5. That if any other Christian shall offend any man belonging to the Kings port the ENGLISH are not to be questioned for it, but if any ENGLISH man doe Commit any offence they are answerable for it.

" 6. That noe land Customs at BAROCH: BRODERA: UNCLEASTAR: KURKEH: BERCHAW[4] places belonging to this king, shall be demanded of them, nor any molestation for matter of Jaggat[5] offered ; but BAROCH being a Port towne, though they ship not their goods but bring them thence by land the customs of that are payable, and order to be given that the English receive no trouble in that particular.

    *   *   *   *   *   *   *

" 8. That their *Coffelas* shall pas freely through the country without molestation," etc.

    *   *   *   *   *   *   *

" 10. That the ENGLISH shall have the free exercise of their own religion. (In case of quarrells between ENGLISHMEN the ENGLISH Captain to decide ; if

---

[1] O.C. 1295.   [2] *I.e.*, coral.

[3] In the other version (O.C. 1179) this is " present or future Governours of *Urpall*". *Orpàr* of the *Aín-i-Akbarí* (*Owrparah* of Gladwin's version) is a pargana' of Sirkár Bahroch, now *Olpàd*, a subdivision of the Surat District, lying immediately north of the Táptí R.

[4] Bahroch (or *Broach*), and Brodera (now *Baroda*), are well known. The third name represents *Ankleswar* (*Aklesar* of the *Aín*), a few miles south of Broach. The two last must be the *Khirkà* and *Párchaul* of the *Aín*, parganas of Sirkár *Súrat* (*Origl.*, Blochmann's Ed., pp. 497-498), but I cannot indicate their position.

[5] *Jaggat* is probably *jagát* (a corruption of Ar. *zakát* ("alms"), which is used in some places for "customs"; see *Wilson's Glossary.*

between ENGLISHMAN and Mussulman the Captain and the Governor together shall decide, etc.)

11. (In case of an Englishman's death his goods shall be taken in charge by English people; if there is no Englishman to take charge, the Governor and "Cozzee" shall take an exact account, etc.)

12. (The English ships to administer aid to the King's ships, and never to pretend to any right or claim to any ship pertaining to the King, etc.)

13. (When the captain or other Englishman desires to go on board their ships, as an acknowledgment to the Governour they shall ask his license, etc.)

14. (About satisfaction to be done to the English on their just demands, etc.)

"Given the 25th Day of the Moone Shahur Noor Allee in the 25 year of the Reigne of SHAW JEHAN GEERE.

"ISSOFF CKAWN Governor,
"KHOZZY MAHMUD KHOSSUM,"
and about 18 others.

A note appears in the old India House Index of these O.C. papers:

"The month intended appears to be the sixth of the ancient PERSIAN Kalendar: But the year must be an Error, as JUHANGEER reigned only 22 years 2 months and 10 days.

"In No. 1180 above, the date is stated to be 1624, Sept. 7, which would fall in the 20th year of JUHANGEER's Reign, and 5 months before President RASTELL sailed for England."

We see by the extract of letter from Rastell and others which follows, that the actual date of the document was the 7th September 1624.

The pending agreement is thus alluded to in a letter from President Rastell and others in "SWALLY ROADS, aboard the *William*, 14th February 1624" (*i.e.*, 1625), to the Company[1]:

"After 7: monthes wretched imprizonment wee, the 7th September last, came to a small period and agreement, wherein for matter of privileges (whereunto SIFE CAUN himselfe, with some 20: or 30: of the principall marchantes etc., of this place have both signed and subscribed) the coppie of our Articles herewith translated, will shew them most reasonably favourable, and not much differing in effect from our formers (the renting of customes etc. excepted) . . ."

The initiation of the trade with Bengal is usually assigned to the circumstance related in a *Letter addressed by* WILLIAM METHWOLD *and the Council at* SURAT *to the Company*, dated 21st February 1633-34 (O.C. 1519).

*   *   *   *   *   *   *

"The 2d present we received from AGRA the Kings *firmand* which gives Libertye of trade vnto Vs, in the whole country of BENGALAE, But restraines the Shippinge only vnto the porte of PIPLYE, the *firmand* was sent unto Vs by a servant of our owne which was dispeeded vnto AGRA with prohibition of the 21st. November formerly mentioned, by which servant soe returned we received noe one ENGLISH Letter or Sillable private or publique, directly or indirectly concerning this or any other busines, except that the ENGLISH Broker advised

---

[1] O.C. 1180.

vnto ours in this place, that Mr. FREMLIN much against their advise had most improvidently bought 3000 *mds. Echobares*[1] of BYANA Indicoe at 64 rups: p. md." . . .

*   *   *   *   *   *   *

But, before this, the Company's agents, recently established on the Coromandel Coast, had taken a distinct step towards opening trade with the Bay. Of this we have some fragmentary notices in the surviving original correspondence from India; but also a more continuous, though speedily interrupted, narrative, which has been curiously overlooked by writers on these subjects.[2] This is the relation of William Bruton, originally published in London, 1638.[3]

WILLIAM BRUTON relates that the 22 March 1632(-3), he being at MASULAPATAM in the Country of CORMANDELL, Master JOHN NORRIS, the agent there, was resolved to send two Merchants into BENGALLA for the settling of a factory, and six EUROPEANS besides, who were then at MASULAPATAM, were to accompany the merchants, and carry a present from the Agent to the Nabob or King of that country. They set sail on the 6th April, and on the 21st anchored before a town called HARSSAPORE. This place I have (vol. II., p. ccxl) to the best of my ability identified with the HURRICHPORE GURH of the Indian Atlas, on the coast of the MAHANADI Delta.

When the party landed there a Portuguese master of a frigate " with the assistance of some of the ribble-rabble Rascalls of the Towne did set vpon Mr. CARTWRIGHT and Mr. COLLEY, where our men, being oprest by multitudes had like to have beene all slaine or spoyld, but that (Lucklip)[4] the *Rogger* (or Vice King there) rescued them with 200 men" (p. 48).

They had an interview with the Nabob at MALCANDY, his residence near COTEKE (Cuttack), and he gave them leave to trade, freely and without paying custom, " off or on the shore in the country of WUDIA (*i.e.*, Odia or Orissa). This took place 3rd May 1633.

In consequence of this permission (though the narrative makes no

---

[1] The *man* of Akbar was (according to Thomas's *Prinsep*) 34¾ *lbs.* (see that work, *Useful Tables*, p. 111).

[2] Except, as I find, by Hugh Murray, in his very interesting but almost forgotten work, *Hist. Account of Discoveries and Travel in Asia, etc.*, Edinburgh, 1820, 3 vols., 8vo.

[3] The title of the work runs : *Newes from the* EAST INDIES, *or a Voyage to* BENGALLA . . . . *written by* WILLIAM BRUTON . . *now lately come home in the good Ship* Hopewel *of* LONDON . . *Imprinted at* LONDON *by* I. OKES . . . 1638.

It is reprinted in vol. v of the enlarged edition of *Hakluyt* of 1809-12.

[4] Probably some Hindu name is meant ; *e.g.*, *Lakhpati* (Lord of 100.000, " wealthy"), or *Lakhadhip* (commander of 100,000).

mention of permission granted to build), the party established a factory at HARHARRAPORE, and whilst some of them remained there to build, Mr. CARTWRIGHT travelled towards BALLAZARY (Balasore), and reached it *viâ* PIPELY.

The next letter is written by Mr. Poule, who appears to have been left in charge of the intended factory at Harharrapore, to his chief.

(*From* JOHN POULE *to* Mr. CARTWRIGHT *at* BALLASORE.)[1]

Dated, "HARRAPOORE the 17th of July 1633."
(Stained and mutilated, difficult to read.)

* * * * * *

" Your opinnion of sending A man to GUGERNAT *Et setera* places, there to procure cloth would very well become our implyment had we but on home we might truste in that bissines but you well know the fallsity and desaytfullnes of our new implyed sarvants is such that we Durst not depose confidence in them to the vallew of 10 *roopees.* Our sarvant NIRANA cannot be well spared from this place. I doo therfoore my Sellfe intend so farr as I can gett musters of *Cussayes*[2] which are now A making to Leave the oversight of this place vnto WILLIAM BRUTON and the broker, and A dress my Sealfe for the greate pogodo, there soposing Likewise to put ofe part such Marchandise as heere Lyeth ded on our hands.

" The Market of Saylls in HARRAPOORE seimes at present as if there were no marchantes in the Contry.

* * * * * *

" Those PORTINGALLS whilome exspelled from HVGLY hath found greate favor with SHAWGAHAN and reentered that place to the number of 20 persones hows Cavidall[3] for their commensing A new investment is the third part of there goods formerly cessed on[4] which with Large priveliges and *tashareefes*[5] with honor, the kinge hath bestowed on them so that our exspectation (of) HUGLY is frusstrayt and I feare likwise PIPPELY will (not?) be obtained beeing A convenient Randyvoes of the(irs?) wherefor som parsones have Latly complained to this Nabob of our seeking to put them from that porte ; have Answered we entended no Svch mater but only for BOLLASARY or HARSSAPOORE, so with good *delassa*[6] they were dismissed."

(The next lines are much mutilated.)

* * * * * *

" The present Afording nought Ellse to my Remembrance worth your knowledge. Our Loving Salute and Remaine . . "

(No signature.)

The capabilities of the trade thus initiated are treated at considerable length, but somewhat vaguely as regards actual proceedings, in the next letter from which I extract :

---

[1] O.C. 1510.   [2] *Khássa,* or *khássá,* a kind of muslin.
[3] *I.e.,* "whose capital"— (?).
[4] *I.e.,* "seized on" (?).   [5] Complimentary presents.
[6] Hind. *dilásá,* "heart-hope", consolation.

Extract of letter to Company, from THOS. JOYCE *and* NATH: WYCHE,
dated MESULAPATAM, *the 25th of October 1634 :*[1]

*   *   *   *   *   *   *

"Mr. NORRIS[2] (if arriued with you) has ere now we assume, shown you the
reason of this dearth's Beginning, which was an Extraordinary drought for
a whole yeare together, that Caused a scarcity of Cotton wooll, and Raised its
price from 4: to 8 and 10 Fs.[3] this *Maund.* The next yeare followinge (which was
since our Comming to this place) here fell such Abundance of Raine as Rotted
not onely a great part of the Corne in the fields, ere twas halfe Ripe, But also
spoyl'd most of the Cotton Wooll, that then was growinge in this Countrey, and
By that meane Brought its worth from the foresaid 8 and 10 Fs. to 25 and 26 Fs.
Pr. Maund (the price Current) which is full 12*d.* the ENGLISH Pound.[4]

"This yeare has hitherto proved very temperate, and if it please the Lord so
to conclude it, there's great Signes of a Plentifull Harvest which will be About
the next March or Aprill, and (we hope) bringe Cotton, and consequently
Cloath to the easy prices it has beene formerly sold at.

*   *   *   *   *   *

"Two of your 3: factors Sent hither on the Shipp *Swann* (vizt. Mr. BAN-
NISTER and Mr. LITTLER) were Continued in her to BENGALA, where the
former dyed shortly after his thither Arrivall, and the other lived there till
Last, and then tooke his leave of this world.

*   *   *   *   *   *

"In the first place the BENGALA factory desires to show it Selfe, Because
(indeed) its Setlinge was the first thinge (of Note) that was Acted after our
Cominge vnto this Coast. Wee presume that you are punctually informed ere
now, As well By Mr. NORRIS (be he liuinge) as By our letters to SURRATT
and BANTAM (if their Coppyes were sent you) of the many Reasons that
impulst the sending of your people into that BAY. It was the forementioned
Scarsity of Cloths here that gave the prime motion (as by a Consultation to that
effect held the 27th June 1633), and then 'twas determined for a Voyage onely,
But after some deliberation it was Computed how Beneficiall to the Company a
Continuall Residence there might Be in many Kinds.

"Ffirst for the trade 'twixt that and this place, in Rice, Sugar, Butter, and
divers other sorts of Provisions and course Commodities.

"Secondly it affords Store of white cloths at Cheape Prices, such as is
Suitable for ENGLAND, PERSIA, and the Southwards. . . .

"Besides it yealdes good Store of exceeding good powder Sugar which Costs
not there above two pence halfe penny the English pound, with all charges
Aboard. As much of this Commodity as may be got timely enough for PERSIA,
we intend for that place by the *Discovery.* . . .

"Gumlacke vppon Stickes is there to be had very Cheape, and is much
required, as well for MACASSAR and PERSIA as for ENGLAND. . . .

"Silke may there be Bought likewise yearely to a great Summe at 4 *in* 5
fanams the English pound.

---

[1] O.C. 1536.   [2] The late chief of Masulipatam factory.   [3] *Fanams.*
[4] It is not easy to verify this reckoning. The maund (*man*) in use on the
Coast is popularly reckoned at 25*lbs.* (actually 23.192*lbs.*) ; whilst the *highest*
value of the *fanam* at this time would be 4*d.* or 4½*d.* Taking the maund at
24*lbs.* and the fanam at 4½*d.*, the price would still be under 5*d.* a pound
instead of 12*d.*

*   *   *   *   *   *   *

" Divers other things it affords for PERSIA, as *Shashes*, Stuffes, *Allyjahs*,[1] fine CHITE Cloths and the like. Some whereof is now in Action for that place, and our Better experience will doubtless Bringe the rest Also within the compass of our future investments.

" These are the Staple Commodities that BENGALA yealds, of which we hope your Worshipps will in short time receive such profitable content, as shall persuade your good liking for the Continuance of the factory.

" Now what goods are there vendible, Experience must better Tutor us ere we can rightly informe you. Most of the Broad cloth and Lead you laded on the *Swann* for this place, was sent thither for a Tryall, and for want of factors (through Mortality) it lay in BALLASARA (the Port Towne) till Aprill last, when 'twas then dispersed for sale to PUTTANA, a months Journey into the Countrey, So as it seems theres Noe great hopes of selling Such Commodities, neare the Sea Side. And what marketts they meet withall further within the land we have not as yet bene Advis'd of. But seinge the same finds no quick vend we forbeare sendinge any of the *Jewells* goods that waye.

" Spices of all Sorts Sells there to good profitt, But the DUTCH freemen from BATTAVIA and PORTUGALLS from MACASSAR, did so stuffe the Marketts therewith last yeare, as now theres little or none required. Hereafter the DUTCH Company (we believe) will doe the like, so we see not any great hope of gains by that Commodity.

" Tobacco, Iron, Tinn, and Sundry other petty Goods is yearly carried thither on the Juncks that Saile from this place ; and if we Receive any encouragement from our friends thereto to be tradinge in the like, we shall not omitt to put it in practice.

" Hitherto have we only shewed you what Commodities BENGALA does Cheifly export and require. Be pleased in the next place to understand that if you resolve the prosecution of this trade, it is very requisite that you Send out two small Pinnaces to remaine on this Coast, of some 80 to 120 tunnes, such as may draw but little water, and carry some 12: or 14: gunns apeece. The DUTCH are never without 3: or 4: such vessells here, wherewith they trade from Port to Port all the yeare longe, some times buying Rice and other Provisions where they are Cheape, and transport to Better Marketts, other whiles they are imployed as men of warr (but never Idle), and by these meanes they cleare at yeares end, all the great charges they are att vppon this Coast.[2]

---

[1] *Shásh*, a turban-cloth, whence our "sash". *Alajah*, a kind of silk stuff corded, or striped with gold or colour. See *Anglo-Indian Glossary*, s. v. *Alleja*.

[2] To the like purpose is this *Extract of a Letter to the Company from Captain* WEDDELL *of the Shipp* Jonah, "*neare* CAPE COMERIN, the 9th Maye 1633." (O.C. 1504) :

*   *   *   *   *   *   *

"If your Worshipps intend to prosecute a trade at the River GANGES, I conceive it were needfull you provide a couple of small Shipps, one of 160 and thother of 120 Tonns, not to drawe above 8 or 10 foote at the most, and to be well fortified the one with 18 and the other with 16 peeces of ordnance, Saker and Minion, that they may be able to defend themselves against frigotts and other Vessells that may assaulte them."

" And now both these and our Small vessells will be more vsefull then ever, for there's noe thought of trade into the Bay without them, our greater Shipps ridinge So farre from the Shoare, and the Kinge of ARRACKANS *Jelliaes* (or Small Boats of warr) ever Scouting twixt them and the land, in so much as neither Goods nor provisions Cann be Brought of without Pinnaces of some defence, Such as we have nam'd, which may goe up the Rivers for the same without feare, and transport it to the Bigger vessells.

*   *   *   *   *   *

" One thinge more is yet to be added touchinge the Setlinge of this BENGALA trade and then wee'le desire leaue to be silent till time letts us know it Better. That's the Mortality of your people there, which is the alone Object that opposes the action ; ffor the last yeare there died 5: of the 6: factors that were left in that place whose roomes were againe Supplyed by 4: that were Spared us from SURRATT on the *Hart,* whome we Sent into the BAY on the *Thomas,* and are told by late Advises from thence that one of them is likewise dead since his Arrivall thither, the Rest (praysed be God) doe yet remaine in health. Your Seamen Also are subject to the same infirmity, for most part of the *Swans* men were there visited with Sickness, and many of them died. The *Thomas* has likewise (we heare) Burried 4: of her Small Company Since her last goinge thither, and the greatest part of the Survivinge lye dangerously weake. The Cheife Occasion of this disease is doubtless Intemperancy (Mr. CARTWRIGHTS letters averr noe less) for 'tis a place that Aboundes with Racke and ffruitt, and these immoderately taken Cannot Chuse But ingender Surfeits. Those that hereafter may receive imployments that wayes will, we hope, practize a more warier diett, and live to report Better of the Country.

*   *   *   *   *   *

" Mr. RALPH CARTWRIGHT who has bene Chiefe in BENGALA ever since that trade has been afoot, and for that he hath bene long out of his Countrey, did earnestly intreat license to depart thitherward the last yeare, but was perswaded to stay till this time, and now againe we have desired his Abode there for the other 12 months, but whether he will Consent thereunto or noe, his answer does not yet Resolve us.

" Some others here are likewise that desire to Be homewards too, But must abide with Patience till their Roomes can be Supplyed. A list of what men are at present upon this Shoare, as Also, how many factors are requisite for this Coast of BENGALA you may please to see here inclosed. . . .

" Last yeare when the *Swann* was in BENGALLA, her boat beinge Sent on Shoare for water was suddenely Surprized by some of the Kinge of ARACKANS *Gelliaes* of Warr : 3: of her men killed, and the rest taken and carryed to a place in BENGALLA called PIPLEE where a PORTUGALL Captain that came thither on a small vessell from MACCASSAR redeemed them for 400: *Ruppes,* which mony was presently sent him from BALLASARRA . . . for which affront we doe awayt all opportunitye to force a satisfaction."

*   *   *   *   *   *   *

The course of proceedings for the next eight or nine years is obscure. The only notice of them that I have met with is in that short account of the rise of Balasore by Mr. Walter Clavell, written for Streynsham Master's information in 1676, which has been printed above (II, p. ccxl). It is perhaps not absolutely accurate, but was probably derived direct from the earliest factors in the Bay. In spite of the repetition it will be convenient to reprint a few lines of the passage here :

"BALLASORE begunn to be a noted place when the PORTUGUEZ were beaten out of ANGELIN" (mod. Hijilí) "by the MOORES, about the yeare 1636, at which time the trade began to decay at PIPLEY and to have a diminution in other places of these parts; and the Barr opening, and the River appearing better than was imagined, the ENGLISH and DANES endeavoured to settle factories here, to be out of the troubles the PORTUGUEZ gave to the other nations and had themselves, the rather because the cloth of HARRAPORE,[1] where our first ffactorye was settled was without much difficultye to be brought hither by land, and the River where our Vessells vsually had laine at being stopt up, itt was noe easy matter to bring the Cloth by Sea, nor soe safe to have vessells ride before that place, as here in the Roade of BALLASORE."

I have not been able to find any evidence of there having ever been an English factory at Pipli. Neither in the Dutch Map of Van der Broucke (c. 1662-64) nor in the chart published in the 1701 edition of the *English Pilot* (see next Part of these illustrations) is there any indication of an English factory there, though both maps show a Dutch one.

How long the factory founded at Hariharpúr was maintained I have found no indication; but voyages to Balasore seem to have been made from time to time, and factors to have resided there, at least temporarily.

Thus (in O.C. 1797) we have "*A Briefe Declaration of some Passages and Observations made by mee Andrew* TRUMBALL *in my last voyage in your Shippe* Hopewell." This is chiefly a series of charges against Mr. FRANCIS DAY. But the writer says:

"1642. August 14th. We arrived at BALLISARA where we stayed 3 monthes and 16 dayes at 180*l.* per monthe charge," etc.

O.C. 1787 shows that a ship called the *Dyamond* had been sent to the Bay (presumably to Balasore) in 1641 to pay debts and fetch off the factors.

Then we have the following:

Letter from FFRANCIS DAY *to the Company, dated* "BALLASARA, November the 3d., 1642" :[2]

* * * * * *

"The 7th August wee left MESULAPATAM and arrived with the above said success at BALLASARA the 13th *ditto*, where having launded the remaines of what left at MADRASAPATAM and MESULAPATAM wee have since arrivall hither made sale of the Glasses, Knives, Lead and some 22 parcel of Cloth, the Lead and most part of the Cloth have bin putt off in truck, for Sugar, *Gurras, Sannoes, Cassaes*,[3] Iron, and Ginghams, all but the last is intended for PERTIA, for willingly I would leave nothing behinde, the returne being soe uncertaine there.

---

[1] I.e., *Harharrapoore* of Bruton, *supra*, p. clxxvii, and II., p. ccxl., *note*.

[2] O.C. 1797.

[3] All names of cotton piece-goods. *Gára* is *now* one of the coarsest of cotton cloths; *sanno*, probably the *sahn* of *Ain* (Blochmann's E. Tr., p. 94). *Cassae*, see *supra*, p. clxxvii.

" There is some *Cassaes* and *Sannoes* providing at HARAPORE, and they are intended for EUROPE, but what quantity of either I cannot certainly nominate· Many you may not expect, the rains having been soe late and so violent.

" Mr. YARD and Mr. TRAUELL doe both intend to goe in your Shipp *Hopewell*, or *Aduice*, for MADRASAPATAM, and soe for EUROPE. Mr. HATCH only remaines and very much discontented in regard his Contracted time is expired, and the small imployment that hee is like to have.

" Accordinge to that small time of my being heer, and that little observation that I have taken, I thinke BALLASARA with the Adjacent places is not to bee totally left, for it is no such dispisable place as is voted, it being an opulent Kingdome and you haveing bin already at great charges in gaininge the free Custome of all Sorts of Goods, beleive it if you had but an Active man, two or three in these parts, you would find it very proffitable, provided you double Stocke the Coast, without which it is impossible to comply to your desires.

" Since I have knowen these parts, for the most parte you have had servants and little or noe means to imploy them, if you should inlarge your trade, you may happely have meanes and noe servants, especially such that should know how to imploy it to best advantage."

A letter of Sept. 8, 1644, from the Council at Fort St. George to the Company,[1] says that Mr. OLTON had been sent to take charge of the Company's business in Bengalla ; and mentions that the factors in that region were this HENRY OLTON, WM. GURNEY, and WM. NETLAND (Netlam), assistant.

The next extract is that which introduces GABRIEL BOUGHTON, the surgeon, under the genuine circumstances of his mission to Agra :

From President and Council at SURAT *to Company, dated* "SWALLY MAREENE, the 3rd January 1644"(-5).[2]

"ASSALAUT CKAUNE, a very great *Vmbra*, gratious with the King and our very good freind haveing long importuned us to supply him with a Chirurgeon, wee Consideringe how advantageous itt may be vnto you, and haueing a fitt oportunity, one GABRIEL BOUGHTEN, late Chirurgeon of the *Hopewell* being therevnto very well qualifyed, and being willinge to stay, wee haue thought fitting to designe him to that service, wherewith ASSAL: CKAUNE is Soe well pleased that lately when Mr. TURNER was to leave AGRA he accompanied Mr. TASH and Mr. TURNER to the King who honor'd them more than ordinary in a long conference he held with them, dismissing them with Vests, and sending vnto the PRESIDENT a *firman* and dagger, which not being yett received wee know not what the former may import or the Latters valew, but shall here after advise, and if the dagger be of any considerable worth it shall be sent you with the jewell before advised the Prince lately sentt vnto the PRESIDENT, both expected by Mr. TURNER."

This is all that we find on the matter. The next Surat letter (March 31st, 1645) has no reference to the subject. In a later one,[3] dated January 3rd, 1645(-6), there is allusion to the dagger and jewel spoken of in the preceding extract, but there is no mention either of Boughton or of the *firmán*.

---

[1] O.C. 1885. [2] O.C. 1905, [3] O.C. 1970.

The next extract but one from the records shows Mr. Boughton transferred to Bengal, and there apparently using his influence to serve his countrymen. Some light is thrown upon this by the latter part of the passage from Stewart's *History of Bengal*, which I have quoted (pp. clxvii-viii) ; but there also the dates are wrong, and circumstances are detailed for which we cannot trace the authority.[1]

I also find from a MS. discourse by " J. B.", a Captain of a Company's ship, who was in India *c.* 1670-1680 (which I have seen just as this sheet is going to press, and which I have the owner's permission to quote), that the story of the acquisition of privileges for his countrymen by Gabriel Boughton (there called *Bowden*) was then current, though some of the particulars are given differently. Indeed, this MS. curiously illustrates the inexactitude of even twenty years' tradition. For it seems impossible that Mír Jumla, who did not come to Bengal till 1659, should have been the Mahommedan patron from whom Boughton (who died some years earlier) obtained trading privileges for his countrymen. The passage in J. B.'s MS. runs as follows :

" In the before mentioned places in these 3 Kingdoms" ("ORIXA, BENGALA, and PATTUNA"—*i.e.*, Behar) " the English nation in generall hath freedome of inhabiting and tradeinge, free from all manner of taxes and customes, in or out, the like priviledges hath noe Other Nation besides. *"Our Nation are free from all Duties and taxes whatever in these 3 Kingdomes."*

" All which was procured by the Ingenuitie of Mr. GABRIEL BOWDEN (One of our owne Nation) and a very Eminent Doctor of Phisick, sometime Doctor in Ordinary to the great Warriour EMIR JEMLA : who took a very great Affection towards him, and was most courteous and ffree to him, and Especially upon a Notable Cure of his owne Lady performed (Vnder God) by the Doctor, the Nabob callinge for him ordered him att that instant to demand what he wold haue giuen him or had most likinge to and it shovld be granted in Consideration of his Loyal Service and care of the best of his familie. *"first Granted by the Great and famous Warriour EMIR JEMLA."* The Doctor highly Surprised with this great Person's Generositie, Soone considered vpon it, yet soe as not to be greedy of any present Gaine (onely for himselfe) and now in the best of time, requested that the ENGLISH Nation might Settle ffactories in what parts of the Kingdomes they pleased and be free off all duties and Customes, which then was 4 per cent. in and the like out for all the goods dealt in, the which was noe Sooner demanded but as readily granted, with *Phyrmands* in the PERSIAN Languadge that the ENGLISH Nation Shold hold that Priviledge soe longe as they pleased to live and Settle in these Dominions, and many Other rewards Liberally bestowed Vpon the Doctor (one beinge very rare among the Mahometants). . . ." But here this part of the MS. breaks off. *"All which priviledge was acquired by that ingenuous and kindhearted Countreyman of ours Doctor GABL: BOWDEN."*

---

[1] Stewart quotes thus : "See *East India Records*, vol. xiv, p. 22". Nothing corresponding to this reference can now be traced in the India Office. The dates given by Stewart, viz., A.H. 1046 and A H. 1050, would be A.D. 1636-7 and 1640-41, which are impossible ; but, apart from the dates, it will be seen that the next extracts from the records seem to corroborate the facts stated in the last lines of the passage from Stewart.

"*Instructions for* Mr. JAMES BRIDGEMAN *Cheife,* Mr. EDWARD STEPHENS
Second, WILLIAM BLAKE *and* FFRANCIS TAYLER *Assistants, in
the ffactories of* BALLASOR *and* HUKELY *for the honoble:* ENGLISH
EAST INDIA *Company.*"[1]

" Srs: Dated at end, " BALLASOR 14th December 1650."

" Principally and above all things you are to endeavoar with the best of
your might and power the advancement of the glory of God, which you will best
doe, by walking holily, righteously, prudently, and Christianly, in this present
world, that soe the Religion, which you professe, may not be evil spoken of, and
you may enjoy the quiet, and peace of a good conscience towards GOD and man
and may alwayes bee ready to render an accompt in a better world, where GOD
Shall be Judge of all.

" Whereas it is the designe of our Masters the honoble: Company to advance,
and encrease the trade in these parts of OREXEA and BENGAL, you are by all
possible meanes to endeavour more and more to informe yourselves how best and
most profitably to carry out the trade thereof, especially for Saltpeter, Silke and
Sugers. To this ende, that you endeavour the sale of those goods remaining in
the ffactories to the most advantage, therebye assoone as may bee, to gett moneys
into your hands that soe you may proceed to invest the same in the best time of
buying the aforesaid goods.

" PATENNA being on all Sides concluded the best place for procureing of Peter,
desire you therefore to make a tryall how you can procure the same from thence,
wherein you may make vse of WB,[2] who you know is able to informe you. You
must soe order that busines, as hee may have proffitt thereby and may bee encouraged, by which meanes you will soonest arrive to our desire. In this commodity invest at least one halfe of your Stock, and endeavour the refineing of the
same at HUKELY. In case you runne into debt, lett it bee for this commodity,
yet I dare not advise you soe to do, vntill you receive order from the Agent, and
Councell, the Interest being (as you know) soe exceeding high.

" In silke you know what great matters are to be done, therefore it doth import
the Company much, that you strive both by relation and your own experience to
know how, and where best to carry on the Manufacture thereof, where the best
Silkes are procured, and where the best conveniences are for fitting, and preparing
the Same for the Sales of EUROPE, that soe if the Company shall require large
quantities you may bee in a posture to fitt them all at the first hand. I suppose
the order of the DUTCH is very good, and will be freest from adulteration, the
properest way will bee to make three sorts, as Head, Belly, and ffoote, each apart
by them Selves. You may also make an experience of the washing thereof at
HUKELY or elsewhere, and Send the Company a maund of each Sort apart by
the next Shipping for a Sample, with an exact accompt of the losse in washing,
and charge of the same. In this Commodity you may invest neare three eight
parts of your remaines.

" As for Sugers, you know they are procured in many places, you may make
a small tryall in each. Herein I suppose you need but inquire secretely into the

_____

[1] O.C. 2186.

[2] So I read these initials, in some form of old Court hand. Perhaps the
person may be Wm. Blake (one of the factors addressed), or " Wm. Benis",
mentioned in Masulipatam letter below (25th Feb. 1651)?

order of the DUTCH, how, where, and when they proceed to buy the said Commodity, and how the seasons doe fall for bringing the same out of the Countrey or downe the Rivers. I am informed that the quantity they last bought at PATENNA is well approved of, therefore I desire also that you procure some from thence by the same way or Instruments that you make use of to obtayne the Peter.

" You know how necessary it will bee for the better carrying on the trade of these parts to have the Princes *ffirman*, and that Mr. GABRIEL BOUGHTON Chirurgeon to the Prince promises concerning the same. To putt matters out of doubt it is necessary that you forthwith after our departure, and the settlement of business here, and at HUKLEY, proceed to RAJAMALL with one Englishman to accompany you; where being come consult with Mr. BOUGHTON about the busines, who hath the whole contents of the DUTCHES last *ffirman*, and together endeavour (if possible) that (according to Mr. BOUGHTON'S promise) the Company may have such a *ffirman* granted, as may outstrip the DUTCH in point of Privilege and freedome, that soe they may not have cause any longer to boast of theirs. You know what I have written to Mr. BOUGHTON about it, who (without doubt) will bee very faithfull in the busines, and strive that the same may bee procured, with as little charge as may bee to the Company, knowing that the lesse the charge is the more will bee the reputation, according to his owne advice in his last vnto me: what you shall present, or expend in the busines I cannot advise, however what you doe, lett it bee done with joint consent, and I pray you bee as spareing as may bee in a busines of this Import.

" ffrom the FFORT you may expect assoone as may bee the Agents further order, with a Supply of Stock for these ffactories, that soe goods may bee procured in readines against the comeing of the next Ships, conforme to his promise.

" The two Assistants WILLIAM BLAKE and FFRANCIS TAYLER being without a knowne salary servants to the Company, you may lett them have five or six pounds a year a peece for their maintenance in clothes vntill further order.

" And whereas the accusations against NARRAND the Companies Broker are without Proofe, and indyed invalid, you are still to continue him, as hee was in the Companies service, and vnder their protection, giving him all convenient encouragement.

" The trade at BALLASOR being now carryed on in *Rupees Morees*,[1] desire you to continue all negotiations there in the same Specie, supposing it most advantagious for the Company soe to doe, And that you endeavour to keep a good correspondence with the Governours of BALLASOR and HUKELY, as also with all such as are the Allies and frends of our Nation.

" In every thing desire you to have a Speciall regard not to putt the Company upon any vnnecessary charge, either of building, or repaireing of houses, or in keeping any more servants than the necessity of their service doth require.

"That all matters of concernement to the Company bee declared to their Servants who thereby may bee the better enabled in the future to serve their masters, soe that in case of sickness, or mortality (which doth often happen in these parts) the successors may alwayes know how, what and where the Companies interests are, and how in all things their busines doth Stand, to avoid the inconvenience, which might arise on the contrary.

---

[1] *Muhri?* I do not find this rupee in Prinsep. It was probably the *round* rupee; see Blochmann's *Áin* (Eng. tr.), p. 31. Akbar had also introduced square coins.

"That either your Selfe or NARRAND procure a donation of that Land on the west side of the DUTCH house, and soe downe to the River and the small Creeke, soe that in case the Company resolve to enlarge trade here they may there build a mansion house, and a house for refineing of Peter close by the River, where meet conveniences for negotiations of that nature doe attend, and lett them digge a trench round about the said land of five or six Rupees charge, to signify our bounds and interest in the same.

"I understand the Nabbob of CATTACKE is to come downe this way. Desire if hee come that you present him with a remnant of fine cloth of the value of tenn pounds or thereabouts and a Sword Blade or two of the best sort.

"These are what I thought needfull to advise you by way of Instructions, doubt not, but you will have such as are more ample by the first from the Agent, with stock to your content from MASULAPATAM, or PEGU, conforme to the advice in my Instructions. And herewith wishing you prosperity, for present take leave, and rest

"Your very loveing frend

"J. B." (*Captain* JOHN BROOKHAVEN.)

Letter from H. GREENHILL *and* ROBERT DOUGHTY *to the Court.*[1]

Dated, "Fort St. George the 18th Januarie 1650."

"After a long and dubious expectation it pleased the Almighty of his goodnes to period our cares, in the safe arrivall of Ship *Lyoness* at this port the 22th: Aug": last, Commanded by Capt. JOHN BROOKHAVEN.

*   *   *   *   *   *   *

We also find 3 other ffactors designed on the *Lyoness* for HUGHLEE in the River GANGES, Mr. ROBERT SPAVIN, Mr. JAMES BRIDGMAN, and Mr. WILLIAM FFAIREFAX, the first of whome lived not to see this place, the other 2 are safely arrived, whose disposure with the other aforesaid ffactors ships and Carga must be the next subject of discourse.

*   *   *   *   *   *   *

. . knowing well the maine bulke of the *Lyoness* her lading was to bee commenced in the BAY of BENGALAH, dispatcht her the next day for BALLASORE with a carg": of monies and goods to the amount of 7336ˡ: 17ˢ: 5ᵈ . . Wee committed the management of the BAY Investment vnto Capt. JOHN BROOKHAVEN in Cheife, appointing for his assistants JAMES BRIDGMAN and EDWARD STEEVENS, which last as more proper for that busines was sent instead of WM. FFAIRFFAX, whom from England you had enordered with ROBERT SPAVIN deceased to the Imployment of HUGHLEE, also vpon WM. NETLAMS petition wee returned him againe for BALLASORE, and wish his services there may bee such as will deserve his wages, as expected from one that hath soe long resided in those parts, but because wee know that Capt. BROOKHAVEN might not have too much confidence in him and that the other two prementioned had little experience in the BAY, wee directed him to vse the Advise and assistance of one RICHARD POTTER who formerly had served you in the *Endeavours* voiage to PEGU, and there fairely acquitting himselfe was gratified with 100ˡ: ster: for his service, and being now somewhere about PIPLEE or BALLASARA, hee was enioyned by letters from the Agent to apply himself to Capt. BROOKHAVEN, and in this vrgency of your affaires to afford him possible help. And whereas from ENGLAND you were pleased to designe that the ship should voiyage it up the River GANGES to

---

[1] O.C. 2200.

HUGHLY, and settle a factory there etca: wee having formerly vnderstood that passage to be full of danger caused it to bee disputed in consultation before the departure, when it was vnanimously voted against the Shipps adventuring thither, therefore our Instructions limited her to the Road of BALLASORE, but for the buying and bringing away of goods or settling a ffactory at HUGHLY, with acquisition of the Princes *Firmand* for free trade, was wholly reffered to the said Captain's discretion."

In the next extract we find the Masulipatam agency testifying their sense of Mr. Boughton's favours, past and to come, by a *peshcash* of gay apparel. The word is a singular one to use in relation to an ex-employé; but it will be seen that it is offered to him as the servant of the Prince Sháh Shujá'.

From MASULIPATAM *Council to* Mr. JAMES BRIDGMAN, &c., BALLASORE.

Dated, " METCHLEPATAM, the 25th February 1650"(-51) :[1]

*   *   *   *   *   *   *

"Alsoe you may take notice of 3 *Guze*[2] of Scarlett and 16 yards of gould and silver lace in WM. BENIS his Coustody the which demand of him and present as a *piscash* from vs to Mr. GABRIELL BOUGHTON whoe being the Princes Servant, wilbe doubtlesse a great help vnto you to gain his *ffirmaund*, which wee cannot coniecture wilbe difficult to bee obtained, considering the very great present you have given already, farr in value exceeding what vse to bee given in preceeding yeares."

In the instructions of Captain Brookhaven we saw the intention to establish a factory at Húglí clearly indicated, and in the following we see that it is accomplished :

From SURAT *Council to the Company.*

Dated, " SURATT, the 10th January 1651"(-2).

" What successe Mr. DAUIDG had in his court affaires, wee have advised you of in former letters ; many faire promises hath hee theare received from Courtiers and others, and some valuable assistance hee had towards the recovery of MERZA MULKES debt. . . . some *phirmaunds* hee also received from the King which haue saued you some thousands of rupees in *Rhadarees*[3] 'twixt LUKCKNOW and AGRA, and 'twixt AGRA and this place, and may saue you much more in BENGALA whither Mr. JESSON (now cheife at AGRA), hath sent it upon the entreaty of Mr. BRIDGMAN and EDWD: STEEVENS factors at HUGHLEY where they are settled for the provission of Salt peeter and Sugar, etca."

Before reaching the date of the following extract we have to pass over several years, during which I have gathered nothing from the surviving papers (except the *Nishán* of Shah Shujá', viceroy of Bengal, which is transcribed further on). We find that Mr. Boughton is now dead, but that his widow is remarried, and her husband is apparently

---

[1] O.C. 2210.

[2] *Gaz* (Pers.), a measure of length, varying in different places from the cubit to the yard.

[3] *Ráhdárí*, transit duty, and those who levied it.

making claims on the Company, on account of the services of his predecessor. We also find misdemeanours of Mr. Bridgman's alluded to, of which we know no particulars.

From Letter of the Court to FORT ST. GEORGE, *of 31st Decr.* 1657:

"It is that wee much desire to be sattisfied in, and that we might haue the certaine knowledge (if possible) in all particulars of those dishonest actions committed by Mr. BRIDGMAN and his Partners, by whose vnwarrantable proceedings (you now write) our ffactors in the BAY are much troubled by one WILLIAM PITTS, who married the Relict of GABRIELL BOUGHTON, who having taken vp Monies at Interest of the MOORES they very much presse the payment thereof out of our estate, but wee hope you have soe managed this businesse, and given such advice to our ffactors that hath armed them with such arguments, as to enable them to withstand and to oppose such vnjust and vnreasonable demands."

From a Paper of same date, being a Commission and Instruction to Mr. GEORGE GAWTON, Mr. THO. BILLEDG, Mr. WILLIAM BLACKE (BLAKE?), Mr. THOMAS HOPKINS, Mr. RICHARD CHAMBERLAINE, and Mr. JON KENN.

  * * * * * * *

" The severall Commodities which wee doe enorder to be provided and retourned on the twoe fore mentioned ships are as followeth, vizt. :

" *By our ffactors on the* COAST.

  * * * * * * *

And by yourselves in the BAY.

Cotton Yarne . . . .
Salt Peeter . . . .
Bengala Silke . . . .

  * * * * * *

Sannoes Adatay[1] . . . .

  * * * * * * *

Cynomon . . . .

  * * * * * * *

Taffaties . . . .
Bowgees[2] and Turmerick . . . .
Gumlack . . ."

Also from same letter :

" Mr. BLAKE who was most able to give you sattisfaction on BRIDGMANS businesse would not be drawne thence to give you any accompt, but deserted our service before he had fairely cleared himselfe thereof, And for Mr. WALDEGRAVE who was then sick in the BAY, and would not come by Sea unto you, but rather made choice to journey by land and bring our Accompts, *Phirmaunds* &ca. along with him, whereby they were vnhappilie lost, and hee neither sending their Coppies by Sea, or leauing Coppies of them behind in the ffactorie, gives us cause to beleiue that Mr. BLAKE deserting our Service, and Mr. WALDEGRAVE bringing away our accompts &c. (and pretending them to be lost) was

---

[1] A kind of piece goods. I cannot ascertain what kind.
[2] *I.e.*, cowries ; Port. *buzios.*

purposely done, that Mr. BRIDGMANS and their own unwarrantable actions, might not be discovered."

From Letter of Court to "Our Agent and Factors at HUGHLY" :

Dated, "LONDON, 27 February 1657"(-8).

"Since dispeede of our prementioned of 31st December, wee haue proceeded and made some good progresse as to the setling of our severall ffactories in all partes of India. And have concluded to reduce all ffactories both to the north-wards and Southwards, PERSIA and the BAY, to be subordinate vnto our PRE-SIDENCIE which wee shall settle in SURATT, Wee have likewise resolved to establish 4 agencies, viz., one at FORT ST. GEORGE, one in BANTAM, a third in PERSIA, and the other at HUGHLY, which last place being your Residence, it most necessarilie requires your knowledge of what wee have determined in relation thereunto, which is as followeth, vzt. :

"At HUGHLY wee doe appoint

Mr. GEORGE GAWTON to be our agent whose sallarie we have settled at 100*l*. p. annum.

(—— second at 40*l*., MATHIAS HALSTEAD, third at 30*l*., WILLIAM RAG-DALE, 4th. at 20*l*., THOMAS DAVIES[1] 5th. at 20*l*.

" At BALLASORE

(THOMAS HOPKINS Chief at 40*l*. ; WALTER ROGERS 2d. at 30*l*.; WILLIAM DANIELL 3d. at 30*l*. ; JOSHUA WRIGHT 4th. at 20*l*.)

" At CASSAMBAZAR

(ION KENN, Chief at 40*l*.; DANIELL SHELDON, 2d. at 30*l*.; JOHN PRIDDY, 3d. at 30*l*. ; JOB CHARNOCK, 4th. at 20*l*.)

" At PATTANA

(RICHARD CHAMBERLAN Chief, at 40*l*. ; —— second at 30*l*. ; WILLIAM VASSELL 3d. at 30*l*. ; —— 4th at 20*l*.)

" These are the 4 ffactories which wee determine shall bee setled in the BAY OF BENGALA, and that they shall be accomptable and subordinate to the Agencie of HUGHLY and from time to time follow all such directions as they shall receive from you."

" *Translate of Sultan* SHAUH SHUJAES Neshaun. *Letters Patent to the* ENGLISH *in* BENGAL."

(*From a transcript by* Sir STREYNSHAM MASTER, *appended to his Diary.*)[2]

" *The Neshaun or Letters Patent of the Most Magnificent Prince Sultan* SHUJA *given the sixth moneth in the yeare of* hegira *one thousand sixty six in the 28th yeare of the Emperour* SHAH JEHANN *his Glorious Reign"; i.e.,* in April, A.D. 1656.)

" BEE it knowne to all great Governours, Chancellors, Farmers of the Kings Rents, Collonells, Captaines, Rent-gatherers, Farmers of Customes, Watchmen, fferrymen, and other Petty officers, that are now in place and hereafter shall be in the Kingdoms of BENGALA and ORIXA, that this day THOMAS BILLIDGE an ENGLISHMAN humbly (laid) his suit before our Splendid Throne, acquainting us that the ENGLISH Companyes goods according to the great Emperours Letter

---

[1] See II., pp. cxxi, ccxcvi.

[2] In India Office marked P.R.FF. B.3.

Patent, which are unalterable, by his free grant therein Specified are custome free all over his great Empire, humbly desireing us that there may a Privilege be granted them by us to trade custome free in these parts, as alsoe complayneing that at present their trade with the Country merchants our Subjects is much hindered by our Governours of Port Townes &ca., demanding the ENGLISH goods at their owne rates, and forbiding any merchants to buy or sell with them unless (they) condescend to their actions, and that the officers in the Port Townes demand four in the hundred custome on all goods imported and exported, as alsoe anchorage[1] in the roads belonging to these Kingdomes of BENGALA and ORIXA.

"Vpon due consideration had of all which wee were pleased to grant, and hereby command you, that according to the abovementioned Letters Patent of the great Emperour, whose words noe man dare presume to reverse, the ffactory (of) the ENGLISH company be noe more troubled with demands of custome of goods imported or exported either by land or by water, nor that their goods be opened and forced from them at under-rates in any places of Government by which they shall pass or repass up and downe the Country, but that they buy and sell freely and without impediment, neither lett any molestation be given them, without anchorage, as formerly has binn, alsoe when ever they have order to build ffactoryes or Warehouses in any part of these Kingdomes that they be not hindered, but forwarded, as alsoe where there shall be any just and due debts comeing to them from our Subjects that all persons in office be helpfull to them in their recovery giveing protection to noe weavers merchants or any other that shall appeare to be really indebted to them. For all the aforesaid matters especiall regard is to be had that you carry your Selves strictly in obedience to the great Emperours Letters Patents, and this my *Neshan* now given the ENGLISH Company, having an especiall care that you faile not (even) a little in your full complyance with our Commands therein Conteyned."

In the appendix to Master's Diary as above noted, are also transcribed in his handwriting the following documents :

(1.) " *Translate of Nabob* SHAUSTEH CKAWN, *Lord of the Noblemen, his confirmation of the* ENGLISH *privileges in the Kingdome of* BENGALA . . . dated this 3d day of the 3d: moneth in the 15th yeare of the glorious reigne of AURUNG ZEEB Emperor of the World.*"[2]

(2.) " *Translate of a Letter from* SHAUSTETH CAUNE[3] (*sic*) *Lord of the Noblemen, Prefect of* BENGALA, *in answer to one received from* WARES CAWNE *the great Chancellor of the Province of* BEARRA (*or* PATTANA[4])

---

[1] *I.e.*, an " anchorage due".

[2] According to Stewart (who gives a copy of this, as well as of the preceding *Nishân*, in the App. to his *History of Bengal*, June 1672).

(It is given on the suit] of Walter Clavell, the English Captain, and refers to the " Letters Patent of the Mighty Emperor and Prince Sultan Shaw Sujah", as also to the *Phyrwana* or order of Meer Jumbla the Cawne of Cawnes (*Mír Jumla Khán-Khánán*), Deceased.

[3] Viz., Sháyista Khán, the Nawáb of Bengal, visited by Hedges (vol. I *passim*).

[4] Bahár or Patna (which city was the seat of government of Bahár).

about the ENGLISH *privilidges in these parts of the Empire of* SHAUH AURUNG ZEEB *Emperour of Hindoustan &ca: . . . . 5th moneth in the 18th yeare of the glorious reigne of* SHAUH AURUNG ZEEB *Emperor of the World, to the most Excellent and Honble.* WAREES CKAUNE *greeting :*

" Your letter have received wherein you write that the ENGLISH have told you that according to the Emperours Letters Patent their Companyes Goods are made Custome free, but they doe not produce any such Original Letters Patent to confirme what they aver and therefore (you) desire advice from me . . . . to which I answer that the ENGLISH have not a *Phyrmaund* or Letters Patent from the Emperour aforesaid upon which I alsoe gave them a grant of the said Privelidges in this Province . . according to which and the said Letters Patent you ought not to trouble or impede their trade on account of paying Custome which is released to them."

(3.) " *Translate of* RUFFEE CKAUNS *Nabob of* ORIXA *his Order or Grant for confirmation of the* ENGLISH *Privelidges in said Kingdome . . . dated the 15th day of the 10 : moneth in the thirteenth yeare of the glorious reigne of* SHAW AVRUNG ZEEB."

(4.) " *An attestation given by the Customers and Broakers of* BALLA-SORE *concerning the* ENGLISH *privelidges in the import and export of their Goods and Disposing of them in that Port . . . . given the 27: day of the third month in the one thousand eighty one yeare of the hegira.*"[1]

. . . . " Sheweth that the ENGLISH for many yeares have used this port of BALLASORE and that they have all along used to unlade their goods from aboard their ships in the roade and to send them on *Purgoes* to their factory in this place without being opened or searcht by any officer or person in Government whatsoever," etc.

(5.) " *Translate of* SHAW AURUNG ZEEB *Emperour of India his* Phyr-maund *or Letters Patents given the* DUTCH *for their Tradeing in his Dominions* 1662   *the 15th of the 3d moneth in the 5th yeare of his reigne.*"

I give one more extract regarding the privileges of trade in Bengal :[2]

Copy of BENGAL *Gen^{ll}, dated the* 9th December Anno Dom. 1678.

" The foregoing was intended as above dated but detain'd by the long stay of Mr. VINCENT at the Prince of BENGALL's Court in fitting out his *Neshaune* till the 10th Octo: last, since which this has bin the first Conveyance to you ; The Princes *Neshaune* is full to all intents and purposes for our Masters privileges in these partes, and more advantageously penn'd then SHA SHUJAHS was ; It is grounded on an *Husbull Hookum* that came from the Vizere ASSUT CAUNE[3] by order of the King to the Duan of BENGALL in answer to the Remonstrance of our Case he had made some months before ; wherein the King interprets SHA JEHAUNS *Firmaund* in the 24th yeare of his Reigne, and his owne graunted in

---

[1] 24th July 1670.   [2] O.C. 4543.
[3] Ibrahím, styled Nawáb Asad Khán, lived to A.D. 1717, dying at the age of 94 (lunar) years. He had been Wazír under Aurang Zíb and Bahádur Sháh.

the 10th yeare of his owne Reigne for SURAT, etca.: to cleare us from paying Custome all over his Empire in any place save your port &ca: on that side ; on which accompt and by meanes of a Present to the amount of 21000 *Rupees* a new *Neshaune* was graunted us ; by which Wee hope we shall not soe immediately want a *Phirmaund;* conceiving that this King will not think it Reason to graunt us a new one aparte since he himself hath already ordered us what we desire, that is, to be custome free in these Parts, by the old one ; If you have by you and could send us a Coppy chopped by The Cozzy of DILLY[1] of each of the forementioned *Phirmaunds,* it may be of use to our Masters Affaires here."

This is indorsed " *Bengal Ext. of a General letter to* SURAT respecting the Nishan *granted by* SULTAN MAHOMMED AZEM".

The remaining letters are only selected as specimens of the private or " demi-official" correspondence which passed between members of the different factories, in those early days of Anglo-Indians in Bengal.

" Loveing friend   " BALLASORE (   ) August 1658.[2]
    " Mr. PICKERING
        " I cannot forgett my freinds though at the greatest distance, but chuse rather to bee impertinently troublsome then vncivilly forgettfull, you have been frequently remembered here by your friends when vpon the bubbing[3] designe which since your absence is not so well carried on as it ought to bee, wee are all generally so sensible of the want of your Company that you have been often wisht for. Your friend Mr. KEN is not yet recouered but has every other day his wonted fitts, and poor JOB begins to droope and simpathize with JON's sicknes. I hope by this time you are acquainted with the Carowsing DUTCHMEN that you may bee able to beare vp against those Melancholy thoughts that assault the solitary. This day I mean to drink your health, with a *vivat Jacobus Pickering,* that hee may suddainly and safely returne to exhilarate the hearts of those that Love him, amongst whome you may please to reckon
                                        " Your reall freind
" If Mr. CHAMBERLAINE (who I knowe has   " THO: BATEMAN.
    no time to stay in CASSANBAZARR)
    should desire you to act any thing in my
    behalfe, pray let mee intreat your care
    therein, and heare from you as Soone
    as you can.
        " Yrs. T. B.
" Mr. REYNOLDS and Mrs. MARY send their loueing respects to you."

        " *To* Mr. JAMES PICKERING, These, CASSANBAZARR."

                            " HEWGLEE, the 14th Octob: 1658.[4]
    " Ciceronian St:
        " Your Elaborate Lines haue so puzled my incultivated intellect that it was some time ere I resolu'd whether by silence to incur the censure of vncivill negligence, or by writing to discouer my foolish impertinence, at length (because thereby I shall least wrong my freinds) and *ex malis minimum Eligendum,* I

---

[1] *I.e.,* " sealed by the Kázi of Dehli."
[2] O.C. 2663.   [3] " Drinking."   [4] O.C. 2673.

fell on the latter, choosing rather to render my selfe ridiculous then my friends displeased. But from a chip of a rough hewn logg hee that looks for better than wooden phrases will starue his expectation, *ex quovis enim ligno non fit Mercurius.*

"I was never yet so good a proficient in the schooles of litterature as to know what Deity to invoke for those Heliconian irrigations which should so sublimate my thoughts as to make mee capable of returning an answer suitable to the sublimity of your style. But in their stead Heaven has been so propitious as to afford mee some divine revelations sufficient to advise you that hereafter you accompt not your solitude a curse since it produced such rare effects in our late Soveraigne. Remember Dr. BROWNE'S . . *Nunquam minus solus quam cum solus.* Now is the only time for you to commune with your owne heart, and by the publishing of your pious soliloquies there may bee hopes in time you may bee preferr'd to be one of MAU · THOMSON'S planters and propagatours of the Gospell in these heathenish parts, which if you may so proove you shall not want the prayers of him who is

"Pathetically yours
"THO : BATEMAN."

The foregoing, both in manner and allusions, indicates recent familiarity with Sir Thomas Browne. And a letter from another member of the service, a few months later, shows that his books were then circulating among the Bengal factories :

Extract letter from THOMAS STEPHENS, *dated* "BALLASORE the 12th January 165⅚."[1]

" *To Mr.* JAMES PICKERING
"Marchant del⁴. In HEWGLY."

*   *   *   *   *   *   *

"Mr. BATEMAN sent by me which is gone as in either Mr. KENNS or Mr. CHAMBERLAYNES Chest for your Selfe, *Vulgar Errours, Religio Medici,* and a *Treatise of Bodies.* I have from Mr. KEN received Satisfaction for the 2 butts of Arack : not else, wishing you Successe in youre approaching journey, Remain
"Yr: verry lo: friend."

(*To the same.*)
"CASSNABAZAR
"or ells where."

"ROJAMALL pr: february ¼⁸."[2]
"JAMES,

"I am sending your namesake James P: to wayte vppon you and to Transport my Lead, Cloth, Tinn, quicksilver, if this Encounter you att HEWGHLY Stay theire, if in the Way stay att CASSUMBAZAR, pray bring all my goods to PATTANA where they'le find the best Markett, your Care and paynes herein will find a thankfull acknowledgment from your very Lo: friend
"RICᴰ: CHAMBERLAYNE.

"It will be 6: *in* 7: dayes before hee can Leave the place because he must disspeede HALL after us. JOB and I goe by water, hee comes vppon my pallenkeene by Land when my *Caharrs*² come.
"Idem R: C:"

---

[1] O.C. 2685.   [2] O.C. 2691.
[3] Hind. *kahár,* a palankin-bearer.

From Mr. HENRY ALDWORTH *to* Mr. THOMAS DAVIES.

Dated, " ROJAMALL, prº : ffebr' : 1658" (·9)[1]

" Mr. THO : DAVIES

" And esteemed freind : yesterday arriued this place where found the Bezar almost Burnt and many of the People almost starued for want of Foode which caused much Sadnes in Mr. CHARNOCK and my Selfe, but not soe much as the absence of your Company, which wee haue often remembered in a bowle of the cleerest punch, hauing noe better Liquor : Mr. CHAMBERLAYNE and Mr. CHARNOCK are going to morrow p. PATTANA ; Mr. CHARNOCKE for the quicker dispatch of his voyage, is now cutting of his haire, and intends to enter into the MOORES fashion this day. I would have sent you one of his lockes too keepe for a antique, but Mr. CHAMBERLAYNE hath promised to doe it ; pray S' : bee pleased to receive of BULLOMALECK 4*r* : and 5*a* : which ouerpaid him, and forgott to remember at CASNABAZAR, as per his accompt inclosed will appeare. Not haueing else at present saue kind respects to your selfe praying to GOD to send you much health and hapynes as my selfe shall cease from troubling you but never from being

" Your assured Loving freind

" HENRY ALDWORTH.

" Mr. CHARNOCK tenders respectes to you and soe wee doe both to Mr. Wm. PITTS."

In addition to the factories mentioned in the preceding extracts, viz., HÚGLÍ, BALASORE, KÁSIMBÁZÁR, and PATNA, there were established at later dates, up to the exodus under Job Charnock in 1686-7, factories at DACCA and MALDA, and an agency of some kind, in connexion with the mint, at RÁJMAHAL.

The preceding extracts enable us to determine pretty nearly the date of the permanent establishment of the factory at BALASORE as January 1651

Though it had been occasionally occupied by Company's merchants and factors, from time to time, before that since 1642

The settlement of HÚGLÍ may also be set down as . 1651

As regards the KÁSIMBÁZÁR factory, I have not been able to ascertain whether it had been regularly occupied much prior to the Court's appointment of factors to it in February 1659. The letter to Mr. Pickering on the preceding page indicates its occupation at least in . 1658[2]

---

[1] O. C. 2690.

[2] In a letter to the company from POWLE WALDEGRAVE, dated " BALLASORE, 28th December, 1654," I find :

" Your servant EDWARD STEVENS, who deceased in CASSNABAZAR at Capt. BROOKHAVENS being here, and very much Insolvent, not onely to your worshipps but severall Creditors in HUGHLY to the Amount of 4200: rupees".   .

So that occasional agency at least seems to have been employed there as early as 1653 or 1654.

The same remark applies to that at Patna.

Prof. H. H. Wilson, in a note to his edition of Mill's *History* (1840, vol. I, p. 79) says: "An attempt was made to establish a Factory at Patna in 1620." I have not been able to recover the authority for this; but in any case such an attempt must have been made from Surat through Agra, long before the settlements were made in Bengal. The letters to Mr. Pickering given above (pp. cxciii-xciv) imply the settlement from Bengal to have been made in . 1659

The date of the establishment of the DACCA Factory may be approximately fixed by the following extract from the Court's letter to the Council at Húglí, dated 24th January 1667-8 1668

" We observe what you have written concerning DECCA that it is a place That will vend much Europe Goods, and that the best *Cossaes, Mullmuls,* &ca. may there be procured. It is our earnest desire as before intimated, that as large a quantity of broad Cloathes as possible may be vended by you. Therefore if you shall really find that the settling a factory in that place will occasion the taking of some considerable quantity of our Manufactures, and that (as you write) the advance of their Sales will beare the charge of the factory, Wee then give you liberty to send 2 or 3 fitt persons thither to reside, and to furnish them with cloth &ca. proper for that place."

The settlement of the Malda factory appears from Streynsham Master's *Diary* (see vol. II, p. ccxxxv) to have taken place in 1676

I conclude this compilation regarding the early Bengal factories with a list of the Company's servants on the Coast and in the Bay, in January 1652; the earliest, I believe, that is to be found.

"A List of such Persons as Serve the Honoble: ENGLISH EAST INDIA Company in MADRASSAPATAM &ca. ffactories on COAST CHORMANDELL and PEGU and Marriners in d{to}. service Voyaging from the COAST to BENGALL and to PEGU."

"January 10th 1651."

"In *Madraspatam* :

HENRY GREENHILL, Agent
WILLIAM GURNEY : Accomptant
THOMAS STEVENSON, Purser
WILLIAM JOHNSON, Godowne Keeper
RICHARD MINORS
WILLIAM BROWNE, Steward
EDWARD WHITING : Chyrurgion
WILLIAM COLTHURST
GUSTAVUS DENNY
DANIELL DENNY
JOHN BRIDGE—died the 12th Jany. inst.
Captaine JAMES MARTINE, Commander of the Soldiers
JEREMY BRADFORD, Serjant
JNO: MORRIS, Gunners Mate (and 16 more Soldiers)

"In the Camp :

JEREMY ROOT, Gunner (and 5 more soldiers)
More Soldiers in Madrassapatam, *but not in the Books.* (8 in number)

"In *Mesulapatam* :

CHRISTOPHER YARDLY : Cheife
THO: CHAMBERS, Accomptant
WILLIAM WINTER }
THOMAS SIMONDS } Assistant
WILLIAM NETLAM } { MICHAEL YATES
EDWARD JARVIS } { JOHN CLIFFE

"In *Verassaroon* :[1]

EDWARD WINTER, Cheife
WILLIAM PALMER, Assistant.
JNO: WHITE
THO: EDWARDS

"In *Pettepolee* :[2]

JOHN LEIGH, Chiefe
WILLIAM BROADBENT, Assistant
WILL. BRADFORD

"In *Ballasore* and *Hewgly* :

POWLE WALDEGRAVE
EDWARD STEPHENS
WILLIAM PITTS

"In *Pegu* :

RICHARD SNIPE
FFRANCIS YARDLEY
SAMUELL ARCHER, Chyrurgion.

" *In the* Ruby *bound for* Pegu :

MASTER BRADGATE, Merchant
WILLIAM JEARSEY, Acct.
THOMAS BLAND, Master
ROBERT SMITH } Masters
WILLIAM MIXER } Mates
(&c).
JOHN ANTHONY, a Mystez."
(etc.)

" *Imploid in the Bay* :

GEORGE BEAKER : a Quarter Master hertofore to the *Lioness.*"

. . . . . .

---

[1] See *note*, vol. II, p. cccxlvii.

[2] PETTIPOLEE (or Peddapalli) was one of the earliest factory-sites of the English Company, occupied about 1613, and abandoned a little after the middle of the century. It was a port of the Gantúr District, below the Kistna, and is now known as NIZÁMPATAM.

VII.

EARLY CHARTS AND TOPOGRAPHY OF THE HÚGLÍ RIVER.

EVEN after the settlement of the Factory at Húglí, it was long before the Company's ships began to ascend the river from the roadsteads in the Bay, nor indeed does this appear to have been practised, unless exceptionally, till after Húglí had been more or less superseded by Calcutta. The lading for the Company's ships was habitually brought down to Balasore from Húglí and Kásimbázár—and, as regards saltpetre, from Patna,—mainly in country craft of various kinds, known as *patellas, boras, purgoes* and what not, and partially in the sloops and pinnaces which the Company maintained on the river.

Still from an early period we see that the Court recognised the possibility and expediency of making their ships proceed up the Ganges (*i.e.*, the great delta branch which we call the Húglí), in order to avoid the expense, delays, and risks of this transhipment, and they repeatedly made suggestions on this subject to their servants in the Bay. They also maintained something of a Pilot establishment for the conduct of the sloops, and of such larger craft as occasionally ascended the River, and with some view no doubt to the eventual realisation of their desire that their sea-going ships should habitually proceed up to the chief depots of their trade.

The following are some of their many utterances in connêxion with this object. The letter of 20 November 1668, with the measures which it announces, may be regarded as the foundation of the Bengal Pilot Service, a body which has done much invaluable work, and which after various modifications of its constitution, still survives, after nearly two centuries and a quarter of existence.

As early as 1650 we find the Court urging that their ships for the Bay should go straight up the Ganges, *i.e.*, the Húglí, as may be seen by the Fort St. George resolution against this, and reply to the Court, as follows :

(O.C. 2179.) *At a Consultation held the 27th day of* August *Anno* 1650, *In* FORT ST. GEORGE :

" Wheras ship *Lyoness* is by order of the Honble : Company designed to goe vp the River GANGES to the Towne of HUGLY the danger of such an vnder-taking being by this Consultation fully debated 'twas resolued by joint consent to avoid soe great a hazard that the ship shall not proceed any further than BALLASORE ROADE, and that Capt. JOHN BROOKHAVEN with the Merchants designed for HUGLY shall proceed thither vpon some other fraighted vessell as they shall find most convenient, to put in execution the generall Instruction."

> "HENRY GREENHILL.
> "JON: BROOKHAVEN.
> "EDWD: WINTER.
> "J: BRIDGMAN.
> "WM: NETLAM."

In accordance with this resolution also the Fort St. George Agent and Council wrote to the Court 18th January 1650(-51), as already quoted in Pt. VI.

Court to HUGHLY.

"22d Feby. 1659(-60).

*   *   *   *   *   *   *

"If it bee necessarie, that a Sloope bee provided to goe vp to HUGHLY, as a Convoy from the Rovers, wee give our Consent therevnto ; And for our Shipping goeing vp into the Riuer of GANGEES, thereby to reduce the Governor of BALLASORE to better ffreindship, and break off his demands for Anchorage, wee also aprove thereof, and recomend its prosecution vnto you, but wee would willingly, that a tryall might first bee made, with Shipping of small burthen, before you venture on such great shiping as the *Smirna Merchant*, or the like. However if vpon Consultation with the Masters and the experiences which you have made of the depths of the River, you shall conclude it to be favorable, and without hazard, wee leave it vnto your discretion."

Court to FORT, 31st December 1662.

"At the departure of Captaine ELLIOTT from you vnto the BAY, wee observe that hee engaged to venture vp with his Shipp for HUGHLY, but was forbidden by Mr. TREVISA &c. Factors, to put the same in exercise, which proved to our damage, and wee hope you have called him to an accompt for the same, whoe was then Subordinate to your Agency, and ought to have Complyed with your directions. Wee take notice that Capt. ELLIOTT hath left a writeing with you, that it is hazardless for Ships to goe vp for HUGELY, and that the DUTCH haue Shipps of 600 Tons, that Tyde it vp thither, soe that you write us, that you intend to contrive that if it bee possible, all our Shipping henceforward shall goe vp for HUGLEY directly, and that then the ffactory of BALLASORE will bee unecessary, and our businesse in the BAY brought into some Decorum. We aprove of this your resolution, and hope you have accordingly put it in practize, that soe when our Shipps the *Castle* Friggatt, and *Royall Katherine* shall arrive with you; which Shipps are engaged in Charter Parties to goe vp as neare to HUGLY as with safety they may, it will apeare a businesse neither Difficult nor dangerous to bee prosecuted, and that then the ffactory of BALLASORE bee totally deserted, if not alreadie done."

Also in *Letter to* HUGLY of 2d Jany. 1662(-3), the Court say that they have agreed to give the owners of the ships just named,

"10s. per Tonn extraordinary, for all goods that they shall take in within the said Barr of GANGEES, and to bee at the charge of Boats and Pylotts, to attend vp and doune the River, and in and out of the Barr, which wee require you to procure for them as you shall see occasion."

To HUGHLY, 24 Januarie 1667.

Announces having built a small vessel called the *Dilligence* " For the accommodation and help of the lading of our Ships in the BAY, and for the discovery of the River GANGEES, that so our Ships may goe vp thereinto, as the DUTCH and Natives doe."

*   *   *   *   *   *   *

" Wee would have you while she is imployed in the lading of our ships, and aftewards as long as you shall find it convenient, that the Master and some other persons doe take notice of the Channell and Depth of the River GANGEES and the entrance thereinto, that so vpon the arrivall of our Ships, in the following years, wee may have alle ENGLISH Pylotts, to bring in our Ships into the River . and let them keepe a journall of their proceedings, and make exact Drafts of their Depths, Reaches, and Currents, as also how the Sands vsually varie, and so when any of our Ships come into GANGEES, you may bee much guided by the practize of the DUTCH both as to their safe goeing out, and coming in." (*See also Court to* HUGLEY, 18th Decr. 1671.)

*   *   *   *   *   *   *

Ext. of a Letter from the Court to their " Cheife and Factors at HUGHLY."

Dated, " 20th November, 1668.

" Wee formerly for the encoragement of those Comanders that would goe into the River GANGEES, allowed them 10s. 6d. per Tonn fraight extraordinary for all goods they should there take in. But for want of Pylotts, They did not then venture, which caused us the last yeare to build the pinnace *Dilligence*, and then gaue you directions that shee should bee imployed in the River, and to take notice of the depths and Shoulds of the Same, and to make Cards or Maps thereof that they may become able Pylotts for the conducting in of our Ships, which order of 10s. 6d. per Tonn wee haue againe this yeare reneued, and have conferred with Capt: GODOLPHIN and some other of the Comanders concerning the same, whome we find willing thereunto, Provided that you have able Pylotts for the bringing of them into the River. Wee therefore doe againe recommend it to you That as wee hope you have already entered upon it, so to proceed to have divers able persons instructed as Pylotts for that service, the which, the better to accomplish, let those that doe command the Vessells, by and downe the River put all persons from the youngest to the Eldest vpon taking Depths, sholdings, setting of Tydes, Currents, Distances, Buoyes, and making of Draftes of the River, or what else needfull for the enabling of them in this affaire, and for a supply of young men, to bee bredd up, wee have entertained as Aprentices for seaven yeares GEORGE HIERON, JAMES WHITE, THOMAS MASSEN, JAMES FERBORNE, JOHN FFLOYD, and THOMAS BATEMAN, the first three yeares at 6l., the next 2 yeares at 7l., and the last 2 yeares at 8l. per annum, The whole to be paid There by you, for their provision of clothes."

In the Court's Instructions to Streynsham Master, when he was going out to India, dated 16th December 1675, we find :

" You are also to consult with our chief and Councell Factors, Commanders and the ablest Pilotts at the BAY touching Ships going up the River GANGES, and how and in what season the same may be best effected, and write to Vs what you can collect materiall to Our Service from all their advizes and informations."

From the Court to HÚGLÍ, 12th December 1677 :

" Wee having so great a desire to have a ship goe up the GANGES, and findeing the *ffalcon* a fitt shipp to make that experiment, and Captain JOHN STAFFORD the Comander willing to undertake it, wee haue ordered her to goe directly to you with a Stock of 37625*l*: 6*s*: 3*d* in Bullein and 30211*l*: 1*s*: 8*d* in Goods, without stopping at the FFORT or MESULAPATAM, and God granting him to arrive safe at BALLASORE you are to accommodate him with so many of our Pilots and Boats as may be there, and he shall desire to carry him up the River as high as HUGHLY, if conveniently she can, or at least as far as CHANNOCK."

We learn from the next extract that the *Falcon* accomplished the ascent of the River.

From the Court to FORT ST. GEORGE, 5th Jan. 1680-81.

"We had a draught of the River GANGES presented to us by Captain STAFFORD, who went up with his ship the *Falcon* unto HUGHLY ; and haue caused three draughts of the same to be delivered vizt : one unto Captain JOHN GOLDSBOROUGH in the *Bengall Merchant*, another to Captain EARNING in the *George*, and another to Captain BROWN in the *Ann* ; hoping they will make such use of them as to endeavour to carry up their Ships into the River." .

From the same, Instructions to Captain SAMUEL LAKE, *of the* Prudent Mary, 2d September 1682.

" . . being arrived in the BAY of BENGALLA you are to sail up the river GANGES as high as HUGHLY."

The same instructions are given to other Captains under date 6th November, *idem.*, and in a letter to Húglí of 17th June 1685.

From the Court to " HUGHLEY", 3d October, 1684 :

" Wee shall endeavour to persuade our 3 deckt Ships to go as high as the Island of INGALEE" (*i.e.*, Hijilí).

From the same to the BAY, 27th August 1688.

" But then considering" (with reference to the selection of ULABARRIA for settlement, (vol. II, pp. lxxi, lxxv) " that you may be at a loss for good Pilots up the GANGES in case of the death of GEORGE HERRON and one or two more of the best of your Pilots, we find it necessary to give you leave at any time to make choice of any of the Soberest of our young Mates or midshipmen that are willing to stay in the Countrey to make Masters of our Sloops, and to bring up for Pilots in the river of GANGES, the rather because now we have such a place of our own as ULABURREA, we would have none of our ships hereafter to ride in BALLASORE Road, spoiling their ground tackle, and wearying out their men with rowing such long stretches." . .

We have seen in two of the preceding extracts the name of Mr. George Herron, who is several times mentioned by Hedges in his *Diary* as chief of the Company's pilots and sloop-commanders. We have given a brief notice of him in vol. II., p. cxcix, to which the two extracts in question supply a substantial addition. We may attribute to Mr. Herron the foundation of the more accurate pilotage and topography of the Húglí, for he must be regarded (as has been said in the notice just referred to) as the author not only (under the perverted designation of "Mr. Herring") of the earliest instructions printed in detail for the navigation of that river, but probably also of the earliest chart of it that has any claim to quasi-scientific character.

The basis, as regards English use, of all the published charts and sailing directions for the Húglí, down to about 1760, seems to have been that supplied by various editions of the *English Pilot*.[1]

Those editions which we have been able to trace and examine are the following :—

Dates.	Titles (abridged).	Libraries in which they exist.
1675.	"THE ENGLISH PILOT : The Third Book, Describing, &ca. . . . . ORIENTAL NAVIGATION. "Collected for the general benefit of our own Countreymen. "By JOHN SELLER, Hydrographer to the King. LONDON, Printed by JOHN DARBY for the AUTHOR, and are to be sold at his shop at the *Hermitage* in *Wapping*"	Admiralty.
1701.	"THE ENGLISH PILOT : The Sixth Book, Describing . ORIENTAL NAVIGATION. * * * * * "London, Printed for *Richard Mount* and *Thomas Page* at the Postern on *Tower Hill*"	Do.
1703.	"THE THIRD BOOK" (as before or nearly so). * * * * * "By JOHN THORNTON, Hydrographer. LONDON. Printed by JOHN HOW for the AUTHOR, and are to be Sold at his Shop at the Sign of England, Scotland, and Ireland, in the Minories"[2]	Do. and British Museum.
1711.	"THE ENGLISH PILOT : The Third Book, Describing," &c. * * * * * "LONDON, Printed by *John How*" (&c., as in last)	British Museum.

[1] In all this matter regarding the charts and topography of the Húglí I am greatly indebted to the assistance of Mr. R. J. Barlow, the amount of which is only to a small extent indicated by the notes bearing his name or initials.

[2] This edition bears a dedication " *To the Honourable the Court of Managers for the United Trade to the East Indies*," etc., etc.

Dates.	Titles (abridged).	Libraries in which they exist.
1716.	(Nearly as the last) "Collected for the general Benefit of our own Countrymen. "By JOHN THORNTON, Hydrographer. "LONDON, Printed for *Rich.* and *Will. Mount,* and *Tho. Page* in *Postern Row* on *Tower Hill*"	Admiralty.
1723.	(Much the same, but without Thornton's name). . " for *Thomas Page* and *William* and *Fisher Mount* in *Postern Row* on *Tower Hill*."	
1734.	⁂ ⁂ ⁂ ⁂ ⁂ . . "for *William Mount* and *Thomas Page*" . . .	British Museum.
1748.	⁂ ⁂ ⁂ ⁂ ⁂ . " Printed for *W* and *J. Mount* and *T. Page,*" etc. -	Admiralty.
1755.	⁂ ⁂ ⁂ ⁂ ⁂ " Printed for W. and J. MOUNT, J. and T. PAGE, on *Tower Hill*"	India Office (Geographical Department).
1761.	"The ENGLISH PILOT, Describing," &c., &c. " Divided into Three Parts," &c. " London, Printed for *W.* and *J. Mount, J. Page* and *Son,* on Tower Hill" - -	British Museum.

The 1675 edition of the *English Pilot* contains what it entitles

"*A* Mapp *of the Greate River* GANGES, *as it emptieth itself into the* Bay *of* BENGALA *Taken from a Draught made upon the Place by the* Agents *for the* English East India Company. *Never before made Publique. By* John Thornton *Hydrographer to the* Honble: East India Company. *At the Signe of* England Scotland and Ireland *In the* Minories London."

Above is a dedication by Thornton to the Governor and Committee of the Company, and below : " Collected by John Seller, Hydrographer to the King", whatever may be the relation between what thus appear to be two claims to authorship. There is no date to the map. But from a collation of it with the Dutch *Map of the Kingdom of Bengale,* published in *Valentijn's Oost Indien,* vol. v, it is clear that the two maps are of common origin ; and the English one we conceive to be derived from the other. Though the Dutch map was not published, we believe, till the issue of Valentÿn's volume in 1726,[1] it purports to have been compiled under the direction of Mattheus van

---

[1] This may require correction. It seems to me almost certain that the author of *Wouter Schouten's* (called *Schulz* in a German edition) *Oost-Indische Voyagie,* Amsterdam, 1676, had a copy of V. d. Broucke's Map before him. But in the British Museum collection there is no copy of the map except that which was published in Valentÿn.

der Broucke, who was Directeur of the Dutch affairs in Bengal from 1658 to 1664. The geographical outline of the Thornton Map, so far as it extends, is an absolute counterpart, including all errors, of the Dutch one ; and though the names in the Dutch map are two or three times as numerous as in Thornton's, there is not, with three exceptions, a name in the latter (allowing for transfer from Dutch to English form) that does not appear in Van der Broucke's.[1] This edition of 1675 gives no pilotage directions for entering or navigating the Húglí.

The edition of 1701 reproduces the same map that we have spoken of, but with the addition of a large and much superior chart of the Húglí channel, in two sections, of which the title runs :

" A CHART *of the Bottom of the Bay of Bengal, with the River Ganges up to Hughly, including the Roads of Balasore and Pipley.*"

The lower section extends from Point Palmyras to the proper mouth of the Húglí, and thence up the river as far as *Calcula,* a name now forgotten, but which we shall see to have attached to a town and creek running eastward, about seventeen or eighteen miles south-west of Fort William. The second section extends from Calcula up to Húglí.

The chart is rough in execution, but has evidently been compiled with care and observation. It is professedly drawn (at least as regards the entrance-channels) to a scale of leagues (twenty to a degree), and a little more than ⅖ of an inch to a league. There are also parallels of latitude, no meridians.

This edition of the *Pilot* has sailing directions, which should probably correspond with those contained in the next edition that we mention, but the only copy of the present edition that we have been able to meet with (in the Admiralty Library) presents but a fragment of these.

In the edition of 1703 we have an improved version of the chart just mentioned, also divided into two sections (of which the N. and S. bearings in this case are at right angles to each other). Of this chart we give a reduction by photo-lithography, on half the original scale.

In this edition we have also very full sailing directions which correspond closely with the indications of the chart. We do not know to whom to attribute the first part of the sailing directions, commencing from Point Palmyras. But after these directions have proceeded as far as Piplí Roads, there commence more detailed *Instructions for carrying Great Ships into the River of* HUGHLEY, after the directions of " MR. DEVENPORT, Pilot" ; followed by *Directions for carrying up Ships from*

---

[1] The three exceptions are as follows :—In the Saugor group of Islands Thornton has " *Id. Rogues*" applied to the most northerly, which is nameless in Van der Broucke ; it has *Nulle* or *Nutte Banglow* on the east bank of the Hoogly, also absent in the Dutch map ; and *Phier Phier* just above Rájmáhl (Pír Pahár), also absent in the Dutch.

BALLASORE ROADS *into the River of* HUGHLEY, *through the* NEW DEEPS, *provided they have no less than two shallops to attend them,* also by " Mr. DEVENPORT, Pilot". And these again are succeeded by "*Mr.* HERRING *the Pilot's Directions for Bringing of Ships down the River of* HUGHLEY."[1]

We have already (II., p. cxcix, and *supra*, p. cci) accepted the suggestion that " Mr. HERRING the Pilot" is to be identified with the George Herron, or Heron, mentioned several times by Hedges in the Diary (*e.g.*, 74, 79), whilst we have as little doubt that " Mr. DEVENPORT" is Francis Davenport, also mentioned by Hedges. And the chart which we have reproduced corresponds so closely to the very detailed directions of " Mr. HERRING the Pilot", affording in fact a full illustration of those details, that we need not hesitate to attribute to him also (GEORGE HERRON), the compilation of that chart, though it probably was helped by Captain Stafford's draughts, mentioned in the Court's letter of 5th January 1681-2 (p. cc, *supra*). Both the text of Herron's directions and the chart itself are clearly of a date anterior to the foundation of a factory at Calcutta, or Chuttanuttee. The latter name appears in the chart (CHITTANUTTE), but with no indication of the Company's occupation, which is shown at HUGHLY and BALLASORE by an English flag. It must therefore have been completed before the occupation of Calcutta by Job Charnock in 1690. And it certainly could not have been compiled in the troubled days, and long absence of the English from the Delta, between 1687 and 1690. Its compilation therefore is to be put under 1686 at the latest, and probably in the time of Hedges (1682-4).

These observations are, we think, conclusive as to the date of the original chart, but one name has been interpolated at a later date, for it exhibits, just above the confluence of the " R. TOMBERLI", or modern *Rupnarain R.*, the name of the JAMES AND MARY Sand, which took its name (as we have seen, II., p. cxxxiii), from the loss on it of the *Royal James and Mary* in 1694, though there is no allusion to the name, or to the shoal, in Herron's sailing directions.[2]

---

[1] The NEW DEEPS were reached by rounding the shoals called the BRACES to seaward, and lay on the East side of the estuary, corresponding in a general way to the GASPAR CHANNEL and BEDFORD CHANNEL of the Admiralty Chart of 1882.

[2] A similar interpolation appears in Van der Broucke's map, which, as we have seen, must have been compiled before 1664, though only published (so far as we know), by Valentÿn in 1726. In this map we find *on the Eastbank of the Hoogly,* below *Soolanotti* (for *Sootanotti, i.e.,* Chuttanutte), and all with flags indicating factories :

1. *Chandernagor.*
2. *Collecatte,* and
3. *Deense Logie* (" Danish Factory").

Collecatte no doubt represents Calcutta, with more or less of the frequent

As regards the later editions of the *English Pilot* up to that of 1761, they continue to present the old maps, including the rude one after Van der Broucke, with the characterization *Never before made Publique!* and the chart of 1703, described as *Carefully corrected and compared with the French charts published in* 1745 (which is a falsehood), and without an indication of Calcutta! The editions of 1748 onwards also contain "*A New and Correct* CHART, showing the sands, shoals, mud-banks . . . with the going over the BRACES from POINT PALMIRAS to CALCUTTA in the River HUGHLEY In the Bay of BENGAL

By $\left\{ \begin{array}{l} \text{THOMAS GREG : WARREN, Surveyor.} \\ \text{WILLIAM WOOD, 'Pilot.'} \end{array} \right.$"

No date is given; but that may perhaps be hereafter ascertained approximately from the names of the authors. The chart is largely based upon Herron's, but it is more roughly executed and does not go above Barnagar. It has fewer names than Herron's, but introduces a few new ones.

We do not know if there was any edition of the *English Pilot* later than 1761. Soon after that date came in the superior surveys of Mr. John Ritchie and others, who worked in aid or collaboration of Rennell, and poor stuff like the Pilot charts must have gone down.

The Herron Chart illustrates all the passages of Hedges' Diary which allude to points in the navigation of the Húglí and its entrance.

He may here observe that the denomination *River of* HUGHLY, or HUGHLY RIVER, was then restricted to the river as terminating at the confluence with the TOMBERLEE River (modern Rupnarain) opposite Húglí Point. Below this the waters form the enlarged and complicated channels of a great estuary.

THE ENTRANCE, OR ESTUARY.

The following names of features between the Shores of the Estuary, occurring in Herron's Chart and Directions, still maintain their ground, or did so quite recently, in modern charts and surveys ; that is to say they have been current for two centuries and upwards, at least.

1. The BRACES, Western and Eastern, or long sands running seaward in the prolongation of the tidal channel, towards the western side of the embouchure.
2. The WESTERN REEF, or Western Reef-head, a seaward prolongation of

---

confusion with *Gholghát* (see II., p. xcvi). In the other two, we have the French settlement at CHANDENAGORE, and the Danish settlement at SERAMPORE, both established long after 1664, and *both here set down on the wrong side of the river.*

the Eastern Brace ; and the Eastern Reef-head, a seaward prolongation of the Long Sand.[1]

3. The Saugor Sand, extending seaward from Saugor Island on the Eastern side of the estuary.

4. Gaspard Sand ; Gaspell in Chart. In the Admiralty chart of 1882, this name is represented only by the *Gasper Channel*.

5. The Mixen, Mizen, or Middle Ground. This remains as the *Mizen* on some modern Charts, and in some older ones (of French origin presumably) as the *Artimon*.[2]

6. Gillingham Sands, or Great Middle Ground, further up. The name Gillingham is also applied on Herron's Chart to a place on the western shore abreast of the sand, and we may suppose it is to be a "Hobson Jobson" corruption of some native name like *Jilinga*.

7. Diamond Sand, on the western shore near Buffalo Point, probably named from some ship.[3] And the sand seems to have given rise to the name of *Diamond Harbour* under the other shore, where the Company's ships down to 1830-40 used often to lie.[4]

---

[1] *Note by Mr. Barlow.*

The Sailing Directions in the *E. Pilot* describe as a peculiarity of the Western Brace that "in the middle of it is 4 Feet more water than on the Edge of it" ; and the chart exhibits this anomaly in both the Braces. This is curiously confirmed by Capt. Lloyd's Survey of 1840.

In Ritchie's time again (1775) the Western Brace was a continuous sand, or he would certainly have discovered a passage ; and I have such confidence in his honest work that I am sure he would have traced the *Reef-head Passage* (between the Eastern Brace and the head of the Western Reef), which Capt. Lloyd so accurately delineated, if it had existed in his time. It had no doubt then silted up,—to reopen, in accordance with some law which we have yet to unravel, and to close again.

In a corresponding *Reef-head Passage*, viz., between the tail of the Long Sand and the Eastern Reef-head, Capt. Lloyd found $3\frac{1}{2}$ fathoms (L.W.) in 1838-39 ; and I know there was a depth of quite 19 feet reduced, in 1858. This passage was actually buoyed the following year, when 18 feet could be found. But it began to silt up as well as to contract in breadth, and about 1876 the approach to it from the N., viz., the (second) Thornhill's channel, had been obliterated ; and once more the Long Sand and the Eastern Reef have united into a single shoal.

[2] Fr. *artimon* = mizen. But mizen was here perhaps a corruption of some Portuguese name, *e.g.*, *mediana* or "middling".

[3] A ship in the Company's employ called the *Dyamond* is pretty often mentioned, *circa* 1620-1640.

[4] "At Diamond Harbour the Company's ships unload their outward, and receive on board the greater part of their homeward cargoes, from whence they proceed to Sagor Roads where the remainder is shipped."—W. Hamilton, *Hindustan.* i., 141.

COMPARATIVE TOPOGRAPHY

From the Sea to Hoogly Point.[1]

Eastern Shore.

SAUGOR ISLAND. This name (from *Ságar*, " the Sea") is now applied to a tract of the Delta isolated between SAUGOR ROADS and CHANNEL CREEK, some 26 m. in length from N. to S. and 7 to 8 in width from E. to W.

In Herron's chart and other old maps the application of the name is limited to what forms the most southerly portion of modern **Saugor Island**, having been then one of three detached islands, which as they succeeded from S. to N. were (1) SAUGOR, (2) COCK'S ID., (3) ISLE OF DOGS, with alternative name of ISLE OF ROGUES.

These have now all become amalgamated by deposit, and Nos. 2 and 3 have long disappeared from charts. But *Cock Island, Cock's Island,* or *Coxe's Island,* is found at least as late as 1807.[2] In the Van der Broucke map it appears as *I. de Gale,* in the 1675 "Pilot" as *Id. de Gallo,* indicating Portuguese *Gallo* (" Cock") as the original designation. In the V. der Broucke map we have also an island E. of Saugor Point called *I. de Galinha* (" Hen's Island").

The last chart in which we have found DOG ISLAND is an anonymous MS. sketch in India Office of 1767

Western Shore.

(KENDOA, not in Herron's chart; but see II., p. cxxxi; probably *Kontai*.)

KITESALL or BARABULLA Trees (in 1701 ed. of chart *Parrasoll*).

KEDGELIE R. and Island should be HIDGELIE, modern **Hidgelee** or **Rasoolpoor R**. and Hidgelee (*Hijilí*) division of Midnapoor district. *Angelin* of Barros and the Portuguese; *Hidgley* of Job Charnock (II., pp. lxii. lxiv-lxx); *Ingellee* of A. Hamilton.

In Warren and Wood's chart, *Ingerly*.

R. COUCOLLY; COCKOLY in Sailing Directions; Warren and Wood, *Cockerles Id.* Mod. **Cowcolly** Light, etc.

(According to *Imp. Gazetteer* properly *Geonkhálí*.)

---

[1] I here drop the correcter orthography of the *Imperial Gazetteer*, which it is inconvenient to use in collation with the rough spelling of the charts. When I desire to indicate the correct native orthography it is given in parentheses and in italics. Names appearing in Herron's Chart and Sailing Directions, or contemporary documents, are printed in small capitals. Names as in modern maps and charts in **loaded** type.

[2] *Note by Mr. Barlow.* "It occurs in a sketch in India Office called ' *A plan of* THORNHILL'S CHANNEL, *so named by the Marine Board after* CUTHBERT THORNHILL, Esq., *Master Attendant, under whose directions it was surveyed March* 1807.' (Sd.) JOHN GARSTIN, Colonel of Engineers, Surveyor General."

Eastern Shore.

(perhaps by Ritchie). But Lloyd's chart of 1837 has, close to its old position, a creek marked as " *Keerpoy Kol* or **Dog's Creek**", called in the 1882 chart "*Fuldulin*" (?) or **Dog Creek.**

In Herron's chart the name OYSTER RIVER is applied to the channel on the east of Cock's Island. This is mentioned by Hedges (p. 64), as well as the oysters.

CHANELL TREES corresp. to **Mud Point.**

CHANNELL CREEK or R. OF JESSORE is still **Channel Creek.**

R. RANGAFOULA } These indicate
ROGUES (R.)   } apparently two neighbouring creeks, near the *Rangaphula Creek* of modern charts. The *Tengra Creek* above the existing Rangaphula Obelisk is still considerable enough for boats. And this is the consideration which gave name to the RIVERS OF ROGUES and of THIEVES which appear in the present chart and sailing directions, and in various documents of the last and preceding century. They were channels admitting navigation from the eastern creeks of the Sunderbunds into the Húglí, and in these the Arakan Rovers lay in ambush, ready to pounce out upon their prey in the great river. Hence the name RIVER OF ROGUES seems to have varied in specific application; sometimes, as here, given to a channel near Rangaphula, sometimes perhaps to Channel Creek, to Kulpee Creek (as we shall see presently), or even to Chingree Khal opening into Diamond Harbour. Hedges mentions the R. of Rogues (pp. 36, 37).

RIVER OF THIEVES.—This is also called RIVER OF ROGUES in the Sailing Directions, and in an old Dutch sketch in the I.O. it appears as *d'Roevers*

Western Shore.

ID. KEDGERYE ; *Kegeria* of Hedges; 1701 edn. of chart, *Gajouri* ; *Kidgerie* of A. Hamilton ; modern *Kedgeree* (*Khijari* or *Kijari* of *Imp. Gazetteer :* but *Khajuri* (*i.e.*, "Date-palm place") of recent Port Trust survey, is perhaps right. The name is *Cajoree* in Bolts's map of Bengal, c. 1770 ; and in Sayers' of 1778.

OLD CROSSING TREES, a name which first appears in Ritchie's Survey of 1770. But in his chart of 1783 they are named *Channel Trees*, and in a MS. chart of 1819 in the India Office, "*Silver Trees*" (R. J. B.).

BUGDEN'S POINT (BUGDEN'S ARBOUR in Sailing Directions). Modern **Huldia Point**, above **Huldia R.**, which is the *Holiday River* of John Ritchie (1770).

R. (OF) TIGERS. This is probably *Bellary* or *Ballari* Nulla, near the G. T. S. Bellary Tower, now insignificant. The name occurs in Tassin's atlas of 1841, but whether from modern information or inserted from one of the old charts we cannot say.

BUFFALO POINT

and

DIAMOND POINT.

The latter name does not occur in the chart before us, but it does in the *Pilot's* chart of 1701, as identical, apparently, with the CUCKOLD'S POINT of the present chart. Both names **Buffalo Pt.** and **Diamond Pt.** have survived. *But their application has been transposed*, and in most of the charts since 1770 Buffalo Pt. applies to the Upper, and Diamond Pt., when it occurs, applies to the lower of the two.

Without noting this, some of Herron's sailing directions will be unintelligible.

Eastern Shore.

Spruyt (" River of Rovers"). It is to be identified with **Kulpee Creek.**[1]

PAGODA R.— Probably **Diamond Harbour Creek.**

HUGHLEY RIVER POINT.—Now known as Hoogly Point ; the prominent point opposite to the confluence of the **Roopnarain R.**, and marking the entrance to the RIVER OF HUGH-LEY, according to the nomenclature of the 17th century.

The reach below this is called the NARROWS in the old Sailing Directions and some charts, now **Hoogley Bight,** and (at its eastern end) **Diamond Harbour.**

Western Shore.

CUCKOLD'S POINT.—Corresponding with **Luff Point** of the modern charts.

GONGA COLLE. — Gewan Kolly Creek and Temple, in modern charts.

About this position the Chart of Warren and Wood has " *Deans Sand*", and " *Deans Town*", which we are enabled to understand by A. Hamilton, who says : " A little below the mouth of it (Ganga or Tumlook R.) the *Danes* have a thatcht House, but for what Reasons . . . . I never could learn" (II., 3).[2]

R. TOMBERLIE (*Tumbolee* of Hedges, p. 175, and *Tumberleen* of S. Master, II., p. ccxxxiii) ; TAMELI of 1701 chart, so called from some form or corruption of the name Tumlook (*Tam-lúk*), a town on its banks, the very ancient port of *Tamralipti*, and no doubt the original of Ptolemy's Ταμα-λίτης (though he has misplaced it desperately). It is the *Ganga* of A. Hamilton ; and is marked as " The

---

[1] In the *Anglo-Indian Glossary* (supplement), p. 849, I have said : " After a careful comparison of all the notices, and of the old and modern charts, I come to the conclusion that the R. of Rogues must have been either what is now called *Chingrī Khāl*, entering immediately below Diamond Harbour, or *Kalpī Creek* about 6 m. further down ; but the preponderance of argument is greatly in favour of Chingrī Khāl."

The opinion of Mr. Barlow, however, a most competent judge of such a question, is so decidedly in favour of Kulpee Creek, that I cannot but accept it. And the transposition of the names of Buffalo and Diamond Points, which Mr. Barlow has pointed out to me, weighs in the same direction.

[2] Mr. Barlow notes : " In *Selections from Unpublished Records*, by the Revd. James Long, Calcutta, 1869, there is the following :

" *Consultation*, Decr. 21, 1749.

" Received a letter from Capt. GEORGE MINCHIN, dated the 19th inst., from *Deans Town*, importing that he should distress the Mahrattas to the utmost of his power, as he looked on the Sloops to be in a state of defence sufficient to secure the men from the shot of the Mahrattas ; he intended to bring them close to the shore,—and that he apprehended he will be able to distress them greatly, if not entirely destroy them."

Dean Sand was identical with what is now named *Hooghly Sand*, or *The Hooghly*.

Eastern Shore.   *Western Shore.*

Ganges" in Warren and Wood's Survey which appears in the *Pilot* of 1748, names arising from some old confusion not easily explained. It is now known as the **Rupnarain**.[1]

In Van der Broucke's Map (and Thornton's of 1675) it is called *Patragatta* River.

TOMBOLI POINT. — **Mornington Point**.

From Hoogly Point to the Site of Calcutta.

JAMES AND MARY SAND.—This must be an interpolation in the original survey, which we have shown to date from about 1684, whilst the wreck which originated this name occurred in 1694 (see II., p. cxxxiii). And though Mr. Davenport's directions in the *Pilot* mention the troublesome eddies about Hoogly Point, as does Streynsham Master (II., p. ccxxxiii), neither these nor Herron allude to any shoal. Some change must have taken place in the relations of the streams between 1684 and 1694, leading to the establishment of this new danger.[2]

---

[1] Rennell says : "Satgong .   now an inconsiderable village on a small creek of the Hoogly river, about 4 miles to the N.W. of Hoogly, was in 1566, and probably later, a large commercial city. .   At that time Satgong river was capable of bearing small vessels ; and I suspect that its then course, after passing Satgong, was by way of Adaumpour, Oomptah, and Tamlook ; and that the river called the old Ganges was a part of its course, and received that name, while the circumstance of the change was fresh in the memory of the people. The appearance of the country between Satgong and Tamlook countenances such an opinion." (*Memoir*, p. [57].) I believe there is nothing highly improbable in this supposition, considering the uniformity of level, and the vast bodies of water in motion during the flood season.

[2] *Note by Mr. Barlow.*—I can throw no light on the cause which led to the existence of this shoal, at a date later than 1676 (the year of Master's voyage), and probably near 1694. If the rivers MOUNDELGAT and TOMBERLIE of Herron (Damooda and Roopnarain) had always been in the same relative positions as at present ; and if they had always discharged the same volume, or if that discharge had always borne the same relative proportion to the flow of the River of HUGHLY that it does now, I should have declared that there must always have been a JAMES AND MARY Sand. But I dare not presume to theorise.

Eastern Shore.

(COURE RIVER, in 1701 chart.)[1]
SIDNEY'S MOORINGS. Somewhere about **Fultah.**[3]

[1] *Note by Mr. Barlow.* Probably the *Neela Khal* (Blue Creek), the modern *Anchoring Creek* of the James and Mary. There is an unnamed creek between it and Hoogly Point, and this I imagine to be the Noorpoor Creek of the 1801 chart, popularly called *Beebee Domingo's* Creek. The Warren and Wood chart has this creek, but omits the name; and gives that of MINGA BIBBY'S CREEK to the upper, or *Neela Khal.*

PORCAS (Creek). Perhaps a corruption of *Porker's Creek.* Herron, in his sailing directions, calls the reach *Hog reaver Reach*, or *Porkus.* "This Reach was formerly the Randez vouz of the Dutch Ships, who had their Pork from that small River on the Larboard side" (*i.e.*, in descending), "and thence gave it the name of *Ferkens Sprent*," i.e., *Varkens Spruijt*, or Hog River; the name applied to two creeks here (*Groete en Kleijne*—"Big and Little Hog Rivers") in the Old Dutch sketch already referred to.[4]

The 1701 chart calls the creek *Rio Parques*, which looks as if the name had gone through a Portuguese alembic (*Rio-dos Porcos ?*)[5]

SAROLL, in 1701 chart.

Ryapore, in Warren and Wood.

Modern **Royapoor.**

Western Shore.

TOULIE'S SAND.[2]
R. MOUNDELGAT. This is the River **Damooda** (properly *Damúdar*).

Mundelghat is still the name of the adjoining tract between the Damooda and the Roopnarain (*Rennell's Atlas*, and *Atlas of India*). In Herron's Sailing Directions it is styled by the Dutch name of "*Rasphuise River*, by the County People called *Mundeggate* or *Mundelgate.*"

BOUGANDA CREEK. This still appears as **Bagunda Khal**, opposite **Brool Point**, in Adm. Chart of 1882, on what is called in the same chart *Hog River Reach.* This name is a survival of the 17th century; see under PORCAS, on opposite side.

[2] Represented now by a mud flat, or the long bank above **Fort Mornington Point·** (R. J. B.)

[3] There is no record or legend of this name. But there was a tradition that opposite Fulta House (or Hotel) of Captain Lloyd's chart, the early Dutch used to discharge their ballast. The clear open anchorage·above the modern Fulta Bazar, was that where the refugees from Calcutta in 1756 were found, and was the rendezvous of Admiral Watson's squadron. (R. J. B.)

---

[4] *Hog-River* (the upper creek) is still a considerable stream in the rains. In Sept. 1823 a small ship (the *Atlas*) displaced her stem by a violent sheer, and could not be kept afloat. They slipt the cable and she was directly placed inside the creek for her repair. (R. J. B.)

[5] On the other hand, the native name assigned by Capt. Lloyd to the vicinity of the *Hog River Point* of the Pilots, is **Pookooreah**, and PORCAS may have some relation to this. (R. J. B.)

Eastern Shore.

CALCULA, and Creek. This is mis-written *Calcuta* on the chart, an error probably due to the engraver, in 1703, having heard of *Calcutta*.

W. Schouten, in 1664 (pub. 1676) speaks of passing the great River of CALCULA, coming from the East out of the Kingdom of Arakan. And A. Hamilton says : "The first (place) of any Note on the River's Side is CUL-CULLA, a Market-Town for Corn, coarse Cloth, Butter, and Oil; above it is the Dutch *Bank's hall* . . . CUL-CULLA has a large deep River that runs to the Eastward" . . . (II. 4). "CALCULA, MONDELGHAT, and some other places below, supply most of the wax and hemp that we require" (*Valen-tyn*, V, 158).

The once navigable channels running eastward out of the Hoogly have evidently all greatly diminished. The name CALCULA (perhaps *Kholkhálí*) seems quite to have disappeared. The creek is probably represented by that now called *Vanzan Creek.* [1]

[1] Now silted up. I imagine the silting of many of the creeks may be in part owing to the *bunds*, which (as in the case of *Chingree Khal*), have been placed across them, not far above the embou-chure, and which of course check the flow of the flood tide. (R. J. B.)

Western Shore.

RANGAMATE. This name still sur-vives in **Rangamate Khal**, opposite to Moyapore Magazine (see Petley's *Sur-vey*, 1882-83).

Hedges mentions anchoring at a little village called RANGAMATE on his first ascent of the Hoogly (p. 32).

WOLLIABEEKE ; more correctly OLOBARIA in 1701 chart; *Willobery*, in Warren and Wood; *Ulbareea* of Bolts's map of Bengal (*c.* 1770). **Oolaberiah** of modern charts (*Úla-baria* of *Imp. Gazetteer*) ; a well-known place on the river, whence a canal runs to Midnapoor. It is the ULABARREAH where Job Charnock at one time thought of establishing the English head-quarters in Bengal (II., p. lxxv).

JOHN PARDO Island and Creek. The Creek is apparently the *Oola-beriah Khal* of the present day. The island has long disappeared. The

Eastern Shore.

MUSKETTO CREEK. Probably at *Poojallee*, of 1882 chart, the *Ponjelly* of Alex. Hamilton, of Warren and Wood, and of Rennell ; *Punghely* of Sayer, and Bennett (1778) ; *Ponjally* of Lacam ; and *Point Jelly* of some pilots (an instance of "Hobson Jobson").[6]

[6] There was in 1858 the same large rice mart at this place which is described by Capt. Alex. Hamilton (II. 4). (R. J. B.)

Western Shore.

first mention of it; so far as we know, is in Streynsham Master's *Diary* (1676, see II., p. ccxxxiii). It is mentioned several times by Hedges (pp. 63, 68, 156, 175). In the 1701 chart we have it entered "R. JEAN PARAD, a river for great ships."

The name in the form *Joahn Petord* survives in the anonymous sketch of 1767, but is there applied to a creek opposite to Budge-Budge, three or four miles above Oolaberiah.

It is not improbable that much of the land on the opposite side, about Atchipoor Point, is new, and that the river about here was much broader in Herron's time, whilst the Island might owe its temporary existence to a deposit of silt in the slack water.

R. BUSSUNDREE. The character assigned to this channel in Van den Broucke's map makes it almost an alternative course of the Hoogly River, bringing it out of that river at Tribeni above Hoogly, the old Saraswati R. in fact. In Rennell's map the most prominent channel leaving the Hoogly as described, and passing Satganw (the *Porto Piqueno* of the early Portuguese), rejoins the Hoogly at Sankral, much nearer Calcutta. But these older maps perhaps indicate that a more important branch of the Saraswati once flowed further to the west and entered near Oolaberiah. See note from Rennell on a still older possible state of the rivers, at p. ccx, *supra*.

Basandhari, or *Balia-Basandhari,* now *Balia* Pergunnah, formed one of the original "24 Pergunnahs", acquired by the Company in 1757. It is mentioned by A. Hamilton (II. 4), who immediately after naming "*Juan Pardoa*", says, "on the west side there is a River that runs by the back of Hughly Island, which leads up to *Radnagur,* famous for manufacturing Cotton, Cloth, and silk *Romaals.* . . . . *Bassundri* and *Tresinddi* . . . . are on that River, which produce the greatest

Eastern Shore.

Western Shore.

Quantities of the best Sugars in *Bengal*."

The 1701 chart has *Sandry Bush*, on which see some remarks in *Anglo-Indian Glossary*, under *Sunderbunds*.

R. SUSANEE ; apparently the **Dowka Khalee**, or *Dingheewala Creek*, of modern charts.

SERANGO TREE. **Sarang Ghat** of *Indian Atlas;* **Peer Serang** Shrine of modern charts.[1]

MORNEEKPORE (also MANNEK PORE in Herron's Directions), Manik-poor opposite Akra. *Mánik Khálí* Point, corrupted into *Moonee Kolly* and *Melancholy Point*, is close to this and no doubt connected in name. N.B.—The reach below Manikpore is in Herron's Directions termed *Crown Reach* (now Jarmaker's Reach), and that below Nutty Bungla Creek, *William and John* Reach. These seem to have taken their names from two noted interloping ships, both connected with " Tom Pitt's " adventures.

NEDDE BENGALLA (NUTTY BUNGELO, etc., in Herron's Directions). *Needle Bengalla* in the sketch of 1767. R. BENGALLA of 1701 chart ; *Bengala* of Rennell. The name had probably nothing to do with a *bungalow* there, as I once thought. It seems to be *Nadí Bangala*, the Bengal or "Bangala river." Probably the **Loonghee Bungla Khall** of modern charts, just below **Jarmaker's Reach.**

EDA HIGHT (?) near Akra Mills (?). Probably more correctly in 1701 chart " EDDY BIGHT."

SANCRELL POINT.—The point opposite to **Sankral**, in some modern charts termed **Hangman's Point.**[2] Sankral itself, which still exists on the west bank, is not in this chart, but is in Warren and Wood's, as *Sangrall*.

(PUDZEPOUR in 1701 chart; *Panchpura* of Rennell probably.)

LOWER CREEK. In 1701 chart " Fresh River."

LITTLE TANNA.

UPPER CREEK. In 1701 chart " The River in which Armenians repair their Ships." These Creeks must be those adjoining Sankral, the Upper Creek being that representing the old Saraswati in Rennell (see above under BUSSUNDREE).

---

[1] Up to a very late date—perhaps still—all vessels manned by Mahommedan sailors, when proceeding to sea, were here met by a *Pir* (or devotee), usually clad in blue. He used to put off from the miniature *Musjid* in the tiniest of boats, and was invariably propitiated by a dole of rice, or a few pice. Inward-bound vessels were by no means so regularly visited ; nor did the custom exist elsewhere on the river. (R. J. B.)

[2] The tradition is that in the early part of *this* century several men were tried for mutiny and murder on board ship and hanged *here*. The particulars are unknown. In Mr. Long's *Selections from Unpublished Records* is a case occurring in October 1754, when two mutineers were hanged (p. 51).

The point has almost invariably been known as *Tanner's Point*, obviously a corruption from *Tanna Point*. (R. J. B.)

See under TANNA below. Both Sankral and Tanna were on the right bank *opposite* to this point.

Eastern Shore.

GOBINPOUR in 1701 chart, but perhaps a mistake, as *Gobernapore* (see next entry but one) seems to represent *Govindpoor.*

KITHEREPORE (in Sailing Directions also KIDDORY-PORE and KIDDERY-POR). The site of the existing *Kidderpore* Dockyard, a name often supposed (and stated) to have been derived from Mr. James Kyd, who established a dockyard hereabouts at the beginning of this century. We see that the name is much older, and indigenous.[2]

In Warren and Wood's Chart we have immediately before Governapore "SURMAN'S GARDEN." This was somewhere about the upper end of Garden Reach. It is mentioned in the curious Charnock legend preserved by Orme (II., p. xcvii): Mr. Surman was a Company's servant, and one of the mission to Delhi in 1717.

GOBERNAPORE. This represents *Govindpoor,* one of the three villages obtained for the Company in 1698, viz. Chatánati, Calcutta, and Govindpoor. The first of these three forms the next entry. Calcutta does not appear on the chart. Its site is now covered by the *Burra Bazar,* and the chief European offices and public buildings. Govindpoor was on the site of Fort William.

Western Shore.

Sankral does not appear in the chart but is mentioned by W. Schouten in 1664, and I have no doubt it is the *Sea Crowle* of Sir John Goldsborough, which puzzled me at II., p. xci.[1]

TANNA FORT.

GREAT TANNA.

All these *Tannas* have disappeared from our maps. Tanna Fort—taken by Job Charnock (II., pp. lxii, lxv), and destroyed by Clive and Watson (1st Jan. 1757), lay, as Rennell's map shows, 3½ miles below the modern Fort William, and we believe just about the site of the house of the Director of the Botanic Gardens.[3]

[3] Tanna Fort was of brickwork. There was a mud fort on the opposite bank (see *Ives,* p. 101).

The log of H.M.S. *Kent,* under Jan. 1, 1757, states in the concise language of the period.

"The *Tyger's* Seamen took possession of *Tanner's Fort,* which the enemy had abandoned, and our boats took the Fort on the opposite side, hoisted English colours, and set fire to them both."

Ives states that 40 cannon were found in the two forts; many of them 23-pounders (p. 101).

I have never seen the slightest trace of these forts, nor heard of any. (R. J. B.)

---

[1] There is still a populous village at Sankral between the two creeks (*Sankrall* and *Rajgunj*). The upper creek was traditionally supposed to have been the highway when Satgong was the terminus of navigation; but it is the merest rivulet imaginable now. (R. J. B.) See a remark at p. ccxiii on the subject of R. Bussundree.

[2] Mr. Kyd was, I believe, a half-caste son of General Kyd of the Engineers, the founder of the Botanic Garden on the opposite side of the River. An older dockyard than Kyd's, in this locality, was founded by Col. Henry Watson of the Engineers in Warren Hastings's time. He was the first to build ships of importance in the Hoogly, but exhausted his means. Both the dockyards eventually became Government property. See an article in vol. iii of the *Calcutta Review* (probably by the late Rev. James Long).

Eastern Shore.

CHITTANUTTE. This is the name *Chuttanutty* (*Chatánatí*) which for the first two or three years was used as the name of the settlement. The village so-called occupied the site of the north part of the present native town. In Valentyn's map it is called *Soelanotti* —the *l* a clerical error for *t*. The name of Chuttanutty was long preserved in that of *Chuttanutty Ghát*, now called Háthkhola Ghát, and in *Chuttanutty Bazar*, a name which perhaps still survives (see *Cal. Review*, vol. III., quoted above).

Western Shore.

SUMATRA POINT. This name still survives ; but the point is often called **Shalimar Pt.**, from a villa of that name adjoining.

From Site of Calcutta to Hoogly.

CHITTIPORE, in Sailing Directions, modern **Chitpoor.**

BARNAGULL. **Baranagar;** still existing as a village about a mile north of the northern boundary of Calcutta. It was a Dutch settlement, and appears as such in Van der Broucke's map. Valentyn (1726) says " *Barrenegger* is a place of ours where the pig-slaughtering for the (Dutch) E. I. Company takes place, just as *Sootanotti* is the place where it is customary to load rice and other grain." (V. 158).

W. Schouten also mentions landing at *Barnagor* on his way up to Hoogly in 1664, but says nothing of Dutch occupation, so that was probably later. ſ.·DIVELL'S LUMP (in Sailing Directions "BRAHMANS OR DIVELL'S LUMP"). Apparently near modern **Duckinsore** (*Dakhineswar*) which is "noted for its twelve beautiful temples in honour of Siva, built on the river-bank". (*Imp. Gazetteer*, s. v.)

Names in which "Divell" or "Devil" is introduced, generally point to Hindu temples (*Dewal*).

CHANEY TREE.

SEAMOURS MOORINGS.

PT. CHOQUET in chart of 1701. Qu. a *Choky* or Station? (R. J. B.)

SIMPLE TOMS TREE.

BOON HUGLEY. This is marked with a R. C. Church. I cannot identify it. The name *Bon Hoogly* is, in a recent large scale survey, applied to a village or township on the *east* side, in about 22° 39′ 15″. Qu. *Ban Húglí*, "Hoogly Wood"?

SLIPPER TREE.

(A tree marked SAPATERRE occurs hereabouts in 1701 chart, which is probably the same; Port. *Sapato*, a shoe. But it is below, not above, BOON HUGLEY, or BANA HUGHLE as in that chart.)

Eastern Shore.

TITTIGUR (miswritten *Tiltigur*). Modern **Tittagurh** (*Titágarh*), a village, and Eastern Bengal Railway Station, near which are several English villas.

" Though now an unimportant place, Titágarh was seventy years ago" (*c.* 1810) " a scene of life and activity. It possessed a dockyard, from which the largest merchant vessel ever built in the Húglí was launched, the *Countess of Sutherland*, of 1455 tons. No vestige of the dockyard remains" (*Imp. Gazetteer*, s. v.)[1]

CHANOCK. **Chanak** is still a place at the east end of the Barrackpoor Cantonment, close to the Railway Station; and *Chának* or *Achának* is the name by which Barrackpoor is habitually known to the natives.

It is a prevalent idea, and it has often been asserted as an undoubted fact, that the place was named after *Job Charnock*.

This is, I believe, purely imaginary, and the derivation historically impossible. See remarks in note at II., p. xcix.[2]

POUTTO (for *Poulto* : in Sailing Directions the reach is called PULTA or POULTO Reach). **Pulta Ghat**; long the ferry on the G. T. Road from Calcutta to the Upper Provinces.

DEVILLS TOWNE. Groups of temples existing now or some years ago opposite the lower end of Chander-

[1] Phipps (*Shipping and Commerce of Bengal*) states this ship to have been built in 1801, afterwards captured, and taken to Mauritius ; and there employed as a hulk, till broken up in 1821. The *Fort William*, 1236 tons, was launched in the Hoogly, but we do not know where. She existed in 1836 as a Bombay trader. I have not seen her since. Phipps names also the *Java*, 1118 tons, built in 1811; the *Castle Huntly*, 1279, in 1812 ; *Vansittart*, 1272, and *General Kyd*, 1200, in 1813.

But the largest ship ever built in the Hoogly was the *Hastings* of 74 guns, tonnage 1732, launched Jan. 8, 1818. She was built by Mr. Kyd. She did not re-visit Bengal till 1851, and then moored at Saugor, bearing the flag of Admiral Austin. I last saw her at Rangoon, a solid and comfortable, but by no means elegant vessel. *C.* 1859 she became one of the screw steam fleet, 200 h.p. In 1863 she was flag-ship at Queenstown ; in 1867, a blockship in the same port; 1868 to 1873 chiefly at Devonport ; in 1874 her name disappears from the Navy List. (R. J. B.)

[2] It is curious that two wellknown places in this list should possess native names, so similar in sound to those of English celebrities as to have created the belief that these accidental residents gave the names—*Kidderpore* and *Chának*. (R. J. B.)

Western Shore.

DEGON TOWNE (in 1701 Chart, DAGON). This appears in Rennell's Bengal Atlas as DIGUM, below Ghyretty ; and in the recent large scale survey of the Hoogly as *Dirghango* above Baidyabhatty.

ELEPHANT TREE.

This must have been somewhere near *Ghyretty*, which figures in Ren-

Eastern Shore.

nagore ; not far from present Sham-
nagar jute factory.

DEVILS REACH, *Hedges*, p. 156.
This seems to have been the reach
opposite the Chandernagore territory,
and terminating at DEVILLS TOWNE.
There are, or were recently, several
great clusters of temples on this
reach.

Western Shore.

nell's Atlas, and now in turn has disappeared from the maps, and is un-
mentioned in the Gazetteer. It was
the site of a country house of the
Governor of Chandernagore (*French
Garden* in Bolts's Map of Bengal, *c.*
1770), and is often mentioned in the
days of Hastings and Sir P. Francis.
Near it was the estate of Sir Eyre
Coote, whither he constantly retired
from Calcutta. *Ghyretty* is marked
in Joseph's *Survey of the Hoogly*
(1841) as "Old French Garden."

BUDDERY. **Bhadresar**, forty years
ago an important mart (see *Calcutta
Review*, 1848) ; still a seat of trade,
and now a municipality ; about 1½ mile
below Chandernagore.

DUTCH GARDEN. This is mentioned
several times by Hedges (pp. 33, 157,
170), who says it was 3 miles down the
river from the English Factory at
Hoogly. Streynsham Master in 1676
(vol. II., p. ccxxxiii) first passes the
Dutch Garden, and then " a large spot
of ground which the French had laid
out as a factory, but which was now in
the possession of the Dutch.'' This
must have been Chandernagore, which
the French are stated to have first
acquired in 1673 (?), but apparently
did not permanently occupy till 1688,
when they got a concession of it from
Aurangzíb (see Malleson's *History of
the French in India*, p. 32). There is
great difficulty in ascertaining the
facts as to the first establishment at
Chandernagore. " About half a mile
northward from the principal ghaut at
Chandernagore, completely overgrown
by trees, is (or was in 1858) all that
remains of Fort Orleans—part of the
N.W. bastion. The bricks and mortar
were then clear, sharp, and hard as
stone—but a mere fragment, 9 or 10
feet high." (R. J. B.)

WHITE HOUSE. The Chart represents this with an English flag. I do
not think it is anywhere mentioned by
Hedges. It seems to correspond to

Eastern Shore.

Western Shore.

the NEW CHANEY of the Sailing Directions. Was it possibly the house which Pitt established in 1682?

DUTCH FACTORY at Hoogly. **Chinsura.**

ENGLISH FACTORY. Herron, in starting his Sailing Directions for taking a ship down from Hoogly to the sea, speaks of GULL GAT. This was the site of the English Factory, *Gholghát*, a name still preserved as a locality about the middle of the length, of the town, and giving name to "Gholghat Dispensary." We find this name used for the English Factory in the quotations from native documents at II., pp. xcvi, xcviii *supra*. And probably some confusion between the English establishments at GHOLGHAT and at *Calcutta* led to the extraordinary forms which we find Frenchmen giving to the latter name, e.g. *Golgonthe* (*Luillier*, 1705). Sonnerat (1782), though he writes the name *Calecuta*, says the English both write and pronounce it *Golgota!*

HUGHLY.

(The ENGLISH GARDEN was some little way above Hoogly. See *Hedges*, pp. 34, 76, 89.)

Notes on sundry places mentioned by Hedges above Húglí:

TRIBBANY. *Tribeni*, see note at vol. I., p. 38.

SANTAPORE (pp. 39, 50, 77). **Santipur** (see Mr. Barlow's note at I., p. 39).

BOGATCHER? (p. 77).

SINADGHUR. Perhaps **Soomoodagurh** of Indian Atlas, 4 m. below Nuddia.

REWEE?

BALLEE (p. 39). On the Jelinghi R., about 28° 42′ Lat. and 88° 30′ Long. (Mr. Barlow's note, and Indian Atlas).

ANDOOLEE (p. 39). **Andooleah** on the Jelinghi, in about 23° 37½′ Lat. (Indian Atlas).

COLCAPORE? (vol. I., pp. 41, 89, 122). There is a **Kullickpoor** on the Jelinghi some 20 m. from Kásimbázár, in about 23° 57½′.

MEERDAPORE, "within 4 or 5 hours travell of Cassembazar" (I., p. 33, also pp. 40, 164). It is shown on the vague Van der Broucke Map, in a position that seems to indicate its being near one of the exits of the Jelinghi from the Ganges. But I cannot trace it on any map later than that of Kitchen (*c.* 1770), in which *Mirdapore* is located N.E. of Cassembazar, near the great Ganges, and some distance below *Bogwangola*.[1]

PULIA, "near (and below) Santapore" (p. 39). There is **Poomleah** on E. Bank, some 4 m. below Santipoor (Indian Atlas).

GOALPARA, "on Cossimbazar River" (I., p. 77)?

MAULA, "3 *cosses* short of Cossimbazar" (p. 77)?

BUGLAGOTTE, on river leading to Malda (p. 77)?

JATTRAPORE (pp. 42, 51). Not in Indian Atlas, but in Tassin's Map of Bengal, about 26 m. west of Dacca.

---

[1] This map of Bengal, professing to be "drawn from the best authorities by Tho. Kitchen, geographer," is in the British Museum. It is evidently copied from a French map. Isle of Dogs is *Ile des Chiens*, Coxe's Island, *I. du Coq.* Calcutta is entered as *Calicotta*, whilst Calcula (see p. ccxii) has been made into *Calcutta.* An English interpolation, quite misplaced near Cassembazar, indicates there the "place where the famous battle was fought between Col. Clive and the *French Nabob* (*sic*) 1757, in which the latter was entirely defeated." It is hardly necessary to say that Plassy is some 20 m. or more south of Kásimbázár. It *does* appear in the same map, unrecognised, as *Plati*.

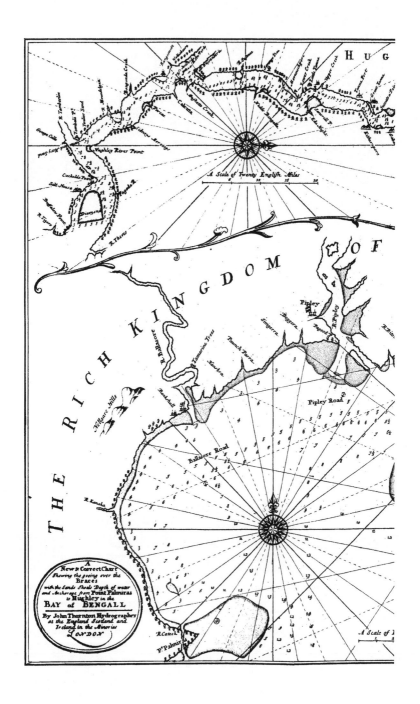

HUG

THE RICH KINGDOM OF

A Scale of Twenty English Miles

Vuhley River Point

Cuchols Point

Salt House

R. Tigers

R. Thoru

Diamond

Pipley Hill

Pipley Road

Singerra

Bugora

R. Pipley

Ballasore Road

Pound Pores

Tamarine Tree

Villgars Hills

Hand Shall

R. Kanula

R. Catch

P. Palmira

A Scale of

A
New & Correct Chart
shewing the going over the
BRACES
with the Sands Shoals Depth of water
and Anchorage from Point Palmiras
to Hughley in the
BAY of BENGALL
By John Thornton Hydrographer
at the England Scotland and
Ireland in the Minories
LONDON

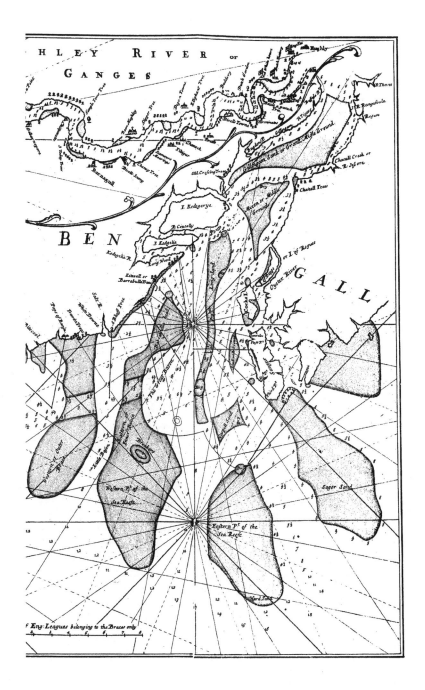

INDEX

TO

VOLUMES II AND III OF "HEDGES' DIARY",

CONTAINING THE DOCUMENTARY ILLUSTRATIONS.

NOTA BENE.—Vol. I, containing the *Diary*, having a separate Index, the figures in this Index, without a separate indication of volume, refer to Vol. II.

Also, though, owing to want of prevision of the bulk to which the illustrations would extend, Roman numerals have been used for the pagination of Vols. II and III, it is to be observed that these numerals are represented in this Index by the usual Arabic digits.

T

l

INDEX ADDENDUM.

Some slips of MS. references were mislaid during the printing of the Index. They have been found when the volume was otherwise complete ; and I think it well to insert the references here.—H. Y.

Printed in Great Britain by
Amazon.co.uk, Ltd.,
Marston Gate.